Reader's Digest

Joy of Nature

Reader's Digest

Joy of Nature

How to explore and enjoy the fascinating
world around you

Published by The Reader's Digest Association Limited
London · New York · Montreal · Sydney · Cape Town

General Consultant:

Durward L. Allen, *Professor of Wildlife Ecology, Purdue University, USA*

Special Consultants:

William H. Amos, *St Andrew's School, Delaware*

Mark R. Chartrand III, *American Museum-Hayden Planetarium*

Harold Gibson, *US Weather Service*

Richard L. Lees, *Earth Science Consultant*

Alfred Leutscher, *Consultant for European Natural History*

Contents

In touch
with
nature

This book is an invitation to become more aware of nature and deepen your understanding of the world around you. Many of the special features listed here will help you to put your knowledge to use. There are eight categories, each with its symbol. Look for them as you read.

Judging a photographer to be no threat, this long-tailed jaeger (a tundra-nesting bird related to the gulls) perches defiantly on the intruder's hat. This amusing picture was the joint product of a mother-and-son team on a photographic trip to Mount McKinley National Park, Alaska.

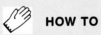

CHAPTER ONE

How to look at nature

Allow the scene before you to take its effect – savour its special character. And put aside, for a while, whatever is on your mind.

We all know people who are very much at home with nature, who seem to fall in with its rhythms as soon as they set foot outdoors. All of us can be like this – capable of shedding the concerns of the workaday world. What it takes is concentration and practice. When a beautiful vista stretches before us, what is there to interfere with the pleasure of its colour and contour? Nothing, really, except our own unfamiliarity. We may feel a sense of wonder tinged with awe, and perhaps a sense of regret at spending so little of our time doing this very thing.

Nature is not remote – limited to parks and wilderness areas. It is abundant and readily available, as close as your own garden. Nature is a year-round source of inspiration. Think of the light that filters through the new leaves in spring, and the pungent scents of autumn. If you are dressed for it, a walk in the teeming rain can be strangely satisfying; perhaps it is a return to the feeling of joy you had as a child, splashing through puddles. A walk through a snow-covered woodland, where you are alone with the sound of the wind and the crunching of your own footsteps, may be a very personal pleasure. Such simple things extend your sense of the pervasiveness of nature.

Much of what you will find in this book may remind you of things your grandparents told you when you were young. Or perhaps you will recall the sayings of a friend who has spent a lifetime deep in the country. Whether your journey is one of discovery or rediscovery, there is infinite pleasure to be had in understanding the land, waters and the skies around you.

Magic at dawn . . . morning mist begins to lift from a forest-rimmed lake, revealing the delicate tracery of the foliage in the foreground, yet still shrouding in mystery and enchantment the green beauty beyond. The appeal of the scene is universal, timeless, like the wonder of nature in all its miraculous manifestations.

Awaken to nature's sights and sounds

About 65 years ago, a Stone Age man wandered down from the mountains of northern California. His name was Ishi and he was the last member of a tribe of Indians who had hidden in the mountains since he was a child. He had never used a metal tool or anything not made from stone or wood. His arrival caused a sensation in scientific circles, but what is often overlooked is that Ishi knew how to look at nature. Within a few minutes after he went into the woods, Ishi would know where the animals were, and where he could find fresh water and edible plants. His senses of sight, smell and hearing were probably no more acute than yours – he simply knew how to use them.

Expert woodsmen like Ishi learn through experience. If there is one main lesson they can teach it is that you do not have to know a lot about nature to be fully aware of it – you simply have to give your senses a chance. For example, sound is the key to seeing wild animals. If, on your next outing, you see an animal you have just heard, think how many times you must have heard it before you spotted it.

Once you see the fine details of a blossom or bud through a magnifying glass, you will want one with you on every nature walk.

For a change in perspective, look up, down and through

A shift in your position can open your eyes to a whole new world. Look straight overhead through the transparent gold of aspen foliage to the blue autumn sky (above) – lie on your back for easier viewing or photographing. If it is spring, look at the fresh green of birches or the red of a copper beech from the same angle. For another viewpoint, kneel or lie on the damp blanket of last year's oak leaves for a close-up of the fragile, fleeting beauty of hepatica blossoms (right) and the leathery texture of their deeply coloured leaves.

Many animals rely on sound to communicate among themselves – and to alert them to danger. Therefore, you will be able to observe even more wildlife by being careful about the sounds you make. If you are talking to companions, speak in low tones (oddly enough, whispers may carry further – there is often a hissing sound to a whisper, which may frighten the very animals you are looking for). You can sometimes see the results of being quiet if you meet a noisy group of walkers clomping down a path. They will often be preceded by a "wall" of frightened animals, fleeing from the noise.

For many people, one of the entertaining features of nature-watching is being observed by the animals themselves. After all, can you imagine how interesting a human being must appear to a tiny rodent or bird? Many wildlife photographers have had the experience of carefully setting up a camera at the entrance of an animal's den or a bird's nest, and waiting – only to discover that the occupant is off in the distance, much too busy observing the photographer to return home. Thus the secret of successful animal-watching is to become part of the natural scene.

The scents of the out-of-doors are nature's exquisite gifts to visitors. There is very little you can do to seek them out. But, when you encounter a noticeable fragrance, make the most of it. Many people forget how acute the human sense of smell really is. Ishi could track an animal by scent. (He refused to hunt with anyone who smoked.)

Occasionally, make a point of analysing what it is you are smelling. You will undoubtedly be surprised not just by the variety of scents, but by your own ability to identify them.

The aromatic odour of wild garlic (whether or not you know its name) undoubtedly enhances the day.

Places as well as things have their own distinctive scents. A Mediterranean seaside resort, for instance, smells nothing like Blackpool. And the fragrance of a tropical night is a far cry from the tang of the wind on Dartmoor.

Smell enables you to retain and savour experiences without collecting a thing. Curiously, odour seems to be connected with memory to an extraordinary extent. Probably the reason why so little is said about the human sense of smell is the difficulty of putting this particular perception into words. But if you are powerfully affected by a scent in a particular time and place, you can trust the scent to take you back again.

When it comes to finding birds, your ears can often be more help than your eyes. The first step in sorting out the medley of bird sounds is to learn the difference between a call and a song. Almost all birds have a number of calls – usually very short bursts of sharp, high-pitched notes. Birds call to communicate with others of their species – to keep in touch, to signal the discovery of food, or to warn of danger. A song is longer, with a recognisable melody or rhythmic pattern. Only males of the songbird species sing. They do so to proclaim their identity and establish a territory.

• Birds of different species may heed each other's warning calls. When a hawk flies overhead, blue jays are quick to sound the alarm. Species may co-operate in calling and diving at a predator. This behaviour, called mobbing, is a great help to birdwatchers in spotting a hawk or an owl.

• Most birds are quiet at midday. You will hear most songs just before or during the breeding season. In midsummer, most birds are silent. Warblers, finches and sparrows often sing during migration.

• Some birds take their names from their calls, for instance the cuckoo and the peewit, whose sounds are unmistakable.

• To attract birds, make squeaking noises by kissing the back of your hand. Birds are curious, and will come out to locate the source of the strange sounds.

A male red-spotted bluethroat is a normally shy inhabitant of northern European swamps and thickets. But in the breeding season he will – when he feels challenged – come forth boldly to defend his territory with song. Usually a visitor, the bluethroat started breeding in Scotland in 1968.

The natterjack has a voice out of all proportion to its tiny body. If you are lucky, you may hear the male's courtship song in July and August. Listen for it in sand dunes or heathland near a pond. Sadly, the species is becoming rare and is even in danger of becoming extinct.

Seeing patterns in nature

Shapes and patterns of living things are functional, helping the species to survive. Their intricacy – or simplicity – seems designed to please the human eye. The inanimate world, too, is full of intriguing shapes that range from canyons cut by swift-flowing rivers to the latticework of ice on a frozen pond. Developing an awareness of this aspect of nature will enhance your enjoyment of the outdoors.

At first glance, the twining tendrils on a vine may seem tangled and haphazard. But look more closely. How perfectly formed are the tiny spirals in the stems,

and how well they do their work of carrying the leaves towards light. If you look for patterns and textures, you will find them all around you, even in the most ordinary rocks and minerals. Split a specimen of slate, and you will see the characteristic layered pattern of this common rock.

Living things cannot be split like rocks or minerals, but you can divide them in your mind's eye. Most of the more complex animals, such as birds and human beings, can be divided down the middle into two matched halves. Leaves with a central vein share this kind of organisa-

tion, called bilateral symmetry. Slit such a leaf along the vein, and you will have almost identical parts. The match is never absolutely perfect, for nature provides many variations within any "scheme of things". If you have a frontface photograph of yourself – say a passport picture – take a square or rectangular pocket mirror and place it at a right-angle to the picture, in the centre of your face. Hold the mirror so that it reflects one side of your face; then turn the mirror and look at the other side of the photo. You will see that your own face would look quite different if it really were perfectly symmetrical.

Another form of symmetry – often three-dimensional – is the spiral. Like the tendrils of a vine, the horns of mountain rams are three-dimensional spirals. So, too, are fiddleheads (the young leaves of ferns). However, once the frond is unfurled, its bilateral symmetry can easily be seen. Thus many organisms have more than one kind of symmetry.

Many flowers are radially symmetrical – that is, the pattern radiates outwards from a central point like spokes in a wheel. Actually, the basis of radial symmetry is the circle, which is a common form in nature. (Think of mushroom caps and daisies.) When a third dimension is added, the circle becomes a sphere – for example, the seed head of a dandelion.

Some shapes in nature are symmetrical polygons. The combs built by honeybees are hexagons – six-sided units that lend themselves particularly well to tight packing. Curiously enough, the first cell that the bees make is circular; but as the chambers are packed together, they become compressed, forming hexagons. Such hexagonal cells, formed into a solid honeycomb, are the most efficient way of grouping cells to share the warmth and protection of the hive and to give access to the working bees.

Pentagons are five-sided forms, and are frequently found among sea animals. Every starfish begins life as a five-sided embryo, no matter how many arms it may develop later. Scientists believe that this particular symmetry is an advantage to such species because pentagons have no natural plane of cleavage; hence they are unusually strong and can withstand considerable buffeting by waves.

Quite often, patterns and forms are marvels of efficiency – as in the aerodynamics of a bird's wing or the shape of a fish that enables it to glide in water with the least resistance. But nature's wonders are not all explicable; its patterns need not be appreciated for utility alone.

Bark flakes off in a jigsaw pattern. This close-up reveals the way bark is replaced from within.

Side-lighting emphasises depth; natural streaks are part of the composition.

1

2

A gallery of symmetries

1. Bilateral symmetry, where the right side matches the left (to a great extent), is so commonplace that we tend to overlook it. But it is worth a second glance, whether in the stern visage of an owl, or in the balance of its wings.

2. Radial symmetry is often complex. A dandelion's seed head is spherical; each feathery "parachute" is radial.

3. Pentagonal symmetry is common among plants, but rare among animals – except for sea creatures such as starfish.

4. The geometric perfection of the spiral in a nautilus shell, seen in this cutaway view, is unusual. Other shells grow in spiral form. But the spiral is more prevalent in plants, ranging from tendrils to the whorled arrangement of branches, like the steps on a winding staircase.

5. The hexagons in a honeycomb are the most economical use of space possible – a shape often found in crystals.

3

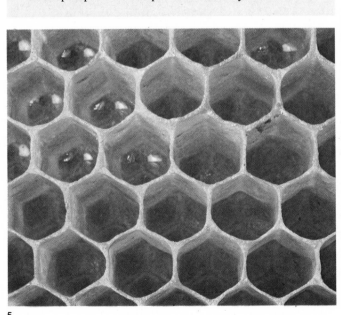

5

4

Colours that communicate

Animals do not see colours as human beings can. To begin with, few species have eyes and brains similar enough to our own for them to see the same spectrum of colours.

But an even greater difference lies in the interpretation of what is seen. The human response to colours in foliage and flowers, butterflies and birds, is aesthetic – we are struck by their beauty. But to many animals, colours are as utilitarian as traffic signals. They are frequently a means of communication – either advertisements to potential mates or warnings to enemies.

Of course, animals do not make a judgment between colours that attract and those that repel. They simply see the message and react instinctively, almost like programmed robots. The colours displayed by a courting male bird cause the female's brain to secrete hormones that make her sexually receptive – no thought is involved.

In some cases, however, the animal may be reacting to what it has learned from previous experiences with creatures bearing the same, or similar, markings. For example, animals that have been injured by the poisonous spines of a brightly

From blossom to child a message passes. That message is the compelling attraction of colour. And the girl, like a bee, responds by moving closer to the sickle-leaved golden asters.

A perfect bull's-eye, at the centre of this peacock gazania (a shrubby South African perennial), is surrounded by a pattern of dots and spots. These direct insects to the flower's pollen-bearing parts.

The shiny red fruits of the holly attract a pine grosbeak, a large northern finch. Home owners who appreciate berries on their holly plants may bemoan the depredations of fruit-eating birds. But by plucking the fruit, such birds help to disperse the seeds inside. The bright colour of the berries is not mere decoration – it serves as an advertisement.

coloured fish may later avoid that species.

The distinctive colours of flowers advertise the pollen and nectar inside. Such colours attract birds, butterflies, bees, and other insects that feed on these substances. At the same time, the animals pollinate the plants (that is, they transfer genetic material from one plant to another, thus fertilising them).

Many insects seem to prefer certain colours. For example, honeybees will usually visit a blue or yellow flower before they visit others. Hummingbirds and other nectar-eating species are attracted to red.

Some animals change colour just before the breeding season. This is true of certain species of fish. In temperate climates, numerous male birds take on bright plumage in the spring. Besides attracting a mate, the vivid colours make the male easily identifiable by other males.

This is part of the process by which a male asserts his territorial rights. To a female rose-breasted grosbeak, for instance, the male's bright, heart-shaped patch is attractive; but it repels males of other species. At times, conspicuous colours may be a disadvantage, making the animal more visible to predators.

Thus many species display their colours only under certain circumstances. A red-winged blackbird, for example, flaunts his red and yellow epaulettes (shoulder patches) when he spreads his wings; normally, the colours are almost hidden.

Many poisonous or harmful animals are vividly coloured; tropical frogs and coral snakes, for example. You might think that animals so well defended with poison would not need to warn away potential attackers. But even though a poisonous animal may emerge victorious in any battle, it is better not to be attacked in the first place.

Many harmless animals gain protection by mimicking the colours of dangerous species – the viceroy butterfly resembles the bad-tasting monarch.

In other cases, one species of poisonous butterfly may mimic another poisonous one. By looking alike, the different butterflies increase the chances that hungry predators will leave them alone.

Some scientists believe that almost every colour found in nature has a function. The bright red of many berries is actually an advertisement to encourage birds to eat them. For the berries contain seeds, and if eaten by birds the seeds will be carried to a new location. Such dispersal is an advantage to the plant species, because it lessens competition.

Resembling a tiny, leotard-clad dancer, this arrow-poison frog can be deadly to predators. Glands in the skins of these Central and South American frogs secrete some of the deadliest venom known. It was used by Indians to paralyse the living targets of their arrows.

Mimicry is borrowed protection

The insect world has numerous examples of sheep in wolves' clothing – harmless creatures that resemble a more harmful species. Certain wasp-like insects are really flies; crickets mimic acid-spraying beetles.

Birds, reptiles and other predators are less likely to attack such mimics once they have eaten one of the models. The harmless ones have a better chance of survival. A model-and-mimic pair is shown below.

Monarch butterfly

The monarch is the model – a bad-tasting butterfly that predators learn not to eat. Its larvae feed on milkweed, which imparts an unpleasant taste.

Viceroy butterfly

The viceroy is the mimic – a palatable butterfly that evolved a pattern resembling the monarch's. Its larvae eat willow and poplar leaves.

Camouflaged by colour and form

In all probability, most wild animals you see in their natural surroundings are moving when you catch sight of them – a deer bolting across a road, an eagle soaring overhead, a squirrel or rabbit scampering away through the woodland.

For many animals are so well camouflaged that you do not notice them unless they move and reveal their presence.

Many leafhoppers, caterpillars, beetles and other insects are the same colour as the leaves or stems where they are usually found. Fish (such as flounder), crabs, snails and other seashore creatures blend with the colour of the sand or rocks.

Many animals have less specific camouflage – they are darker on the back (or top) than on the underside. This is called countershading. At first glance, countershading may not seem to provide much protection. But most objects in the outdoors – animals included – are lighted from above, by the sun; the portions below are shaded. Countershading compensates for the effect of light.

In water, a penguin's dark back makes it harder for predatory seals to spot from above against the gloom of the water. From below, the penguin's light belly makes it harder to see against the glare of the surface.

Some animals actually wear their background. Caddisfly larvae, which live in streams, build cocoon-like protective cases with twigs and tiny pebbles from the stream bed. Decorator crabs are so named because they place bits of seaweed and sponges on their backs. These decorations continue to grow on the animal's shell.

Certain masters of disguise appear to be something they are not. A stick insect, for example, looks like part of a twig. Other animals adopt their disguises only when needed. When some birds are threatened, they assume a posture that helps them blend with the foliage.

Certain caterpillars rear up when disturbed – a position in which they resemble parts of leaves or stems.

Many tropical fish are so brightly coloured that one might suppose they could easily be seen. But when such a fish swims close to a coral reef, the colour and pattern of the fish merge almost invisibly with the brilliantly coloured background.

Zebras are camouflaged in a similar way – when they are in a group, their stripes make it difficult to see where one zebra ends and another begins.

Contrary to popular belief, however, the chameleon does not change colour to camouflage itself. The colour changes reflect changes in light, temperature and emotions – for example, sudden fear.

The effect of animal camouflage is often so dramatic, it seems as if the creature planned it that way. But the colours and patterns of a species are the result of millions of years of evolution. In many cases, animals that were not well camouflaged were preyed upon in large numbers, and thus left fewer offspring than their camouflaged relatives.

Some present-day species are difficult to detect even among themselves; other signals – such as sounds and scents – are the principal means by which they make their presence known to potential mates or competitors.

Some predators are blind to certain colours. What looks like a conspicuous pattern or colour to a normal human eye may escape the notice of an owl. Like other nocturnal birds, owls are believed to be sensitive only to black, grey and white.

Of course, many predators are also camouflaged, thereby gaining an advantage when stalking prey. Witness the leopard. As Rudyard Kipling wrote of this magnificent cat, "You can lie out on the bare ground and look like a heap of pebbles . . . you can lie right across the centre of a path and look like nothing in particular. Think of that and purr!"

Key to camouflaged insects

Few habitats in the world have the abundance of species to be found in a tropical rain forest. The painting opposite illustrates a number of insects that flourish in the jungle near Rio de Janeiro, Brazil. (Of course, you would never find them clustered in this way.) It is a challenge to locate all of the 11 insects without referring to the key below – each one is so camouflaged. Not only do their colours blend into the background of bark and lichen; their shapes and postures also help them to hide.

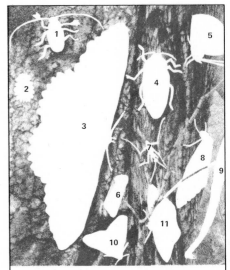

1. Long-horned beetle	6. Prominent moth
2. Stink bug	7. Praying mantis
3. Owlet moth	8. Sphinx moth
4. Metallic wood-boring beetle	9. Section of stick insect
5. Brush-footed butterfly	10. Noctuid moth
	11. Noctuid moth (different species)

The least bittern often relies on its uncanny "reed posture" – neck extended, bill straight up, feathers flattened. Not even its eyes move. Thus it blends with its marshy habitat.

Glowing light, shimmering colour

If you have ever caught a glow worm or a firefly, you know that the little insect's "fire" does not burn – in fact, it is one of the coldest lights on earth. Most man-made illumination gives off not just light, but a great deal of heat as well. In contrast, the insects' tiny lanterns are nearly 100% efficient; little energy is wasted as heat.

In Britain the insect that brings pin-points of light to the late summer evenings is the glow worm, the flightless female of a species of beetle found on grassy banks. Its signals attract the flying but unillumi-nated males. In most of the rest of Europe, however, for about two weeks fireflies streak through the air like miniature shooting stars.

Firefly flashes are actually signals that enable males and females of the same species to get together. The female rarely flies (her body is heavier because she car-ries the eggs). So in the evening, she takes a position on the ground where she can see and be seen – perhaps on a blade of grass. The males flash signals to her as they fly over the area.

The female responds only to a particu-lar pattern of flashes; she signals back. Different species have different patterns, and when a male sees the right pattern flashing below, he descends to the ground and the two mate.

Scientists have discovered that firefly signals are not as simple as they seem.

Biologists lurking in the grass with tiny torches found that they could attract male fireflies by imitating the signals of females.

They also discovered that female fire-flies of a certain species can mimic the patterns of other species. However, such behaviour is not by any means a technique used for courtship. The female of this mimicking species is apparently predatory – when the males arrive, she devours them.

Surprisingly, bioluminescence (the ability of an organism to produce light) is not rare, although people seldom see it. Certain bacteria, toadstools, sponges, cor-als, marine worms, clams, snails, squid and deep-sea fish can make their own light.

In the darkness of the ocean depths, rows of luminescent organs on a fish's body may look like tiny portholes. These lights are believed to be useful in com-munication and in the search for food. Sometimes they may also help to warn off enemies.

Some animals that seem to be biolumi-nescent are actually reflecting light, not producing it. The eyes of cats, deer, owls and many other creatures do not really glow. A silvery reflective layer in the back of their eyes helps them to see at night by collecting weak light from the moon and stars. This layer, in effect, acts like a mir-ror, reflecting outwards. Human beings have similar layers in their eyes, although

the reflecting surface is not so large. One of the few times you can see "glowing" eyes in human beings is in the pink eyes that often show up in colour photographs taken with a flashbulb.

Another distinctive phenomenon is iridescence – colours that seem to shim-mer over the surface of birds' feathers, particularly those of hummingbirds and peacocks. Many insects – beetles, moths and butterflies – are also iridescent. This kind of colouring differs from other col-ours in nature.

For example, the green in plant leaves is caused by pigmentation, and the micro-scopic green cells appear green no matter the angle at which light strikes them. By contrast, iridescent colours depend on the angle at which the light strikes – a feather may shimmer from blue to purple to green. Such colours are called structural. On close examination, there may be little or no pigment there.

Iridescence is an optical illusion. The colours are produced by tiny grooves and ridges on an animal's feathers or scales. These structures act somewhat like a prism, separating light into its component colours. A similar illusion is produced on gramophone records – if a record is deeply scratched, you can see it is black, not multi-coloured. The same is true of the purple flashes on the throat of a starling – the colour is in the eye of the beholder.

NATURE OBSERVER
Watching the flashing patterns of fireflies

In continental Europe you may see fireflies for a period of about two summer weeks, especially on a warm, moist night. Some species spend about two years as larvae, burrowing through the soil and feeding on slugs, snails and worms. The larvae have a bite that anaesthetises their prey. Some look like short centipedes, and many have tiny spots of light on their abdomens. These lights may play a role in keeping the animals together. At a certain stage, the larva builds a little "igloo" of mud and spins a coat inside it. There, the larva changes into a winged adult. The adults live only long enough to mate and reproduce. In fact, some do not eat at all during their brief existence. Others feed on pollen and nectar.

If you catch a firefly, do so carefully and release it after you have studied it. These insects are declining because of pollution, so every one should be handled with care.

Spectacularly coloured plumage generally belongs to the male of the species, like this broad-billed hummingbird. The bright colours of male birds are thought to serve two important functions – attracting the females and warning off competing males.

The wings of a moth (or butterfly), such as the Urania below, are an iridescent mosaic of millions of minute, tile-like scales. The moth is named after the Greek goddess Urania, whose name means heavenly one.

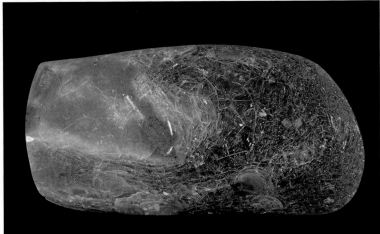

The sparks of colour that seem to leap like flames from an opal (above) are caused mainly by impurities in this glass-like mineral. Yellows and reds are produced by iron oxides; trapped gas bubbles create the milky sheen.

The silvery layer that causes the eyes of many animals to glow (such as the deer, left) helps the animals to see in the dark. The "mirrors" are visible only in dim light, when the pupils are dilated – another aid to night vision.

What is ecology all about?

Ecology is the present-day name for what used to be called natural history. (The word ecology began to be used about a century ago, but did not come into common usage until the 1960s.)

In their time, men like Charles Darwin, Alexander von Humboldt, John James Audubon and Henry David Thoreau were known as naturalists; today, they would probably be called ecologists. These early ecologists studied how plants and animals lived in relation to their total environment, not as isolated organisms.

The concept of evolution, which was explained by Darwin, had the unexpected effect of diverting many scientists from the study of natural history. Darwin's ideas on how species had developed caused some scholars to concentrate on particular species, instead of observing them in relation to the environment as a whole. The British biologist Charles Elton, who established the principles of ecology, wrote that Darwin's discoveries sent "the whole zoological world flocking indoors".

Today, ecology has become something of a catchword. In almost any newspaper, you can find a story describing a controversy between "ecologists" and advocates of a new dam or power plant. Actually, this is a misuse of the word. Ecology is the study of the relationships of organisms to their environment (including all other organisms present).

The word environment should not be intimidating. It is a very flexible term – we often speak of the *total* environment (the earth) or the *home* environment (which is really a sociological idea).

When ecologists use the word, they are generally describing a *particular* natural situation, and are including all the animate and inanimate components of the place – the air, water, soil and living things, both plants and animals. As a matter of fact, the living and non-living parts of an environment are so intertwined – by the food chains they are part of and by a particular species' choice of home – that it is almost impossible to separate them.

Of course, the total environment – the earth – is not the same throughout. The *biosphere*, the thin outer shell that supports life, is part sea, part land. The terrestrial environment is further divided into grassland, desert, forest, and so on. Each of these major divisions of the land areas is called a *biome*. Specific biomes have many things in common.

For example, deserts in Africa are much like those in Asia; rain forests in the Amazon region are similar to those along the Congo River.

The borders between biomes are called *ecotones*. These zones of transition, such as the seashore, harbour species from the biomes on either side. You may find a tiny crab that is temporarily living above the tide; many birds spend as much time on the water as on land.

In spite of the wide adaptability of most organisms they usually inhabit specific neighbourhoods, or *habitats*. In the sea, for example, there are numerous habitats – the tidal zone, the shallow

Few biomes are as clearly defined as these tiny, forest-covered islands that dot a lagoon in the western Pacific. Here, through the nearly transparent water, you can see another biome – the coral reef that fringes the shoreline and encroaches on the shallow, sandy areas. There is a relatively sharp transition between these biomes; the ecotone, or zone of blending, is not extensive in this region because there is so little variation in the tides. Most biomes, such as grasslands, forests and marshes, blend almost imperceptibly into neighbouring zones.

offshore regions, the ocean floor, and others.

Habitats are often likened to the addresses of plants or animals. Unlike biomes, habitats are not restricted to physical surroundings. A dog may be the habitat of a flea; a flea's digestive tract may be the habitat of a microbe.

These small habitats are often called *microhabitats*. For example, the underside of a fallen log is a microhabitat within a forest, as are the leaves of certain plants (see the pictures on the right).

Most of the organisms living in a specific habitat are affected in some way by the others. Together, these interrelated plants and animals are called a *community*. Each species uses the habitat differently, depending on such things as time of day.

A hawk is a daytime hunter; a moth is a nocturnal nectar-eater. The role an organism plays in its habitat is called its *niche*. It could also be called its profession – or its way of life.

Microhabitats are worlds within worlds

An entire community can live in the little pools of rainwater that collect in the hollows formed by the leathery leaves of bromeliads (a type of epiphyte, or air plant). These short-stemmed plants often retain water for long periods. A scientist who drained one of these miniature reservoirs found over a dozen kinds of insects in the water, even tiny crabs. Many creatures, such as tree frogs and mosquitoes, grow to adulthood in these pools, and others may remain all their lives. Not all microhabitats are as stable as the ones in bromeliads. Those that may develop in a snowbank next to the shelter of a rock sometimes produce a small population and then die out.

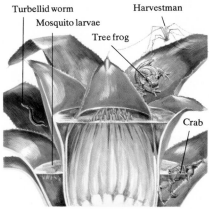

Turbellid worm
Harvestman
Mosquito larvae
Tree frog
Crab

The home range of these brilliant Anthias fish is the craggy, vertical wall of a coral reef in the Red Sea. Nearly every animal has a home range – a familiar area where it feeds and breeds.

 NATURE OBSERVER
A niche is more than just a place

In architecture, a niche is a recessed place that contains a statue. In nature, a niche is more a role than a place. The niche of any species is its position in the community – what and where it eats, who its predators are, where it nests, and when it is active. The squirrel, for example, is a woodland-dweller that nests in trees, eats buds, pine seeds and nuts, and is preyed upon mainly by martens.
• An animal's niche may change with time. A frog egg hatches into an aquatic plant-eating tadpole; later, it adopts a terrestrial, insect-eating way of life. Many ducks and geese hatch on the tundra (where they feed on insects); they fly south, feeding on freshwater weeds along the way. They spend the winter in saltwater bays.
• It is a basic assumption of ecology that no two species occupy the same niche in a community at any one time. So you can think of niches as a natural means of lessening competition. Consider two closely related water birds – the shag and the cormorant. These birds are large, dark, and long-billed. In fact, they evolved from a common ancestor, but they have different niches. The shag fishes in shallow waters, the cormorant out at sea; the shag nests near the base of cliffs, the cormorant at higher locations. In spite of their similar appearances, competition between the two species is not fierce, because they have evolved different ways of life.

Adaptation: built-in survival mechanisms

An elephant's trunk, a giraffe's neck, a kangaroo's pouch, and a humming-bird's ability to hover have one thing in common – they are all adaptations.

An adaptation is any characteristic of form or behaviour that aids an animal's survival. Plants, too, are adapted to their environments. These adaptations took countless generations to develop, probably through many small changes. This is the essence of evolution.

The dynamics of adaptation can be demonstrated in a classic example of the way one kind of bird diversified into many species. When Charles Darwin studied the finch populations on the Galapagos islands, he found that these islands had a variety of habitats. Within the habitats, the niches (opportunities for making a living) were filled by finches that had evolved in different ways.

They developed bills of different shapes, depending on the type of food available. Some retained the short, seed-cracking bill typical of finches. Others developed long, curved bills suitable for picking insects from crevices. One insect-eating species even took to using a long cactus spine for digging out insects.

All species of plants and animals are thought to have originated in much the same way, though not all continue to diversify. Ginkgo trees, ferns, dragonflies, opossums and crocodiles have changed very little from their ancient forms, which we know from fossils. On the other hand, scientists believe that the perching birds (including finches) may still be evolving as they adapt to their treetop life.

The eastern and western meadowlarks of North America are examples of recently developed species. Their plumages and behaviour patterns are almost identical, and their ranges overlap, but they have recognisably distinct songs and calls – and most important, they rarely interbreed.

Many different groups have developed similar structures. For example, birds, bats and insects all have wings. Conversely, similar life-forms often develop in different directions. The marsupials (pouched animals) of Australia are all closely related, but they are adapted to many different life-styles. Even the ways they move vary – they run, hop, climb, burrow or glide.

Populations are held in balance by natural factors. Among these are the food supply, predators and disease. If a species is moved to a different environment, the natural checks may be absent. In that case, the introduced species may threaten to take over. The starling of Europe and the walking catfish of Asia, both introduced to North America, are now regarded as serious pests for this reason.

Sometimes plants and animals develop adaptations that prove to be a trap. For example, the Australian koala bear is dependent solely on a few species of eucalyptus for its food; it cannot live beyond the range of these trees. The distribution of many rare wildflowers also seems self-limiting, perhaps because they thrive only on an unusual balance of minerals in the soil. In other words, for some species a precarious existence is a result of evolution and not the fault of mankind.

Two methods of feeding

Two birds that feed in water are the brown pelican (left) and the American avocet (below). But the ways they have adapted to their environments are vastly different. The high-diving pelican, a ponderous, web-footed bird, uses a pouch of skin on its lower jaw to scoop fish from the sea. (True to the popular rhyme, the bill of the pelican indeed holds "more than its belly can" – up to 3 gallons.) The graceful, long-legged avocet feeds while wading through the shallow waters of tidal marshes and alkaline lakes. It moves its long, upturned bill from side to side, thereby dislodging the small aquatic animals which form its diet.

Seeds give a plant mobility

One adaptation that enables plants to survive is their ability to travel. In the form of seeds, many are capable of extended journeys. Coconuts drifting on the waves have colonised remote oceanic islands. Dandelion and milkweed seeds are carried for miles by the wind. Winged fruits of maples twist through the air like miniature helicopters. Burrs and tick-seeds hitch-hike on the fur of animals and the clothes of people; small seeds cling to the feathers and feet of birds. Seeds are often carried thousands of miles by car, train, plane and ship. These wanderers are tough. Some seeds that are centuries old have actually sprouted. Many can survive long exposure to extreme heat and cold. Some stay viable when immersed in salt water. Many withstand the digestive juices of animals that have swallowed fruits, which attract them as food and, of course, contain seeds.

Witch hazel has ballistic seeds

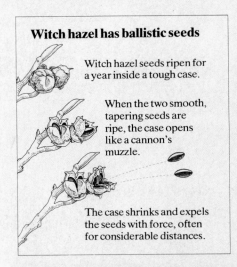

Witch hazel seeds ripen for a year inside a tough case.

When the two smooth, tapering seeds are ripe, the case opens like a cannon's muzzle.

The case shrinks and expels the seeds with force, often for considerable distances.

Rough-surfaced, pointed pods of green milkweed open up when ripe and brown, launching wind-borne seeds into the air. The fluffy parachutes – modified parts of the seed coat – carry seeds for many miles. The silky fibres are so buoyant that they have sometimes been used by human beings to fill life-jackets.

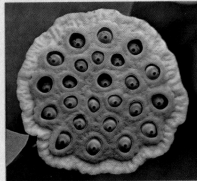

The sacred lotus of Asia (left) is prized world-wide by owners of garden pools. Its blossoms rise a foot or more above the water. The centre is the seed holder. As the seeds mature (above), this part grows heavier and changes colour. The "seed carton" breaks off, turns over, and drifts – allowing the seeds to drop out and plant themselves in the shallow water.

The varied life-styles of animals

Most animal species live in comparative peace. Much of the noisy squabbling among birds and sparring among mammals is only ritual fighting – bluffing rather than the real thing. Such activities are signalling systems that enable the animals to assert their claims. It is only after the signals have failed that animals come to blows. This is especially true of fights between individuals of the same species.

Within any species, there is generally a definite social system. Some animals are solitary for most of the year. Others live in groups – wolves in packs, lions in prides, antelope in herds, and penguins in tremendous colonies. The most complex social systems are those of some insects, such as termites and honeybees. These social insects are so strictly organised that they almost seem to possess a single identity

Within each social system, rules of conduct give order to the group. For example, many gregarious animals will not allow another of their kind to come too close.

When swallows perch together, they do not bunch up, but look as if they had precisely measured the spaces between themselves. Walruses, on the other hand, lie all over one another on an Arctic beach, noisy but peaceful.

In the breeding season many animals, especially birds and mammals, become snappish about space. Male songbirds proclaim ownership of a territory – a segment of field or wood. Seabirds nesting in colonies also hold a territory, but it is usually small and can be measured by how far a sitting bird can jab with its beak.

The chief purpose of a territory is to attract a mate and then to rear offspring. The animals do not know this consciously, of course, but they act as if they do, and strongly defend their territories against intruders.

Solitary animals do not always have a territory. However, they may have what is known as a home range. Each animal hunts and pursues its other life habits in the area with which it has become familiar.

A home range is like a home town, where you know all the important places.

Tigers, like many big predators, have enormous ranges. For many species, home ranges overlap, but there is no problem so long as two individuals do not meet.

Among most mammals, the females care for the young without help. Male elk, antelope and elephant seals round up large temporary harems, but totally ignore their offspring. Only a few species – wolves and some monkeys, for example – share parental tasks. The duration of male-female relationships and the length of infancy vary with each species.

Most animals of different species are indifferent to one another. An elephant pays no attention to a zebra. Then there are animals that compete for the same food. Hyenas have first choice at a kill, while vultures wait. Actually, plant-eaters (herbivores) greatly outnumber meat-eaters (carnivores). So many animals live long, relatively peaceful lives.

Parasitism is a further interspecies relationship. A true parasite is an animal that lives at the expense of another species. Many kinds of worms are internal parasites, which damage their hosts but seldom kill them outright.

In another form of relationship, the guest is aided, but the host is not seriously inconvenienced – for example, the barnacles that hitch a ride on a whale. In a different, more amiable relationship, each partner benefits. Small tropical fish remove and devour parasites from the skin of larger species, which stay still while the service is being performed.

Sometimes a solitary hunter, sometimes part of a pack, a coyote may hunt co-operatively with other species. Coyotes probably pair for life. A family stays together from spring into autumn; in the middle of winter, the adults mate.

Penguins are colonial birds that spend most of their lives in close contact – millions may live in a single colony. These are king penguins. Note the fuzzy youngsters, some with tufts still clinging to their emerging adult plumage.

A playful predator, the agile river otter may spend as much time cavorting as it does fishing. If you are lucky enough to catch a glimpse of an otter, you will probably find at least one other near by. Otters sometimes team up to drive fish into shallow waters.

NATURE OBSERVER
Seeing animals through binoculars

To get the most from binoculars, you need to know how to use them. Practise with them on still targets.
• Find the quarry by watching quietly for movement. Once you have spotted a bird or mammal, note a point of reference, such as a forked limb or tree stump.

• Without taking your eyes from the spot slowly lift the binoculars into position.
• To tell someone else where to look, describe your point of reference. *Do not lower your binoculars.* Identify the place using a clock system – "nine o'clock" if it is halfway up the left side, and so on.

To scan a large area quickly and systematically, sweep your binoculars from left to right and back again, as in the diagram on the right.

Special relationships

When you think of interactions between species, the predator-prey relationship comes to mind first. But animals have evolved many other interdependencies, some beneficial, others detrimental.

This red-billed oxpecker appears to be whispering into the ear of an impala, but the bird is actually removing parasites, such as ticks and fleas, from the impala's skin. This type of relationship, called commensalism, benefits both sides.

A European cuckoo dwarfs its "parent", a hedge sparrow. This cuckoo, like North American cowbirds, is a nest parasite; it lays eggs in nests of other species. The sparrow cannot distinguish an interloper, and instinctively feeds any gaping bill.

Cycles of birth and renewal

Nature is dynamic. The expression "balance of nature" is somewhat misleading – it suggests a stability that does not exist. True, much in nature *seems* the same and much can be predicted, but no two days and no two summers are alike.

Though we are vaguely aware of certain patterns, only in comparatively recent times have scientists discovered fundamental cycles that affect our lives. The rhythms of day and night, the tides, the seasons are familiar to us all, but most other cycles escape notice because they are more subtle or occur over longer periods of time.

One man who noticed a recurrent cycle was Charles Greeley Abbot, an American astronomer. About 40 years ago, he predicted that a severe drought would hit the US central plains, "beginning about 1975". The drought arrived on schedule – crops were seriously affected, and topsoil was blown from thousands of acres.

Farmers in the area were aware that droughts occurred every now and then, but had no idea when to expect them. From weather records, Abbot realised that the dry spells had a cycle of about 20 years.

He suspected that the earth's climate – especially the amount of rainfall – was greatly affected by the changing energy-output of the sun. Today, scientists believe that the solar output is cyclical, and that drought cycles have regularly afflicted the great crop-growing areas of the world.

The longest cycle yet discovered (called an epochal cycle) is that of the earth's Ice Ages, which have occurred about every 250 million years. There are innumerable lesser cycles. The populations of many animals rise and fall every eight to ten years. Lemmings generally migrate every three or four years.

The land, too, has cycles, and perhaps these are the most important of all. The soil nourishes plants, which feed the plant-eaters, which in turn support the predators, including mankind. Thus, a decrease or increase in the productivity of the land is felt throughout nature. (Minerals washed from the soil by increased rainfall even influence similar cycles in the oceans.)

Most plants sprout or resume growth in spring, when the soil is rich with accumulated nutrients and moisture. On the African plains, most grazing animals give birth to their young at this season, when the grasses are at their lushest and before the long, dry summer gets under way.

In the course of a relatively long rainy cycle in temperate zones, grasslands may become moist enough to support trees. The first trees are likely to be conifers such as pines. These will eventually be shaded out by broad-leaved trees, in a natural sequence called succession. Forests can continue to grow for centuries, but if the weather cycle swings back towards less rainfall, the forest may dry out and perhaps be set on fire by lightning, leaving the land open to become grassland again.

Because cycles of birth and renewal start with the land, it is the land that ultimately determines how much plant and animal life can be supported in any particular place. This is called the land's carrying capacity, and it is a basic concept that we are just now beginning to understand.

Farmers, ranchers and hunters have frequently attempted to increase the carrying capacity of their land. But if the vegetation becomes overgrazed, erosion sets in, and the land can no longer support the herds and flocks that once thrived there. The carrying capacity of farmlands can be increased by fertilisers and irrigation, but these have limits because they, too, are affected by weather cycles. It is better, it seems, to discover – and follow – nature's cycles than to fight them.

A venturesome fox cub, still wobbly on its legs, sets out to explore a buzzing, green summer world. The prosperity of any animal species ultimately depends on the fertility of the land and the abundance of vegetation. From year to year, all animal populations fluctuate.

 PHOTO TIPS
From bud to flower

You can capture development from bud to flower by taking a sequence of pictures. Usually you will need close-up attachments – a bellows, extension rings, or a second lens. Almost any illumination will work – sunlight, flashbulbs, electronic flash. The light must be bright enough to let you stop down to about f/11 for sufficient depth of field. You can produce a sequence by shooting the same bud, such as this pussy willow, over a period of days. Or photograph different buds at different stages.

The tenacity of plants serves us all

Central Park in New York was planned by an American nature-lover named Frederick Law Olmstead. In the 1850s, he won the land for the park in the face of bitter opposition.

Human beings depend on oxygen, and all of it comes from plants. Yet for decades, by some incredible lapse of reasoning, the builders of cities have regarded parks and clumps of trees as impractical amenities. Many people are now insisting that urban trees be protected. "Pocket parks" are being established, making everyone aware of the renewal of spirit that is created by these green oases. Not only do trees constantly replenish the oxygen supply – they also help to cleanse the air of dirt particles, cool it on hot days (they are tireless, absolutely free air-conditioners), and conserve heat at night. Trees are also excellent sound-absorbers, a boon to any city or town with heavy traffic. It is time for town dwellers to be vigilant on behalf of trees and other plants – even weeds.

A crack in the pavement is filled and enlarged by the exuberant growth of a young ailanthus (which will become a tree, if allowed). With it are a number of other city-adapted plants.

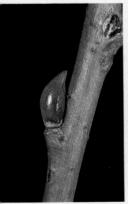

Your awareness of time

Clocks and calendars are ways mankind has invented to measure time, but nature goes by more intricate measures and rhythms. Time of day, the waxing and waning of the moon and season of the year come to mind first. But each of us is concerned with a larger time-scale as well – our own lifetime.

Oddly enough our conscious awareness of this unique, personal time-span seems to be the first casualty in the hurry of everyday living. On a grander scale, presiding over all the others, is geological time – the millions of years it takes for mountains to form and wear away.

There are other kinds of time, always present but often forgotten. Lunar time is one. The moon makes its rounds, pulling on the surface of the earth, and creating the powerful, rhythmic rise and fall of the tides. All living things – plants as well as animals – seem to follow inner timers.

These so-called biological clocks govern periods as diverse as the customary time of day that a bird will begin to sing, a lion will doze, and a flower will open. One American flower is known as a four

o'clock, because that is when its blossoms open every afternoon. There are also biological clocks that tell 17-year locusts (or insects on other schedules) to emerge from their underground burrows and whir about in the world above.

Human beings are strongly influenced by daily rhythms. Everyone recognises the "owls and larks" among us – those who are most active at night, and those whose energies are stimulated by the rising of the sun. These are personal patterns that seem to be inborn. But regardless of this tendency, when a traveller flies over long distances to a different time zone, turning night into day (or vice versa), the individual usually feels uncomfortable.

Time might be thought of as absolutely democratic because a day gives each of us exactly the same allotment of hours. But this is not accurate. Time is subjective – a very personal perception. For example, a child and an adult together on a trip will experience time in vastly different ways. A very young child may barely understand what "again" means, or "tomorrow", or "when I was your age".

As an individual matures, the patterns of time become more coherent in his mind. The snows of winter do not come as a surprise. In fact, unless there is a toddler around discovering what wonderful stuff snow is, an adult may think only about shovelling it away.

A person's perception of time keeps shifting. As the very old can tell you, time goes more swiftly the longer you live. An old man may look at a forest and remember when, in his childhood, the land was a ploughed field. Time becomes telescoped, not by failing faculties, but by overlapping images. Each age offers a different vision, which you can capture, borrow and savour.

The point is this – somewhere along the way each individual needs to recognise that there is such a thing as personal time.

Immediate events – ranging from toothaches to far-reaching political crises – cannot be set aside. But we really have a great deal of leeway in choosing what we do with our time. If you have been thinking about getting outdoors more often, have you set aside the time?

Seeing time in four different perspectives

Many ancient peoples attempted to develop calendars that included the major elements of time – length of day, phases of the moon, and return of the seasons. For the most part, the calendars were faulty because these three elements cannot be synchronised. The most accurate calendar was that of the Maya of Central America. They recorded each kind of time separately – although they often checked one against another. In a sense, the Maya recognised the true complexity of time. Their intricate calendar is a parable for us today – time has many faces. Subjectively, for any one individual, time can be recollections of important moments, best-loved seasons, the stages of a lifetime, and those memorable occasions when we suddenly become aware of the deeper etchings of geological time.

Night gives way to day over Prince William Sound in Alaska. The morning light has penetrated the hovering bank of thick fog, and now glitters on the gently rippling waters.

A sparkling winter sun turns the graceful birch branches into a filigree of crystal-clear ice.

Reading sundials – ancient and modern

Sundials are believed to be the oldest time-telling devices in the world. Some are known to be 4,000 years old. You can make one yourself by simply putting a stick into the ground at high noon. Fix it firmly in place, at an angle, so that you get a shadow. Tilt it northwards in the Northern Hemisphere, southwards in the Southern Hemisphere. Put a pebble at the tip of the shadow. An hour later, put another pebble at the tip, and so on during the afternoon. The next morning (if it is sunny), repeat the hourly placement of pebbles until you have reached high noon once again. Set an alarm clock at hourly intervals so you will not lose track of time and miss out a pebble.

● Thereafter, the pebbles will tell the time by themselves. You will see that the shadow moves faster in the morning and evening than around noon. This is why numbers on a sundial are unevenly spaced. On the type of sundial usually seen in gardens and parks, the stick is a stone or metal angle called a gnomon. The study of sundials is called gnomonics, and the dial face is called the plane. Your advantage over all primitive sundial-makers is that you know the right time from the start, from a mechanical clock or watch; *they* had to arrive at it by the painstaking method of trial and error.

● Of course, sundials can be constructed in many different forms – some are rings, spheres, curved bars, cylinders or indented plates. All sundials function because, as the earth rotates, the sun seems to move across the heavens and causes shadows to shift precisely. Because of the tilt in the earth's axis which causes the seasons, a sundial will be exactly on time only twice a year, when the sun is directly over the equator. It will also be out by a few seconds more each year because of the almost imperceptible changes in the earth's orbit round the sun. But sundials are certainly accurate enough for everyday use, though obviously not on cloudy days. Hence, many of the inscriptions, which seem to be traditional on sundials, read, in many different languages, "I show only sunny hours".

Sundials like the one at the left are so sturdy, they are almost part of the landscape. They will tell time for centuries, although every year their accuracy decreases a few seconds.

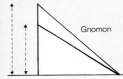

Gnomon

The angle of the gnomon depends on the location – the further from the equator, the higher the gnomon.

A tree you plant in childhood will soon tower over you. Here, two pine seedlings begin life.

The span of geological time is clearest at places like America's Grand Canyon. The oldest known rocks are at the base; these rocks, at the top, were once on the bottom of an inland sea.

CHAPTER TWO

Trees and forests

What plants do – how they live and adjust – is so ingenious, that it is hard to believe they cannot think, plan or co-operate consciously.

The plant kingdom comprises more than 95% of the living substance on earth. Trees – especially when massed in forests – are the most impressive members of the plant world. Because most species of trees live longer than human beings, they seem timeless to us. We assume a serenity in their lives that is far from the truth. As animals do, trees compete vigorously for the necessities of life – space, light and water.

Their struggle for survival is beset by drought, fire and various pests. But trees have many systems of defence. They are amazingly resilient (a chestnut tree with a dead trunk will go on sending out new shoots for decades); some exude a chemical repellent to discourage competitors (few plants can sprout beneath a eucalyptus tree); one species even has insect guardians (the bull's horn acacia is host to fiercely biting ants that ward off all animal invaders, large and small).

Just what is a tree? Or a forest? Dictionaries do not provide satisfying definitions. They say a tree is a "woody perennial" – which means a plant that develops woody tissues and that continues its growth year after year.

But the same can be said of shrubs. Some definitions specify a height of 15 ft, but shrubs such as rhododendrons often exceed this height. A forest is called a dense concentration of trees, but how many is meant by "dense"?

It is tantalising to know what a tree is, and what a forest is, yet to find their definitions so elusive. We know what trees do. They give off vital oxygen. They moderate temperatures, hold soil and prevent erosion. They are beneficial to the animal world, including man. Not the least important thing about trees and forests is their power to influence the human spirit – somehow to soothe and inspire.

Standing within the ramparts of a forest, looking out at the world, you are in a perfect place to contemplate trees. How strong and beautiful they are! A choir of bird song fills the morning. There is stillness at noon. Then, in the evening, the setting sun turns the fringe of rustling leaves to pieces of stained glass.

Every woodland is unique

When you inhale the odours of a forest, the mixture of scents is dominated by its most numerous trees. Pine forests have an unmistakable, resinous aroma.

Other woodland scents are often harder to define, but no matter how subtle the fragrance, there is usually something distinctive about a particular woodland. Even years later, a single whiff is often all that is needed to recall the times spent there.

The seasons have scents of their own. There is the invigorating air of spring, tinctured by new growth and pools of melted snow; the mixture of midsummer smells, when the thatch of ground-cover and humus keeps the soil musty and damp; the hearty autumn odour of drying vegetation and fallen leaves.

Many parts of the world share the same types of trees, especially in the Northern Hemisphere where the continents are close together.

Hundreds of Scandinavian families who moved to America with the early settlers made their homes around the Great Lakes, perhaps because the region's giant pine forests reminded them of Europe.

But more commonly, a traveller is struck by the vast differences among regional forests and woodlands. Tropical rain forests such as those near the Amazon River in South America have such a diversity of species that they are difficult to classify.

At far-flung sites, there are odd pockets of one particular species, such as the giant sequoia (a conifer native to small areas of California) and the coco-de-mer (a palm found only on a few islands in the Indian Ocean).

Australia furnishes a prime example of unique native forests – and many other unusual plants and animals as well because of its position.

Isolated from other continents for millions of years, Australia is dominated by one group of trees, the eucalyptus or gum trees. In response to local differences in soil and climate, these trees have diversified to such an extent that today there are some 600 different kinds of them.

So impressed were early European explorers by the vegetation of Australia – not just the eucalyptus but such novel flowering shrubs as banksias – that an inlet was named Botany Bay to celebrate the variety of plants. This one area had some 1,000 unfamiliar species.

Some botanical expeditions were intended to enhance the beautiful gardens of wealthy Europeans. Other voyages were more commercial. When certain prized plants were lacking in newly colonised places because of geographical barriers such as oceans and mountains, people supplied the transportation. (The famous mutiny on HMS *Bounty*, which took place in 1789, interrupted the collecting of breadfruit plants. Not only was Captain Bligh set adrift by the mutineers; the plants were also tossed overboard.)

In spite of the widespread introduction of alien species from one continent to another, native forests remain diverse, individual, and typical of their locales.

The leaves of many temperate-zone trees change colour before they drop in autumn. But in no part of the world is there so spectacular a show of autumn colours as in the broad-leaved forests of Europe and the eastern United States. This is because the climate there often provides perfect weather conditions for producing such effects: sunny autumn days, cool nights, and not much rain.

Some forests are marked by mankind. For centuries, the European attitude towards nature was that it was unruly and could be much improved by planning.

Hence many magnificent old parks lend a special – if formal – grace to the world of woodlands. Strictly speaking, they may not seem natural because they have not been allowed to grow wild. But the workings of nature can readily be seen in such places – and enjoyed just as much.

 PHOTO TIPS
Taking silhouettes of trees

What does silhouette photography show that ordinary pictures do not? For one thing, it gives a simplicity that sets off the line of the subject – in this case, a tree. Its symmetry tells you that this tree has grown alone during its formative years, unpruned, uncrowded by other trees. This is an easy clue to identifying a good subject for your photography – choose a tree that is free-standing, free-moving.

• Take photos at times of day when the background sky is most colourful. Sunset and sunrise can be equally dramatic.

• Try different exposures: one photo while standing in the shadow of the tree, then at the edge of the shadow, then in direct light (which may give you bright flares). There is no one "right" exposure, only an expression of mood.

• You do not need to know the species of tree. But the chances are that, if you have taken a real beauty, you will want to know its name. Before long, you will be on your way to learning much more about trees.

Orderly rows of trees are features of many European landscapes. They were planted to dignify the entrances to great estates and mark the highways of kings and noblemen. The inspiration for planting such groves has vanished, but their charming remnants delight the eye.

Slender mountain ashes, trailing long strips of shed bark, emerge like ghosts from the winter mist in an Australian eucalyptus forest. A dense undercover of tree ferns and antarctic beeches provides the damp, shady habitat favoured by lyrebirds.

The fragile look of birches, with their chalk-white trunks and pale green leaves, stands in marked contrast to the environment that fosters them. It seems almost impossible that something so airy looking can dwell in a Finnish woodland, so near to the icy Arctic region.

Brilliant autumn foliage is a special glory of North American forests. At a distance, it is possible to guess at the identity of trees, based on colour. The scarlets are probably maples; the yellows are likely to be birches or poplars; the dark greens are almost certainly conifers.

Where the trees are

Most people know that climate determines where certain trees can grow. What is less apparent is that it also works the other way around: trees have a significant effect on climate. All stands of trees, even narrow hedgerows, have a part in the great water cycle which is essential to the survival of life on this planet.

For trees collect water with their roots and give off water vapour from their leaves, so a forest and the surrounding area are usually more moist than areas of grassland.

This map shows where different types of trees dominate the vegetation. Human beings have cleared off trees for farming, for living space and for timber, so much of the land is no longer fully forested. Human activities, going back to prehistory, have progressively destroyed great stands of trees, thereby creating a climate drier than before.

The body plan of a tree is organised to gain maximum exposure to sunlight. Not only do the trees compete with one another for the light, but leaves on the same tree are also in competition. This is apparent not just among broad-leaved trees such as oaks and maples, but also among other species, with needle-like leaves, such as pines.

Broad-leaved trees prosper in tropical and temperate regions. In the tropics, where maximum sunlight strikes the earth, leaves – which, by temperate-zone standards, are sometimes huge – can frequently be seen crowding one another in a dense canopy high above the ground.

For similar reasons, although sunlight strikes less directly in temperate zones, a broad leaf is still advantageous.

Conifers dominate the high latitudes. Here, the light of the sun strikes the earth at an oblique angle (because of the tilt of the earth on its axis). In effect, the light has to take a longer path through the atmosphere, and the sunlight is diffused.

Under these conditions, the narrow needles of a conifer come into their own, able to capture light from any angle. Needles also lose less water into the air than do wide, flat leaves. During winter, when the water supply is locked up in ice or snow and therefore unavailable, such water conservation is important.

Where winds are harsh and frequent, as at high altitudes, conifers usually do better than broad-leaved trees, regardless of latitude.

The tough needles withstand gusts of wind that would tatter the leaves of such trees as maples. The wind's influence on trees is evident not only on wind-whipped coasts and mountains but also in your own garden.

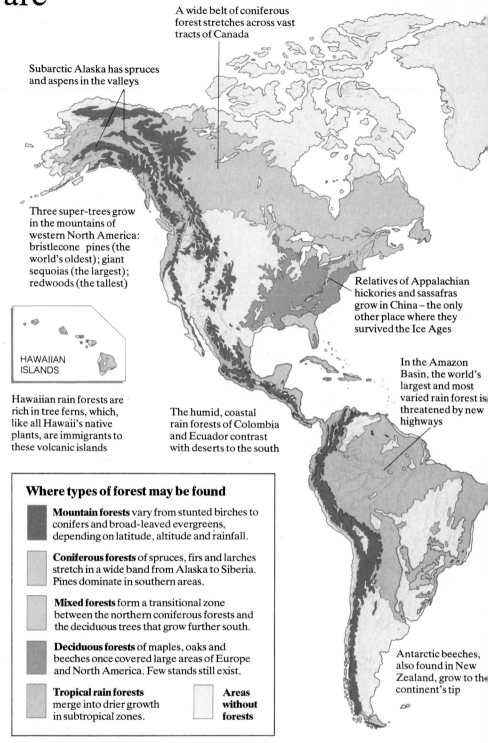

A wide belt of coniferous forest stretches across vast tracts of Canada

Subarctic Alaska has spruces and aspens in the valleys

Three super-trees grow in the mountains of western North America: bristlecone pines (the world's oldest); giant sequoias (the largest); redwoods (the tallest)

HAWAIIAN ISLANDS

Hawaiian rain forests are rich in tree ferns, which, like all Hawaii's native plants, are immigrants to these volcanic islands

The humid, coastal rain forests of Colombia and Ecuador contrast with deserts to the south

Relatives of Appalachian hickories and sassafras grow in China – the only other place where they survived the Ice Ages

In the Amazon Basin, the world's largest and most varied rain forest is threatened by new highways

Antarctic beeches, also found in New Zealand, grow to the continent's tip

Where types of forest may be found

Mountain forests vary from stunted birches to conifers and broad-leaved evergreens, depending on latitude, altitude and rainfall.

Coniferous forests of spruces, firs and larches stretch in a wide band from Alaska to Siberia. Pines dominate in southern areas.

Mixed forests form a transitional zone between the northern coniferous forests and the deciduous trees that grow further south.

Deciduous forests of maples, oaks and beeches once covered large areas of Europe and North America. Few stands still exist.

Tropical rain forests merge into drier growth in subtropical zones.

Areas without forests

Curious trees of the world

Most of us have a preconceived idea of the way a tree should look: single, narrow trunk, a leafy crown and spreading branches. But certain trees do not conform to this "lollipop" pattern. Scientists believe that shape helps the survival of a species – as, for example, when it aids in water conservation. The advantage is easy to see in some cases; at other times, the "value" to the tree is more of a puzzle.

Bristlecone pines of the high Rockies, twisted and half dead, outlive all other trees.

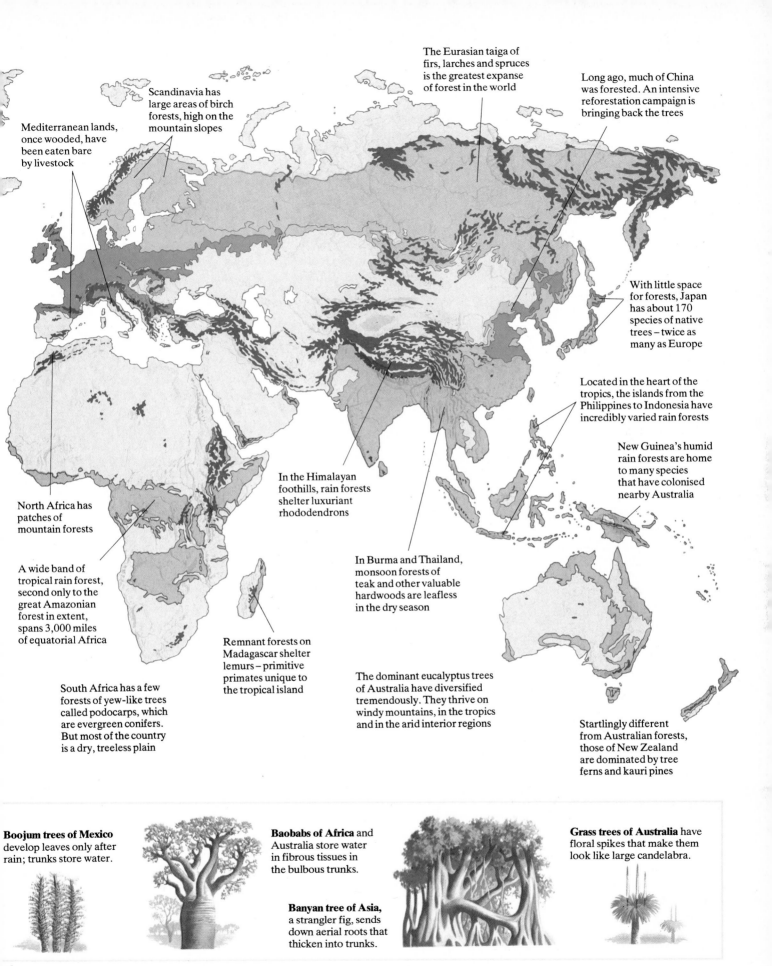

The Eurasian taiga of firs, larches and spruces is the greatest expanse of forest in the world

Long ago, much of China was forested. An intensive reforestation campaign is bringing back the trees

Scandinavia has large areas of birch forests, high on the mountain slopes

Mediterranean lands, once wooded, have been eaten bare by livestock

With little space for forests, Japan has about 170 species of native trees – twice as many as Europe

Located in the heart of the tropics, the islands from the Philippines to Indonesia have incredibly varied rain forests

North Africa has patches of mountain forests

In the Himalayan foothills, rain forests shelter luxuriant rhododendrons

New Guinea's humid rain forests are home to many species that have colonised nearby Australia

A wide band of tropical rain forest, second only to the great Amazonian forest in extent, spans 3,000 miles of equatorial Africa

In Burma and Thailand, monsoon forests of teak and other valuable hardwoods are leafless in the dry season

Remnant forests on Madagascar shelter lemurs – primitive primates unique to the tropical island

South Africa has a few forests of yew-like trees called podocarps, which are evergreen conifers. But most of the country is a dry, treeless plain

The dominant eucalyptus trees of Australia have diversified tremendously. They thrive on windy mountains, in the tropics and in the arid interior regions

Startlingly different from Australian forests, those of New Zealand are dominated by tree ferns and kauri pines

Boojum trees of Mexico develop leaves only after rain; trunks store water.

Baobabs of Africa and Australia store water in fibrous tissues in the bulbous trunks.

Banyan tree of Asia, a strangler fig, sends down aerial roots that thicken into trunks.

Grass trees of Australia have floral spikes that make them look like large candelabra.

The evolution of trees

Forests seem to us to possess a timeless and enduring quality – yet they have not always been as we see them today. The evolution of trees has taken some hundreds of millions of years. And when forests first evolved, they were low-growing, swampy, silent places, shrouded in stagnant mists. It is strange to think that trees came before insects – and even before the grasses of the world.

The long drama of plant evolution began in the primeval seas, where the waters contained every element needed for growth and reproduction. Algae were probably the first plants to leave the water and colonise the mineral-rich land.

Over the millennia, algae developed certain characteristics they had not needed in the sea – a tougher coat that retained water in the plant; pores that absorbed and gave off gases; and supporting tissues that helped them withstand the pull of gravity.

About 400 million years ago there appeared the rootless, leafless progenitor of all trees – a plant called psilophyton, from Greek words meaning naked plant. Little more than a spiny stem with branches, psilophyton had one remarkable characteristic: it stood erect, unlike the fragile algae, and reached a height of some 1–3 ft.

This is not much by modern standards, but it meant that the psilophyton was taller than its low-growing neighbours. The added height enabled it to capture sunlight – at the expense of any other plant in its vicinity.

Slowly, over countless generations, some plants grew still taller, evolving woody tissue that supported their height. One primitive kind of woody plant, called the Gilboa tree, grew as tall as 40 ft. Gilboa trees developed long, fern-like leaves and reproduced themselves by means of spores.

Spores are produced by a single plant. They may be dispersed by wind or animals, and can develop into new plants without having a second "parent".

Most spore-producing species have, at some point, a sexual stage, where male and female traits are mixed. But clusters of spores are what one can usually see on plants such as ferns.

Many scientists object to mention of sex – male and female reproduction – in connection with plants. True, it is an oversimplification, but it is also a long-standing tradition, and a convenience.

Essentially, what sexual reproduction accomplishes is the mixing of inherited traits. This means that each offspring has a different combination of traits from the others, and so there is greater variety. Such variety enables plants (and animals) to adapt to changing conditions over long periods of development.

When sexual reproduction takes place among the more advanced plants, a seed is eventually produced. The seed is a tiny plant embryo with a built-in food supply: this is an important advance over the microscopic spore because the food gives the young plant a head start. Among the first trees to produce seeds were the cordaites, ancestors of the conifers.

Conifers have survived to our day, but they have lost ground, literally, to flowering trees. These trees, including the widespread family of maples, have taken over the temperate and tropical zones.

Two adaptations of flowering trees seem to have been especially important in giving them the advantage over conifers: a more efficient water pump and a more advanced reproductive system. Rather than depending on wind pollination alone, some flowering trees attract insects and other animals by colour or scent, enlisting their aid in pollination.

From spiny stems to leafy abundance

A comparison of modern trees with fossils of their ancestors shows that big changes have occurred. Most obvious is the great increase in height and girth. Another significant change is in the method of reproduction – modern trees produce seeds, not spores. Diversity of shape seems to be greater now than in the past, but because the fossil record is incomplete, this is a matter of speculation.

Psilophyton was not a tree, but it did stand upright, higher than mosses near by. This leafless, spiny plant produced drooping cases of spores after its branches had unfurled.

The Gilboa tree, named after the American site where its fossils were found, was one of the earliest plants that seems tree-like by modern standards: it reached a height of 40 ft.

The cordaites are important to the story of tree evolution because they were some of the first trees to produce seeds instead of spores. The seeds developed in the leafy crown.

The heyday of the conifers, which bear their seeds in cones, ended millions of years ago. Once giant sequoias had an extensive range; today they grow wild only in California.

The two great categories of present-day trees

Though there are thousands of species, the living trees of the world can be divided into just two groups. A tree (like other plants) is classified by the way in which it reproduces – in this case, whether it has cones or flowers. Mature cone-bearing trees are easy to identify: look for their woody cones high in the branches or scattered on the ground. The identification of flowering trees is no problem for such species as magnolias, especially when they are in bloom. But there is greater variety among flowering trees than among conifers, and some tree flowers are so inconspicuous that they escape notice. Then, too, most flowering trees blossom only once a year (usually in spring), so this botanical habit cannot always be observed. If you see a tree that is not in flower, look around it for fruit, berries or nuts. A tree that has any of these is undoubtedly a flowering species: these varied structures are the end-products of a flower's development.

Conifer means cone-bearing

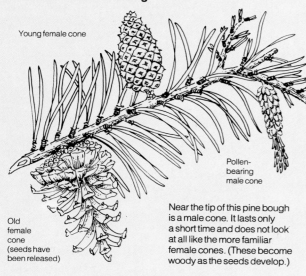

Young female cone

Old female cone (seeds have been released)

Pollen-bearing male cone

Near the tip of this pine bough is a male cone. It lasts only a short time and does not look at all like the more familiar female cones. (These become woody as the seeds develop.)

Most trees reproduce with flowers

That most trees have blossoms may come as a surprise, for people often overlook the tiny flowers on many species (right). Tulip trees, which are close relatives of magnolias, have showier flowers (below).

Flower of a tulip tree

Curved "fingers" on a tulip-tree flower bear pollen; seeds develop in the centre.

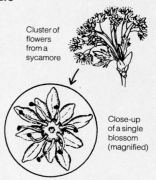

Cluster of flowers from a sycamore

Close-up of a single blossom (magnified)

Look for the clusters of small flowers that hang from a sycamore in spring. (You can also find them beneath the tree.) Each flower is either male or female; the one above, with pollen, is male.

Flowering trees dominate the world's forests, except on mountain slopes and in the far north. Sycamores bloom in the spring, although their flowers are often overlooked.

Ginkgos: "living fossils"

Noted for its exquisite fan-shaped leaves, the ginkgo stands by itself among living trees. Long before the evolution of modern conifers or broad-leaved trees, ginkgos populated temperate forests all over the world; below, a fossil shows the imprint of a distinctive ginkgo leaf. Ginkgos survived the Ice Ages only in the Orient – but today the stately and pollution-resistant trees are planted in cities around the world. Look out for them in any towns you visit.

What is an evergreen?

Evergreen is a gardener's term that is more descriptive than scientific: it means that a plant has leaves throughout the year. But the word evergreen causes confusion when it comes to learning about trees, because both of the basic types of trees – conifers and flowering varieties – have evergreen representatives.

To many people, the word evergreen means the same thing as coniferous, or cone-bearing. It is true that most conifers *are* evergreen. And because the leaves of conifers take the form of needles or scales, most conifers resemble one another. But some conifers, such as larches, are not evergreen: in autumn, they drop their needles.

Some broad-leaved trees, especially tropical species, *do not* drop their leaves seasonally. If an oak or maple is transplanted to the tropics, it may abandon its leaf-shedding winter habit and become an evergreen like its new neighbours.

Some of the most popular garden evergreens are broad-leaved plants, but many are shrubs, not trees. Certain hollies, laurels and rhododendrons fall into this group of plants.

The leaves of these evergreen shrubs remain on the branches until the individual leaf dies, regardless of the season, so the plant is never bare. So the word evergreen actually describes the habit of a plant, not the plant itself.

As botanists have discovered, the most reliable way of classifying plants is by their reproductive structures. Among trees, the critical question that scientists ask is: does the tree bear cones or flowers?

Conifers have female cones and male cones, which are distinctively different but are usually present on the same tree. The female cone holds the ovules (egg cells), which must be pollinated in order to develop into seeds.

Pollen, produced by male cones in enormous quantities, is carried in the wind to the female cones. Most people recognise the female cones, but the male cones are there too. Often they are smaller, bright yellow or red, and borne on the lower branches of a mature conifer. Male cones have a short-term existence in spring and early summer and never become woody later in the year like their female counterparts.

Before pollination, the egg-bearing scales on a female cone are open. After pollination, the scales swell up and the cone enlarges dramatically: witness the sugar pine of North America, which has a cone that reaches a length of some 2 ft.

When the seeds are ripe – which in some species takes more than a year – the once green and resinous cone becomes dry, brown and woody. The scales separate and the seeds fall.

Coniferous trees are the earth's oldest and tallest inhabitants. Some bristlecone pines (mountain trees in the western United States) are more than 4,000 years old. Redwoods in California reach a height of more than 350 ft, rivalled only by the Australian mountain ash (which is not a conifer).

Some 500 kinds of conifers exist; nearly all are evergreen. Among the strangest conifers are the yew-like podocarps that grow mainly in the Southern Hemisphere. The pygmy pine, a New Zealand podocarp, is the tiniest conifer; it begins producing cones at 3 in. high.

Just three of these conifers – pine, spruce and fir – make up about one-third of the world's forests. Conifers furnish nearly three-quarters of all timber and nearly all our paper. In fact, the page you are now looking at almost certainly came from a coniferous tree.

Three plants that appear to break the rules

Larches are not typical conifers because they change colour in autumn and lose their needles. This American larch, called a tamarack, has already turned gold and is shedding needles.

Juniper foliage is scaly and branching, not at all like needles – but the juniper is a true conifer. The fleshy, blue-grey structures look like berries but are really modified cones.

Most hollies are actually evergreens, for they keep their leaves all year round. But hollies have broad leaves, not needles, and their berries reveal they are flowering plants.

Different ways of identifying conifers

Telling one conifer from another is simply a matter of narrowing down the many possibilities. First decide whether or not a particular tree is indeed a conifer. All conifers have needle-shaped or scale-like leaves.

Look at the needles to discover the major group (such as pine). Tree shape may provide some clues. A cone by itself, away from the tree that produced it, is often difficult to identify precisely.

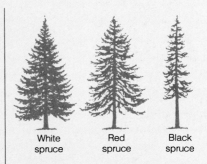

White spruce   Red spruce   Black spruce

Guide to needles or scales

Needles are the easiest way to identify a conifer. Compare them with the ones shown here which represent the major groups. A guidebook will help you to determine the precise species. If the branches are too high off the ground, look at the fallen needles.

Larches
(Tamarack)

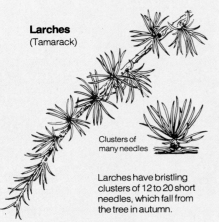

Clusters of many needles

Larches have bristling clusters of 12 to 20 short needles, which fall from the tree in autumn.

Pines
(Scots pine)

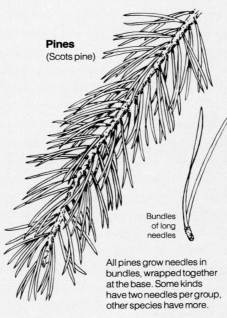

Bundles of long needles

All pines grow needles in bundles, wrapped together at the base. Some kinds have two needles per group, other species have more.

The shape of a conifer

Experts can often identify conifers, such as spruces, by shape – the density and arrangement of branches. But individual trees vary greatly. For beginners, shape may be less helpful than needles in tree identification.

Cones confirm a tree's identity

Each kind of conifer produces cones of a unique size and shape. The selection of cones below shows the tremendous diversity within one group – the pines. The cones have been drawn to scale, each at about half its natural size.

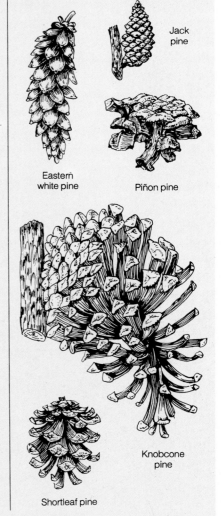

Jack pine

Eastern white pine

Piñon pine

Knobcone pine

Shortleaf pine

Firs
(Balsam fir)

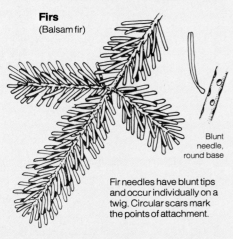

Blunt needle, round base

Fir needles have blunt tips and occur individually on a twig. Circular scars mark the points of attachment.

Spruces
(Norway spruce)

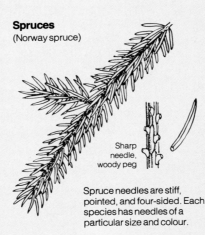

Sharp needle, woody peg

Spruce needles are stiff, pointed, and four-sided. Each species has needles of a particular size and colour.

Cedars and Junipers
(Northern white cedar)

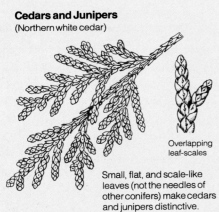

Overlapping leaf-scales

Small, flat, and scale-like leaves (not the needles of other conifers) make cedars and junipers distinctive.

Yews
(English yew)

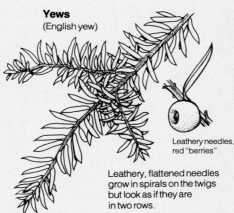

Leathery needles, red "berries"

Leathery, flattened needles grow in spirals on the twigs but look as if they are in two rows.

The "family tree" of a flowering tree

As a game, ask a friend or relative to name three flowering trees other than magnolias or fruit trees. The chances are that few people will mention oaks, maples, beeches or elms.

Such trees do have flowers, but their blossoms are often inconspicuous. For example, the tassel-shaped flowers of sugar maples are greenish-yellow and appear at the same time as the leaves.

The short-lived flowers of many kinds of trees may be overlooked entirely, not just because of their small size and camouflaged colour, but because they may bloom only in the higher branches. You can often get a better look at these tree flowers from an upstairs window or by viewing them with binoculars.

Many trees bloom after the leaves have come out, so you do not notice the flowers.

And sometimes, too, because of their shapes, you may not recognise a tree flower for what it is. The flowers of birches and willows are catkins, which are usually fuzzy, caterpillar-shaped clusters of flowers without petals.

Flowers are reproductive structures. Although they bloom only for a brief time, from generation to generation flowers are the most consistent part of a tree.

Leaves may be large or small, even variable in shape – one sassafras, for example, may have leaves of several different shapes. Bark and branches help in identifying many trees. But only the flowers are always the same. Consequently, botanists rely on flowers as a means of telling trees apart.

The magnolia family, generally believed to be the oldest of flowering trees, includes not only the various kinds of magnolias, but also the stately tulip tree.

The magnolia flower is complete, which means it has all the four components that go to make up a flower: sepals, petals, and both stamens (male parts) and pistils (female).

Another group of plants with complete flowers is the pea family. The flower itself is shaped like a butterfly, with a large, showy, insect-attracting petal on top, two side "wings", and two fused petals at the base. The remarkable thing about the pea family (which includes many trees as well as trailing vines) is its great diversity. One member, the black locust (also called false acacia), is grown for its lovely drooping clusters of sweet-scented flowers.

The golden-flowered broom and gorse shrubs that are native to European hill-

Catkins are clusters of incomplete flowers

Most people have seen catkins (though they might not have been recognised as such), for the furry, grey parts of a pussy willow are really catkins. A catkin is a dense cluster of tiny blossoms reduced to the essentials of reproduction. Unlike a complete flower, a catkin has no petals and sepals (modified leaves); a catkin is either male (pollen-bearing) or female (seed-producing), never both. The photo below shows male catkins from a poplar, one of the many plants that develop these clusters. In the close-up (right), note the purple structures; these produce pollen.

sides, the peanut plant, the Japanese wisteria, and the sweet pea itself all belong to the pea family.

Flowering trees have diversified over the long span of their development. There are many trees with incomplete flowers, simplified to petal-less, sepal-less, or single-sex flowers.

In the main, these varieties of trees are pollinated by the wind, and it is to this large group that catkin-bearing birches and poplars belong. Male and female flowers may be on one tree (as in the case of beeches) or on separate trees (as among cottonwoods).

Learning about trees by their family relationships makes identification more entertaining. With the help of a guidebook, survey local trees; then look to see if they have any relatives near by.

Roses and fruit trees are close relatives

The rose family, with some 3,000 members, includes many more kinds of plants than just roses. Some of the best-known fruit and ornamental trees belong to this group. The flowering cherry shown above does not produce edible fruits – it is considered an ornamental. Other members include apple, plum, strawberry and hawthorn. These seemingly diverse plants are classified into one family because of the similarity in the structure of the flower. Each blossom has five petals and five sepals; both stamens (the male components) and pistil (female) are present. The bulbous ovary, at the base of the flower, is where the seed grows. Many different types of fruits grow from this basic type of flower. Below is a selection of cross-sections of flowers and fruits from the rose family.

After a rose is pollinated, seeds develop inside the rose-hip – a bright structure slightly larger than the base of the flower. A rose-hip is really a group of fruits called achenes; each achene has a single seed. Cross-sections of both rose and rose-hip are shown (right).

Botanically, an apple is known as a pome – a fruit that has a central core. Usually there are five seeds inside the core. If you compare an apple with an apple blossom (left), you can see that the base of the flower (around the seeds) has enlarged greatly. Pears and quinces – both in the rose family – are pomes.

Though the plum's botanical name – a drupe – may be unfamiliar, drupes are easy to recognise. At the centre of a drupe is a single seed, which is surrounded by a hard pit; this, in turn, is covered by a thick, juicy layer. Peaches, cherries and apricots are drupes.

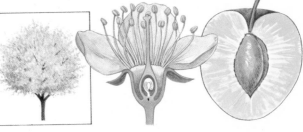

Two oddities: bamboo and palm

A forest without trees sounds about as plausible as a city without buildings. Yet in warm, wet places, there are many treeless forests – populated by bamboo. These plants, with their hollow, jointed stems divided by watertight partitions, are more closely related to grasses.

Bamboo reproduces by means of fast-growing sprouts sent up from underground stems called rhizomes (see below).

Within months after new shoots appear, stands of bamboo reach their full height; in a single day, growth may be more than 3 ft. Unlike a tree, a bamboo grows only at the upper 2 ft of the vertical stem: from its sides, it produces a few small branchlets.

The flowering of a bamboo is amazing. Depending on species, the intervals may be 20 years or more. *Madake*, a common Japanese bamboo, is an extreme example – it blossoms about once every 120 years.

Incredibly, all *madake* bamboo produce flowers at nearly the same time, no matter where in the world they may have been planted. The flowering is the "swan song" of the bamboo. After it blossoms, a bamboo stalk usually dies. Only the underground portion stays alive, capable of renewed growth.

Bamboo forests flourish not only in the tropics, but also in temperate zones. They spread rapidly and will quickly take over any available space. Such impassable thickets are natural sanctuaries for the giant panda of Asia.

Palms share some traits with bamboo. Although palms are classified as trees, they lack the branching habit and woody structure of ordinary trees. Like bamboo, a palm has only one growing point – a single bud at the centre of the crown.

This bud, which first appears at ground level, consists of tightly folded, cabbage-like leaves. In the early part of the palm's life, the leaves unfurl close to the ground for several years.

Then, as the plant develops, the bud is carried upwards, concealed deep within the spiral of fronds. As long as the bud is intact, the palm tree will continue to grow. If it is removed or damaged, however, the whole tree dies.

The circulatory system of a palm is different from that of an ordinary tree. The transportation of water and nutrients is not confined to the outer part of the trunk, as in a pine or an oak; it takes place throughout its fibrous interior. When a palm is cut down, its stump shows none of the growth rings characteristic of other trees.

Palms have no bark. When fronds die and fall off, they leave successive scars, visible the full length of the trunk. These leaf scars protect the palm, just as bark does. But because a palm tree grows upwards, rather than outwards, this "skin" does not expand.

Palms yield two important foods: dates and coconuts. Date palms are remarkable for their capacity to prosper in dry regions where most other trees would fail.

In many desert or semi-desert parts of the world, date palms are grown near oases, and on land otherwise dependent on irrigation. By contrast, the coconut palm is almost the symbol of tropical coastlines (though it grows abundantly inland, as well).

The world's largest fruit – the 40 lb. coco-de-mer – is produced by a palm which is native to the lush Seychelle Islands in the Indian Ocean.

How bamboo shoots develop

When a bamboo emerges, it reveals – right at the start – the full width that the adult plant will achieve. The shoot is the edible part of the plant. As the bamboo grows, the soft tissue of the shoot is replaced by a tough, jointed stem more suitable for furniture than for food.

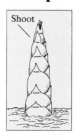

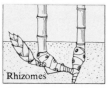 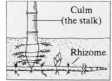

Bamboo grows either in clumps or as single sprouts. The growth pattern (shown left) results in clumps. The underground stem (right) produces stalks that grow separately.

The quality of bamboo that makes it a useful and versatile building material – the extremely tough fibres in its stalks – creates hardships for anyone trying to cut a path through a bamboo thicket. Bamboo resists all but the strongest cutting tools. The floor of this Ugandan forest (right) is criss-crossed with fallen stalks, which create further problems for the hiker.

Coconut palms are great voyagers. These natives of the South Pacific have tough fruits that can float for as long as four months without damage. Thus currents explain their wide distribution – human beings have also provided transportation. Here, on a Polynesian beach, several young coconuts can be seen sprouting.

A single date palm bears thousands of dates (below). To begin with, there may be as many as 10,000 flowers in a single cluster. When a female tree flowers, it is pollinated by bees – and is often aided by date-growers, who place male flowers on the female tree to ensure productivity.

 LIVING WITH NATURE

The palm: an all-purpose tree

People in many tropical areas have within reach one of the most useful trees in the world – the palm. The palm family produces not only coconuts and dates but also oil, sago, betel nuts and wax, enabling human beings to maintain life in places that would otherwise be deserts. The peoples of the South Seas, in particular, have learned how to make the most of these living storehouses as the mainstay of a pleasant, relaxed life.

• The huge leaves provide material for both shelter and bedding. The hard midribs of leaves make good kindling, and can be used as skewers for holding food over a fire. The fronds and the sacking-like fibres at the base of a leaf can be woven into ropes and mats.

• Most species of palm provide fluid and food as well, often highly nutritious food. Of course, some parts are too tough or dry to eat. But the soft and cabbage-like new leaves, when accessible, can be chopped up for salad. The sago palm of Africa and Asia has a soft, white pith that produces a flour after it has been pounded and kneaded with water.

• Coconuts are the most useful of all palms; and though the husk of the fruit is extremely hard, it is simple to break one open by smashing it against a rock. Once open, a mature coconut yields about a pint of clear, sweet liquid; and since it is sterile, too, it can be drunk safely without any precautions. The

meat of the nut is jelly-like when it first develops; later it becomes firm and white. Either way, it is usually too rich for a steady diet and should be mixed with other foods if possible.

• Coconut oil is a good lotion to prevent sunburn, and an effective insect repellent. It can be extracted from the nut by boiling small pieces in water and allowing the water to cool. When it does, the oil – which is also a staple cooking oil – can be skimmed off the top of the water.

• Hollowed-out shells also make sturdy spoons and bowls. Some effort and skill is required in providing them, however. Climbing palm trees is a job for experts.

The way a tree works

If you were to write a science-fiction story, complete with incredible organisms, you would find it hard to invent anything more unlikely than a factual description of a perfectly ordinary tree and the way it is constructed.

Trees can live for hundreds (sometimes thousands) of years – longer than any other living thing. They are able, annually, to launch millions of miniaturised offspring, each able to colonise a favourable location. Trees are able to live on nothing more than sunlight, air and water (with a number of necessary minerals).

But this hardly begins to tell how amazing trees are.

Trees have an elaborate body plan, adapted through the ages. Only a small percentage of a mature trunk is actually alive. At its core is the heartwood, its cells filled with resin or similar materials.

One might describe heartwood as dead, but inactive is a better word. Heartwood is often in a splendid state of preservation, and it performs a vital function: it provides a sturdy support that enables the growing tree to reach upwards and catch the sunlight.

A tree is the most effective pump in the world. Silently and with no moving parts, it can transport an incredible amount of water. Even a sapling only a few feet high may move up to 10 gallons of water from the soil to its leaves in a day. A medium-size oak tree may pump 150 gallons a day to supply its needs, raising more than half a ton of water.

How can trees raise water against the pull of gravity? Water tends to stick to most surfaces it touches. This characteristic causes it to climb the walls of hair-fine sapwood tubes in the trunk.

Water molecules are also strongly attracted to one another. As a molecule of water evaporates from a leaf, another moves up the sapwood to take its place. It is followed by another, and so on. Thus the trunk acts as a natural pump, and its force is powerful enough to lift a column of water to the top of a 350 ft redwood.

Sapwood tubes eventually fill up. With use, they are plugged with resin and growth by-products, and become inactive heartwood. New tubes form in the thin growing layer, the cambium.

Replacement occurs in the growing season (spring and summer in some regions, the rainy season in others). As long as a tree lives, it grows. And when growth stops completely, death is not far behind.

The growing layer also supplies cells to the outer layer, called the phloem. This layer carries sap throughout the tree,

Close-up of a leaf

A leaf is a sugar factory. When the sunlight hits the tightly packed palisade cells, the chlorophyll in them changes water and carbon dioxide to sugar (and also oxygen). To a lesser extent, photosynthesis occurs in the spongy layer, where vital gases diffuse through large air spaces. On the underside of the leaf, tiny pores called stomata open and close, letting gases move between the leaf and the outside air. Veins carry sugar and water, and have the effect of stiffening the leaf much as water stiffens a hosepipe.

Upper layer is waxy and transparent

Palisade cells

Vein

Spongy layer

Stomata act as valves

especially to the tips of branches (where new growth occurs) and to the roots. Sap is a sugary juice that supplies all living parts of the tree with food. Surplus food is usually stored in the roots. This reserve will carry the tree through its dormant period of winter or seasonal drought.

Tree roots are remarkable. Tiny root tips can penetrate soil so rocky and resistant it hardly seems possible. The ability of roots to detect and grow towards water is a recurrent feat we take for granted. But the mystery remains: how do roots know where to go? When they do find water, roots extract it through their delicate hairs and pump it up through the trunk to reach the leaves.

The word that describes the capture and use of the sun's energy by trees and other green plants is photosynthesis. The site of capture is the leaves, in cells with green chlorophyll.

Here, with water and carbon dioxide, the plant produces energy-rich sugar, which fuels its life processes and growth. (Scientists know a great deal about this process but have never been able to duplicate it in the laboratory.) A by-product of photosynthesis is oxygen. It is upon this oxygen supply that the life of the world's animal kingdom depends.

There are three kinds of roots: tap-roots, lateral roots and feeder roots. The mighty tap-root, which goes straight down, is an anchor for the tree. Not all trees have them. Trees in rain forests, which rise to heights of 120 ft or more, lack tap-roots; often these trees are supported by buttresses – thick structures above the ground. Lateral roots, which extend outwards from the trunk and tap-root, are usually close to the surface. They supply some or all of the bracing for the tree, and also absorb oxygen. Intricately branched feeder roots (at the ends of the laterals) take in water and dissolved minerals through microscopic hairs near their tips. Roots can function at a lower temperature than any other part of the tree. Thus it is in the roots that spring really begins.

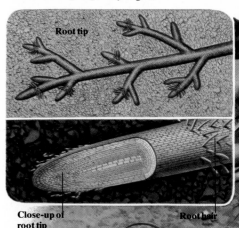

Root tip

Close-up of root tip

Root hair

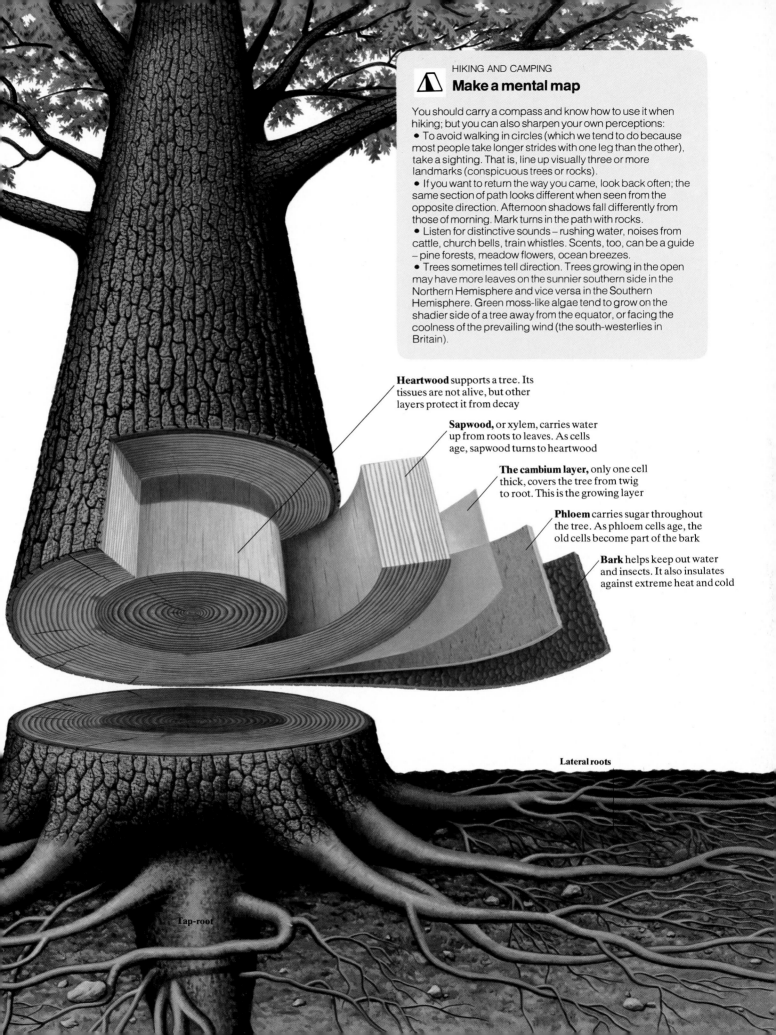

HIKING AND CAMPING

Make a mental map

You should carry a compass and know how to use it when hiking; but you can also sharpen your own perceptions:
- To avoid walking in circles (which we tend to do because most people take longer strides with one leg than the other), take a sighting. That is, line up visually three or more landmarks (conspicuous trees or rocks).
- If you want to return the way you came, look back often; the same section of path looks different when seen from the opposite direction. Afternoon shadows fall differently from those of morning. Mark turns in the path with rocks.
- Listen for distinctive sounds – rushing water, noises from cattle, church bells, train whistles. Scents, too, can be a guide – pine forests, meadow flowers, ocean breezes.
- Trees sometimes tell direction. Trees growing in the open may have more leaves on the sunnier southern side in the Northern Hemisphere and vice versa in the Southern Hemisphere. Green moss-like algae tend to grow on the shadier side of a tree away from the equator, or facing the coolness of the prevailing wind (the south-westerlies in Britain).

Heartwood supports a tree. Its tissues are not alive, but other layers protect it from decay

Sapwood, or xylem, carries water up from roots to leaves. As cells age, sapwood turns to heartwood

The cambium layer, only one cell thick, covers the tree from twig to root. This is the growing layer

Phloem carries sugar throughout the tree. As phloem cells age, the old cells become part of the bark

Bark helps keep out water and insects. It also insulates against extreme heat and cold

Lateral roots

Tap-root

Bark: a tree's protective skin

Like human skin, the bark of a tree is a barrier that protects against any invading diseases. And, like skin, bark "breathes" – regulating the escape of moisture from within – and has the capacity to repair itself. However, while human skin constantly wears off and is replaced, the bark of a tree often accumulates to a great depth.

Growth in the trunk and twigs of a tree originates in a remarkable layer called the cambium. But unlike human skin, with which it is often compared, the cambium layer grows in two directions.

The inner side of the cambium adds to the girth of the tree (woody tissue), and the outer side eventually adds to the bark (also called cork). This may be hard for us to grasp because our conception of skin is geared to the kind we have ourselves, which replaces itself if it is damaged (human skin has no part in the building of inner bodily tissues such as muscles).

The cambium is only one cell thick – a fact that becomes amazing when you consider the cambium's many feats. Cells reproduce by splitting. In this growth process, a cambium cell will contribute a daughter cell to one side or the other (either to the inner part that will become heartwood, or to the outer part that will eventually become bark).

But before they reach these stages, the daughter cells perform activities that are essential to the tree.

For a time, the cells developed by the cambium serve as the circulatory system for the whole plant. The inner layer (the sapwood or xylem) transports water from the roots to the leaves.

The outer layer (the phloem) circulates the sap – the nutrient-rich products of photosynthesis that enable a tree to grow. It is this organisation of layers that allows sap to be "harvested" without damaging the tree. The skilful tapping of a tree depends on carefully preserving the essential growing layer (the cambium). This is often done, and entire industries depend on it – the rubber industry, for instance, which has cultivated great plantations.

A homely example of the difference between human skin and bark is in the adolescent child who, while growing, may split a clothing seam. The gradual expansion of human skin as a child grows to an adult can be detected only under a microscope. But trees do split their seams, quite literally. The ridges and striations on a tree are from the pressures of growth, which usually affect only the dead portions of the bark.

These patterns of growth – stretch marks or furrows – are special characteristics of individual species, and are often used in identification.

Appreciating the variety of texture in bark

Bark grows from the inside outwards. What we see is the dead tissue that has been displaced by new growth underneath the bark. This growth process produces the different textures and patterns of bark – ridges, flat plates and deep furrows – that characterise each kind of tree. Knowing the various types of bark helps in tree identification, especially in winter.

The satiny red-brown bark of the cherry is marked by long, horizontal pores (lenticels) through which the tree breathes in winter.

Peeling layers of chalky white bark split and curl on the trunk of a mature paper birch. The young tree (left) will turn white with age.

Deep furrows form ridges in the bark of some species of maple and oak. (Ash trees, too, are heavily ridged, in an unusual diamond pattern.)

Shagbark hickory is a perfect description for this member of the walnut family. The thin, splintery plates curl outwards at the ends.

The surprising bounty from bark and sap

Trees have a remarkable ability to repair damage and compensate for losses. It is this characteristic that allows man to make use of trees on a continuing basis, tapping a variety of trees for their fluids and bark. Today, of course, man-made products have replaced many substances that were once extracted from trees.

The maple syrup that North Americans traditionally pour over pancakes is still, however, made from the sap of the sugar maple. This sap rises in the trees during late winter and early spring. The best "runs" take place when nights are cold and days warm; a tree may yield 100 drops a minute under these conditions. Though this rate is impressive, the liquid is so watery that some 40 gallons of sap must be boiled down to make 1 gallon of syrup.

Sap refers to a specific substance – the sugary liquid that flows through certain plant tissues (phloem). Not all liquids made by a tree are really sap. The latex that drips from cuts in rubber trees is believed to be a protective substance, similar to the milky fluid that oozes from other wounded plants. An individual rubber tree can be tapped for a period of more than 20 years. But between tappings, the tree requires a rest period; often tapping is done every other day.

Cork comes from the cork oak, a tree native to the Mediterranean regions of Europe and Africa. The cells of its bark are filled with air, making it a good insulating material. In harvesting cork, the bark is carefully peeled off; to avoid permanent damage to the tree, this is done only about once every ten years. The tree will produce for 150 years.

Cinnamon, the fragrant spice from India and Sri Lanka (Ceylon), is obtained from the bark of certain trees in the laurel family. Because the most productive bark grows on the twigs, trees are continuously pruned to stimulate twig growth. Quinine, used in treating malaria, is a bark product (from a South American tree); the active ingredient in aspirin formerly came from willow bark, but is now made synthetically.

A worker harvests latex from a rubber tree in Liberia. This liquid oozes from a recent cut into a cup; as the cut heals, another diagonal slice is made near it.

Sharp, three-branched spines sprout on the trunk of a honey locust. They develop from deep buds; leaves may grow at their bases.

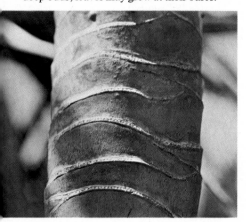

Spiralling scars left by the successive rows of leaves give the tropical pandanus its name of screw pine. Palm bark also shows leaf scars.

NATURE OBSERVER
Reading bark marks

Many wild animals and birds are secretive and elusive. While walking in woods, however, you can see signs of some that leave characteristic marks on the bark of trees, usually when they are in the process of obtaining food.

Squirrels feed on bark, usually in spring to reach the sap, leaving torn pieces hanging in shreds from the branches.

Rabbits can kill a sapling by "ring barking" Clues are the size of the teeth marks and position low on the tree.

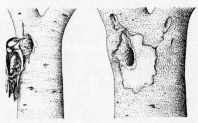

Holes chipped into a tree, especially into dead wood, may show where a woodpecker has been searching for grubs.

Deer use the bark of young trees as an emergency food supply, tearing it off with upward movements of their teeth.

Claw marks and mud at the base of a tree can indicate that a badger from a nearby set has been cleaning its paws.

The autobiography of a tree

Every tree keeps a permanent diary of its growth, recording the passage of the years, droughts, temperature changes, and even the death of neighbouring plants. This history lies in the rings of wood added each year.

A ring of new wood is laid down just beneath the bark in the growing season. In temperate regions, there is only one period of growth (during the spring and summer months). Thus every ring represents one year in the life of the tree, and the total number of rings gives its age.

Normally, the annual rings are visible only after a tree has been cut down. Fortunately for trees, scientists have developed techniques for counting the rings while the trees are still alive and growing (see far right).

A tree may "lie" about its age. If cut near the top, it reveals only the number of years since it reached that particular height. To tell the true age of a tree, the annual rings must be counted on a section near the ground. Even then, the age may be only an approximation. A short period of drought during a growing season may create an extra, "false" ring that makes a tree look older than it really is.

Look at the rings on a tree stump, using a magnifying glass. Some kinds of trees, such as oaks and elms, actually have *two* distinct layers within each annual ring. The inner layer, known as early or spring wood, is laid down at the beginning of the growing season. Early wood is soft and light-coloured; its cell walls – the microscopic structures that give wood its characteristic hardness – are very thin. Late (or summer) wood, which has thicker cell walls, is harder, darker, and more compact. Wood made at the very end of the season forms a narrow, dark band.

The more wood laid down in a year, the wider that particular annual ring. Thus a broad ring reflects favourable growing conditions, such as warm temperatures and adequate rainfall. A drought or insect infestation means narrow rings. Annual rings are rarely perfect circles, because different sides of the tree do not always grow at precisely the same rate.

The most interesting annual rings develop on trees in areas where growing conditions are most limiting. Bristlecone pines, for example, are found only in arid mountain regions where rainfall is never abundant; even minor fluctuations are reflected in their growth rings. These patterns offer scientists a precise measure of climatic conditions. (By contrast, trees in the tropics, where growing conditions are more stable, may show little variation from one year to the next.)

Archaeologists and antiquarians, who have compiled lists of year-by-year growth patterns in various parts of the world, are often able to date ancient buildings by studying wood growth rings.

NATURE OBSERVER
What a twig reveals about a tree

Only in winter, when trees are leafless, can the beauty and variety of their twigs be appreciated. Examining a twig will tell you something about a tree's history. Closely spaced rings mark the end of each year's growth; the further apart they are, the more the twig grew that year. Twigs also help to identify a tree. Buds on the twig, which contain tiny leaves or flowers, are especially useful. Beech buds look like inch-long spears; flowering dogwood has onion-shaped buds. The labels (below and at right) point out other structures; the twig shown is from a sycamore.

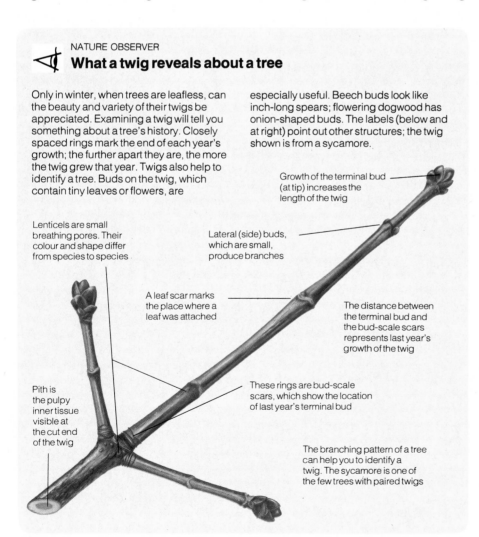

Growth of the terminal bud (at tip) increases the length of the twig

Lenticels are small breathing pores. Their colour and shape differ from species to species

Lateral (side) buds, which are small, produce branches

A leaf scar marks the place where a leaf was attached

The distance between the terminal bud and the bud-scale scars represents last year's growth of the twig

Pith is the pulpy inner tissue visible at the cut end of the twig

These rings are bud-scale scars, which show the location of last year's terminal bud

The branching pattern of a tree can help you to identify a twig. The sycamore is one of the few trees with paired twigs

Characteristic sizes and shapes

Each kind of tree has a distinctive growth pattern, though no two trees of a species are ever identical. The ones shown here are classic examples of trees that have adhered to their inherent pattern of growth. Trees of the same type also have similar life-spans – yews are long-lived, poplars are not.

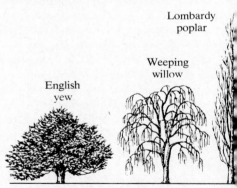

Lombardy poplar

Weeping willow

English yew

Variability within a species

Although the vigour of an individual plant is always a factor in its development, the quality of its growing conditions can make a great difference in how large and how quickly it grows. The influence of sunlight, moisture and richness of soil can best be seen by comparing trees of the same age and species. In a study of 100-year-old redwoods, the best sites yielded trees about 240 ft tall; second-best sites had trees 220 ft tall; but the average was about 100 ft.

In the case of the bristlecone pines, which are the world's oldest trees, the history shown in their rings goes back more than 4,000 years. Trees alive today were saplings when Nero burned Rome (in AD 64) and in the year 800, when Charlemagne became emperor. The fascinating aspect of such records is the constant revision they must undergo as more tree-ring information becomes available. Comparison of irregular growth patterns in tree rings relates not just to human history but to the history of climatic conditions on earth. Fossil trees extend records even more.

In America, logs are occasionally taken into court, and their annual rings used in evidence. Because surveyors often mark trees with axe-cuts when land is purchased, cuts can be used to establish the year a survey was made. Such information may settle a dispute concerning the title transfer.

Core sample shows growth rings

A record of growing conditions in the past

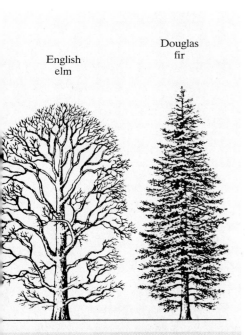

English elm

Douglas fir

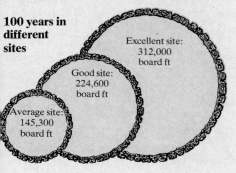

100 years in different sites

Excellent site: 312,000 board ft

Good site: 224,600 board ft

Average site: 145,300 board ft

A tree keeps a record of its growing conditions in annual rings, but the information is not only about the general environment. A tree also records incidents in its own life. In this cross-section, past weather conditions may be observed. So, too, can particular events that make this tree's life unique. Four major incidents are identified on the stump, and also in the story below. How is it possible to reconcile the two records – the general climatic conditions and the events that touched one tree?
Samples taken from other trees in the same region help scientists draw conclusions.

Comparing growth-ring patterns

Core is taken out with a boring tool

Core from stump shows similarity

Third sample is from fallen log

Slim columns, called cores, are taken from several trees. When the cores are laid side by side, it is often possible to match patterns. One tree of known age leads to data on nearby trees:

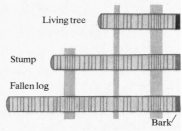

Living tree

Stump

Fallen log

Bark

1. In the cross-section (top), a few major events in the life of a tree have been numbered. When this tree was a sapling, it was knocked to one side by another tree. The young tree bent, but it survived. It grew vigorously, and as the old tree decayed, the sapling resumed its upright growth.

2. Later, a forest fire damaged the bark and growing layer on one side of the tree; but years of growth healed the wound, eventually covering it.

3. The tree's growth-rate leaped when the forest was thinned out, and it was no longer deprived of sunlight.

4. Thin rings often indicate a long period of drought. But here, a cutting damaged the root system on one side, and produced a similar effect. This shows how the "evidence" in rings can be interpreted in more than one way. A single tree reveals only part of the history of regional climate.

Where forest meets meadow

The edge of a forest is a transition zone between two communities. On one side is the forest itself; on the other, a field, meadow or marshy area. Each community has characteristic plants and animals, and the forest edge is the crossroads for wildlife from the two neighbouring worlds. Forest-dwellers venture forth into sunnier regions to feed, and meadow animals seek food, shade, and hiding places. So a forest edge is richer in animal life than the areas on either side. It has not only its own residents, but also visitors.

A barrier to hikers, a forest edge is often a dense tangle of blackberry bushes, hawthorn trees, hazel shrubs and bracken. The plants that grow here need more sunlight than those inside a forest, but less than meadow plants. Their water requirements are generally intermediate, too – less than a forest, but more than a meadow.

Berry-laden brambles are a rich food source for fruit-loving animals. Such thorny plants also provide excellent cover – animals take refuge among the thorns. A nest in a thorny shrub is far safer than one in the open.

The cluttered appearance of a forest edge masks the structure of the forest interior. But if you know what to look for, you will be able to see – even at the forest edge – distinctive zones of life. Holes in the ground mark the entrances of nests and dens in the subterranean layer. The ground layer is covered with plant litter and populated with insects; ground-nesting birds and those that feed on the ground can be seen during the day. Because most small mammals such as mice are nocturnal, they are seldom seen.

The shrub layer, with its berry and nut-bearing plants, often has the most animal traffic on any forest layer. Above the shrub layer, there is a region called the understorey. It is relatively dark because it is shaded by the top layer, or canopy. More birds nest in the understorey than in any other layer in the woodland areas.

It is relatively easy to spot a grey squirrel or a blue tit in a forest edge. However, if you want to see other, more timid animals, you will probably have to sit quietly for a while and wait. Not only will animals appear, but you will be able to see more as your eyes adjust to the dimmer light beneath the trees.

The works of modern man have increased the areas covered by forest edges. Every clearing for a farm creates four edges. Whenever a road penetrates a forest, each side of the road becomes a forest edge. Thus there is more space today for animals that flourish in such places. For example, the robin of North America (really a thrush) is more numerous now than before European colonists arrived.

Hedgerows, which separate cultivated fields in many places in the world, have plants and animals similar to those of the forest edge. So hedgerows might be thought of as forest edges without forests.

Key to wild life at the forest edge

1. Sparrowhawk (European)
2. Tawny owl
3. Green woodpecker
4. Wood warbler
5. Grass snake
6. Woodcock (European)
7. Bank vole
8. Red admiral butterfly
9. Seven-spot ladybird
10. Banded snail

An old oak in a British woodland provides a home for a tawny owl, which drowses during the day in its branches. For other animals – passers-by or residents – the oak is part of the "edge" habitat. A green woodpecker drills for insects in the bark of the tree. A subtly coloured wood warbler nests on the ground, but comes up to feed, while a red admiral butterfly pauses briefly on a blackberry. A banded snail, crawling slowly across a leaf, may fall prey to a bird or even a beetle. Grass snakes are common at the forest edge and often come out to bask in the sun. Russet feathers are an effective camouflage for a woodcock, as it hunts among the fallen leaves and grasses. A bank vole scurries behind a bush to hide from a sparrowhawk.

Watching a spider build its web

Most spiders build webs of some type to catch prey (a few do not – they pounce on a victim, or build a trap). Of all spinners and weavers, the orb-weaver spider, shown below, is the easiest to watch at work. Its webs are often visible at a forest edge, where they may be lit from behind. Webs are made of a silk-like liquid substance, which the spider draws from its undersides, using its hind legs. The strands are pure protein, which the spider can recycle; when a line is no longer needed, the spider eats the silk. The strength of silk is shown by the drops it supports, as seen here.

The first, "bridge" line is either carried by the spider or blown by the wind.

This close-up of the web shows two different spirals. The inner one, with widely spaced strands, is laid down first. The second, outer spiral has a special adhesive quality, and turns in the opposite direction. As the outer spiral is spun, the inner one is eaten.

From the midpoint of the bridge, the spider establishes a third anchor.

As the spider goes back and forth, it adds spokes and reinforces boundaries.

From any point on the finished web the spider feels the slightest touch of an insect, and quickly pounces on it.

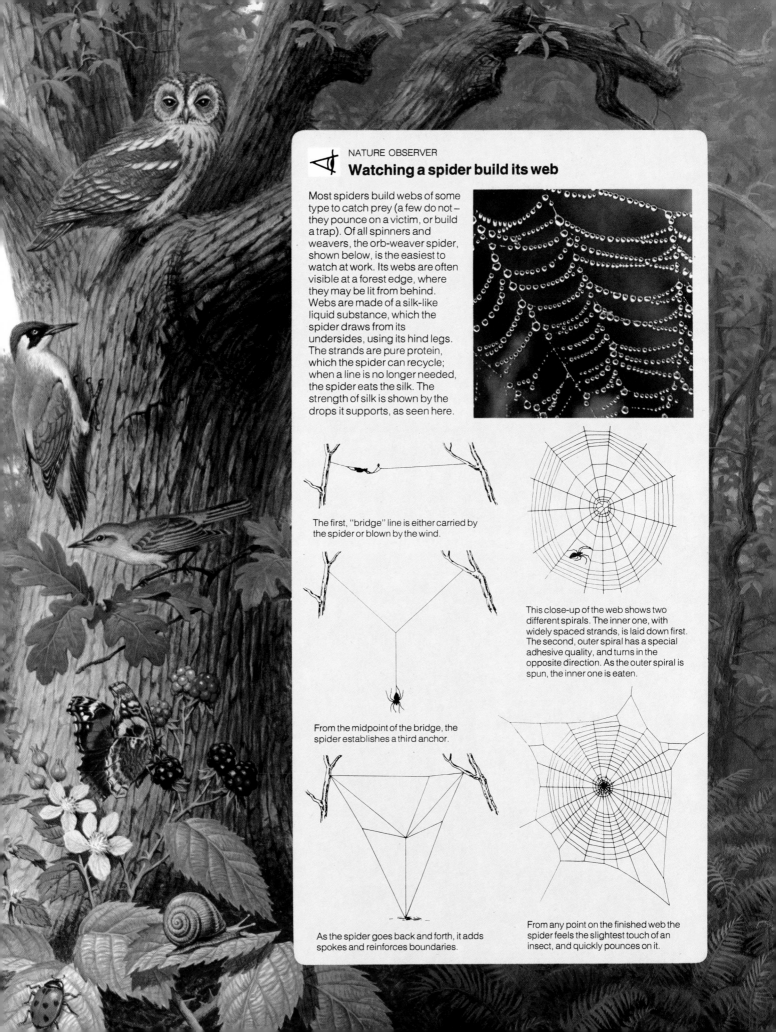

The ever-changing forest

Suppose you were to plan a picnic in the country, choosing to go to a picturesque abandoned farm you remember from the recent past. On arrival, you will more than likely be startled by the tall weeds, sprawling shrubs, and even trees that have taken over.

What you are witnessing at such a moment is the phenomenon called succession – a predictable series of changes. Such changes occur in a forest that has been cut down or been ravaged by fire. There, the bare soil is an open invitation to new plant life.

From roots and seeds already in the ground, and from seeds carried by winds or wildlife, pioneer plants sprout, and soon occupy untended fields. Couch-grass and rosebay willowherb are often pioneers. Such plants have seeds that germinate quickly, and all can survive drying winds. Characteristically, they also thrive in strong sunlight, like the wild poppies that sprang up in the war-torn fields of Flanders.

By providing shade and protection, pioneer plants change the growing conditions near the ground. Their presence creates a more hospitable world for other kinds of plants that are not able to survive in bare, sun-baked soil. This is the ironic aspect in any story of plant succession: as pioneer plants grow, they make conditions worse for themselves, and better for other species that follow them. Newcomers such as thistles and ragwort overshadow the pioneers. Later, young trees sprout. First to appear are fast-growing, sun-loving species such as pines, birch, rowan and hazel.

As the forest in western Europe matures, some further changes take place. Birch and hazel, for instance, do not grow well in dense shade beneath the larger trees. The older trees take up much of the water near the soil surface, and the young trees that do best at this stage are the oaks and beeches. Their roots grow below those of the birches and bring water from deep in the soil. When the birches die off, more sunlight reaches the saplings of oak and beech and their growth rates speed up. The birches, now at a disadvantage in the competition, do not reproduce so well, and are gradually replaced. After some 150 years, an oak forest will stand where pioneer plants once grew.

The final, climax stage of succession over those parts of Britain that have been left to nature is oak forest on the heavier clay soils and beech on the lighter chalk. Ash prefers limestone and pine still grows naturally in the Scottish Highlands. In other continents, in cold regions and in the tropics, the tree species that make up the climax forest are different from those in the temperate zones, but the principles of succession are the same.

A climax stage lasts for centuries. Thus, in theory, there is no limit to the life-span of a climax forest, only the minor, constant replacement of dead trees. But such forests may be destroyed by a lightning-sparked fire, by flooding when a river changes course, or, more commonly, by the activities of man.

People affect succession in many ways. We keep millions of acres of land in the pioneer stage called a lawn. To grow desired species of trees quickly, foresters plant seedlings on open land. The resulting tree plantation is a crop, not a true forest. In both instances, human efforts prevent the natural succession to a climax forest.

How plantations differ from wild woodlands

Tree plantings can be considered crops in the same way as fields of wheat. But because trees grow slowly, compared with ordinary crops, people fail to see the essential similarity of these two forms of agriculture. Like a food crop, a plantation is controlled throughout its life. Often, the land is prepared by clearing; then it is planted, tended and eventually harvested. Fast-growing species such as pines and larches (above) are suitable for commercial use. A 30-year-old pine plantation (below) shows the orderly look of such cultivation. Hikers are often welcome, but there is less diversity of animal life than in a wild forest.

As habitats change, so do the bird populations

The place to find birds is at natural feeding places where they congregate. In the meadow stage of plant succession, seed and insect-eating birds find plenty of food among the grasses and other flowering plants. As shrubs spring up, seed-eating birds such as larks take over. When pines succeed shrubs, nuthatches and

crossbills search the trunks for insects. In a climax forest, large, broad-leaved trees with dense foliage offer insect food and nesting sites for many species. There is a further change in bird populations with the coming of winter (insects die off, and the birds that depend on them migrate elsewhere).

Succession from meadow to forest in the temperate zones of Europe

Meadow and shrub
Most meadow birds nest on the ground or in low, tangled vegetation. Such birds are often protected from enemies by their plumage; mottled patterns and colours provide camouflage.

Skylark

Meadow pipit

Song thrush

Pine forest
Lacking dense undergrowth, stands of pines do not attract many birds. The crossbill is able to extract seeds from cones. Tits may nest in pines, and owls may occupy old crows' nests.

Crossbill

Crested tit

Long-eared owl

Climax forest
Among the many birds that nest in a deciduous forest are the nuthatch, the shy woodcock (which is a ground-dwelling species), and the strikingly marked green woodpecker.

Woodcock

Nuthatch

Green woodpecker

A closer look at the forest floor

On your next walk through a wood or forest, look down and give a thought to the living world at your feet. Although little sunlight filters down to this level, a carpet of small and exquisite plants covers the forest floor. A few, such as trilliums, trout lilies and wood anemones, may be wildflowers, but most of the plants that thrive there have no flowers at all.

This is where mosses thrive – especially if the woodland is damp for much of the year. Water is essential for the reproduction of mosses and many other non-flowering plants. As part of their life cycle, reproductive cells must "swim" to join other individuals of their species. The stems of mosses are sponge-like reservoirs that conserve water and foster reproduc-

tion. So mosses are hardy plants, able to withstand drought for considerable periods of time. When the rains come again, mosses resume growth and are once again springy under the visitor's feet.

Mingled with the mosses are ferns, fungi and lichens. Ferns are a highly diversified group. Some climb like vines; others, such as staghorn ferns and

Exquisite flowers that grow in the half-light

Ramsons (*Allium ursinum*) is a form of wild garlic and its bulb smells strongly. It can usually be found in the damper parts of woodlands.

Lords-and-ladies, or cuckoo-pint (*Arum maculatum*) sounds and looks attractive. But appearances are deceptive: its berries are poisonous.

The primrose (*Primula vulgaris*) sometimes flowers as early as Christmas when the winter is mild, and grows in great yellow carpets.

The common dog violet (*Viola riviniana*) flowers from April to June and grows under hedgerows and on open heaths as well as in woodlands.

Wood sorrel (*Oxalis acetosella*) produces its clover-like leaves in autumn and its delicate flowers in April and May. Fruit forms later.

polypody, grow perched on rock ledges, stumps or tree trunks. Most ferns native to a temperate forest lose all their leaves in autumn – but polypody and Christmas ferns keep their shiny green fronds throughout the year.

The parts of a fungus visible above ground – which most people call mushrooms or toadstools – are always short-lived. By contrast, lichens endure for years. A lichen is actually an alliance between two different plants, an alga and a fungus. The forms that lichens take are as varied as any in the plant kingdom: in some instances, they look like smudges of paint on a rock; in other cases, they look rather like an olive-green salad.

The low-growing plants in one forest may be dramatically different from their counterparts near by; it all depends on what trees shelter them. Coniferous forests have a sparse population of ground plants and shrubs because the cushion of fallen needles makes the soil acid. The crunchy litter in a broad-leaved forest is more hospitable to plants, and so this kind of forest is more likely to have thick undergrowth.

Litter is a forest's security blanket. It protects the soil from successive thawing and refreezing in winter, and acts as a mulch that prevents the ground from becoming parched by the sun. Eventually litter becomes part of the topsoil, which fosters plant growth.

No matter what the season for your forest walk, there is something to be seen. And remember that there is a bonus to forest rambles. Every now and then the trees thin out and you find yourself in a clearing or on the edge of a marsh or pond, where wildlife is permanently protected from human interference by the surrounding forest. You will find these silent undisturbed "islands" are among the most fascinating haunts of nature.

How to look at a fern

The "fruit dots" on the underside of this fern are clusters of spores.

Ferns and mosses are often grouped together because they have much in common, including habitat and method of reproduction. But ferns have characteristics uniquely their own. New leaves of some types of ferns uncurl from soft, downy protective scales in the spring. Ferns have leaf forms that range from very feathery to coarse and undivided; such patterns are an important means of identifying the different kinds. Although the leaves of ferns are usually green, those of certain species have a bluish tint, others are very dark, and some even turn a bronze colour in the autumn. Another way of identifying ferns is by the location of their spores. The common polypody above, a fern widely distributed throughout the British Isles and Europe, has spores on the undersides of its leaves; some other species have separate spore-bearing leaves.

Diminutive world of moss and lichen

Bristling like a miniature pine, a stalk of hair moss is surrounded by bluish-green lichens which are often found in the company of another type of lichen, called British soldiers (because of the bright red reproductive caps on their inch-high stalks). When you find one of these lichens, look for the other. Such associations of plants are undoubtedly based on the growing conditions, but the exact reason has still not been established by botanists, in spite of careful study.

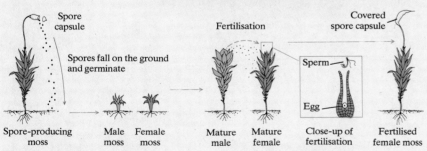

The spores from hair moss grow into separate male (sperm-producing) and female (egg-producing) plants. A sperm swims to a nearby egg (at the top of the female moss), and fertilisation occurs. The fertilised female then grows a stalk, with a spore-bearing capsule. When the spores are released, a new cycle begins.

Magical, mythical mushrooms

Awareness of the curious properties of mushrooms – the widely used name for the fungi – goes back to antiquity. There are biblical references to these strange plants, and they were also known and eaten by ancient Greeks, Romans and Chinese. Although many are edible and delicious, a fair number are poisonous. The Roman Emperor Claudius is thought to have been poisoned in AD 54 with mushrooms administered by his wife, Agrippina.

Some species of mushrooms have a powerful effect on the human mind – they cause hallucinations. Small wonder, then, that superstitions have grown up around them, and not a little fear. Among some Indians of Mexico and Central America, hallucinogenic fungi are part of religious rituals.

In the English language, the word toadstool is often used to identify poisonous fungi. The name was apparently applied because toads were believed to be poisonous; and because fungi appeared in the same sort of damp, dark places, it was a case of guilt by association. However, the distinction between toadstools and mushrooms is not a scientific one, and more important, gives no assurance that the particular specimen will not cause illness or even death.

Fungi were thought to be magical because of their unusual, often bizarre shapes, and also the fact that they seemed to materialise out of nowhere. As you may have observed on your own lawn, mushrooms often pop up within hours after a rain. It is easy to see why primitive peoples believed mushrooms were a result of lightning. Until a century ago, they were associated in many European country districts with "the little people" – gnomes, goblins and fairies – and sometimes with witchcraft.

The main part of the fungus lies under the ground. The mycelium, as this part is called, performs all the functions normally carried out by the roots, stem, and leaves of other plants. The white, web-like mycelium (which you occasionally see when you pick up a layer of decaying leaves or bark) has no chlorophyll, which means it cannot make its own food. As it grows through the soil, the mycelium absorbs water and nutrients present there. Nutrients in this case usually means material from dead plants and animals.

To bear fruit, a mycelium needs plenty of food and moisture. Typically, a button-like bud forms and pushes its way upwards through the soil. Even though it is mostly water, the emerging mushroom is strong enough to break through the cracks in a pavement. As it grows, the button rises on a stem, then unfolds like an umbrella.

On the underside of the umbrella are tissues, called gills, that release millions of microscopic spores. A tiny fraction of these spores will land where growing conditions are favourable, and a new fungus will become established. Often these plants will radiate in an ever-widening pattern, producing the circular "fairy ring" that figures in folklore. Some fairy rings have reached the age of 600 years.

Mushrooms vary greatly in size, shape, colour and toxicity. Some are tiny, but one Australian specimen measured more than 5 ft in circumference and weighed 17 lb. "Bird's-nest" fungi resemble their namesake, complete with egg-like spore sacs; puff-balls are spherical, and give off a cloud of spores when tapped. Some are luminescent – the gills of the oyster mushroom glow greenish-white, and the honey fungus gives off blue "fox fire".

Unfortunately, there are no clear signs to guide inexperienced mushroom hunters as to the safety of unfamiliar species. Some "edible" mushrooms become poisonous with age. Others are toxic only to certain people. Still others are harmful only if eaten day after day.

The only mushroom hunter that never seems to make a mistake in the quest for wild species is the pig that is trained by the French to root out truffles, a delicious mushroom that grows completely under the ground. A truffle-hunting pig may even be seen riding to "work", comfortably settled in its owner's wheelbarrow.

Oyster mushrooms, which may measure more than 5 in. across, grow in clusters of dead tree trunks and branches. Note the fluted gills.

A mushroom is the fruiting body of a subterranean plant

Covering called universal veil ruptures

Emerging mushroom

Partial veil

Spore-bearing gills

The growth of the amanita mushroom, some species of which are poisonous, resembles the hatching of an egg. Initially, a membrane called the universal veil covers the mushroom. As the amanita pushes its way up through the soil, the universal veil ruptures; the stalk and the cap are exposed. Another membrane, called the partial veil, gives extra protection to the gills on the underside of the cap. This veil also ruptures as the mushroom matures.

The "fly agaric" mushroom is poisonous, though rarely fatal. Its cap can vary in colour between scarlet and orange-red, but it always has its characteristic white patches.

Two flowering plants that live like fungi

Some flowering plants are frequently mistaken for mushrooms. These curious species have no chlorophyll – the green substance necessary for photosynthesis. Recently, scientists have discovered evidence that certain of these plants actually obtain their nutrients from mushrooms near by and would fail without them. The mushrooms, in turn, extract nutrients from decaying material or the roots of other plants.

Broomrape is a parasite that feeds on other plants. It attaches tubers to the roots of its hosts, especially clovers or members of the daisy family.

A rainy-weather species that appears on lawns and pastures, these mushrooms belong to a group named Leucoagaricus (white agaric).

Scarlet cups are heralds of spring. These inch-wide mushrooms, which thrive on fallen logs, appear much earlier than most other species.

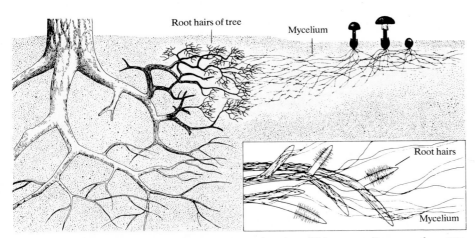

Root hairs of tree

Mycelium

Root hairs

Mycelium

A hidden but important part of any mushroom is its mycelium – the network of filaments that spreads through the soil, absorbing water and nutrients as it grows. Certain mycelia form a joint network with the root hairs of trees or other plants. This merger allows a mushroom to "tap" a tree for its nutrients, since the mushroom cannot make its own food. This does not seem to harm the tree – in fact, some trees do poorly if no mushrooms are present.

The bird's-nest orchid, which grows in beechwoods, takes its name from its mass of short, swollen roots. It lives on dead plant and animal matter.

A fallen log is full of life

When an old tree falls, human beings are likely to see only the death of something beautiful, and not recognise that this event is part of a continuing cycle. During its lifetime, the tree collected and retained many materials from its environment. The energy from the sun, water, and minerals extracted from the soil were all converted into the substances that form wood, leaves and sap. When the tree dies, all the nutrients that were locked in the tree become available again.

Bark kept out many insect invaders and disease organisms during the tree's lifetime. But now there are no more defences; the hard, dry bark that protected the interior of the tree becomes loosened – perhaps by damp, fire or wind damage. Many animals and plants arrive, taking advantage of the opportunity. The succession of invaders is not haphazard. The first to arrive are pioneers such as fungi and wood-boring beetles and termites. The tunnels and egg-chambers made by insects serve as channels by which water, bacteria and other species of insects may enter. Occasionally, the tunnels carved by young beetles can be seen as delicate "engravings" on the bare surface of the wood.

The log is gradually softened as the structure becomes a source of food and shelter for increasing numbers. Snails and insect larvae eat fungi and bits of log; each new wave of creatures attracts a new set of predators. With constant wear and tear, the entry points are expanded until the cavities are large enough to accommodate such animals as birds and snakes. Hollow logs often house red foxes.

Even before a tree falls, shelf or bracket fungi may appear. Once the tree is down, it may support these and many other species of fungi. Mosses, too, flourish on and around a fallen log, especially in damp environments. In time, the edifice is so hollowed out and weakened that it collapses gently, merging with the soil around it. This rich mound of humus encourages growth of ferns and wildflowers.

A falling tree may even give life to another tree. Seedlings of spruce, for example, find it hard to compete with vegetation on the ground, but will sprout readily from a rotting log above the undergrowth.

The rate of decomposition of trees varies according to species – some have more porous fibres than others, and so are "dismantled" more quickly. And, of course, a big tree lasts longer than a small one. Temperature and moisture also play a role. Fallen trees in hot places "disappear" more rapidly than in the cold.

The goat moth takes its name from its caterpillars, which bore through wood and smell like goats.

The wood mouse, field dwelling cousin of the familiar house mouse, may shelter in a barn during winter.

Male fern is so called because it looks tougher than lady fern.

The little wren stays through the British winter.

Bracket fungus looks like brackets on a wall.

The common salamander, cousin of the newt, lives in wet places throughout Europe.

Fly agaric, a poisonous fungus.

The chaffinch is a colourful dandy of bird society.

The black slug has twin sets of tentacles.

The elusive animals that visit or colonise logs

A fallen log is attractive to wildlife because it provides shelter (including nest sites) and food for a variety of species. In fact, as time passes, a food chain becomes established in and around the log. Insects that feed on the wood attract nuthatches and other insect eaters; these animals, in turn, encourage owls and other predators to visit the log. The illustration above depicts some of the wildlife that might be found near a decaying log in one particular region – a deciduous forest in Western Europe. (Of course, all these creatures would never be in the same place at the same time.) When you come upon a fallen log, do not be disappointed if it looks more like the one in the photo on the right, which shows a decaying tree in an Australian rain forest. Logs and stumps only appear to be lifeless – most of their residents are insects or other small animals, visible only if you poke the log or remove bits of loose bark with a stick. If you sit motionless near a fallen log, larger animals may come to visit, especially if the tree has been on the ground for a long time. Such a log in a secluded place is an ideal spot for bird-watchers.

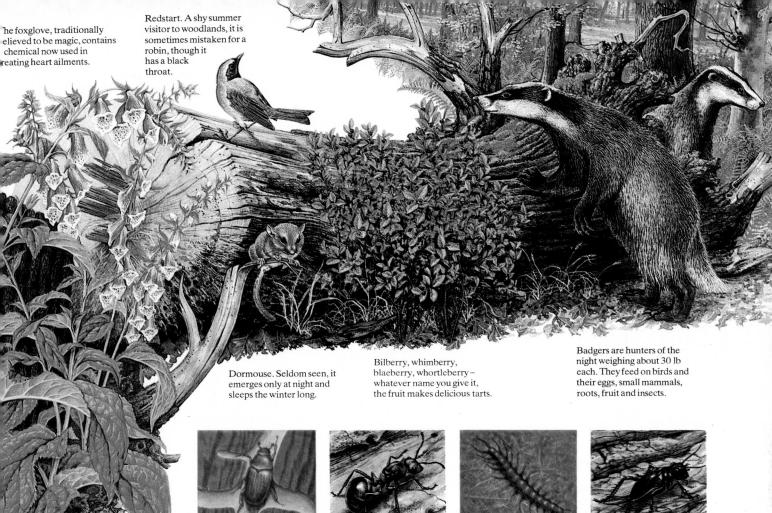

The foxglove, traditionally believed to be magic, contains a chemical now used in treating heart ailments.

Redstart. A shy summer visitor to woodlands, it is sometimes mistaken for a robin, though it has a black throat.

Dormouse. Seldom seen, it emerges only at night and sleeps the winter long.

Bilberry, whimberry, blaeberry, whortleberry – whatever name you give it, the fruit makes delicious tarts.

Badgers are hunters of the night weighing about 30 lb each. They feed on birds and their eggs, small mammals, roots, fruit and insects.

stag beetle seems to have antlers. But these are jaws. And they can draw blood with a nasty nip.

Less than ¼ in. long, an engraver beetle eats through the wood, hastening decay.

Although wood ants tunnel in logs, they do not eat wood; they feed on other insects.

Centipedes, which often live under loose bark, prey upon insects and other small animals.

Field crickets eat more or less anything, including rotting wood. They prefer dark places.

HOW TO
Build a compost heap

Nature constantly recycles material. In building a compost heap, you are simply putting nature to work on your own behalf.

- Choose a relatively sunlit place where the compost heap will be inconspicuous. A space about 4 ft square will be ample; however, you can adjust the dimensions to fit your space.
- Set up the compost heap by fencing in the area; the fencing material should have holes for ventilation. Or you can dig a pit – although this arrangement does not bring about decay as quickly.
- The best compost has a variety of ingredients. Start with lawn debris – grass clippings, leaves, weeds. Add potato or carrot peelings, coffee grounds, and other kitchen waste. The "fluff" from a vacuum cleaner can also be used. Newspapers, cartons, and other paper should be shredded before they are added. Do not include meat scraps, tins or bottles.
- To speed the composting process, add an activator – the manure of horses and cattle; even of dogs and cats. Or sprinkle on one of the chemical powders made especially for the purpose and sold in gardening shops.
- Build the compost heap in alternating layers of lawn debris, kitchen waste, activator and soil. Soak each layer well, and tamp it down firmly.
- When the pile reaches a height of 4 ft, stop adding material. Let it sit for six months; if it dries out, spray it with a hose. If you have the space, you can start a second compost heap at this time.
- Bacteria will go to work on the material in the compost heap. When the heap is dark-coloured and shows no traces of the materials that you put in, it is ready for use. If the outer portions have not decayed, shovel them on to the second heap.
- Sprinkle your new humus in the garden. If you mix it with a few inches of topsoil, your garden will be greatly enriched.

Autumn changes in the woodland

Plants and animals seem to know that winter is coming because they do so many things that prepare them for the approaching rigours of that season – shortages of food and water, and exposure to cold. But animals do not know about the future; unlike human beings, they apparently do not even recognise the implications of cooler weather. They respond to something far more reliable than the chill of autumn. Their behaviour is governed by the amount of sunlight present.

In temperate regions, the length of day decreases in late summer and autumn; this occurs consistently every year, for it is a result of the earth's annual movement around the sun. Animals respond to the shorter days by a complex mechanism. Among the more advanced species (such as birds and mammals) the change in the length of the day registers in the "master-control" gland in the brain, the hypothalamus. The hypothalamus secretes hormones that trigger other systems throughout the animal's body.

The specific form of the adjustment varies widely. Some animals embark on breeding behaviour. For example, autumn is the rutting season for many kinds of deer, the time when bucks lock antlers in competition for the does. Deer, like many other animals (such as porcupines and weasels), have about a six-month interval between mating and giving birth. This pattern of behaviour ensures that the young will be born in the spring, when food is abundant.

Another animal adjustment to the waning days may be the urge to eat more, thus building up layers of fat that will tide the animal over the winter. In autumn the most important source of food is seeds. Seed-eating animals are actually beneficial to a forest. Birds that digest only the coverings around seeds help plants to reproduce: they inadvertently disperse the seeds (in droppings) at places the seeds might not otherwise reach. Though squirrels eat nuts, their caches – buried and covered with leaves – are often abandoned. Instead of serving as food, the seeds grow into new plants.

Plants also respond to the shorter days – but without the help of a central controlling gland. Instead, the leaves of deciduous trees change to a reddish-brown and then fall. Left in the open, autumn-flowering plants like chrysanthemums will bloom only when the days start to grow shorter. Commercial growers can trick chrysanthemums into flowering at other times by shortening or lengthening the hours they are exposed to light.

An autumnal display such as this one in Britain's New Forest may last for weeks. The next time you have a chance to watch leaves change colour, notice which trees change first. Larches and maples start their transformation relatively early.

 COLLECTOR'S TIPS
Pressing, preserving and printing with leaves

Preserving leaves can be the basis of two hobbies – one, using leaves decoratively, the other, learning to identify different species. Autumn leaves make especially colourful collections; but in order to get good specimens, be sure to gather leaves while they are still supple. Collect as many types of leaves as possible (and their twigs). Make a note of the dates, names and locations of your specimens.

How to press leaves

To preserve your collection, make a simple leaf-press. First, arrange leaves between thick layers of absorbent cardboard or blotting paper. Be sure layers do not overlap. Place entire stack between two flat, heavy boards or plywood, and bind tightly with straps or cords. Store in a warm, dry place for about ten days, checking often and tightening straps.

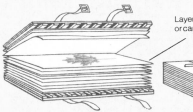

Layers of pulpy paper or cardboard

Note the arrangement of absorbent layers and how leaf is placed between them.

A tightly bound press ensures maximum release of moisture and flat leaves for display.

Why leaves change colour and drop with the waning year

Although leaves contain several substances that give them colour, the influence of green chlorophyll in spring and summer is so great that other colours are obscured. But as the production of chlorophyll declines in autumn, the other colours begin to show, and some new substances even develop. In the close-up (upper left), chlorophyll is still along the veins, but a red hue predominates elsewhere; in the photo below it, the entire maple leaf has turned a brilliant gold. A leaf changes colour because a layer of cells dries out at the base of the leaf stalk, where it attaches to the twig. Called the abscission layer, these cells seal the leaf from the circulatory system of the tree. Deprived of water, the leaf stops producing chlorophyll and dies. Autumn winds do not really tear a leaf from the twig – they snap it off at the abscission layer (see below). The leaf-shedding habit conserves water in winter, when it may be frozen and unavailable. The needle leaves of conifers do not have to be shed because their smaller surface loses far less water.

Chlorophyll's green colour predominates in spring and summer

Other colours are revealed in autumn as production of chlorophyll stops

Abscission scar, where leaf was attached

HORSE CHESTNUT
(Aesculus hippocastanum)

Old horse chestnut in full flower on farm near Arundal, Sussex. May 14, 1976.

A preserved leaf is shown with twig and a photograph of the tree; also its scientific name.

Display leaves under plastic

Use two equal-size pieces of clear plastic – the type that is adhesive on one side. Choose leaves and plan their placement before peeling off backing. Handle adhesive only at edges; finger marks will show. Position leaves on to adhesive.

Remove backing from the second sheet. Smooth plastic sheets starting from one end, working air out as you go. Then trim edges.

Leaf impressions in ink

Put a dab of printer's ink or endorsing ink on a square of glass and spread with a small rubber roller. Place leaf on blotting paper (vein-side up) and ink with roller. Turn inked leaf down on page to be printed. Cover with paper; press firmly; peel off paper and allow to dry.

For very detailed prints, like the one on the right, use plants with leaflets on which the veins stand out prominently, such as ferns and laburnums.

How animals adapt to winter

The less you do, the less energy you need – that is the key to winter survival. Activity uses up energy, which comes from food; and food is in scant supply during a northern winter. Then, too, activity requires water, and near-drought conditions prevail when water is locked up in ice and snow.

Sleeping through the winter saves energy. Brown bears and badgers, for instance, are winter-sleepers and conserve their body fuel by not moving about; they doze much of the time, but are easily awakened by intruders into their dens. Typically, mammals that adapt to winter by sleeping through most of it must keep their temperatures much higher than that of their surroundings. But it takes some energy to do this.

Unlike winter-sleepers, true hibernators such as hedgehogs have drastically lowered body temperatures. Reduced temperatures mean that everything happens at a slower speed, so pulse and breathing rate drop. (Hibernating hedgehogs breathe only once every six minutes, which is about 200 times slower than their normal rate.) At this slow pace, life requires a minimum of energy, and a hibernating animal's fat layers can usually meet the slight demand.

Snow is a protective blanket for small mammals that neither hibernate nor winter-sleep. Snow is ten times lighter than liquid water and traps air; thus it is an ideal insulator (it also allows ventilation). Soil with a snow cover may be as much as 10°C (18°F) warmer than the air above it. Under the blanket of snow, mice, voles, and other small mammals lose little body heat to their surroundings. They stay active and feed on plant food, including some they may have stored during autumn.

The chill of winter inactivates most "cold-blooded" animals. These creatures, whose body temperatures are invariably tied to that of the environment, do not move about when it is cold. Reptiles and amphibians – such as terrapins and the vociferous European green tree frogs – remain covered and dormant during the coldest part of winter. So, too, do adult tortoiseshell butterflies, which stay immobile in the comparative safety of attics, decaying logs or hollow trees.

Another adaptation to winter is common among plants and insects. The adults reproduce and then die as winter sets in. All that remains of some species of insects are their offspring, which live out the winter as eggs or larvae. Similarly, plants known as annuals exist during winter as seeds that are capable of withstanding both frost and drought.

Migration is yet another solution to survival in winter. Warblers, swallows and other insect-eating birds fly to warmer climates, where insects thrive. Some of the large, hoofed mammals – moose and reindeer – also migrate, but not to the south like the birds, and only to places where there is enough vegetation throughout the cold weather on which to feed.

Although the winter forest may seem

Thick, downy feathers preserve the body heat of the ruffed grouse. On freezing nights they may dive into snow banks; at other times they simply fluff their feathers and sit in a tree.

Black bears awaken periodically in winter and leave their homes – usually in caves. Their normal temperature of 37°C (99°F) drops only a few degrees during periods of rest, which is why bears are not considered true hibernators.

64

silent, life goes on above ground. Tracks reveal the comings and goings of grouse, wildcats and mountain hares. But you can find more than tracks, if you know where such animals seek food, in thickets and similar places.

Winter is good for birdwatching – the leafless trees allow better visibility than in spring and summer. There are visiting birds – late migrants, perhaps. Waxwings and finches, jays and crossbills feast on seeds.

If you carefully scan the branches of a conifer, you may discover a silent, motionless owl; other clues to the residence of an owl are small, oblong pellets of undigested food under a tree. Woodpeckers and nuthatches extract insects from trees, especially dying or injured ones. Ducks and eagles feed in open water, but they also favour places where warm water is discharged. And, of course, a bird table, offering scraps of food and, even more important, water is an ideal place for watching birds.

Active throughout winter, a bobcat pounces on small rodents, which live in tunnels and burrows under the blanket of snow.

Broad, heavily furred feet support a snowshoe hare as it hops across soft snow. Its fur – white only in winter – camouflages the hare in snow.

A hibernating ground squirrel awakens in spring

Rising body temperatures arouse a hibernator, such as the golden-mantled ground squirrel (below). Hibernation is a physical state where all the animal's body functions slow down. For example, the temperature of this squirrel drops from an average of 32°C (90°F) to about 4°C (39°F). Its digestive and hormonal systems appear to stop; the heartbeat is too faint to be detected with an ordinary stethoscope. Essentially, hibernation is a means of conserving energy. While in this state, a squirrel can be picked up and brought into the light and still not wake up. In spring, however, the squirrel begins to stir; its breathing rate increases, as do its circulation and heartbeat, until it is completely awake.

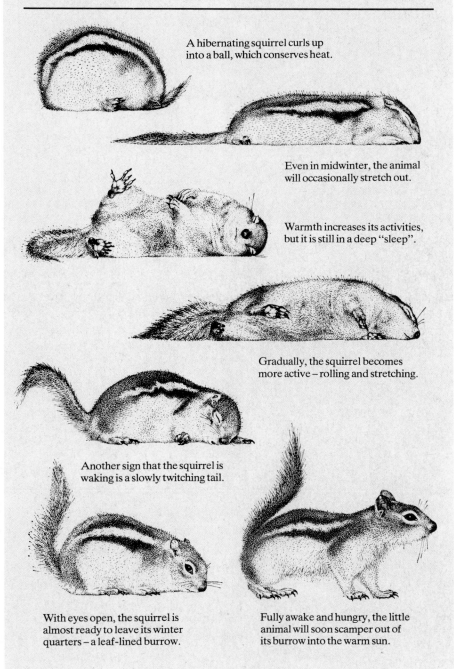

A hibernating squirrel curls up into a ball, which conserves heat.

Even in midwinter, the animal will occasionally stretch out.

Warmth increases its activities, but it is still in a deep "sleep".

Gradually, the squirrel becomes more active – rolling and stretching.

Another sign that the squirrel is waking is a slowly twitching tail.

With eyes open, the squirrel is almost ready to leave its winter quarters – a leaf-lined burrow.

Fully awake and hungry, the little animal will soon scamper out of its burrow into the warm sun.

Where summer never ends

Imagine a time when palms spread their leafy fronds on what is now Alaska, when crocodiles swam in the rivers of England and Wales, when tropical bread-fruit trees grew in Scandinavia. One-hundred million years ago much of the earth was hot, humid, and covered with lush rain forests. Today the warm and wet climate that nurtures these forests exists primarily in the relatively narrow belt around the equator.

The most unvarying conditions on the surface of the earth are in a tropical rain forest. Lacking seasons, rain forests are ever-wet, ever-warm and ever-green worlds of endless summer. Eighty is a key number: the annual rainfall averages more than 80 in., temperatures hover near 27°C (80°F) throughout the year, and the relative humidity rarely drops below a muggy 80%.

The result of this constantly warm and wet climate is an elaborate profusion of plant life. Tropical rain forests support more living material than any other natural community. Nearly all of this is plant life – and trees predominate over all other plant forms. The trees, in fact, prevent most of the sunlight from reaching the forest floor, thus inhibiting other plants.

Many trees in a tropical rain forest look startlingly alike. Their trunks are straight, slender and smooth-barked; they branch and produce leaves and flowers only near the top, where there is the most light. Their bases often have immense buttresses, which may support them in the moist and shallow soil.

Not all of the fragrant and bright-coloured blossoms that festoon tropical trees belong to the trees themselves: they are, instead, the flowers of epiphytes ("air plants") that perch on tree trunks and branches – plants adapted to a lofty life because of the lack of light below. In one instance, an Australian tree had a load of some 50 species of epiphytic plants.

Tropical orchids are generally epiphytes, but many other kinds of plants have also taken to the trees. Some epiphytes, such as bromeliads, grow rosettes of leaves that trap water and soil; the centre of the rosette becomes an aerial breeding-site for insects and amphibians. Other epiphytes have roots that absorb water directly from the humid air.

Though the word "jungle" is often used as a synonym for a ruthless and competitive world, this is not a valid description of a tropical rain forest. Of course, there is competition (especially for sunlight and soil nutrients), but a remarkable diversity thrives here. Many relatively fragile species are able to exist. A Malaysian rain forest may have more than 200 kinds of trees; contrast this with a typical temperate forest, which may contain a dozen species.

Diversity has a surprising side-effect. Although there are many different kinds, members of a particular species may be few and far between. For example, one equatorial forest in Africa has only a single mature mahogany tree in 25 acres. This widely scattered distribution means that once a tropical rain forest is cut down, it may take centuries for all the different kinds of trees to recolonise the area – and some species may never return at all.

Often forests have been recklessly destroyed in garnering the occasional valuable species of tree, such as teak in South-East Asia. Conservation and replanting have far to go to repair the damage.

A tropical rain forest justifies the name jungle only at its edges, where it borders a river or clearing. The interior of this African forest is drastically different: deprived of light by the profuse growth of treetop leaves, the interior is dark. The forest floor has only a small amount of undergrowth.

Spectacular Encyclias from Central America are pollinated by male carpenter bees. But it is not the orchids' vivid colours that attract the insects: the flowers smell like the female bees.

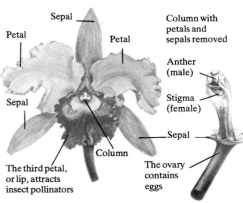

Sepal

Petal

Petal

Column with petals and sepals removed

Sepal

Anther (male)

Stigma (female)

Sepal

Column

The third petal, or lip, attracts insect pollinators

The ovary contains eggs

How to look at an orchid

Although there are more than 25,000 species of orchids, it is possible to recognise any member of the orchid family, regardless of superficial differences. Each flower has three petals, with one that is different from the others (usually larger and more elaborate). This specialised petal attracts insects to the centre of the flower, where male and female reproductive organs are fused into a column. Only orchids have this column. All orchids also have three sepals, which may be brightly coloured. Although tropical orchids are the most spectacular and diverse, you can find orchids in nearly every terrestrial habitat.

The graceful Epidendrum is one of a group of New World orchids that usually live on trees; in fact, Epidendrum means "upon a tree".

An Asiatic lady's slipper (which is an orchid) temporarily traps insect pollinators in a pouch. Similar species grow in temperate forests.

Different growth forms divide orchids into two groups: with horizontal stems (left), and those with upright stalks. In the tropics, most species of orchids grow perched atop rocks or other plants, rather than in the soil.

LIVING WITH NATURE

Tribal life in a tropical rain forest

Surprisingly, the lush hothouses of the tropical rain forests are not able to maintain large populations of humans. This is not because of jungle terrors such as jaguars, tigers, crocodiles, snakes, flesh-eating fish and poisonous insects, for men soon learn to cope with all these.

The obstacle is lack of food. This seems odd when the jungles are often thick with birds and animals, the rivers are teeming with fish, and wild fruits hang from the trees, ready for the plucking.

But this natural bounty is usually seasonal. The native peoples can catch fish when waters are low, or kill animals with bow and arrow in their seasonal migrations. But they cannot keep these food supplies fresh.

To stay alive, forest dwellers must often be nomads, moving on to new sites when they have exhausted the resources of fruit and game in one area. For this reason tribes in tropical forests of South America, Africa and Asia usually number only a few hundreds, or even a few score.

They live in easily erected huts of timber, roofed with a thatch of leaves, often near to a river, which serves them as fishpond, bathing pool and highway. In most regions they have learned to sleep off the ground for safety and comfort – in hammocks in the Amazon region and in houses on poles in South-East Asia and New Guinea.

All over the world, jungle communities are threatened by the intrusion of civilisation. Roads are driven through the jungle; forests are torn down to make farmland; birds, animals and fish are slaughtered with modern weapons. Worst of all, the forest people are infected with diseases of civilisation, against which they have no in-built resistance.

67

Zones of life in a rain forest

Walking in a tropical rain forest is surprisingly easy. The tall trees that make up most of the vegetation branch only at their tops, forming an umbrella-like canopy that may be 200 ft overhead. Thus the traveller encounters ranks of tall pillars in a dark, sheltered interior – a far cry from the tangled jungles of fiction.

Sounds in a tropical rain forest are tantalising. They are loud and varied, but the creatures that scream and squawk are usually far above and can be glimpsed only through binoculars.

Unlike temperate forests, the floor of a rain forest has no thick carpeting of dead leaves and branches. When an organism dies, fungi and scavengers of all kinds convert the dead material (plant or animal) into nutrients for themselves. The result is that the rain forest soil receives little enriching humus from its own dead leaves. Thus, in spite of its luxuriant vegetation, the soil of a tropical rain forest is far less hospitable to plants than it seems. When cleared for farming, such land seldom produces abundant crops.

Tropical rain forests are usually divided into five distinct layers. Starting at ground level is the dark Herb Layer, which has tree trunks and a sprinkling of ferns and saplings. Only an estimated 1% of the sunlight that strikes a rain forest ever touches this layer of it, although it is possible occasionally to see slender daggers of light stabbing the sombre ground.

Next is the Shrub Layer, which extends from about 2 to 20 ft above the ground. Although this layer has relatively sparse growth, you may find cauliflorous trees and vines here. These plants have flowers that grow out directly from the bark, with no branch or twig, and do, in fact, resemble cauliflowers.

The Understorey – the layer you see when you look upwards – is about 20 to 40 ft above the ground. The foliage here is thick enough to hinder movement of most animals, although some creatures do pass through on their way to and from the upper layers. Many small birds feed here and at lower levels, in spite of the obstructions to flying.

The Canopy Layer is alive with birds – the boisterous macaws (whose cries can be heard a mile or so away), parakeets, parrots and many others. Sloths (only in the Americas), monkeys and other climbing mammals are common here. This layer usually includes the intermeshing crowns of trees and numerous perching and climbing plants.

Bromeliads and other epiphytes grow on trees and vines, getting their sustenance from dust and rain. A tree limb may hold several tons. Although epiphytes are not parasites (they take no nutrients from the trees), they sometimes strangle their hosts with their grip.

Unlike the other levels, the Emergent Layer is not continuous. "Emergent" refers to a scattering of trees that project far higher than the others. This "attic" has the most variable conditions of any place in the rain forest. It is more exposed to the elements and gets the full force of sun, wind and rain. Many animals climb or fly between the Emergent and Canopy Layers, but it is difficult for human beings to find a place from which to observe them.

Rivers are the main highways of the rain forest. Often changing course, they cut through the dense walls of vegetation that grow along their banks. In this Liberian forest (right), the trunks of emergent trees are visible above the canopy.

Buttress roots are a remarkable feature of this Venezuelan forest giant (below). These woody growths form between the trunks and roots near the surface of the ground, and may serve as supports for tall trees during heavy storms. The angles between these high roots make shelters and homes for many kinds of animals.

How vines reach for the sunlight

1. Clinging vines are usually air plants with finger-like anchors that stick to tree trunks, branches and other vines.

2. Lianas, sometimes called monkey ropes, are fast-growing twiners. Their woody stems wrap tightly around trees as they push up towards the sunlight.

3. The lawyer vine is a scrambler. It puts out slender auxiliary vines with curving thorns that hook on to smooth tree bark or other neighbouring plants.

4. Vines with tendrils possess multiple shoots so sensitive they can reach out and cling to the tiniest twig for support.

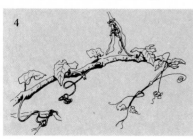

Parallel lives though worlds apart

Many animals of different species that live in similar environments have evolved along similar lines. These residents of tropical rain forests have strong resemblances and almost identical habits and life-styles.

EMERGENT LAYER

Living at the top of the tallest trees, the large birds of prey can scan lower treetops for potential quarry or take off in soaring flight.

Monkey-eating eagle
Asia

Harpy eagle
South America

CANOPY

The canopy is colourful with flowers and fruits, which are delicately plucked and eaten by these birds with enormous, light bills.

Great hornbill
Africa

Toco toucan
South America

UNDERSTOREY

The bushbaby's suction-like grasp and the woolly opossum's prehensile tail are adaptations to life among slippery branches.

Bushbaby (galago)
Africa

Woolly opossum
South America

SHRUB LAYER

Tapirs and other large animals often race through the shrub layer at amazing speeds.

Malayan tapir
Asia

Brazilian tapir
South America

HERB LAYER

Pittas are among the elusive ground dwellers whose loud calls echo through the forest.

Fulvous pitta
Asia

Black-crowned ant pitta
South America

CHAPTER THREE

Mountains and highlands

Though mountains and hills loom majestically over every continent, they conceal far more about themselves than they reveal.

Mountains were once believed to be eternal – mainly because their life-spans are so much longer than our own. Mountains rise, grow old and wear away, but on a time-scale that is almost beyond human comprehension. Even when we see a mud-slide or rock avalanche, it is hard to believe that such seemingly minor events can eventually bring down anything as massive as a mountain. Gravity is an unrelenting force, which affects everything. So, too, is the process of weathering that crumbles rocks.

The spectacular behaviour of volcanoes was generally regarded as something apart. That many other mountains are still gradually rising was not even suspected until comparatively recent times. And the complex composition of mountains was not fully understood either, until engineers began tunnelling through mountains. As the work progressed, there were often violent explosions as the pressures on particular segments of rock were relieved. Though such explosions were common in mines, few people realised that tremendous pressures are present within mountains as well.

Nowadays, many people approach the airy heights with a new understanding. But one important fact is still not fully grasped – that mountains are fragile. The rocks themselves are vulnerable, and so are the pockets of soil lodged there, and the plants and animals dependent on the soil. The clearing and farming of steep slopes has imperilled many mountainsides. Even temporary loss of vegetative cover invites the disaster of a landslide – the soil accumulations of centuries can be lost in a matter of minutes. When this is widely understood, mountains will have a better chance of survival.

To stand on mountaintops, as on this promontory in the French Alps, climbers must take frightening risks. Yet the lure of mountains is so great that even those of us who only dream of such adventures can share the feeling of exhilaration.

Mountains new and old

When exploring a hill or a mountain, what you see depends on how good a detective you are. You might be able to discover evidence of major geological events, for many of the forces that shaped mountains have left clues. You do not even have to go to the hills to get information. It is practical and very rewarding if you begin by consulting geology guidebooks.

If someone were to ask you about the hills or mountains nearest your home, could you say how they were formed? You might be surprised to discover that you are living on land that was once under the sea, or that is covered by the remains of extinct volcanoes.

People sometimes learn about geology accidentally, for example when drilling a well or excavating the foundations for a new home. If the bedrock of a worn-down mountain lies near the surface, the digging may be very expensive. The underlying geology of large cities influences the kinds of buildings that can be erected. Sometimes this, too, is discovered the hard way. For example, in Mexico City, high in the Sierra Madre mountains, many buildings are slowly sinking because part of the city rests on a former lake bed.

Like any good detective, you must be ready to look for clues in many ways. If you take photographs, you may be able to get a view of the mountain structure that would be hard to analyse simply by looking at it. Collecting rock samples from an actual site is extremely useful, too (of course, only in places where collecting is permitted). You can later compare the clues you pick up with geology books, or perhaps with someone else who is interested and informed about the geology of the region. This is the key to enjoying such a pursuit – concentrating on specific places and not trying to learn about the whole world all at once.

Mountains can be intriguing because their histories are complex. Few people will mistake the classic cone-shaped form of an active volcano. Extremely high mountains, such as the Himalayas, are clearly new formations. Old mountains, such as the Grampians in Scotland, some of the oldest rock in the world, the Appalachians in the eastern USA and the Urals in Russia, are likely to be lower and less imposing. This is the best clue to their antiquity. They were formed 250 million or more years ago and have been greatly worn down in the intervening centuries.

But there is a further element that has to be taken into account in studying mountains – immense shifts in the earth's crust sometimes cause tilting of great layers of rock. The Himalayas and the Alps, for instance, were probably formed by the collision of great continental plates thrusting layers of rock upwards. You might expect that in a mountain range, the older rock would be at the bottom. But this is not a reliable assumption. As layers are pushed up like waves, the buckling layers may flop over on each other, burying newer layers under the old.

Exposure to the elements takes its toll. Weathering can cover the trails left by mountain-raising forces; but weathering leaves clues, too. In many places – in cities as well as on mountains – you may be able to discover the grooves scratched in rocks thousands of years ago by glaciers.

A good detective must expect the unexpected. Recent glaciers (that is, recent in geological terms) have chiselled portions of the northern Appalachian mountains, with the result that peaks such as Mount Katahdin in Maine have acquired the sharp, jagged look of much younger mountains.

The jagged silhouette of the Cordillera Real, looming over the high plateau of Bolivia, is typical of the relatively young Andes system. Its beginnings go back 100 million years, when the earth's crust buckled and folded. Much later, only 2½ million years ago, intense volcanic activity thrust up the long chain of towering peaks that runs down South America's west coast.

The giant domes (some 30 in all) that make up Mount Olga rise 1,000 ft or more above Australia's central desert. These sandstone outcrops are composed of some of the world's oldest sedimentary rock – first deposited in an ancient sea, then tumbled into boulders, and ultimately compacted into solid masses.

The low contours of the Great Smokies (below), which are part of the Appalachian range of eastern North America, testify to their age. The upheaval that produced these mountains began some 200 million years ago. More millions of years went by as rains wore down the heights and filled valley floors with soil. The Smokies were never covered by glaciers; many rare plants have survived there.

 PHOTO TIPS
Composing landscapes

When you photograph a mountain, your first impulse may be to move forward, freeing the subject from obstructions. Take this shot, but then, if there is foreground foliage, try using it as a frame or point of reference. Later, compare results.

• If the subject is near a body of water, as in this landscape, try using the reflection as part of the composition of the picture.

• Because mountains often turn cold fast, camera and film need protection. Load the camera indoors. Freezing makes film brittle; to prevent cracking, be sure to advance the film slowly. Be careful not to breathe on the lens or view-finder; ice might form, obscuring your field.

• Before returning to warm conditions, put the camera into an airtight plastic bag. Any condensation will form outside, on the bag, and not inside the camera.

How mountains wear down

When you look at a mountain, even a snow-capped peak, what you are seeing may be just a fraction of the original land mass. For example, an estimated 25,000 ft have been worn off parts of the Appalachian Mountains, and also from the once-great mountains of the Lake District of Britain. Some 50,000 to 60,000 ft are gone from the Simplon Pass in the Swiss Alps. All the mountains of the world are constantly being worn down – even those that are still being formed.

What whittled the mountains down? The answer is weathering – the process by which natural forces such as rain and wind wear down the surface of the earth. The process is slow; on the average, the height of a mountain is lowered less than one-thousandth of an inch a year. But because most mountains are millions of years old, the long-term effect is impressive.

Running water has done more to change the face of the earth than anything else in nature. Anyone who has ever aimed a garden hose at a patch of earth knows how quickly the force of the stream will dig a hole. Every time it rains, a similar thing happens; each raindrop is a tiny projectile striking the ground. The drops loosen and remove particles of rock. Rivers and streams, laden with particles, scour the land.

Water weathers rock in still another way. When water is in liquid form, it invades the cracks in a rock. Then, when the water freezes, its volume expands by about 10%. Whenever freezing occurs, expansion exerts tremendous pressures – the ice may push with a force of 2,000 lb. per square inch.

Alternate freezing and thawing of water is only part of the crumbling process. Unlike water, other substances, such as rock, will contract when cold and expand when warm. Rocks have a tendency to crack when subjected to sudden changes in temperature (just as glass or china may do in the kitchen). Thus, when the sun heats the rocky surface, the rock expands slightly, and the exposed part may flake off.

Then, too, the sheer weight of accumulated ice and snow will wear a mountain down by abrasion. A glacier 1,000 ft thick exerts a force of 30 tons per square foot. As this massive weight moves down a mountain, it gouges out earth and rocks, eventually depositing them in the valley below. In Scotland and the Lake District there are several examples of corries – bowl-like structures on mountain-sides scooped out by glaciers.

Wind plays a role in the wearing down

Sheer on one side and rounded on the other, Half Dome (in the American Rockies in California) owes its helmet-like shape to ice and weathering of the granite. When the rocks above it eroded, the newly exposed surfaces peeled off as well. The "missing" part, which weathered especially quickly, apparently collapsed; a cliff was left behind.

of mountains, although it is a far less significant agent of change than water and ice. The wind carries away particles of rock that have been chipped off by other forces. A blast of mountain air carries a light but steady burden of pulverised rock.

Different kinds of rock weather at different rates. (If they did not, mountains might "melt" away evenly, the way ice cream seems to subside in a bowl.) Some rocks weather quickly because their components are particularly susceptible to chemical attack: limestone, for example, is readily dissolved by the acids in rain or groundwater.

Sandstone and other porous rocks often contain a great deal of water and consequently weather at a faster rate than dense rocks. In dry climates, where water evaporates quickly after rainfall, sandstone outcrops become immense "wicks"

that soak up water. When temperatures drop enough to freeze the water, such rocks are especially vulnerable.

But not all weathering is done by inanimate forces. Mountain plants are slow, steady agents of weathering. The roots of trees prise cracks apart, and some plants – notably lichens – actually dissolve the rock. Burrowing animals, insects and worms also scrape away material and expose the rock to weathering processes.

Although mountains are created by mighty shifts of the earth's crust, it is weathering that gives most mountains their distinctive shapes. The wearing-away process often reveals the geological history of the mountain. Softer layers go first; pillars and caps of harder stone, laid down in other periods, often stand out, creating fanciful-looking natural sculpture such as can be seen on Dartmoor.

Fractures occur in rocks when a change in temperature is too abrupt for normal expansion or contraction to take place.

Into every crack in the rock, particles of soil will drift, bringing with them seeds and spores. At first, only plants with small root systems are able to grow there. But under steady assault by infiltrating ice, changes in temperature and plant roots, the rocks split further.

Weathering reveals the structure of rocks

Exfoliation is the onion-like peeling of rock. It occurs after release of pressure or after changes in temperature.

Block separations, often found in limestone, reveal the tendency of rocks to break along weak seams.

Granular disintegration may occur when coarse-grained rock (such as sandstone) weathers; it simply crumbles.

The round, pitted look of this limestone rock is the result of chemical weathering: rainwater, which contains a mild acid, has gradually dissolved and washed away part of the stone.

  HIKING AND CAMPING
Do's and don'ts on rugged mountain paths

A mile-long walk does not sound like much, unless the direction is up. Everything changes as you hike higher up a path – the temperature is colder, the winds are stronger, the air is thinner, and you may discover that you tire more easily (the reason for this is a combination of extra exertion and lower concentrations of oxygen in the air; you have to work harder to get enough to breathe). You are more likely to get sunburn in mountains than on lower ground because ultra-violet (UV) light penetrates the thin air more readily, and it is UV that gives you the tan. It is fun and exhilarating to go hiking in the hills, but it takes preparation – and practice, too – if the trip is to end well.

● Never climb alone. Most accidents can be avoided by staying with a party – preferably with a knowledgeable leader. Even expert climbers notify others of their whereabouts. If you sign into an area, remember also to sign out to avoid concern over your absence.

● Wear the right clothes – ones that are comfortable. Boots are especially important; never wear new boots on a trek, only ones that you have tried out. Mountain weather changes rapidly, so carry waterproof clothing, an extra sweater, socks, gloves, a hat and sunglasses.

● Prepare for emergencies. Take along a first-aid kit. A compass is essential, and so is a whistle. The latter is an easy, effective device for locating a lost member of your party. Carry a water bottle and a supply of quick-energy foods, such as chocolate bars. If you have a feeling of light-headedness, which is often caused by high altitude, lie down on a warm, sun-exposed rock and prop your feet up. If cold, pull your hat down firmly and keep your torso well covered; your extremities will soon warm up.

● Study (and take along) a map before going into an unfamiliar area. Plan your route, avoiding smooth, steep slopes and any landslide areas.

● Do not go out in poor weather. Hazards increase with rain and fog. If mist suddenly obscures your path in a dangerous area, wait for it to blow away before continuing. Never stand on a ledge; it may break off under your weight.

Mountains and plateaux

Except for isolated volcanoes, such as Kilimanjaro in Tanzania, Fujiyama in Japan, or Etna and Vesuvius in Italy, mountains seldom stand alone. They are usually grouped in belts or ranges; and several connected ranges form a mountain system. The Himalayan Mountains are a system, with the Karakoram as one of its ranges; the Rocky Mountain system has, as two of its components, the Brooks and Wasatch Ranges.

Some great plateaux stand independent of mountain systems. Such regions may have been formed by the tilting and shifting of huge plates in the earth's crust millions of years ago. In northern Australia, the Barkly Tableland is an elevated sea-bed, where some of the most ancient rock on earth lies exposed. The Deccan Plateau in India, and vast regions of Mongolia and Siberia are highlands of volcanic origin.

Mountains have influenced history. They have caused the isolation of peoples, which has resulted in a greater divergence of cultures. The Andean Indians, often living in remote, isolated valleys, are an example of people who developed a unique language and culture. So, too, are the Basques, inhabitants of the foothills of the Pyrenees who speak a language different from the Indo-European ones of France and Spain, in whose territories they are incorporated, and fiercely maintain a separate national identity.

For most of recorded history, the power of mountains to block invaders was so great that military historians have made much of the few conquerors able to cross them. For example, Alexander the Great is noted for his invasion of India through the Hindu Kush; Hannibal is famous for having invaded Italy from Spain, first by crossing the Pyrenees, then the Alps, with elephants carrying his military stores. Conversely, the lack of mountains has converted many a region into a crossroads, a market-place and, unfortunately, a battleground.

In summer, many species of animals migrate to the Brooks Range to breed

The name Rockies is sometimes used to refer to the entire North American mountain system, but at other times to specific sections of it, such as the Canadian Rockies

The Hawaiian Islands are tips of volcanic peaks in the middle of the ocean. Some volcanoes, such as Mauna Loa, are still active.

The Central American land bridge, which links the two continents, is volcanic in origin. The chain extends from Mexico's Sierra Madres down to the Isthmus of Panama, then to the Andes

The Andes Mountains have a characteristic volcanic rock (called andesite). The mineral composition of lava varies widely throughout the world

Aconcagua is the highest peak in the Americas; off the coast is a deep oceanic trench. From mountaintop to ocean floor is the earth's greatest vertical distance – 9 miles

The Appalachians are old worn-away mountains. Long ago in earth's history, these mountains were entirely submerged by an inland sea

Many rivers flow from Brazil's two highlands – the Mato Grosso and Brazilian Plateau

Famous mountains world-wide

Height alone is not the measure of a mountain's fame. Though Everest is the highest, the Matterhorn and McKinley attract more climbers. All by itself on a plain, Kilimanjaro commands notice. So do active volcanoes, such as Mount Etna. Religious significance gives an aura to many – Popocatepetl, Cotopaxi, Ararat, Sri Pada, Fujiyama.

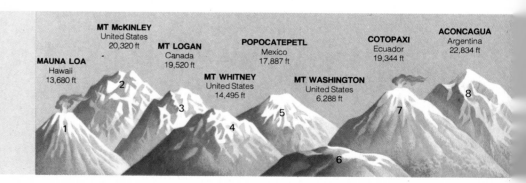

MAUNA LOA
Hawaii
13,680 ft

MT McKINLEY
United States
20,320 ft

MT LOGAN
Canada
19,520 ft

MT WHITNEY
United States
14,495 ft

POPOCATEPETL
Mexico
17,887 ft

MT WASHINGTON
United States
6,288 ft

COTOPAXI
Ecuador
19,344 ft

ACONCAGUA
Argentina
22,834 ft

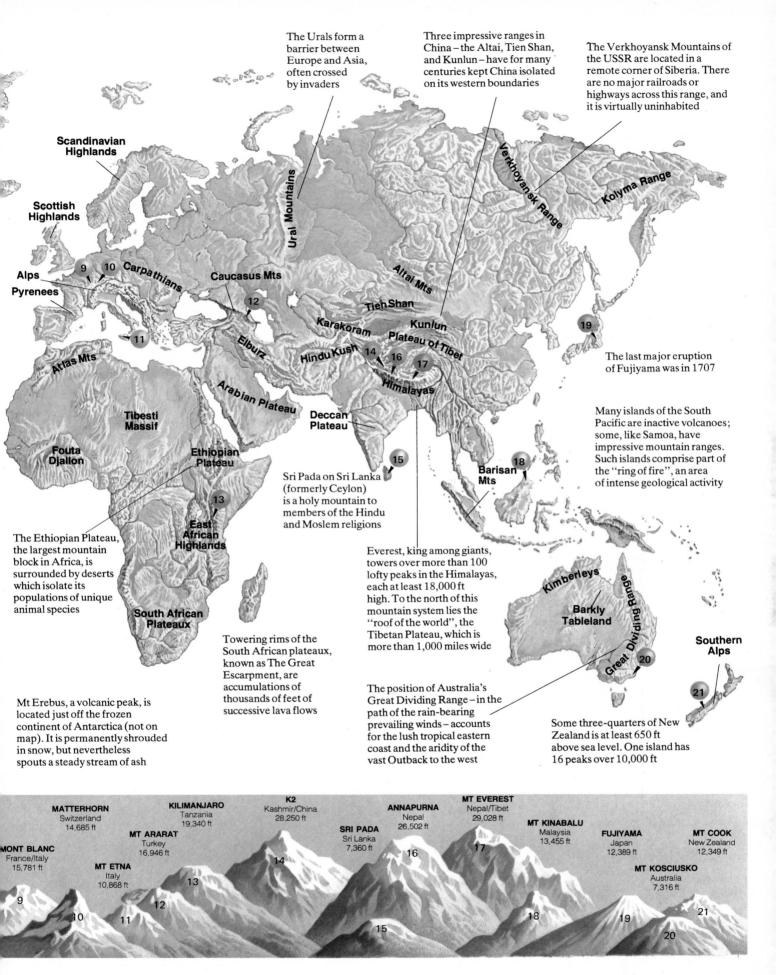

The Urals form a barrier between Europe and Asia, often crossed by invaders

Three impressive ranges in China – the Altai, Tien Shan, and Kunlun – have for many centuries kept China isolated on its western boundaries

The Verkhoyansk Mountains of the USSR are located in a remote corner of Siberia. There are no major railroads or highways across this range, and it is virtually uninhabited

Scandinavian Highlands

Scottish Highlands

Alps

Pyrenees

Ural Mountains

Verkhoyansk Range

Kolyma Range

9 10 **Carpathians**

Caucasus Mts

12

Altai Mts

Tien Shan

Karakoram

Kunlun

Plateau of Tibet

19

Elburz

11

Hindu Kush

14 16

17

Atlas Mts

Arabian Plateau

Himalayas

The last major eruption of Fujiyama was in 1707

Tibesti Massif

Deccan Plateau

Fouta Djallon

Ethiopian Plateau

Many islands of the South Pacific are inactive volcanoes; some, like Samoa, have impressive mountain ranges. Such islands comprise part of the "ring of fire", an area of intense geological activity

13

15

Barisan Mts

18

East African Highlands

Sri Pada on Sri Lanka (formerly Ceylon) is a holy mountain to members of the Hindu and Moslem religions

The Ethiopian Plateau, the largest mountain block in Africa, is surrounded by deserts which isolate its populations of unique animal species

South African Plateaux

Everest, king among giants, towers over more than 100 lofty peaks in the Himalayas, each at least 18,000 ft high. To the north of this mountain system lies the "roof of the world", the Tibetan Plateau, which is more than 1,000 miles wide

Kimberleys

Great Dividing Range

Barkly Tableland

Southern Alps

20

21

Towering rims of the South African plateaux, known as The Great Escarpment, are accumulations of thousands of feet of successive lava flows

The position of Australia's Great Dividing Range – in the path of the rain-bearing prevailing winds – accounts for the lush tropical eastern coast and the aridity of the vast Outback to the west

Some three-quarters of New Zealand is at least 650 ft above sea level. One island has 16 peaks over 10,000 ft

Mt Erebus, a volcanic peak, is located just off the frozen continent of Antarctica (not on map). It is permanently shrouded in snow, but nevertheless spouts a steady stream of ash

MATTERHORN Switzerland 14,685 ft

KILIMANJARO Tanzania 19,340 ft

K2 Kashmir/China 28,250 ft

ANNAPURNA Nepal 26,502 ft

MT EVEREST Nepal/Tibet 29,028 ft

MONT BLANC France/Italy 15,781 ft

MT ARARAT Turkey 16,946 ft

SRI PADA Sri Lanka 7,360 ft

MT KINABALU Malaysia 13,455 ft

FUJIYAMA Japan 12,389 ft

MT COOK New Zealand 12,349 ft

MT ETNA Italy 10,868 ft

MT KOSCIUSKO Australia 7,316 ft

9 10 11 12 13 14 15 16 17 18 19 20 21

Volcanoes and volcanic clues

An erupting volcano is the only place in the world where you can watch a mountain under construction. In 1943 a Mexican farmer witnessed such an event – in his own cornfield. One evening there was a little smoke and an odour of sulphur coming from his field; next morning there was a hill some 30 ft high, spewing smoke and ashes. After a year, his cornfield had become a 1,000 ft high volcano – Paricutín.

The famous "ring of fire", an area of intense volcanic activity that encircles the Pacific, runs along the western coast of the Americas, skirts the tip of Antarctica, and continues along the Pacific coast of Asia. Many relatively recent volcanoes are near coastlines or in the sea – as for example Krakatoa, which is an island in Indonesia.

Some geologists believe that the continents themselves began as groups of volcanic islands that had been built up from the bottom of the sea. The areas between these islands were later filled in by lava and eroded material, forming continental masses.

There are several thousand volcanic mountains around the world, some of them millions of years old and no longer active. Volcanic activity does not seem to be as great today as in the past. Nevertheless, there are about 500 volcanoes still active. One of the youngest, Surtsey, was born off the coast of Iceland in 1963.

What forces create volcanoes? No one is certain, but most scientists believe that

Hidden layers of a volcano

Sangay in Ecuador (left) is one of the few almost continuously active volcanoes in the world. Ecuador has at least 20 other active volcanoes within a 200 mile stretch, but none gives off clouds of ash as frequently as Sangay. Intense volcanic activity along the Pacific coast of South America accounts for several chains of volcanoes. Such areas are constantly threatened by earthquakes. Some volcanoes have more violent eruptions than others – these are easily identified by the conical necks and relatively steep sides.

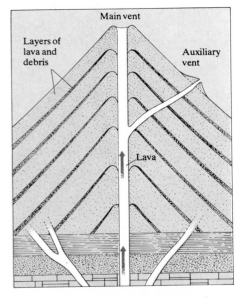

This diagram shows the general structure of a stratified volcano (such as Sangay). That is, its steep slopes were built up by alternating layers of lava and debris. This type of volcano is known as a composite or strato-volcano. In its centre is a wide, cylindrical vent that extends down into the bedrock. Much of the material escapes through this main vent. With each eruption, lava flows out (settling mostly at the vent) and down the sides of the volcano. Rocks and other volcanic debris accumulate on top of the lava. Auxiliary vents, or fissures (also called parasitic or lateral cones), often break through the sides of the volcano.

hot molten rock, known as magma, located some 20 to 40 miles beneath the surface of the earth, is pushed upwards through cracks in the crust. The magma contains great amounts of steam and other gases. As the gases near the surface, they leave the magma like bubbles from an uncapped fizzy drink.

Gases escape with great force, breaking a hole in the earth's crust, which is called a crater. These gases carry huge quantities of dust and ashes. Molten magma also pours from the crater. Once magma reaches the surface, it is called lava. Tons of lava and other debris pile up, forming an unmistakable volcanic cone.

No two volcanoes are alike: shape is a clue to a volcano's past behaviour. If a volcano has a steep cone, such as Ecuador's Sangay (see photograph, left), its eruptions were probably violent; but if it is low, with gentle slopes, its eruptions were probably more quiet. These gently sloping volcanoes are sometimes called shield volcanoes because of their low profile; the Hawaiian volcanoes are good examples. The main reason for the different kinds of volcanoes is the type and consistency of materials that erupt from them. Some release a lot of gases, thereby producing cinders and ashes; others are mainly lava and rocks. The viscosity (or fluidity) of the lava varies from place to place.

Different volcanic mountains contain different minerals. The Andes, for example, consist mainly of andesite – a rock formed from very thick, slow-moving lava. Occasionally a volcano has accumulations of lava down at its base. This type usually stands alone or near larger volcanoes; examples of these are found in Mexico. The strange shapes of the Giant's Causeway in Northern Ireland, on the other hand, were caused by the rapid cooling of lava as it entered the sea. The local people believed it must have been built by an earlier race of giants.

Sometimes an entire volcanic mountain blows up, leaving a large depression known as a caldera. The caldera may fill up with water. This is the way Crater Lake in America was formed.

Volcanoes are feared by man. However, scientists believe that the steam and gases that escaped from volcanoes millions of years ago may have been the source of most of the earth's water. (Volcanoes are still making a minor contribution to the water supply today.) Another surprising gift from volcanoes is the millions of acres of farmland created and fertilised by tons of minerals from the earth's interior.

Specialising in volcanic rocks

The rocks formed from a volcanic eruption are quite varied, as in the three specimens shown below. Even in areas throughout Europe where volcanoes are no longer active, you may still find traces of them.
• Texture is the key to identification. Look for grains of embedded glass and air holes – caused by gases as they escaped from the cooling lava.
• Rocks made of solidified ash are usually light in colour. They differ from other kinds of volcanic rock because they were blown into the air instead of flowing down on to the surface. Some volcanic fragments – called bombs – are pieces of lava thrown into the air by explosions.
• Catalogue your finds carefully and only take specimens if you are sure that collecting is permitted. In any case, a photograph of the site – including the specific location – can be helpful if you later use a reference book to identify the rocks you have found.

Scoria is a porous cinder; its cavities are sometimes filled with bits of minerals.

Obsidian is a relatively rare dark, volcanic glass formed of fast-cooling lava.

Pumice is a grey volcanic froth so light that it can float on water.

Unmistakable evidence of volcanic activity

As inactive volcanoes erode, their remains often take on interesting patterns and shapes. Several factors contribute to the various forms of these remnants: the climate of the region, which influences the rate of erosion; their mineral content; and the rate of cooling and hardening of the different volcanic rocks. The examples shown here are three of many volcanic remnants throughout the world.

Shiprock is a volcanic remnant some 1,400 ft high in New Mexico in the USA. All but the hardened lava core has been worn away.

Swirling lava, from Hawaii's Mauna Loa, is called pahoehoe. The brownish colour beneath indicates lava from a previous eruption.

The Giant's Causeway in Northern Ireland has famous hexagonal columns; such columns are formed of basalt – one kind of volcanic rock.

Folded mountains large and small

When Charles Darwin was trekking over the South American Andes in 1835, the great naturalist was impressed by a fossil sea shell he found embedded in a cliff. At the time, Darwin was about 13,000 ft above sea level. Yet here were the remains of shells like those he had found on beaches. Darwin could have found similar fossil shells on many of the world's large mountain ranges – the Appalachians, Alps or Himalayas.

This is evidence that not all mountains were made from the outpourings of volcanoes, as had been thought previously. Scientists believe some mountains were formed of sediments laid down hundreds of millions of years earlier, on the bottom of ancient seas.

According to this theory, the first act begins when sediments settle in the troughs of shallow seas. Much of the debris is washed from land and mixed with the limy skeletons of sea creatures. As the debris accumulates, it becomes heavier and sinks into the sea-bed. Gradually the sediments are cemented together, forming layers of limestone, shale or other sedimentary rock. These layers may contain fossils.

How do sediments change to mountains? Two tremendous forces are believed to be responsible for raising these flat-lying beds: pressure from the sides and pressure from below. This squeezing and lifting acts on the sedimentary layers the way ripples form on your skin if you squeeze a section between your thumb and forefinger. The size of the ripples in the earth's surface varies from microscopic folds to those that make up mountains, measuring miles from crest to crest and from top to bottom.

There are many theories to account for the squeezing, folding and lifting. Change may have occurred when the crust of the earth cooled and shrank (the way the skin of a baked potato wrinkles as it cools). Another theory of mountain formation is that the folding resulted from the collision of huge, shifting plates in the earth's crust. The Himalayas are thought to be the product of a collision between the Indian subcontinent and the main bulk of Asia. Similarly, the Alps were thrust up by the northward motion of the Mediterranean plate.

Or the folds may be the result of the up-and-down movements of the fluid interior of the earth, which tugs and pushes on the surface. Whatever the causes, the bending and sinking of great masses of rock often created so much heat that segments of the rock melted. Many folded

Ripples in the landscape

Ridges of limestone undulate across the face of Mount Timpanogos in the Rockies. This rippling illustrates the way the forces of compression wrinkled the earth's rocky crust. In many places the folds were pushed so high that they formed mountains such as this one. When you look at such folding, an obvious question may occur to you: how can solid rock be bent like toffee? When the folding took place millions of years ago, the layers of rock were under tremendous pressures, and were often heated to a point where the rock became relatively plastic. Not all rocks bend easily. At the base of many folded mountains, there are cracks where the rock broke instead of bending. The folding of rock layers is still going on in many regions of the world, but so gradually that the change can be measured only with sophisticated instruments.

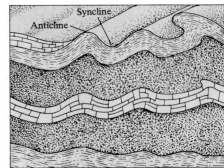

This diagram shows how folding in the layers of rock resembles waves in a body of water. The top (or crest) of a fold is called an anticline; the bottom (or trough) is called a syncline. Sometimes the anticline may rise so high it flops over, like a wave breaking on the beach, as shown at the right of the diagram.

mountains are composed of granite and other types of rock, formed by melting.

You can often see the folds in rocks at major roadworks, and on cliffs where the formation is not yet covered with vegetation. But even then you are not seeing the folds as they were originally formed. Thousands of feet may have been worn away over the centuries by the scouring action of wind, rain and ice.

Most mountains are a mixture of hard and soft rock. Whatever its structure, a mountain is most vulnerable to the forces of weathering at its summit (and also on its windward side). As ice and temperature changes wear away the mountain top, the rock formation is invaded – rather like waves pounding through and widening a break in a sea wall.

In fact, mountains generally erode faster than nearby valleys, especially if extensive deposits of soft rock are present. It is the nature of erosion that ice and water will take the easiest path downwards, which generally means an ever-widening of already established gouges and cracks. Thus mountains keep losing ground; a mountain becomes a valley.

But even as the mountains are worn away, others are forming. At present, the Mississippi River is depositing tons of sediments every day in the Gulf of Mexico. Millions of years from now, these deposits may become the raw materials for a new range of folded mountains.

What is now a valley was once a mountain peak

Sometimes a mountain that was created by folding of the earth's crust is worn away and replaced by a valley. Canada's Mistaya Valley (above) is believed to have once been the site of a very high mountain. Folded mountains are particularly susceptible to the forces of erosion because the folds in the rock may expose soft layers. Erosion wears away any soft vein, like a miner following a lode into the earth. This process can bring down an entire mountain. Rock at the side of the mountain may be relatively protected from erosion. Eventually, as the valley deepens, the sides may become separate mountains.

This artist's conception shows how, long ago, the tilted strata on one side of the valley may have connected with those on the other side.

NATURE OBSERVER
Roads are prime places to see geological formations

Road cuttings and seaside cliffs often reveal landforms that are otherwise hidden by vegetation or worn down by the forces of erosion. The way a road is designed must take into account the basic, underlying structure of the rock. As you drive along, you can often see – in miniature – such folded structures as the one shown left. Two roads pass in opposite directions, with a remnant of the fold separating them – a small, perfectly matched continuation of the fold on the wall beyond. You will be able to see many such forms, different only in size and not in kind from the larger formation on the facing page. A road like this is relatively simple to design; engineers often have more serious construction problems – as when a road is literally blasted out of solid rock, with a jagged face on one side and a steep drop on the other. When you travel, examine the contours of roads, and you will gain insight into both geology and engineering.

Fault-block mountains

Some of the world's most spectacular mountains are not necessarily the highest. For sheer drama, few mountains can match those that rise abruptly from the surrounding plains: no foothills distract from their soaring grace.

These starkly beautiful mountains are often precisely what they appear to be – great blocks of rock pushed up by the massive pressures beneath the surface of the earth.

Sometimes the raised block is flat-topped, like the battlement of a castle. More often one side is pushed up higher than the other to form a wedge-shaped mountain. Both types are known as fault-block mountains because they occur along faults, or cracks, in the earth's crust.

The land bordering an active fault does not stay put. At intervals ranging from a few days to several hundred years, the ground moves. Each shift releases pressures from deep within the earth.

Although each displacement usually amounts to no more than a few inches, over a long period of time the movements along a fault may cover great distances.

The San Andreas Fault in California is a famous example of a fracture where the land is slipping jerkily, but unstoppably sideways. Streams, roadways and rows of trees that were once aligned are now displaced. If you look down on such a fault from an aeroplane the whole landscape seems to zigzag crazily.

But there are vertical shifts, too, and fault-block mountains may be the result. The land bordering these fractures has moved up or down, not sideways; sometimes both sides have slipped (one up, the other down). In any case, these movements may create a huge step – not immediately, of course, but probably over a long period of time.

Fault-blocks can be deceptive: they are readily identified only if you see them from certain directions. The classic fault-block has a distinctive profile. The side facing the fracture is steep (unless the forces of weathering have worn it down); the back of the mountain (the part away from the fault) usually slopes down to flat land. Thus unless a fault-block mountain is seen from the front or side, it might not be recognised as such.

Certain areas – including Utah, Montana and Mongolia – have spectacular ranges of fault-block mountains. But you do not have to travel to any of these places to see this type of formation: look for small-scale displacements, produced by miniature faults, beside roads or on the face of a cliff.

Faults generally do not occur singly: movement along two nearby faults may leave characteristic marks on the surface. Sometimes the land in between is pushed up, forming mountains that resemble huge bricks lying on the ground. These

"bricks", called horsts (from a German word meaning heap or mass), are relatively uncommon: The Vosges Mountains in France and the plateau of the Black Forest in Germany are extensive neighbouring horsts, separated by the Rhine.

Land between two faults may sink. This creates a ditch-like depression – a graben, the German for grave. Large grabens are also called rift valleys. The Rhine Valley is a graben, bordered by two horsts; so is America's Death Valley. A graben about a mile deep makes up part of the Jordan River valley, near the Dead Sea.

Although the depth of a fault is difficult to determine, some fractures are believed to extend downwards over 30 miles.

Faults also act as channels that conduct heat, water and molten rock from the earth's interior. Thus hot springs and geysers, or a line of volcanoes indicate the presence of a deep fault.

When fractures and uplifts make mountains

A profile of Mount Rundle (left) from across a lake in Banff National Park, Canada, is a classic example of a fault-block mountain, recognisable when seen from the proper angle. If seen from any other angle, it may look like another type of mountain. Distinguishing features of a fault-block mountain are a steep, jagged front-slope – the edge of a large fracture – and a more gradual down-slope, or back. Pressures within the earth fractured the even layers of rock, thrusting a section into the air. Many sections of the Rockies of North America were formed in this way.

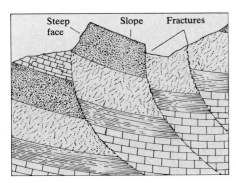

It is not possible to see the exact underlying structure of any given area, but the diagram (above) is a rough model of the bedrock layers found beneath a fault-block mountain. Note the order of the layers, and how they have slipped along the fractures and are now mismatched as a result of violent earth movements. The highest part, in the centre of this drawing, represents Mount Rundle.

Why fault-blocks are hard to detect

Faults are something of a paradox – they are so clear in textbooks, but so difficult to identify out in the field. Mountains along faults are not made of any one particular kind of rock; it is the sharp fracturing of the land that gives them their identity. Soon the forces of erosion begin to wear them down. Why be concerned with faults at all? Partly because the wall of a fault may extend deep into the earth, and that wall sometimes influences the land around it. For example, if underground water collides with such a barrier, water may rise and form a spring (either cold or hot). Pressures within the crust of the earth are variable, and so are the substances that rise along faults – petroleum is another example. Beyond that, the structure of landforms has a fascination of its own, once you become interested in the living rock.

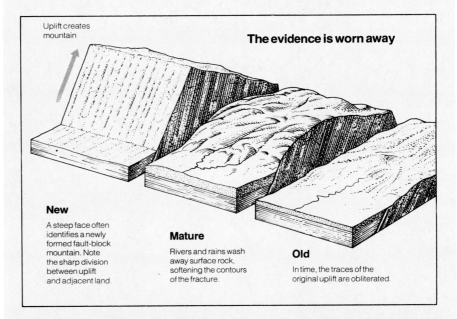

The evidence is worn away

New
A steep face often identifies a newly formed fault-block mountain. Note the sharp division between uplift and adjacent land.

Uplift creates mountain

Mature
Rivers and rains wash away surface rock, softening the contours of the fracture.

Old
In time, the traces of the original uplift are obliterated.

If it were not for the fact that these two sections of land (above and right) were recently cut, there would be no way of knowing that they contain fault structures. The stepped formations probably made the ground above them uneven for a while, but now the fractures are best seen in cross-section. The levelling effect of erosion has prevailed.

Landscapes carved by glaciers

For centuries naturalists were baffled by curious landforms found in many parts of the world – huge boulders strewn across the countryside, deep grooves gouged in solid rock, strange hills and depressions in otherwise level plains.

The prevailing explanation was that these curiosities were evidence of a worldwide catastrophic flood. Yet this explanation did not match all the geological evidence.

It was not until the early 1800s that a Swiss naturalist, Jean Louis Agassiz, found the answer in the mountains. By studying glaciers sliding slowly down mountain valleys, Agassiz learned that glaciers could produce the landforms that had been attributed to an ancient flood.

He was the first to suggest that long ago much of the earth was covered with glaciers during a great Ice Age.

The idea of an Ice Age was ridiculed at first. Who could believe that areas now occupied by Paris, London, Boston and Moscow once lay beneath an ice sheet perhaps 5,000 to 10,000 ft thick? But by using the remaining glaciers as an outdoor laboratory, Agassiz and his followers were able to prove that ice had indeed carved the land into its modern shape.

For reasons no one knows, millions of years ago the climate turned cold for the first time in earth's history. There have been three, four or perhaps more major Ice Ages. In these periods, more snow and ice accumulated during the winters than melted during the summers. The glaciers eventually spread over enormous portions of the globe. The immense ice sheets advanced and retreated several times, as the earth's climate fluctuated – possibly because of changes in the sun's output.

There are few great glaciers today (except in polar regions). Not all mountains form glaciers – some simply do not have sufficient snow. But there are a few mountaintop remnants of the Ice Ages.

These mountains have natural catchbasins that trapped the snow. As the snow accumulated, it gradually compacted to form ice and eventually became heavy enough to begin a slow, long journey downhill, moving out through a low spot in the basin wall. As it slipped away, the glacier often enlarged the depression to form a cirque (French for circus, because it resembles an amphitheatre).

Sometimes three or more cirques were scooped out on the slopes of a rounded peak, transforming it into a jagged pyramid called a horn, like the Matterhorn in the Swiss Alps.

A river of ice is pushed from behind, as well as being pulled downwards by gravity. It can move over level areas in the valleys and even up slight slopes. It may create steps in the valley. If the glacier eventually melts, these steps may fill with water, forming a chain of lakes called "paternoster" lakes, perhaps because from above they look like the string of beads in a Catholic rosary. When a single lake forms in a cirque, it is called a tarn. Finger lakes may occupy depressions in the valley.

Glaciers do not follow fine contours in the land as rivers do, and so tend to straighten and widen valleys. These valleys are easy to recognise because they are usually U-shaped, contrasting with the V-profile of most mountain river valleys.

The main valley is scooped out more quickly than the shallower tributaries that join it. If the glacier melts, the floors of the tributaries may be left "hanging" hundreds of feet above the main valley.

Often streams of glacial meltwater flow down the hanging valleys, creating waterfalls, some of the most spectacular of all glacial scenery.

Immense glaciers grew during the Ice Ages

Melting glaciers were the mighty geological agents that sculptured the landscape during the Ice Ages. As massive sheets of ice shifted downwards, they whittled mountains, scoured the lowlands, and scattered large rocks far and wide. Tributary glaciers sometimes joined the main glacier, forming a common bed of ice.

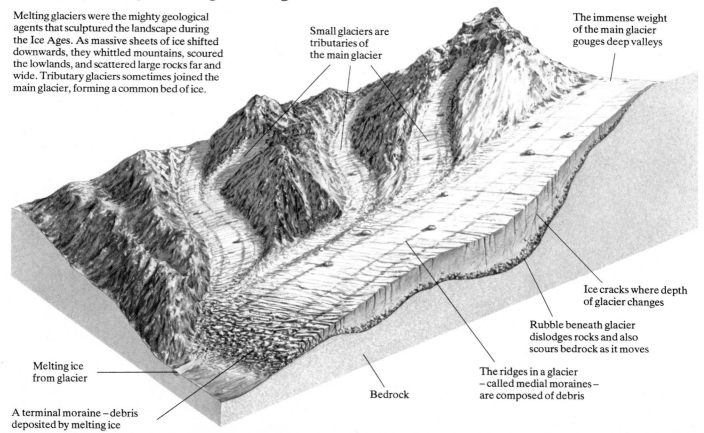

Small glaciers are tributaries of the main glacier

The immense weight of the main glacier gouges deep valleys

Ice cracks where depth of glacier changes

Rubble beneath glacier dislodges rocks and also scours bedrock as it moves

The ridges in a glacier – called medial moraines – are composed of debris

Bedrock

Melting ice from glacier

A terminal moraine – debris deposited by melting ice

This wide, U-shaped valley in the Pyrenees is characteristic of a once glacier-covered landscape. The stream, fed by melting ice from snow-capped peaks and nearby ice fields, meanders down a valley carved thousands of years ago by an advancing glacier.

Boulders known as erratics are also evidence of moving glaciers. As a glacier advanced, it plucked boulders from underlying rock and moved them far from their original sites. Such boulders usually have a different mineral composition from that of surrounding rocks.

When the earth warmed, the glaciers receded

Today, glaciers cover only about one-tenth of the earth's surface (mostly at the poles), but many rugged landscapes still reflect their work. Mountain lakes are filled by water from them; beautiful waterfalls cascade from hanging valleys. Some of these glacial effects can be seen in the Alps and Rockies.

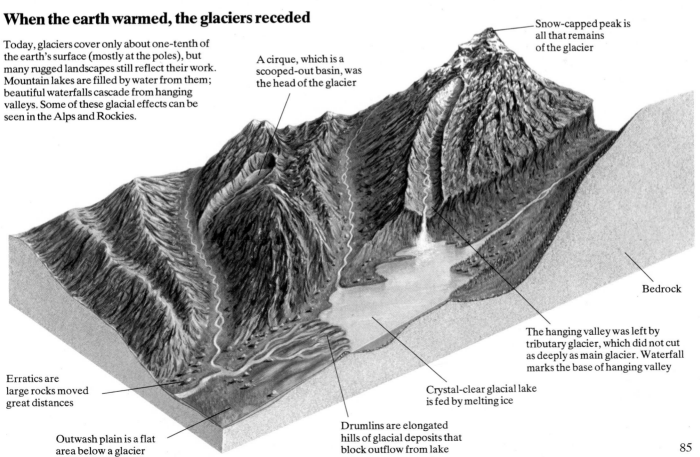

A cirque, which is a scooped-out basin, was the head of the glacier

Snow-capped peak is all that remains of the glacier

Bedrock

The hanging valley was left by tributary glacier, which did not cut as deeply as main glacier. Waterfall marks the base of hanging valley

Erratics are large rocks moved great distances

Outwash plain is a flat area below a glacier

Drumlins are elongated hills of glacial deposits that block outflow from lake

Crystal-clear glacial lake is fed by melting ice

85

Glaciers: slow-moving rivers of ice

Once a glacier forms, it tends to be self-perpetuating. As moist winds pass, the cold may cause condensation of vapour, adding new snow. Even if the air is not cold enough for that, it will tend to form clouds which shield the glacier from the sun. Cold mountain air also produces powerful downdraughts that drive away warmer air, so keeping the glacier cold.

When snow reaches a depth of about 100 ft, its weight compresses the deeper layers into a granular snow called firn. If snow continues to pile up, the firn melts under the pressure and then refreezes into ice. This hard glacial ice may weigh nearly 20 times as much as newly fallen snow.

Something happens when snow and ice accumulate to a depth of about 200 ft. The seemingly solid mass starts to flow, spreading like a spoonful of pancake batter dropped in a hot frying pan. Steep slopes accelerate the movement of the ice, but the glacier can move on flat land, and even up slight inclines.

Tremendous pressures exist at the bottom of a glacier (28 tons or more per square foot), transforming ice from the brittle substance we know in everyday life to a substance that can flow like cold treacle. This is because ice melts under pressure. You can prove this by pressing a cold metal object into ice – a knife or the tines of a fork.

How a glacier advances

The great weight of a glacier makes it move down a mountain. Because of the pressure on the lower part of a glacier, this portion may thaw (and then refreeze), causing the entire sheet of ice to slip downhill. Glaciers flow in crescent-like waves (see photo, at right, of a glacier in America's Olympic Mountains). Such waves develop because the centre of a glacier moves more quickly than the sides. A measuring technique has been designed to plot the motion of a glacier: stakes are driven into the ice (see surface view diagram at right). As the ice moves, the stakes are carried along with it. The ones at the centre move further down the slope than the others, and the straight line becomes a curve. By using this method, scientists can determine the distance a particular glacier moves in a given period of time. They have discovered that the ice at the surface flows rather slowly – from a fraction of an inch to several feet a day (depending on temperature, steepness of the mountain, and width of the valley). But the ice at the bottom of a glacier moves even more slowly (see side view diagram, right).

Deep glacial crevasses present a special hazard to mountaineers. Some crevasses may be more than 40 ft wide and 100 ft deep, and may be hidden by a thin layer of snow. The cracks develop as the ice travels over an uneven surface. The masses of ice split – though not usually as far down as the floor of the glacier (where the ice flows like treacle).

The ice will melt gradually under the weight, and the metal will sink in. Similarly, the weight of an ice skater actually melts the ice beneath his feet, producing a thin layer of water that lubricates the passing of the blades over the ice. Much the same thing is believed to occur at the bottom of a glacier.

Glaciers may also "roll" on natural ball bearings. Tiny cracks occur between the individual ice crystals, crumbling the ice into pieces about $\frac{1}{2}$ in. in diameter. Thus the glacier may slip on crystals the way your foot might slide if you stepped on some marbles.

But while the bottom layers of a glacier may flow and slip, the upper layers, which are under less pressure, remain brittle.

As the ice sheet moves, some areas crack, forming crevasses as much as 100 ft deep. Crevasses are normally bow-shaped, with the convex part facing downhill. This is because glaciers, like rivers, tend to move more quickly at their centres than along their margins, where they are in contact with the valley walls.

As a result, the centre of a crevasse, extending across a glacier, soon gets ahead of its edges. Some glaciers have so many deep and dangerous crevasses that travel over them is impossible.

Crevasses make mountaineering especially treacherous, and sometimes skiing as well. A crust of recently fallen snow may bridge over a region that is sliced with crevasses. The crust may be thick and strong enough to support a person's weight; but then again, the crust could give way without warning.

The powdery snow that makes for good skiing often builds up on mountain slopes. This accumulation may move downhill, too – but far more rapidly than a glacier – in the form of an avalanche.

Some of these snow slides have been clocked at speeds up to 200 mph, sweeping almost everything in their path. When this powder builds up on a slope steeper than about 45 degrees, it is often called an avalanche waiting to happen. Almost anything can trigger an avalanche on such a slope – a falling branch, a hopping animal, a skier, or even a passing aeroplane.

Tens of thousands of avalanches occur annually in the Alps, where the snow is sometimes brought down deliberately in small, harmless avalanches by the firing of shells or rockets. Occasionally, the sound alone is enough to trigger the cascade of snow, but contrary to popular legend, there is no documented evidence that a human voice can start a snow slide.

Nowadays local authorities in mountainous regions keep a close watch on their snow. An avalanche in the Andes once killed 5,000 people.

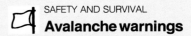

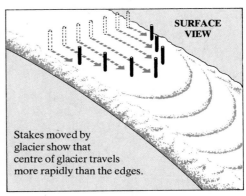

SURFACE VIEW

Stakes moved by glacier show that centre of glacier travels more rapidly than the edges.

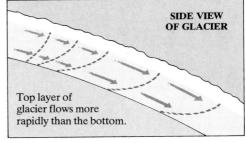

SIDE VIEW OF GLACIER

Top layer of glacier flows more rapidly than the bottom.

Zones of life on the mountainside

When you climb a mountain, you see and feel change – the most obvious is usually in temperature. For every 1,000 ft you go up, the temperature drops about 2°C (3.5°F). Thus the summit of a mountain 10,000 ft high, such as Mount Olympus in Greece, is about 20°C (35°F) colder than its base. This is because the gases that make up the atmosphere are denser at sea level and retain more heat.

In effect, the earth's insulating blanket of air provides a mountain climber with less protection as he goes higher, even as a thin blanket holds warmth less well than a thick one.

The physical conditions on a mountain – temperature, wind, exposure to sunlight, and amount of moisture – shape the environment for many plants and animals.

There are distinct zones of life, which correspond roughly to the zones you would encounter if you were to travel thousands of miles from the temperate latitudes to the frozen poles. On a mountain, you can go from a temperate world to the arctic tundra by simply climbing upward.

Unlike these diagrams, real zones are not sharply delineated; the transition between two zones is gradual. Starting at the bottom of a pair of mountains in temperate latitudes, there is a Mixed Forest Zone – with coniferous and deciduous (leaf-shedding) trees. Next comes the Conifer-ous Zone, where the environment is harsher.

Above this is the Alpine Zone, where conditions are too cold and windy for any but dwarf varieties of willow and other low-growing plants. The line of demarcation between the Coniferous and Alpine Zones is frequently a ragged line of conifers trailing across a mountain – the timberline. Above the Alpine Zone lies a frozen, virtually lifeless region.

The types of vegetation anywhere on earth will determine to a great extent the kinds of animals that will be able to live there. However animals such as bears and deer, eagles and hawks move between zones to find prey and pasture.

Wildlife communities in the Rocky Mountains and

Life above the timberline in North America

Strong winds, little water and low-growing plants characterise the zone above the timberline where few animals are residents.

Golden eagle · Dwarf willow · Bighorn sheep · White-tailed ptarmigan · Hoary marmot · Rocky Mountain goat · Pika · Water pipit · Mountain dryad* · Purple saxifrage · Moss campion · Crowberry

Where coniferous trees dominate

Stands of conifers lend a park-like quality to this evergreen zone. Here many predators find prey.

Cougar · Red crossbill* · Northern three-toed woodpecker* · Engelmann spruce · Lodgepole pine · Elk · Wolf · American marten · Black bear · Clark's nutcracker · One-flowered wintergreen · Mountain gentian · Pasqueflower

Mixed forests flourish

On lower slopes where conifers and deciduous trees mingle, abundant food attracts animals.

Porcupine · Red fox · Hermit thrush · Steller's jay · Western larch · Quaking aspen · Douglas fir · Pine squirrel · White-tailed deer · Short-tailed weasel* · Varying hare · Blue grouse · Harebell

*The same species has a different name in North America and Europe.

The amazing thing to notice here is the similarity of life forms in each zone, no matter how far apart their respective mountains may be.

Matching marmot for marmot, ptarmigan for ptarmigan, crowberry for crowberry, these two places, worlds apart – in North America and in Europe – are more alike than different.

Zonation is world-wide, but there are interesting variations. For example, the Alpine Zone may begin at about 7,000 ft in the Alps, but the comparable zone in the Himalayas occurs at 15,000 ft. What is worth considering is not the statistics, but the patterns of plant and animal adaptations to local conditions.

✋ HOW TO
Make your own zonation chart

As a family activity or a school project, you can work out a zonation chart for a nearby mountain or hillside. You can get started without knowing the specific altitude. However, in some instances, as a clue to vegetation, this information will help. You can consult road maps, or, if available, geological survey maps.

● Begin with a narrow segment, going all the way to the top. Other segments may be different because of variations in winds and exposure to sun and rain. Establish a regular path, taking notes on each trip.

● As you get to know your own area, you can branch out, comparing one part of a hill or mountain with other segments, or with the adjacent hillsides.

● If they are available, regional guidebooks

to plants are great time-savers; they eliminate all the species of plants that are unlikely to be in your area, and tell you what to expect.

● Animals are often easier to guess at than plants, but their mobility makes a positive identification harder. Many are shy, some are migrators that can be seen only occasionally, and others are mainly nocturnal. A good guidebook will describe the mammal, bird or insect, and also its behaviour, habitat and feeding pattern.

● As you collect data (perhaps on cards), plan your chart. You can pattern it on one of the mountains shown here (especially if you like to draw). Or use gummed labels with names of species written on them, ready for putting into a specific zone.

their plant and animal counterparts in the Swiss Alps

compared with a similar region in Europe

Life is rugged among the peaks and crags. The sparse vegetation is sheltered among the rocks, and only hardy animals survive.

certain species take up residence

Many birds live only in the pines, extracting seeds from the cones or searching the trunks for insects.

low on the mountainside

The milder climate at the base of the mountain encourages constant activity during most seasons.

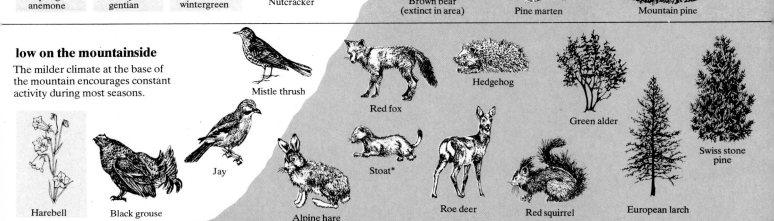

Crowberry · Moss campion · Purple saxifrage · Mountain avens* · Water pipit · Ptarmigan · Golden eagle · Ibex · Dwarf willow · Snow vole · Chamois · Alpine marmot

Spring anemone · Trumpet gentian · One-flowered wintergreen · Nutcracker · Three-toed woodpecker* · Crossbill* · Wolf (extinct in area) · Brown bear (extinct in area) · Pine marten · Red deer · Lynx (extinct in area) · Mountain pine · Norway spruce

Harebell · Black grouse · Jay · Mistle thrush · Red fox · Hedgehog · Green alder · Alpine hare · Stoat* · Roe deer · Red squirrel · European larch · Swiss stone pine

Remote gardens of alpine flowers

One of the most pleasant surprises in the mountains are the little verdant valleys, tucked away between the rugged mountain peaks like precious jewels.

Travellers often hear the echoes from a valley before they reach it – the shrill whistle of a shepherd or the jingling bells of grazing animals. In the mountains of Greece, these bells, on sheep or goats, frequently sound like distant choirs, because the shepherds take pride in carefully tuning the bells. In the Alps, the sound is commonly a deep-throated gong from cow-bells as a herd browses across the tilted lushness of a mountainside meadow.

Grazing animals and mountain valleys go together because certain grasses with dense networks of roots are often the only crop that can be grown on slopes. It is impossible to use farm machinery there; the crop must be harvested by animal or by hand.

During spring and summer, many of these high pastures are dotted with colourful clumps of delicate-looking mountain (or alpine) flowers. The apparent fragility is deceptive, because flowering – as well as non-flowering – mountain plants are among the hardiest in the world.

Many such plants grow in ground-hugging mats, or tussocks, thus keeping out of the wind and taking advantage of the warmth absorbed by the ground. The next time you see some of these flowers, such as cushion pinks, notice how their thin stems, leaves and flowers intertwine. This intermeshing enables them to trap air near the ground, in much the same way that spun glass is used to insulate homes. The temperature inside such a cluster may be as much as 11°C (20°F) warmer than the air outside.

Fuzzy stems trap air, which is another insulating device of many alpine flowers – such as the red campion. On some flowers the bright fuzz is almost as colourful as the flower itself. The downy willow has two-toned fuzz on its buds – dark at the base and a light translucent colour at the tips. Warm rays of the sun, passing through the window-like tips, are absorbed by the dark-coloured base. The principle is basically the same as that used in solar-heated homes.

Many alpine flowers are insect-pollinated, as are those of the lowlands, but the cold mountain air often inactivates the insects. On a cloudy day you can see many bees lying numb on the ground, unable to move. When there is a break in the clouds, however, the pollinators revive with surprising speed, and are soon up and around the flowers, collecting alpine honey.

Insects living in the mountains also take advantage of the warmer microclimates that exist near the ground, and in nooks and crannies. Many species of butterflies found in mountains fly close to the ground, thus avoiding being carried away by gusty winds on the unsheltered slopes of their habitat.

Perhaps the most amazing adaptation of alpine flowers, however, is their ability to manufacture a kind of "antifreeze". The fluid content of such plants is often high in salts and other chemicals.

These high concentrations keep the fluids – and thus the plant – from freezing at temperatures that would kill other plants. Some mountain plants even generate small amounts of heat during their growth, melting their way through the snow to reach the sunlight of early spring. Because the growing season in the mountains is short, plants also set seeds quickly.

Certain alpine flowers, such as the edelweiss, sometimes develop unseen beneath a snowbank. On the first warm spring day, snow-clad mountain slopes may seem lifeless. Then, in a matter of a few hours, as if by magic, there is a carpet of bright blossoms.

Red campion flourishes both in the lowlands and on mountain heights up to 7,500 ft. This colourful, downy-stemmed plant is native to Europe and Asia. When introduced to America as a garden flower, the red campion "escaped" to the wild. No longer restricted to gardens, it now blooms along roadsides in the north-eastern United States and Canada.

Fuzzy stems and leaves of pasque flowers trap heat. This apparently enables them to open their delicate buds in early spring before other flowers – when snow still covers the ground.

High in the Himalayas, these gentian flowers look quite similar to related species. But these plants do not grow as tall as the typical gentian – an adaptation to alpine life.

Mountain modifications

Many alpine flowers bear little resemblance to their lowland relatives. On the other hand, they often look like their neighbours on the mountainside – cushion pinks, rock jasmine and dotted saxifrage have all adapted to harsh conditions by developing a rounded form. This shape is advantageous to plants in exposed locations – they are not so easily buffeted by the wind. The compact shape also retains heat. Deep roots provide anchorage.

This forget-me-not (left) is distributed world-wide. Usually, the flowers are borne on tall stems.

An alpine variety of forget-me-not (right) is most easily identified when in flower.

Wildflowers carpet an alpine hillside in the Olympic Mountains of north-west America. Asters, lupins and paintbrushes are just a few of the meadow flowers that seem to be present all summer long. In fact, plants on the lower slopes blossom earlier. Then, as the season advances and the snows retreat, the same species will bloom at a higher altitude.

The beauty of highlands

Highlands are, in actuality, a middle ground between the mountains and lowlands, whether they are the rolling, heather-clad Scottish Highlands, the arid South American altiplano (high plains), the high country of the western United States, or the teeming equatorial heights of East Africa. So, in a way, the term "highland" is a misnomer. The Andean altiplano, for example, is about 12,000 ft high, yet is surrounded by much higher peaks that soar to more than 20,000 ft.

Most highland regions are damp, cool, and frequently foggy. They are sometimes dotted with moors, lakes and streams. Even arid highlands such as those in South America are pitted with lakes because of saucer-like depressions that collect rainwater and melted snows.

Lake Titicaca, one of the world's highest lakes, is a classic example – it fills a depression in the Bolivian altiplano, even though it lies at an altitude of more than 11,000 ft.

For many people, the Scottish Highlands epitomise the austere beauty of these special regions, and localised terminologies for land formations enhance their charm.

Rocky plateaux in northern Scotland are trenched by deep, narrow valleys – or glens – such as the Great Glen of Scotland, which splits the Highlands diagonally from north-east to south-west. Deep firths, similar to the fjords of neighbouring Scandinavia, run many miles inland from the coast.

The Scottish moors are characteristically thick with low-growing vegetation which can resist the driving rain and winds of the Highlands. In late summer some sections are carpeted with the distinctive purple or white flowers of the evergreen heathers.

These small, bell-shaped blossoms are so abundant that bee-keepers often bring their hives on to the moors during this season for a special feast.

Wildlife abounds in the highlands, though the terrain is generally too rocky and infertile for farming. Some lightly forested areas of the Scottish Highlands are called "deer forests", because of the large numbers of red deer found there.

Red grouse are also plentiful in these areas of Scotland. However, small mammals such as field voles, wood mice and shrews, hares and rabbits make up most of the animal population.

In South America, the guinea pig – prized as a pet and laboratory animal the world over – is a native of the altiplano. Kruger National Park in the South African highlands has representatives of most of the wild animals of Africa – from aardvarks to zebras.

Highland regions have long been a preferred home for the human species. Some of the oldest human fossils ever found – dating back several million years – were discovered in the famous Olduvai Gorge in the African highlands of Tanzania.

A feudal keep, Castle Varrich, stands guard over the Kyle of Tongue, a sea channel in the extreme north of the Scottish Highlands. This austerely beautiful land has deer and grouse.

The comeback of the deer

Once close to extinction, the deer of the Scottish Highlands – the large red deer and the smaller roe deer – have made a truly spectacular comeback. At one time, Scotland was covered with forests. But as the human population grew, and especially since sheep were introduced, most of the deer's habitat vanished. Red deer retreated to the moors and mountaintops; roe deer made a last stand in the remaining forests of the north. In the 19th century, however, enthusiasm for deer stalking led landowners to establish huge deer forests. These reserves ensured the deer's survival. Without large predators, both species prospered so well that they were a threat to their environment. Today a successful management system controls their numbers. During the autumn breeding season, stags are jealous of their territories. In the picture on the right, two red stags fence with their antlers.

The noisy grouse family enlivens highland regions

Superbly adapted to the highlands of Europe and the colder mountains of North America, grouse and ptarmigans are protected by feathers on nostrils and feet. Most grouse are polygamous and compete for females with leaps and raucous calls. Ptarmigans have only a single mate.

At a mating ground, male European black grouse engage in strenuous, ritual combat.

The mottled spring plumage of the female ptarmigan is excellent camouflage at the nest.

A strutting blue grouse of the American West emits loud booms from inflated throat sacs.

Wildlife at high altitudes

The sure-footed chamois, a member of the goat family, found in the mountains of Europe, moves with care on narrow ledges, but its jumps seem audacious – it can leap across a chasm more than 20 ft wide.

Mountain sheep and goats are pioneers at the edge of the world, in regions where it is bitterly cold and windy, where food and water are scarce and even the air is thin. One kind of Asiatic wild goat (an ancestor of domestic goats) lives up to 13,000 ft, a superb example of nature's ability to adapt to almost any extreme.

These mountaineers can survive on land that will support no other large mammals. Sheep and goats are ruminants, which means they have a four-chambered stomach.

They can stuff themselves with a meal of plants very quickly, then bring the food up again and chew their cud like cows. Unlike most other ruminants, they can digest extremely low-grade plant materials – including lichens and twigs.

This capacity to eat every scrap of food has had an unfortunate effect on large areas of the earth. The indiscriminate appetites of domesticated sheep and goats have turned many places – especially the once-green Middle East – into deserts. For these animals eat ground cover to the roots, killing the plants.

Archaeologists have found evidence that sheep and goats have been providing man with food and wool for six or seven thousand years. During the great Age of Exploration, these animals were carried aboard sailing ships to provide fresh milk and meat.

You are lucky if you chance to see wild sheep or goats in the mountains. It is almost impossible to get close to them; their vision is amazingly keen, and they avoid people. However, if you see one individual, keep watching: you may see others, for sheep and goats are social animals.

You may even be able to work out their social relationships from close observation of a herd. Rams associate in all-male bands except during the mating season. If you see a group with large horns, and if no young are present, it is probably an all-male band. With the arrival of the mating season, male and female bands join. This period is easy to identify; there is much spirited chasing and fighting.

Can you tell sheep from goats? Usually, the horns of *goats*, both male and female, grow from near the top of the head and curve up and back; their foreheads are convex. The horns of *sheep*, generally prominent only in males, grow from the sides of the head; foreheads are concave.

Horns are often used in battles between males during the mating season. Surprisingly, horns and human fingernails are made from the same material – a substance called keratin. The horns of sheep and goats are permanent (unlike the bony antlers of deer, which are shed annually). The number of rings on a horn is sometimes a clue to an animal's age.

Visit your local zoo or a farm to get a really good look at these impressive animals. Usually you will find several representatives of this large sub-family, or tribe, of hoofed animals, the *Caprinae*. The list of animals in this group includes not only domesticated varieties, but also ibexes, mouflons, chamois and many others.

Notice the cloven hoofs. They are hard and sharp and grip rock almost like pincers. Between and behind the hoofs are padded soles that cushion the animal's sure-footed leaps from ledge to ledge. Also notice their heavy, water-repellent coats, ideally suited to high altitudes.

Rocky Mountain bighorn sheep winter below the timberline, where the climate is warmer and food more plentiful than at higher elevations. These heavy animals climb mountain slopes in spring, and descend from them in autumn. Such movement is called vertical migration.

BIRDWATCHING TIPS
The great gliders

Mountains are the only places you can get a really good look at the great birds of prey: hawks, eagles, falcons and their kin. Instead of craning your neck and squinting into the sun, you can watch them from above, as they ride the updraughts with effortless grace.
• Notice that these birds seldom flap their wings, but take advantage of wind currents, banking and turning like gliders. These truly magnificent birds seem to cut the skies with their wings.
• Shape is the key to identifying birds of prey in flight. Buteos (a type of hawk) have broad tails and wings; accipiters (such as goshawks) have longer tails and rounded wings. Falcon wings are pointed.
• Autumn migration is the best time for watching hawks and eagles. There is a better chance of seeing one on the move than at any other time. Choose a windy day, especially one after the passing of a cold front.
• The flight routes of these birds are often well known. Some return year after year to the same spot, or fly regularly over the same town on their twice-yearly voyages across the world.
• Ospreys are among the first birds to migrate, starting in August; golden eagles are often last, departing for the south as late as November.
• Except during migration, you will rarely see more than one or two birds of prey. As their name indicates, they are hunters and need a lot of space.

Small, furry mountain mammals

There is an amazing similarity among the small mountain mammals on different continents. The ones shown here are all plant-eating animals that live in large groups; they have short legs and thick fur, which reduce heat loss. Unlike mountain sheep and goats, these little creatures remain at high altitudes throughout the year, hibernating in winter or sometimes moving about under the snow.

The North American pika has a variety of names, including whistling hare, rock rabbit and coney. Other pikas live in Asia.

The rock hyrax of Africa, some 12 in. long, looks and behaves like a rodent – but it is really the elephant's closest living relative.

The chinchilla, long-whiskered and covered with extremely soft fur, occupies burrows and rock crevices in the Andes Mountains.

The alpine marmot, found near the timberline on many European slopes, has relatives all around the world.

Cold-weather vegetation

It seems hard to believe that anything could live on mountain peaks where the wind may howl at more than 200 mph, and where temperatures often fall far below freezing.

The little moisture present is usually frozen solid, and so is useless to most life-forms. Yet certain plants have developed amazing adaptations that allow them to survive under such extreme conditions.

Lichens, probably the hardiest of all plants, live where virtually nothing else can – not just on rugged mountain peaks but also on sun-baked desert rocks. They are usually the first life to appear on the mountainside that has been scraped bare by an avalanche or incinerated in a volcanic eruption.

Unlike other members of the plant kingdom, lichens are actually a symbiosis, or partnership, between two plants. The framework of a lichen is usually a network of minute hair-like fungus that anchors the plant (shown in the diagram below).

The other component is an alga (similar to the green film of plant life that grows on stagnant pools), which is distributed throughout the fungus. Being green plants, algae are capable of photosynthesis – that is, using energy from the sun to manufacture their own food. The fungi are believed to supply water, minerals and physical support to their partners.

Lichens are famous for their ability to survive a water shortage. When water is

Lichens grow in a variety of shapes and places

It may come as a surprise that lichens are so varied, flourishing from the Sahara to the polar regions. There are some 16,000 species, which are classified into three types: crustose (crusty), fruticose (shrubby) and foliose (leafy). All three are common in mountain regions. Crustose lichens form patches on solid rock and are often the first plants to colonise barren, rocky soil; they actually help to make soil for other plants by secreting acids that eventually disintegrate the rock. Fruticose species such as beard lichen hang from branches or, like reindeer "moss" (the winter food of caribou), cover the ground. Foliose lichens grow on tree trunks, dead logs and rocks. One species is shown below.

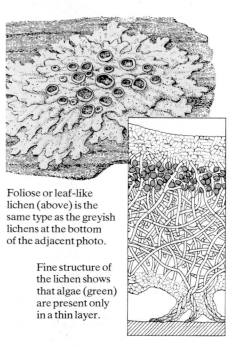

Foliose or leaf-like lichen (above) is the same type as the greyish lichens at the bottom of the adjacent photo.

Fine structure of the lichen shows that algae (green) are present only in a thin layer.

A lichen tapestry (left) of subtly interlocking forms enlivens a highland rock slab. In this community of several lichen species, each one has a characteristic colour.

scarce (as is often the case on a mountain), lichens may become dormant and remain in that condition for extended periods of time. Some lichens can even grow where there is no rain at all, surviving on only occasional dew. And unlike most other plants, lichens are little affected by the strong ultra-violet rays in the sunlight at high altitudes.

Lichens use little energy, for they grow slowly. Some grow so slowly and are so old that they are called "time stains".

You may find lichens that are centuries old; certain lichen colonies have been established for an estimated 2,000 years.

For decades, scientists wondered how the offspring of an alga and a fungus got together to form a new lichen. It seemed unlikely that they would just happen to meet completely by chance.

It was finally discovered that in many cases the two partners have never been separated. Stalk-like "buds" that form on certain lichens are broken off by the wind, or by animals; these tiny offshoots roll or are blown to a new location where they take root and begin a new colony.

Another long-standing puzzle was how the two components established their partnership in the first place. Under certain conditions, scientists were able to grow the alga and the fungus separately, but they could not combine the two to make a "test-tube" lichen. It is now believed that the two plants will form a partnership only if conditions are unfavourable. It is as if they agree to the partnership only when they cannot survive on their own.

Most mountain plants – the lichens, wildflowers, grasses, and even trees – have a low profile that helps them take advantage of whatever protection rocks and ridges may provide. Near the timberline (the highest altitude at which trees can grow), woody plants become gnarled.

These gnome-like plants are called krummholz, which means, appropriately, "crooked wood". Here, trees such as firs and pines are so contorted and dwarfed that they resemble an enchanted forest from a fairy tale. But the chilling, drying wind is the true architect of these shapes. The parts of the plants that would normally grow on the windward side have been frozen, dried, and even torn off.

At the upper edge of the timberline the krummholz-effect is even more extreme. Trees may be so dwarfed and intertwined that you can walk on top of them. A hiker in the mountains who says, "Today I walked over a forest," may be telling the absolute truth.

Veteran pines, growing near the timberline on steep mountain slopes, still cling stubbornly to life. The fresh green of new summer growth contrasts strongly with the silver-grey of weathered trunks and branches that have been damaged by the onslaught of wind and frost.

Stunted trees of the timberline are shaped by winds

Severe spring ice-storms, blistering summer sun, and sub-zero winter temperatures combine with ever-present winds to prune timberline trees into bizarre shapes called krummholz. The timberline is not a rigid boundary that circles a peak at a certain altitude. It will extend higher up in sheltered areas and on southern slopes.

A young pine grows on the protected side of a rock. Even there, some branches are bent down by the wind and will eventually take root.

In winter, a blanket of snow protects the tree from freezing, but new shoots that protrude are soon killed off by the dry, cold wind.

The tree has grown as tall as it can. Only the side branches, protected from the wind, continue to reach outwards along the ground.

As the tree ages, older portions near the rock are the first to die. However, as the younger branches take root, the tree gradually creeps away from the protected site where it started. Strong prevailing winds create flag-like forms by shearing buds from the windward side.

The unstable world of permafrost

The tundra terrain in summer has been described as "too thin to walk on, but too thick to swim in". If you pause for a moment's rest, you are likely to discover how soggy it can be, as your boots sink slowly through the slushy "active zone" of melting ice.

There is water everywhere – in mud, puddles, ponds and lakes. Paradoxically, the tundra gets less rain than many deserts – only about 8 in. of rain a year. The explanation is that the upper layers of soil and ice lie upon permafrost, the almost impermeable layer of ice-impregnated soil and rock. As the name suggests, permafrost remains frozen all year round. Consequently, there is little drainage. The active layer melts and shifts in summer, but not much water enters the still-frozen layers deeper down.

Tundra country, with its underlying permafrost, is found mainly in the far north, where it forms a belt around the top of the world between the northern forests and the Arctic Ocean. The arctic tundra cuts across Alaska, Canada, Greenland, Scandinavia, and into Siberia, covering an area of about 5 million sq. miles. This kind of terrain is also found above the timberline in high mountains all over the world. Here, it is called alpine tundra.

In northern Alaska, the permafrost layer is about 2,000 ft thick; in Siberia, the permafrost is an estimated 1 mile deep. Usually, the permafrost is not influenced by activity on the surface. All the fluctuations – freezing and thawing with the seasons, and, to a lesser extent, by night and day – occur above it. Primitive people did not often settle on permafrost, so its very existence was not discovered until fairly recent times.

You cannot walk for long on the tundra without noticing the countless sharp fragments of rock. During thaws, water seeps into cracks in the rock, shattering the rock as the water freezes and expands. Gradually, the rock is pulverised and becomes part of the soil. The repeated freezing and thawing also has the effect of sorting and separating debris into coarse and fine particles. The larger particles are pushed outwards and settle into patterns called polygons. The polygons may be a few feet to 300 ft wide, and clusters of polygons may stretch for several miles. Often the interior of the polygons fills with water. On mountain slopes, this sorting process forms stripes of coarse and fine materials.

During the brief summer, when the active layer is thawed and soggy, the layer tends to slip downhill like treacle. This action, called solifluction, is particularly pronounced on the steep slopes of mountains, but it occurs even on slight inclines in the arctic region. The movement may be sluggish – only a few inches a year in some areas – but gradually this movement changes the whole face of the tundra, moving rocks and plants, rounding off projections and filling in hollows.

Although tundra covers nearly one-fifth of the Northern Hemisphere, the permafrost in Antarctica is almost entirely under ice with scant vegetation.

A soggy arctic world of mud, ice and meltwater

This bird's-eye view of a square mile of arctic tundra shows hillsides and streams, and also unique formations called pingos. Pingos are believed to be derived from pockets of water trapped in the permafrost (perhaps the remains of lakes that lost their waters through seepage). The water froze, expanded, and was forced to the surface by pressure from the permafrost. A pingo lifts a layer of vegetation as it rises. This uplifting cracks the covering soil, opening the way for the icy core to melt. Collapse of a pingo may take 1,000 to 4,000 years.

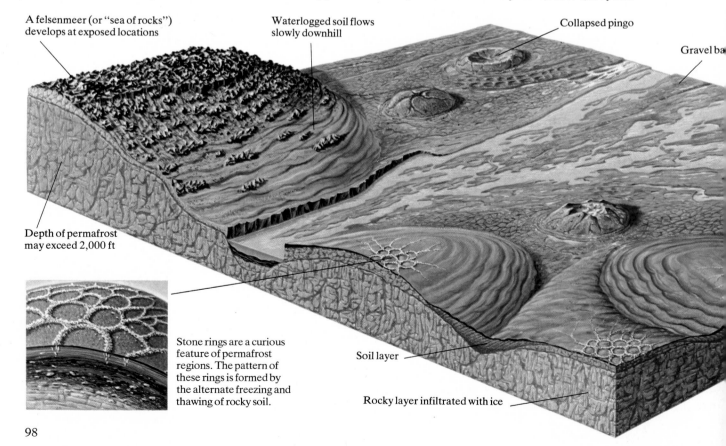

A felsenmeer (or "sea of rocks") develops at exposed locations

Waterlogged soil flows slowly downhill

Collapsed pingo

Gravel ba

Depth of permafrost may exceed 2,000 ft

Stone rings are a curious feature of permafrost regions. The pattern of these rings is formed by the alternate freezing and thawing of rocky soil.

Soil layer

Rocky layer infiltrated with ice

An exposed ice lens on the winding Atigun River in Alaska is only a few feet thick. Such lenses are of varying depth throughout the tundra, and, in the summer, they thaw at different speeds. This makes for soggy, unpredictable surface conditions. Meltwater from this source supports tundra plants and animals. Oddly enough, this icy layer actually insulates the deeper permafrost region below it from thawing out in summer.

Cut-away of pingo

Covering of soil

Ice core

Silt layer

Permafrost

A pingo is a mound of earth thrust up by ice. Some are 300 ft in diameter.

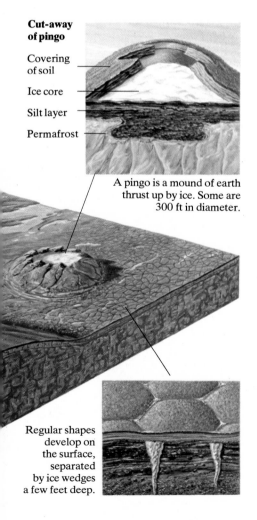

Regular shapes develop on the surface, separated by ice wedges a few feet deep.

LIVING WITH NATURE
Of permafrost, people and pipelines

The discovery of vast petroleum deposits in the arctic region of North America began a modern-day "gold rush". In the early days of surveying these resources, many problems were uncovered, and many paradoxes as well. For example, the land appears to be rugged, but it is actually delicate. Most people expected the working conditions to be physically taxing; what came as a surprise were the psychological drawbacks of living in the far north. Many were dismayed by the dark winter days and the lack of darkness during summer nights.

• Everyone concerned with construction – whether working on buildings or pipelines – must be careful to avoid damaging the thin layer of soil. This soil protects the permafrost below. The heat of human dwellings and the engines of construction equipment jeopardise the stability of the ground. If melting occurs, the effect is like a small, local earthquake; the ground becomes soft, buildings sink, and pipelines are in danger of cracking. To preserve the permafrost, insulation may be necessary. Homes can be placed on top of gravel beds or pilings; or cold air can be piped beneath them to refrigerate the ground. Excavations for the pipeline must be filled in and the surface restored as far as possible. One characteristic of this terrain is that any damage to the thin, fragile vegetative layer takes years to restore itself to healthy growth.

• In many places, the trans-Alaskan pipeline runs above the ground, on pilings. The foundations of the pilings are vulnerable, too. In addition, they must be engineered in such a way as not to interfere with migratory animals, such as the herds of caribou that have to travel in search of seasonal food supplies.

• The construction season for the Alaskan pipeline extends into the winter, when unwanted warmth is carried off by chilling winds. The wind-chill factor is a measure of just such an effect – how much colder it seems at a particular temperature under windy conditions than on a windless day. The one advantage of working in the winter is the absence of biting insects, which are abundant in warmer weather.

• Snow often brings all work to a halt, whether snow falls from the skies or is blown from snowdrifts. Even when all is still, snow affects the lives of residents. Snow reflects sunlight, and sunburn is a hazard of arctic life. So is snow blindness, which can be prevented by wearing protective goggles. A combination of snow and diffused light (as on an overcast day) causes a whiteout – a loss of depth perception that makes it difficult for the individual to see irregularities in the terrain or to estimate distance. Snow also reflects sound, so you can hear surprisingly far on a cold, clear day.

Animal life on the arctic tundra

Summer on the arctic tundra is brief; thawing begins about June, and freezing conditions return in August. It is the movement of the earth around the sun that brings the seasons. Because the earth turns on a tilted axis, light from the sun strikes the surface of the earth unequally. The greatest seasonal variation is apparent at the poles. Polar winters are dark even during the day; at midsummer, the sun does not dip below the horizon.

The arctic tundra region, which is near the north pole, also experiences drastic seasonal changes. The temperatures, which may have been as cold as −57°C (−70°F) in winter, rise to summertime peaks of 21°C (70°F) to 27°C (80°F), producing humid, balmy conditions. At night, temperatures seldom go below 5°C (40°F).

Even before the snows have melted, clumps of grass begin to grow, and dense, spongy carpets of moss and lichen come to life. Hordes of insects hatch in the pools of melting snow that dot the landscape.

The stage is set for many animals – residents and transients alike – to breed, rear their young, and build up their physical strength for the hardships of winter. Some birds, such as ptarmigan, are year-round residents. In winter, these birds have white feathers, which provide camouflage against a snowy background. With the changing season, their plumage changes too, to a mottled pattern that blends perfectly with the summer tundra. Ptarmigan eggs are also mottled. When the tiny chicks hatch, they are so well camouflaged as to be almost invisible.

Like most of the larger tundra nesters – such as geese, swans and ducks – young ptarmigan are capable of feeding themselves from the time they hatch. So are the chicks of nesting shorebirds, such as sandpipers and plovers. The young of these species are called precocial. The parents' role is to guard, guide and brood them (providing warmth at night) until they achieve independence.

But there are other species of tundra-nesting birds with different patterns of infant development. Tree sparrows, for example, have altricial nestlings – helpless young that stay in the nest and must be fed by adults. The abundance of insects on the tundra allows parent birds to feed their offspring hundreds of times during a long arctic day. Meanwhile, hidden nests provide protection from foxes and other predators.

Hawks, eagles and falcons soar overhead, searching for prey. Other birds account for much of their diet. But multitudes of small rodents are also available prey. Lemmings, voles and marmots, which live in burrows and tunnel systems throughout the winter, come out to bask in the sun and feed on the new vegetation. These little animals respond to favourable conditions by increased breeding. Some are capable of producing four or five litters a year, with five or six offspring per litter. Their numbers climb for as long as the food supply holds out. This wealth of prey attracts snowy owls, arctic foxes, and other predators from outlying regions. The predators, in turn, successfully rear more offspring.

The end of a population explosion comes when the prey animals exhaust their food supply. High mortality follows – caused partly by starvation, partly by stress, which leaves the animals vulnerable to disease. Soon after, predators experience the same downward trend in population.

For most birds, the tundra is only a temporary feeding and breeding place. When food runs short they flock south to the conifer belt or the temperate zone beyond.

BIRDWATCHING TIPS
Tundra nesters that visit us

Have you ever wondered why birds travel thousands of miles to nesting sites on the arctic tundra? Scientists believe they are attracted by the incredibly rich food supply – grasses, berries, aquatic plants and myriads of insects, such as mosquitoes and blackflies. Long daylight hours allow young birds to feed and be fed almost around the clock. Thus the young birds fledge quickly. When the breeding season is over and the food supply dwindles, these tundra nesters head south. The map shows the approximate breeding range and migration routes for three species of birds.

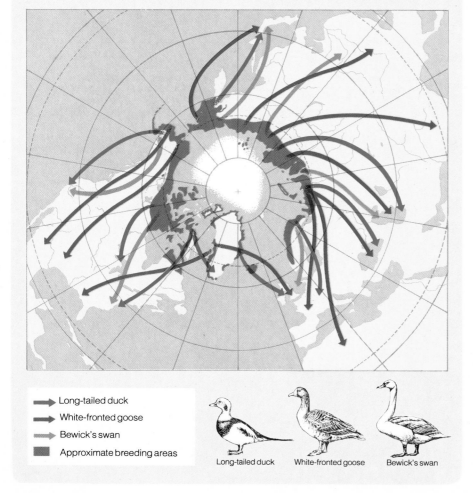

→ Long-tailed duck
→ White-fronted goose
→ Bewick's swan
▪ Approximate breeding areas

Long-tailed duck   White-fronted goose   Bewick's swan

Lemmings are extremely prolific rodents that literally eat themselves out of house and home. Periodically, the stress of crowding sends them swarming over the tundra.

A snowy owl on the alert for lemmings – its main food. Snowy owls have begun to breed again in the Orkney Islands.

Caribou are the nomads of North America. Following routes that are centuries old, these deer migrate from forested wintering areas to calving and feeding grounds on the tundra.

CHAPTER FOUR

Sea and shore

*The ocean is a giant circulatory system
for the earth. And the motion of currents and
tides lends vitality to the waters.*

No part of the planet exerts a more powerful emotional pull than the sea. Poets and painters, writers and photographers, have sometimes captured a measure of the sea's attraction, but none has explained it fully. Restless, unfathomable, a constant challenge to adventurers, the sea is the cradle of the animal world from which, scientists tell us, our distant ancestors emerged hundreds of millions of years ago to begin life on land.

The waters themselves are a source of wonder – far from being a uniform mixture of water and salts, the ocean environment has many different zones and provides varied habitats for plants and animals. The waters around a tropical reef have a wealth of local life forms. These influence both the water and one another. Transport a tropical fish to another environment – even to one of the same temperature – and the chances are it will not live. Stranger still is the fact that the jostling of the waters seems to be essential to its vitality; if you take part of the sea home in a jar, it will soon become stale and lifeless.

The odours of the sea are infinitely varied. The basic scent comes from sodium chloride, which is ordinary table salt. But in some places its smell is medicinal (like iodine), in others, pungent with seaweed. The high amounts of dissolved salts make seawater sting when blown across our faces, and give it an astringent taste. The sea captures all our senses.

The movement of oceans over two-thirds of the globe acts like a huge heat engine, stirring the atmosphere and affecting the weather all over the world. Thus the influence of oceans, so apparent on the coasts, extends even to remote inland regions, where seas are the stuff of story and legend.

*It is only at the shore that waves break in this way – dashing
against an underwater slope, then erupting. The result is a
magnificent spray that looks like a fan of etched glass. As a wave
topples, sunlight on the shallow waters transforms the deep blue
colours of the open ocean to pale, translucent tones.*

Rocky, sandy and marshy shores

Seashores are narrow margins on the vast ocean world, but they are the only part of this realm that people can easily explore. At the shore, you can see the endless contest between land and sea. In some places, the sea is winning – dune fences and even buildings have toppled into the water as the surf cuts deeper into the land. In other places, the land seems to win. Sometimes, in just a matter of hours, a storm may pile up countless tons of mud, sand and rock against the shore, creating land where there was none before.

For convenience, you can classify a particular shore into one of three types – rocky, sandy or marshy. Rocky coasts are the most dramatic; jagged cliffs often rise sharply above the seas. The seething water seems to be ripped apart by sharp fingers of rock. But just the opposite is actually happening; the waves are slowly wearing away the rock, breaking it into fragments, sculpting it into arches, ledges and caves.

The waves often cut the rocks like a huge horizontal saw, undermining the face of a cliff and causing it to collapse. Then the waves break down the rubble, grinding boulders into pebbles and pebbles into sand. Sometimes you can even hear a grinding sound as waves wash a rocky beach.

It has been estimated that the sea may take several hundred years to reduce a boulder about 1 ft in diameter to sand. Ocean currents may carry this sand far from the site where it originated, or it may be caught and held near by in cup-shaped depressions in the rocks. Sometimes the currents drop particles washed from cliffs at the end of a long, rocky shore, and a sandy beach develops at that point.

Though many times smaller than boulders, the tiny sand particles usually last much longer on a shore. You can discover why as you walk along a sandy beach. Your feet will sink in dry sand; damp sand supports your weight and provides a natural pavement between the shifting dry areas and the submerged beach. This is because a thin film of water envelops each grain in damp sand. The film acts like glue, holding the grains together and also insulating them from one another so that the waves do not grind them down.

This watery insulation protects many animals that live on sandy shores. These species are different from the inhabitants of a rocky coast, which tend to attach themselves to rocks. The more mobile creatures of the sandy beach – crabs and clams, for instance – occupy burrows. Some even live in the minute spaces between the grains of sand. This is a more cushioned world than a pebbly beach.

Eventually – probably after thousands of years – sand grains are broken down into smaller pieces and become mud. The pulverised material – silt and clay particles – is readily swept away by shore currents,

Rocky coasts are wonderful places for photographers, philosophers and geologists (not to mention gulls and other birds). The pounding of waves steadily dissects the rock – water infiltrates along the seams, where it is weak. Here, slightly tilted horizontal layers of sandstone can be seen.

but in a protected area (such as a bay or inlet), the material may accumulate and form a muddy shore. Mud flats also form where rivers flow into the sea.

Mud flats are quickly colonised by plants and animals. Eelgrass grows on the muddy sea floor just beyond the surf, and marsh grasses gain a foothold on the shore. The maze of roots and intertwining stems traps more mud and provides a sanctuary for creatures of sea and land.

Salt marshes are relatively short-lived. The more sheltered world, created by plants capable of clinging on to the sea-edge, bears the seeds of its own destruction. As more soil is accumulated, conventional land plants are able to flourish and gradually over the years the salt marsh turns into a field, particularly if local farmers have an eye to improvement. While the marshes exist, they provide superb natural wildlife refuges and bird-watchers flock there like the birds themselves.

A sandy shore may seem desolate, almost devoid of life, but beneath its wet and glistening surface is an incredible variety of tiny animals. The most important factor in their lives is the water that surrounds them: it brings them food, keeps them cool and moist, and may eventually wash them away.

Salt marshes are also shores, though their outlines are less defined than those of other coasts. Man has been slow to appreciate the importance of these productive regions. Some animals (including fish) use marshes as incubators for their young; other species (such as egrets) live here all year round.

Warm currents, cold currents and climate

Currents are like rivers in the sea. Some of the currents that circulate in oceans are more than 50 miles wide and transport about 50 million tons of water a second. Ocean circulation has a profound effect on climate. Heat from a current is transmitted to the winds that pass over it; the net effect is that of a gigantic hot-water heating system for the whole globe. Were it not for the Gulf Stream bringing warm water from the Caribbean, West Europe would be an icier place.

Energy from the sun drives the currents – surface waters are heated, which causes them to expand, especially in the region around the equator. This increased volume of water flows outwards, towards the poles, where it gradually cools and sinks. At the same time, cold water from the ocean depths comes up, replacing waters that have flowed away.

The motion of the earth stirs the seas. Many currents become part of immense, slow-motion whirlpools. For example, the Gulf Stream flows into the Canaries Current, which branches west into the North Equatorial Current and (to a lesser extent) south into the Guinean Current. The currents flow mainly clockwise in the Northern Hemisphere, counterclockwise in the Southern Hemisphere. This general pattern is greatly influenced by the winds, and is modified by the contours of continents and the presence of islands. Many currents fluctuate in their range. The Humboldt Current, for example, sometimes turns towards the west before its cold, oxygen-rich waters reach the coast of Peru. This adversely affects fishing off the Peruvian coast.

Warm air holds more moisture than cold air. When two temperature systems collide, the result is usually water vapour in some form. When warm winds from the Gulf Stream strike cooler air from the arctic near the British Isles, fog results. So, too, when the cold winds from the Labrador Current touch the Gulf Stream off Newfoundland – the seas are blanketed by notorious banks of mist.

Whale-watching close to land

One of the joys of ocean-watching is the surprising frequency with which whales can be sighted, both from shore and (more often) from ships. Whales regularly visit waters off California, eastern Canada and Norway for breeding, or during migration. They often reveal their presence by spouting – in fact, most species have an identifiable spouting pattern. If a whale is near by, look at the curve of its back to identify the species, and also at the shape of its fins and flukes (tail). Widely distributed whales, from the largest (the blue) to the smallest (dolphin), are shown at right.

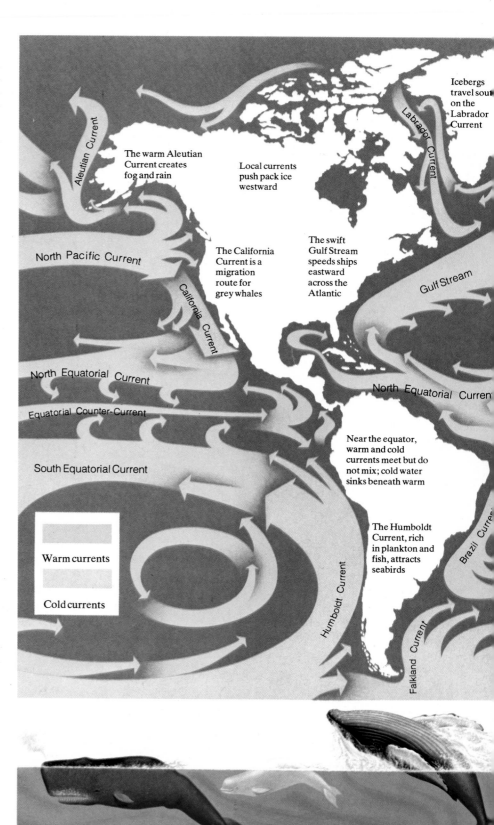

The warm Aleutian Current creates fog and rain

Local currents push pack ice westward

Icebergs travel south on the Labrador Current

Aleutian Current

Labrador Current

North Pacific Current

The California Current is a migration route for grey whales

The swift Gulf Stream speeds ships eastward across the Atlantic

Gulf Stream

California Current

North Equatorial Current

North Equatorial Current

Equatorial Counter-Current

South Equatorial Current

Near the equator, warm and cold currents meet but do not mix; cold water sinks beneath warm

Warm currents

Cold currents

The Humboldt Current, rich in plankton and fish, attracts seabirds

Brazil Current

Humboldt Current

Falkland Current

The sperm whale, named after spermaceti, the oily wax in its enormous head, is a tropical species. The fictional Moby Dick was an albino sperm whale.

The beluga, or white whale, travels in large groups, usually in arctic waters.

The humpback whale, famous for its underwater singing, often leaps high, hitting the water with its flukes as it submerges.

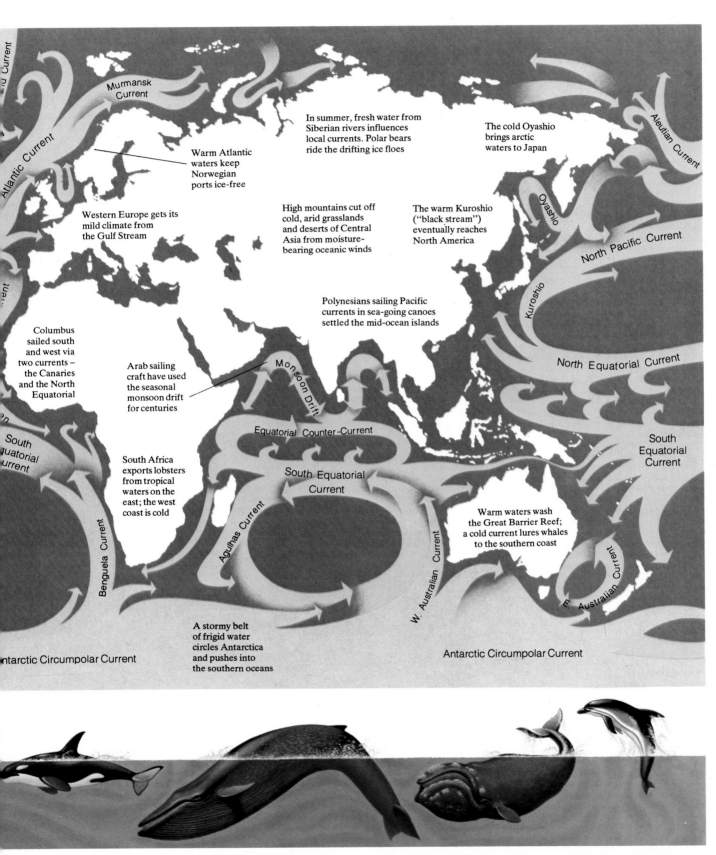

Current

Murmansk
Current

Atlantic Current

Atlantic Current

Warm Atlantic
waters keep
Norwegian
ports ice-free

In summer, fresh water from
Siberian rivers influences
local currents. Polar bears
ride the drifting ice floes

The cold Oyashio
brings arctic
waters to Japan

Aleutian Current

Western Europe gets its
mild climate from
the Gulf Stream

High mountains cut off
cold, arid grasslands
and deserts of Central
Asia from moisture-
bearing oceanic winds

The warm Kuroshio
("black stream")
eventually reaches
North America

Oyashio

North Pacific Current

Kuroshio

Columbus
sailed south
and west via
two currents –
the Canaries
and the North
Equatorial

Polynesians sailing Pacific
currents in sea-going canoes
settled the mid-ocean islands

Monsoon Drift

North Equatorial Current

Arab sailing
craft have used
the seasonal
monsoon drift
for centuries

Equatorial Counter-Current

South
Equatorial
Current

South
Equatorial
Current

South Africa
exports lobsters
from tropical
waters on the
east; the west
coast is cold

South Equatorial
Current

Agulhas Current

Warm waters wash
the Great Barrier Reef;
a cold current lures whales
to the southern coast

South
Equatorial
Current

Benguela Current

W. Australian Current

E. Australian Current

A stormy belt
of frigid water
circles Antarctica
and pushes into
the southern oceans

Antarctic Circumpolar Current

Antarctic Circumpolar Current

The killer whale is the only
species of whale that attacks
large prey. In aquariums, these
whales are surprisingly friendly.

The blue whale is the largest of all
mammals – the record length is
108 ft. It is a filter-feeder, straining
its food through baleen plates.

The right whale was named by
whalers because it was so easily
captured. Right whales live in
northern and southern oceans.

The common dolphin is a
small, friendly and gregarious
whale that often accompanies
ships at sea.

The open ocean

On an ocean voyage, as land drops from sight, a sudden sense of isolation often overtakes a traveller – an awareness of the immensity of the sea. Washington Irving, the 19th-century American writer, experienced a "delicious sensation of mingled security and awe" when he climbed to the ship's main-top during his first transatlantic crossing. That was in 1804. Although ships have changed a great deal since that time, few modern travellers are immune to the experience described by Irving.

A sea voyage offers valuable insights into the marine world. For example, the colour of the ocean varies widely. The reddish colour sometimes seen in antarctic waters may reveal the presence of millions of krill, shrimp-like creatures on which many great whales feed. Vast numbers of tiny aquatic plants colour many coastal seas green or blue-green. Such intensive plant growth occurs near the mouths of rivers, where the flowing waters deposit their load of nutrient-rich sediments.

In contrast, the typical colour of the open ocean (the region beyond the coastal seas) is a deep blue. Too far from the land to receive much in the way of nutrients, the open ocean has relatively little microscopic life. Any sea (or deep lake) that is not coloured by plants, animals or dissolved materials looks blue. Although no one knows exactly why this is so, the reflection of the sky is believed to play a role.

Lights twinkle on and off beneath the surface of the night-time sea. The poet Coleridge, in "The Rime of the Ancient Mariner", called these ghost-like flashes witches' fire; today, the light is known as bioluminescence. Usually, the light comes from tiny animals that rise to the surface at night. Although some larger animals – certain fish and squid, for example – are also luminous, this light is often produced not by the animals themselves but by bacteria living on or inside them.

During the day you can see other, larger animals from the deck of a ship, especially near islands, shoals or patches of seaweed. Flying fish leap in the path of a ship. Occasionally, sea turtles paddle by; these massive reptiles must come to the surface to breathe. Shearwaters (birds named for their habit of skimming low over the waves) fly across the ship's wake; birds known as storm-petrels patter on the water as they feed. Away from the land, sharks may follow a ship to scavenge on food thrown away by the cooks. And a sight that will always bring passengers thronging to the rail is a school of porpoises or dolphins at play.

One curiosity of the ocean is that few insects have managed to colonise its vast surface. A few sea-going gnats are identified by scientists from time to time, but even though there is a steady stream of insects as the wind blows from the land, insects have never made a substantial contribution to the populations of the seas. Their absence may be one reason for the popularity of cruises, and of sailing in craft of all sizes.

A pod of dolphins leaps across a quiet sea.
Though the names dolphin and porpoise are often used interchangeably, it is usually easy to tell one from the other: dolphins have beak-like snouts, porpoises have blunt ones.

The Ancient Mariner's seabird is the albatross, a long-winged bird famous for its habit of following ships. The word seabird usually refers to species that live far out to sea, returning to land only to breed. This species of albatross, called a light-mantled sooty albatross, roams southern seas and nests on islands near New Zealand and Antarctica. Other seabird species include fulmars, gannets and puffins, but not gulls, which are birds of the shore.

NATURE OBSERVER
Reading the waves

The surface of the sea responds to the movement of the wind – high winds transform a smooth, placid sea into a tumultuous swirl of whitecaps or driving spray. With the help of the Beaufort Wind Scale (right), you can gauge the approximate wind speed just by looking at the open ocean. Simply select the description that best suits the sea; the scale will give you the corresponding wind speed in knots. (A knot is 1 nautical mile per hour; a nautical mile is slightly longer than a standard mile.) The Beaufort scale was devised by an officer of the British Navy in the 19th century, when sailing ships depended on wind speed and direction for manoeuvring in the open sea. Modern ships have anemometers, which measure wind speed with greater precision.

Beaufort number	Sea description	Wind speed (in knots)	Wind description
0	Sea like a mirror.	0–1	Calm
1*	Scale-like ripples; no foam crests.	1–3	Light air
2	Small wavelets; glassy crests, not breaking.	4–6	Light breeze
3	Large wavelets; crests break; few whitecaps.	7–10	Gentle breeze
4	Small waves; frequent whitecaps.	11–16	Moderate breeze
5*	Moderate waves; many whitecaps; some spray.	17–21	Fresh breeze
6*	Larger waves; whitecaps everywhere; more spray.	22–27	Strong breeze
7*	Sea heaps up; foam from breaking waves.	28–33	Near gale
8	Moderately high waves; crest edges break into spray; foam blown in streaks.	34–40	Gale
9*	High waves; sea begins to roll.	41–47	Strong gale
10*	Very high waves with overhanging crests.	48–55	Storm
11	Exceptionally high waves; sea covered with foam patches; reduced visibility.	56–63	Violent storm
12	Air filled with foam; sea completely white with driving spray; visibility very poor.	64–71	Hurricane

*Shown below

1

5

6

7

9

10

Edges of the continents

Continents do not end at the seashore. They continue under the water, where, on gently sloping plains, there are hills, valleys and other features much like those on land. This shallow underwater region is called the continental shelf, and it is considered to be the true edge of the continent. Beyond the shelf, the land drops steeply down to the deep, dark ocean floor.

On the average, the continental shelf is about 45 miles wide. But in some places, it stretches hundreds of miles out into the sea. The underwater descent from the shore to the edge of the shelf is gradual, dropping only about 10 ft for every mile. The outer edge of the shelf is usually covered by about 450 ft of water. Beyond that region, the sea floor plunges steeply (this incline is called the continental slope) and does not level off again until it reaches the bottom of the ocean basin.

Many of the continental shelves were formed millions of years ago, when forces deep within the earth pushed up underwater mountains near the coasts. In some places, the mountains rose above sea level, creating islands that have lasted to this day. Sediment washed from the land filled in behind these island dams, forming an undersea shoulder at the edge of the land mass.

During the Ice Ages, the oceans were lower because much of the earth's water was frozen. Glaciers gouged the exposed parts of the shelves. As the sea level gradually changed, the surf gnawed at the edges, creating terraces. Some parts of the shelves that were exposed during the Ice Ages were covered with forests. Fossils collected by research submarines and dredges indicate that mammoths, mastodons and giant moose foraged in the vegetation there.

Today the continental shelves are once again covered with water. In some places, there are canyons cut by rivers. For example, an underwater extension of the Hudson River valley off New York forms a canyon nearly three-quarters of a mile deep and more than 5 miles wide. Occasionally, underwater avalanches race down the canyons, scooping them out and making them deeper.

⚐ SAFETY AND SURVIVAL
Beware of sea creatures that sting and pinch

When you set out to explore a beach or a rock pool, take some simple precautions to avoid a sting, pinch, bite or jab:
- Wear plimsolls when wading. Sharp edges of rock, as well as broken shells, can inflict painful cuts. Sea urchins, the brown, spike-covered creatures on rocks, can even penetrate plimsolls.
- Do not pick up sea creatures with your bare hands. Some crabs may pinch severely if they are disturbed.
- Never stick your hands into a hole or crevice. It may be the home of some animal that will defend itself with a nasty bite or sting.
- If you see a jellyfish, get out of the water – these stinging animals usually swim in groups. Some species are harmless to humans, but others can cause reactions that vary from a rash or welt to a violent allergic attack. More dangerous still is the Portuguese man-of-war – its tentacles (as much as 50 ft long) can ensnare a swimmer. A dead jellyfish on a beach may still have active stinging capsules – do not touch it!

Buoyed by a gas-inflated "sail", a Portuguese man-of-war is not a jellyfish; it is actually a colony of many specialised animals. Here, its tentacles are wrapped around its prey.

Like a pulsating flower, the moon jelly swims by contracting its shallow bell. This species, common in shore waters of Europe and North America, is not as harmful as other jellyfish.

The shelves are rich regions of the ocean. Sunlight penetrates the shallow waters, stimulating photosynthesis – which is the basis of all life. Microscopic floating plants are the start of the food chain in the sea; they are eaten by microscopic animals and a host of larger creatures. Consequently, coastal seas are by far the most productive habitats – almost four-fifths of all plants and animals on earth live here. At first, this may seem surprising (if, for example, you had supposed tropical rain forests to have the largest populations of living things). But even on the relatively shallow shelves, the ocean is far deeper than a forest is high, so there is much more living space in the sea.

Although the shelves underlie only a small fraction of the oceans, their waters furnish nearly all the world's seafood. Hence the importance of the fishing restrictions imposed by many nations in the mid-1970s. The aim was to preserve fish stocks endangered by modern fishing methods, and maintain national sources of supply.

Petroleum deposits are valuable resources of the shelves, especially in the northern Gulf of Mexico, the North Sea, the Persian Gulf and Australia's Bass Strait. This substance is a by-product of the bountiful life in ancient coastal seas. Then, as now, minute plants and animals drifted in the water. After these organisms died and sank to the bottom, they were buried by sediment washed from the land. Over millions of years, these dead plants and animals were converted into petroleum and natural gas. Today the shelves yield more than one-fifth of the world's total production of these fuels – a figure that is sure to increase in the future.

Afloat in its spiral shell, the chambered nautilus enlarges its home as it grows. The animal itself lives in the outer chamber; the inner segments provide buoyancy. (See cross-section, p. 15.)

Where the octopus and its relatives live

The octopus and other cephalopods (meaning head-foot) are members of an ancient group. The ancestors of present-day nautiluses were larger in size and amazingly abundant. Now, however, cephalopods without shells are more numerous. These animals live at varying depths on the continental shelves. Octopuses occupy holes in the rocks, mostly in shallow water. Nautiluses are bottom-dwellers. Cuttlefish (with an internal, vestigial shell) inhabit warm, coastal waters. Many species of squid swim near the surface; others are deep-sea denizens.

Common octopus

The varying profiles of the continental shelves

The shelves that edge the continents seldom show the same profile from one section of a coast to another. Coastal charts record great variations in width of shelf and depth of water. The surface of some shelves is irregular, with deep troughs and shallow banks. In the arctic, a smooth shelf slopes gently for hundreds of miles. Elsewhere, a narrow platform may end abruptly in rocky, underwater cliffs. An extreme example of such a drop occurs off the coast of South America (where there is a deep trench). The pitch-dark ocean floor, called the abyss, varies in depth throughout the world.

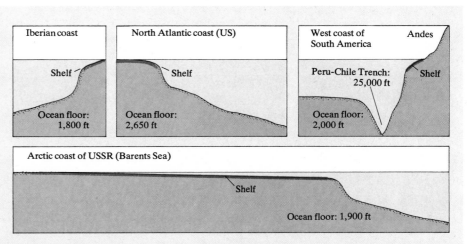

Iberian coast | Shelf | Ocean floor: 1,800 ft

North Atlantic coast (US) | Shelf | Ocean floor: 2,650 ft

West coast of South America | Andes | Peru-Chile Trench: 25,000 ft | Shelf | Ocean floor: 2,000 ft

Arctic coast of USSR (Barents Sea) | Shelf | Ocean floor: 1,900 ft

The rhythm of the tides

Day in, day out, the tides advance upon the shores, only to retreat again at predictable times. So regular are these rhythms that in ancient times some people believed them to be caused by the breath of a monster at the bottom of the sea. We now know that the tides are, in fact, governed by a huge object, but not one on this planet. The moon is the main cause of the tides. Its gravity tugs at the oceans and creates a bulge on the side of the earth nearest to itself. The sun also exerts an influence, but the moon is dominant.

In addition to daily tides, twice a month the tides are extremely high. They are called "spring" tides – but not because of season. They are higher because the moon and sun are jointly exerting a pull on the seas. (To jog your memory, think of high tides as "springing up".) The opposite condition, where there is little tidal variation, is called neap. Neap tides reflect the situation when the moon, earth and sun are at right-angles to one another, which also occurs twice a month.

The movement of the earth also contributes to tidal action. The rotation of the globe, with its irregular distribution of continents and islands, causes the water to "pile up" when the land masses collide with the tidal bulges. (Ocean waters do not race around the world, but instead rise and fall in a much more localised way.) In a sense, you can think of the waters as being under the ever-changing influence of the moon and sun, and of the continents as doing all the moving – into tides and out of them.

The different sizes and shapes of the ocean basins have a profound effect on tidal movements. Everyone who has walked across a room carrying a glass of water or cup of coffee knows that if you hold the container level, you can go fairly quickly without spilling. But if you were to carry a pan of water of equal depth but greater diameter, you would have to go much more slowly; the sloshing effect is magnified.

Similarly, oceans react differently to the tidal bulges. For example, the tides at the Pacific end of the Panama Canal are 12 to 16 ft, while at the Atlantic end, only 40 miles away, the tidal range is only 1 or 2 ft in height. In some oceans, such as the Atlantic, the tidal bulges produce two daily tides of about equal magnitude. In the Pacific, successive highs and lows are often unequal. In some areas, such as South-east Asia, one of the tides is barely detectable.

Shorelines also affect tides. As tidal waters enter the relatively narrow mouth of the Gulf of Mexico, they spread out and are diminished. Just the opposite happens at the Bay of Fundy on Canada's Atlantic coast. As tidal waters move in the funnel-shaped bay, they are squeezed higher and higher. In part of the bay the water rises more than 50 ft – the world's highest tide.

A further complexity is the tides in smaller bodies of water. The Mediterranean, for example, does not have tides in the ordinary sense. Evaporation lowers the water level, and the influx of water at the Strait of Gibraltar seems to be a tide.

Experiments are being made to produce electricity from tidal power. By damming the Rance estuary near St Malo in Brittany, the French are generating much of the current used locally.

What causes the tides?

Tides are the result of the moon's pull (and, to a lesser extent, that of the sun) on the oceans. Bulges form where the pull is greatest.

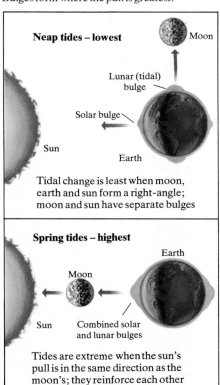

Neap tides – lowest

Moon

Lunar (tidal) bulge

Solar bulge

Sun

Earth

Tidal change is least when moon, earth and sun form a right-angle; moon and sun have separate bulges

Spring tides – highest

Earth

Moon

Sun

Combined solar and lunar bulges

Tides are extreme when the sun's pull is in the same direction as the moon's; they reinforce each other

Sea caves are formed by the pounding of waves. Starting as a crevice, a cave may grow so large that it undermines the rocky face of the cliff, causing it to collapse. Sea caves attract visitors; it is essential to know when the tides will be high, as the influx of water may cover the exits.

Tide flats are coastal regions where changes in water level are frequent. Like most muddy regions, this broad expanse, located on an arm of a wide sea inlet, is protected from the pounding of the open ocean.

Knowing when tides will go out is important for anyone boating near tide flats. If marooned by the dropping water level, a skipper may well have to wait for the next tide in order to float free.

Taking advantage of tides for boating and fishing

Tides alter the seashores significantly for boaters and fishermen alike. (Even if you do not intend to boat or fish, you can observe the working of tides, starting with the high-tide marks on piers, rocks and beaches. You can also follow human activities, which the tides alternately "encourage" and "prohibit".)

• At high tide, relatively large craft can cross shallows and negotiate channels that might otherwise be hazardous. On the other hand, low tide may enable a tall ship to pass under a bridge where there is usually too little clearance.

• When anchoring, lines have to be adjusted to match the variation in tidal levels over the next few hours (or however long the vessel will be there).

• Many ships leave port on outgoing tides, taking advantage of the current. Low tide is also the time when boat and ship owners repair damages.

• For fishermen, the incoming tide is a boon because it stirs up sandbanks and mud flats, rousing many of the burrowing animals there. This attracts fish to feed. The presence of circling seabirds over a patch of water is often a clue to where fish are feeding near the surface.

• As the tide goes out and shores are exposed, fishermen go after clams, crabs and shrimps, and also dig for bait. If you do the same, keep a sharp look-out to make sure you are not cut off by the incoming tide, while preoccupied with your search.

• Information on tides is usually given in local newspapers in coastal towns. The hours of low and high tide are also shown on notice-boards at the sea-front and published in motoring handbooks. Or you can ask local boatmen or fishermen who know the idiosyncrasies of the underwater landscape, which affect the tides.

Living conditions on a rocky coast

A receding tide on a rocky coast uncovers one surprise after another. As the water falls, previously hidden plants and animals come into view – crusty barnacles and limpets, filmy red algae, slippery rockweed, and long strands of kelp. Unlike shifting sandy beaches, the more stable rocky coasts provide both plants and animals with many places to attach themselves. But when the tide goes out, they may be left stranded – to be heated by the sun, dried out and chilled by the wind, and washed in a freshwater bath if it rains.

As the tide ebbs, horizontal bands of differing colours appear on the rocks – as if a giant paintbrush had swept across the shore. These bands are most apparent on steep rocky coasts where the rise and fall of the tides is at least 3 or 4 ft.

Each band is a zone of life. It takes its characteristic colour mainly from the dominant plants in that area. The upper zone often has two tones – greyish-green

lichens at the top, black lichens and algae below. Yellow-brown bladderwrack enlivens the middle zone; strands of dark-brown kelp and other algae, commonly called seaweeds, hold fast to rocks in the lowest zone.

The zone in which a particular organism grows depends on how much wave action it can withstand and how long it can survive out of water. The extremely high tides that occur twice a month may be the only times when the top zone is covered with water. Lichens, for example, are rarely under water, but sea urchins, crawling over the bottom, are seldom out of water.

Where crevices or rock pools disrupt the pattern, the bands may blend. These areas are usually cooler, darker, and wetter when the tide is out than the face of the rocks. Plants and animals that cannot survive much exposure to air, such as sea anemones, can sometimes live here.

Some residents seem permanent – almost as enduring as the rocks themselves. But many of them were once drifters in the sea. For example, mature barnacles, which cannot move to a new location, release milky clouds of larvae into the surf. The young barnacles spend weeks floating before settling down on rocks – or on the hull of a ship. Similarly, many mussels, limpets and snails cast their eggs into the sea. Many algae, too, release tiny reproductive bodies, which drift in coastal waters, then attach themselves to rocks.

Unseen and usually unnoticed, there is yet another animal population – several quite distinct creatures that bore holes in the rock and live there behind the visible colonies. Usually nothing can be seen of them except the entrances to their holes.

As you climb down a rocky shore, you are, in a way, travelling backwards in time, for hundreds of millions of years ago the land was first populated by aquatic animals. Periwinkles (which are snails) illustrate the transition from sea to land. One species – the smooth periwinkle – lives near the bottom of the rocky shore and can survive only short exposures to air; it reproduces by shedding its eggs into the water. In contrast, the rough periwinkle, which lives at the top of the tidal region, will die if it is covered by water for too long. It can breathe oxygen from the air, and it bears live young on dry land. But apparently the rough periwinkle is not yet completely ready for a terrestrial life – it still requires periodic dousings of sea water. The ancestors of land snails made this transition ages ago.

Rocky shores in temperate regions have the greatest variety of life. The submerged portions of tropical coral reefs may have more species, but exposed areas are not as rich. Cold regions, too, have less variety. Under arctic conditions, the scouring action of ice denudes rocky surfaces, and what little life there is survives in crevices.

Limpets cling tenaciously to their places on a rocky shore. They are remarkable because they seem to remain in one place for weeks or even months. These molluscs move around at high tide, often at night (their movement is snail-like). They feed on algae, then go home.

Barnacles attach themselves to sea vessels by secreting a glue of amazing strength. As more barnacles accumulate, the ship is slowed – this is called fouling. On a rocky shore (right), examine these crusty little animals in their closed-up state, then try to dislodge one.

As the tide ebbs on a rocky Atlantic shore, this surf-washed rock reveals a layered community. The lowest layer here is fringed with bladderwrack, a yellow-brown type of algae.

Next comes a band of black lichen, then a wider, still-damp zone inhabited by greyish-white barnacles. At the top, patches of lichens and algae are browsed by periwinkles.

HOW TO
Know your own shore

Choose a relatively small, well-defined area for your survey – a large boulder or two at the edge of the water – not a whole stretch of shore. Eye-catching bands of colour often mark a likely spot.

● See if you can sort out the major classifications of plants and animals – lichens, algae or seaweeds, barnacles, limpets and snails. You might make a zonation chart like the one below.

● As an amateur naturalist, you may find a scarcity of information about common seaside animals and plants. There are several guides to the shells that help in identifying the molluscs, but you will probably have difficulty with lichens and algae. Your public library may be able to suggest sources. You might chip off a hard-shelled specimen or collect empty shells and compare them with displays in a natural history museum.

● Colour photographs of your chosen rocks are perhaps your best record. A sketchbook of the seaweeds and sea creatures is also worthwhile. Or you could press and dry some of the delicate seaweeds as you would leaves.

Zones of plants and ranges of animals on a rocky shore in Britain

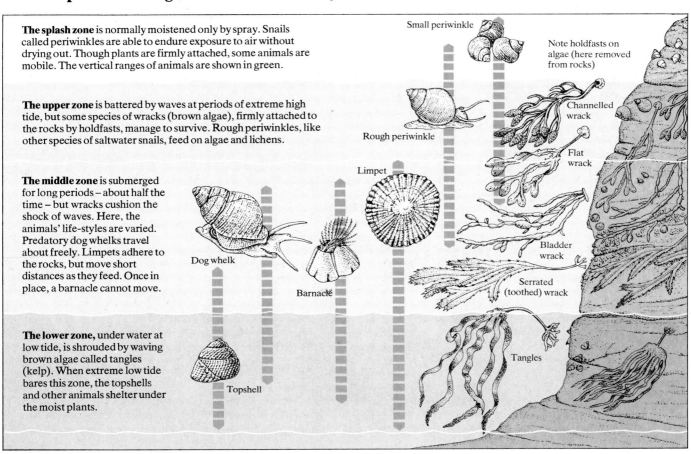

The splash zone is normally moistened only by spray. Snails called periwinkles are able to endure exposure to air without drying out. Though plants are firmly attached, some animals are mobile. The vertical ranges of animals are shown in green.

The upper zone is battered by waves at periods of extreme high tide, but some species of wracks (brown algae), firmly attached to the rocks by holdfasts, manage to survive. Rough periwinkles, like other species of saltwater snails, feed on algae and lichens.

The middle zone is submerged for long periods – about half the time – but wracks cushion the shock of waves. Here, the animals' life-styles are varied. Predatory dog whelks travel about freely. Limpets adhere to the rocks, but move short distances as they feed. Once in place, a barnacle cannot move.

The lower zone, under water at low tide, is shrouded by waving brown algae called tangles (kelp). When extreme low tide bares this zone, the topshells and other animals shelter under the moist plants.

Small periwinkle

Note holdfasts on algae (here removed from rocks)

Rough periwinkle

Channelled wrack

Flat wrack

Limpet

Bladder wrack

Dog whelk

Serrated (toothed) wrack

Barnacle

Tangles

Topshell

Life in a rock pool

A rock pool is a fascinating pocket of life at the edge of the sea. Tucked into a rocky crevice, often camouflaged or rendered inaccessible by slippery algae, these pools are the secret treasuries of the rocky shore. Once you know about them, once you have seen beneath the deceptive reflections of the sky, it is almost guaranteed that you will become entranced by their inhabitants.

Some of the world's most adaptable creatures live in rock pools, where they are alternately drenched (and often pounded) by salty seas, then left landlocked by the outgoing tides.

This is an enormous adjustment for any plant or animal to make: to change environments daily, and so drastically. Despite this, some large pools have such a rich supply of plants and animals that they seem almost to be jungles. Plants predominate – filmy mats and miniature forests of algae. Animal inhabitants, which often lurk among the algae or in crevices, may include crabs; periwinkles; dog whelks or drills, which are predatory snails; small barnacle populations; shrimp-like animals of all sizes from the visible to the microscopic; and limpets.

Not all the animal life in the pool will reveal itself, even if you wait unobtrusively for the crabs and small fish to lose their fear of you and start moving again. Many creatures live under rocks. If you lift a rock to examine them, remember to replace it exactly where you found it and the same way up, otherwise they may die.

No two rock pools are the same. The life forms that a pool supports depend on its size and location on the rocky sea wall. Pools high up on the wall are usually the least populated. Not only must they rely on high tides for their existence – supplemented by water that is splashed up by the waves – but they also have the further problem of being vulnerable to excessive freshwater run-off from higher ground. If a pool receives too much fresh water, even the hardiest of its animals will die.

Pools in the middle of a tidal zone are probably the best to explore. This is because they are likely to be rich in plant and animal inhabitants, and because they are relatively safe to visit. Rock pools located low on the rocks, which are thoroughly washed by sea water and are exposed only for brief periods, are often difficult to explore. Surrounding rocks are likely to be extremely slippery. Such pools should be approached with caution (sometimes even on hands and knees). And beware of getting caught by an incoming tide.

In middle-zone pools, it is easy to dis-tinguish between permanent residents and visitors. Transients such as jellyfish may be trapped in a pool for a while, only to move out with the next tide. You can check on this by visiting the same pool on several consecutive days, seeing which animals have left, which have remained behind, and which are new to the pool.

The depth of a rock pool influences its inhabitants greatly. A deep pool is not likely to have good circulation; fresh water (from rain or run-off) lies on the surface, while the denser salt water accumulates in the deeper part of the basin. This layering limits the travels and in-teractions of the inhabitants, but it may mean that the pool has a greater diversity of species.

Like a flat pan of water, a shallow pool heats up more rapidly than a deep one. Warm water holds less oxygen than cold water, but higher temperatures speed up the metabolism of plants and animals. Consequently, the little oxygen in a warm pool is used up rapidly. Such a pool may choke on its own productivity. Tides and storms, which fill pools, govern their lives. A pool that disappointed you on one visit may be full of life the next time; similarly, an interesting pool can soon deteriorate.

Rock pools are transition zones between sea and shore. The land is alternately soaked in salt water, then left high and dry. Erratic rains and occasional flooding complicate the lives of all inhabitants. Scientists believe that this zone is where some marine forms invaded dry land.

At low tide on a Pacific shore, a turnstone (named after the way it finds food) pauses on a rubbery carpet of green sea anemones.

Flower-like anemones are actually animals. The white tentacles on this Pacific coast species retract during digestion, and only a smooth button is seen.

Which ones are plants, which ones are animals? Lavender coralline algae are slender, twig-like plants, so named because of their resemblance to coral (tiny animals with a brittle skeleton). Royal purple sea urchins, near by, are animals with bristling spines. Lower left is a turquoise sea anemone. Its soft tentacles are armed with minute stinging structures that paralyse small prey; the greenish centre is its mouth.

NATURE OBSERVER
Explore a rock pool with an underwater viewer

All bodies of water, large or small, have a "skin" on them. The molecules of water at the surface adhere more firmly to one another than do molecules surrounded completely by water. From the standpoint of the shore explorer, the effect of this skin-like surface is that light bounces off and dazzles the eye. Even on a grey day, it is hard to see into a rock pool.

• The problem is solved if you put a viewer into the water, one with sides high enough to block out reflected light. A snorkelling mask is ideal for this. It is waterproof, has shielded sides, and may already be part of your beach equipment.

• But an ordinary clear plastic box or cylinder will do just as well – the bottom goes into the pool, and your face stays out of the water. You can also make a viewer by substituting clear plastic for the bottom of a container and attaching the plastic to the sides. (The simplest viewer would be an ordinary soup tin with both ends removed.) Attach the plastic firmly to one end by means of a sturdy rubber band.

• Light travels at different speeds through air and water. So what you see in a pool will be distorted. For instance, when you reach into a pool, the water may turn out to be deeper than you guessed it to be. The snorkelling mask or plastic box will help counteract this distortion.

• Be careful not to damage any plant or animal you pick up. Replace it in the position in which you found it. Even better, just watch it without touching.

117

The amazing world of sea shells

We call them sea shells, but shells, and the living animals that produce them, are distributed world-wide on land and in water. The mollusc group ranges from common garden snails to giant clams on Australia's Great Barrier Reef. And though these huge clams (which may grow to 3 ft in length and weigh several hundred pounds) probably never trapped a diver, as popular legend insists, there are dangerous molluscs: a 2 in. cone shell of the Pacific has killed human beings with its venom.

There are five categories of shells, and it is easy to tell one from another. The *univalves* have a single shell that is usually coiled. *Bivalves* always have two sides, hinged together. Most shells you will find fall into these two categories. *Chitons* have eight overlapping plates and can curl into a ball like a frightened armadillo, *Tusk* or *tooth shells*, which are also few in number, look like conical tubes. The fifth category

is *cephalopods*; although they are numerous, few people think of them as shells because most species (including squid and cuttlefish) grow their "shells" inside their bodies. The spiral-shaped chambered nautilus (shown on p. 111) is the only cephalopod that has an external shell.

About 100,000 species of animals have shells. Each region has its characteristic populations. The cool regions produce shells of subdued colour. In Europe, the mussel, scallop and razor shell are examples of this. Warmer climates produce a greater variety of vividly coloured species, including the great West African land snail, the fluted giant clam from the Philippines, and the deep-purple noble scallop from Japan. Colour pigments are obtained by each animal from food and transported to the shell-forming layer.

Molluscs crawl and leap. Snails have given molluscs a reputation for slow movement, but there are many species,

such as scallops, that are jet-propelled. When a starfish (which consumes a scallop meal as readily as any human being) approaches, the scallop expels a stream of water. This jet-action carries the scallop away in leaps. The foot of some species, like the cockle and the razor shell, can dig an instant home in sand. It becomes a most effective and fast-working spade.

Some molluscs have plagued man: burrowing shipworms have sunk many a wooden-hulled ship, and their close relatives can bore through solid concrete. But people have always treasured shells. Shells have often served as money, and they have been found in ancient tombs, sometimes far from the sea.

A treasury of sea shells washes up with each tide on the beaches of the world. Each region has its own distinctive shell population. These are just a few of them.

Univalves are molluscs with one shell

Most univalves have a spiral shell, though the spiral is not always obvious. A muscular foot enables the animal to move about.

Tentacles

Respiratory holes

Sand collar (egg mass)

Lewis' moon snail is common on the Pacific coast. Eggs are laid in a mucous collar that collects sand.

The green abalone, one of eight Pacific coast species, is now rare. Sea otters seek them out; so do human gourmets.

Inside of shell

Cut-away view

Foot

Alphabet cones, of varied colours and patterns, are favourites with collectors, but the living cones are poisonous.

Egg case

The lightning whelk lays egg cases in long strings. Other whelks lay similar egg cases, which often wash up on shore.

Foot

The knobby keyhole limpet resembles a barnacle and clings just as tightly to a rock.

Inside of shell

Operculum (lid)

The flame auger is rare and highly prized. Like many univalves, it seals its shell with a lid on its foot.

Cone with poisonous barb extended

A shell collection is easy to start. You can find interesting shells in fresh water and even on land, but the seashore offers the greatest variety and largest number of specimens. Even if you do not live near the sea, hunting for shells can add interest and amusement to your holidays.

• Shells that wash up on beaches are usually empty and clean, although they may be damaged. With persistence and luck, you will be able to assemble a fine collection without disturbing any living molluscs or their environment.

• Take a small rake or shovel to uncover shells. A kitchen strainer is useful for sifting small shells out of the sand. You will need some plastic bags to carry your treasures home. Wear plimsolls if you are collecting on a rocky shore.

• The hours before and after low tide are the best for shell hunting. Local newspapers usually publish the times of tides in their area. They change each day as well as varying from place to place.

• When you get home, scrub your shells in warm, soapy water. To remove algae and stains, soak in laundry bleach. Dry shells out of doors, out of direct sunlight so that the colours will not fade. Rub lightly with mineral oil to restore lustre.

• Each shell should be identified by a number in indian ink, protected by a coat of clear nail polish. Record this number, name of the species, date and location in a loose-leaf notebook or card file. You will need to consult a reference book to help in identification.

• You can display your finds by cementing them to glass, or by arranging them in labelled carboard trays or wooden drawers in a cabinet. Keep tiny shells in vials plugged with cottonwool or in small plastic boxes. If you have many large shells like conchs and whelks, display them prominently on coffee tables and bookcases.

• If you care to turn some of your shells into brooches, ear-rings and necklaces, you will be carrying on a practice thousands of years old.

ivalves have two hinged shells

bivalve's left and right halves may look alike, but e always different. A ligament connects the shells.

llop swims by pping shells ejecting ter

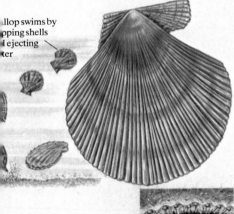

e Iceland scallop is a lourful Atlantic species. allops have up to 100 blue es set around the edge of e fleshy part (the mantle).

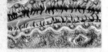

Mantle edge with eyes

Mantle

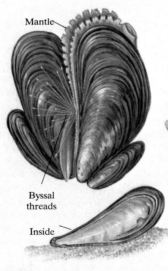

Byssal threads

Inside

Common blue mussels spin a tough thread (byssus) by which they attach themselves to rocks and piers. In Europe, mussels are prized as seafood.

The jackknife clam swims well and burrows quickly out of sight, using its extensible foot. Razor clams are related species with broader shells.

Jackknife clam burrowing

Extruded foot

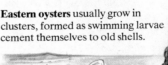

Eastern oysters usually grow in clusters, formed as swimming larvae cement themselves to old shells.

Oyster clusters

hitons have eight plates

overed with plates (valves) instead of single shell, the primitive chiton clings intertidal rocks with a suction foot.

he West Indian chiton is ed locally for food. Most itons are small, but one ant Pacific species may ow to 12 in. in length.

Side view

Underside shows oval foot

Tusk shells have open ends

Water moves in and out of the tusk shell through the narrower opening; feeding threads extend through the wider end.

The Indian money tusk digs into the sea floor and feeds on minute animals. The shells were used as money by Pacific tribes.

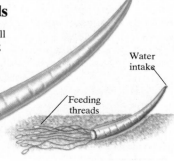

Water intake

Feeding threads

Birds of the rocky shores

The world's great seabird colonies, which crowd the precipitous cliffs and boulder-strewn edges of rocky shores, are established there for two reasons. One is the availability of suitable nesting sites; the other is the abundant supply of fish in nearby waters.

Both sides of the North Atlantic – from Labrador to Maine, from Iceland and Spitsbergen south to the British Isles – have their famous seabird colonies, often many centuries old. For the most part, the North Atlantic seabirds are chunky, short-winged species called auks or alcids (members of the family *Alcidae*). In general, these birds correspond to the penguins of the Southern Hemisphere; and with their half-black, half-white plumage and upright stance, they certainly resemble penguins (though they are not related).

There are many kinds of auks, and you often see them together in one colony – razorbills, common guillemots (called murres in America), black guillemots, and the familiar, irresistible common puffins. The Pacific coast of North America has

Yellow-plumed rockhopper penguins breed on remote islands in the cold seas near Antarctica. More easily visited colonies, with other kinds of penguins, dot the coasts of South Africa, Australia, South America, and even the Galápagos Islands, which are near the equator.

Noisy northern gannets crowd cliffs on both sides of the Atlantic. Offshore, these strong fliers and spectacular divers are easy to spot.

tufted and horned puffins, auklets (small auks), and murrelets.

Whether or not you are a seasoned birdwatcher, a visit to one of the well-known bird cliffs – such as Skomer off the Welsh coast, Noss in the Shetland Islands or Bonaventure Island off Canada's Gaspe Peninsula – is an experience to be treasured. When seen from a small boat (the best way to get the full effect of the teeming colony), layers upon layers of gleaming, white-breasted birds tower above you. Every ledge, every cranny, has its contingent of birds.

At the water's edge, boulders are animated by adult birds, relieved for the moment of the tasks of brooding eggs or young. The parents take turns bringing home quantities of small fish to feed their ravenous chicks. The swelling surf on which your boat bobs up and down is carpeted with swimming and diving auks; you can follow them underwater by the flash of their brightly coloured feet and legs.

Meanwhile, hundreds of others go whirring over your head on stubby, fast-beating wings. There may also be a mass flight of dove-like kittiwakes (a small species of gull), touched off by some sudden alarm.

The noise produced by a seabird colony is indescribable. Each species contributes its own raucous or piercing cry, caw, kik-kik-kik, growl, or snarl. And through-out the tumult, streamlined gannets, the largest birds in the colony, cut the air in their stupendous, straight-down dives.

Chaotic though a bird cliff may appear, it is really an organised, orderly community. Each species of bird has its own preference as to location on the cliff. For example, black guillemots lay their eggs in crevices among the boulders at the foot of the cliff; if cormorants are present, they build their untidy nests in this area. Narrow ledges along the steep face are crowded with row after row, by species, of razor-bills and guillemots, which lay a single, large egg directly on bare rock. Gannets occupy wide ledges at the top of the cliff.

Harsh though the conditions of life on a rocky shore may seem to a human observer, the birds obviously thrive and multiply. Living in a crowd stimulates mating activities. Seabirds are very curious – watching the neighbours and following their example, whatever they may be doing. Within the huge colony, the birds of each neighbourhood are thus stimulated to mate and lay their eggs in the space of a few days. The greater the number of breeders, the earlier they tend to mate. (Pairs on the outside of the colony tend to mate last.)

This synchronised behaviour makes for a co-ordinated defence against the inevitable egg robbing and chick snatching by predators, such as herring gulls, that haunt the colonies.

Clown-like common puffins burrow in turf or dig nests under rocks in Europe and eastern Canada. (Other puffin species live on Pacific shores. The Southern Hemisphere counterparts are penguins.) Once the breeding season is over, their gaudy beaks become paler.

🦅 BIRDWATCHING TIPS
Seaside techniques

The most important tip for birdwatching on the shore is to make sure you will be comfortable. Take along insect repellent, sun lotion, sunglasses, and a brimmed hat to shade your eyes (intense glare reflected off the water can be very tiring). A long-sleeved shirt and a sweater (or jacket) are advisable. Early morning or late afternoon are the best times to observe gulls, terns, and other shorebirds.

● On cliffs and rocky shores, wear sturdy shoes with rock-gripping soles – a sprained ankle means trouble. The edges of a cliff may be undercut, and can crumble beneath you. A strong gust of wind may throw a child or lightweight adult off balance. So keep well back from the edge. A cliff is no place to go by yourself.

● You can usually get a good look at cliff-dwelling birds by approaching from below. Check for high tide if you go on foot. Viewing from a boat is even easier. At some of the better-known birdwatching islands, boat trips can be arranged to take you near the nesting sites of seabirds.

● On beaches and mud flats, plan your excursion during migration periods in spring or late summer (shorebirds leave for the south early). Time the visit so you will arrive at low tide (local newspapers give tide tables). Low tide exposes small marine animals that attract numerous birds.

● The upper beach is the place to look for plovers and other small shorebirds. Dunes may shelter colonies of gulls and terns, or sea swallows. Never walk through a breeding colony, and never let a dog run loose. The adult birds will inevitably leave in a panic, and eggs and chicks will be exposed to predatory gulls and hot sun. If a tern attacks you by diving at your head, you are too close.

● A beach trip in winter can be rewarding. A jetty or pier makes a good place from which to sweep the ocean with telescope or binoculars for diving ducks and grebes. Pay attention to rocks and breakwaters for small flocks of birds such as sandpipers.

● At any time of year, a visit to the beach after a severe storm may turn up rare oceanic or tropical birds blown far from their usual range. It is worth getting in touch with the local birdwatching organisation before you visit an area. Hides for birdwatchers have been built in many of the best sites round the British coast, and genuine nature-lovers are usually welcome.

Birds on the beach

Twice a year, the beaches of the world are flooded with shorebirds – long-distance migrants from the tundra and uplands of the far north. In late July and early August, after a mere six weeks of hatching and rearing a family, tiny sandpipers, sturdy plovers and long-legged waders begin their southward journeys. Some travel to the tip of South America or Africa, to Australia, or to islands in the Pacific.

Birds have impressive navigational skills. Often parent birds depart for the south earlier than their offspring. Young birds travelling in juvenile flocks find their own way to ancestral feeding grounds.

Then, after having the benefit of a second summer of sunny days and abundant food in the Southern Hemisphere, many return to the north using a different route from their first journey. Nevertheless they arrive back in the regions of their birth.

Travelling in either direction (north or south), shorebirds land frequently to feed and rest. Because they come in wave upon wave, with many leaving or arriving during the night, they seem to be full-time summer residents. For many European birds, the resting place may be on a beach by the Adriatic, a Corsican cliff, a rocky headland on the Côte d'Azur, or by the Bay of Biscay. Further north, migrants may linger in the sheltered coves of England's south coast.

The best place for novice birdwatchers to identify shorebirds that look alike is a sandy shore where mud flats are exposed by retreating tides. The small birds, that busily scurry about or rest in compact flocks can be confusing. But a mixed flock can actually be of assistance in identification. Field guides often tell you which birds tend to associate with one another. When you have identified one species, you have a size comparison, and some hint as to the others in the flock.

Identification can be aided, too, by the fact that some species do not form flocks,

The differences between a gull and a tern

Compare the herring gull (right) with the common terns shown below. Gulls and terns are close relatives – they make up the family of long-winged, web-footed birds called *Laridae*. Typical adult birds in this family are grey and white, accented with black. Gulls and terns nest in large colonies and are found all over the world, except in some deserts; they live on inland waters as well as near the sea. Here are some tips to help you tell one from the other:

• Although both gulls and terns vary in size, gulls are usually large, robust birds. Terns are smaller, more slender and streamlined.

• Gulls have long, stout legs and are good walkers. Terns have short legs and seldom walk about.

• Gulls are scavengers – they pick up scraps from the water or shore. Terns dive for living prey, often submerging completely when they dive.

• Gulls swim or float in the water. A tern's feet are not adapted for swimming; after capturing prey, terns fly upwards immediately. They alight on water only to bathe.

• Gulls croak harshly or mew and scream at one another. Terns squawk raucously or utter rasping kee-ars or staccato kik-kik-kiks.

• Gulls build nests of dry grass or sticks. Terns simply scoop out shallow holes in the sand, or among pebbles and broken shells.

• Newly hatched gulls and terns are covered with down. Gulls take several years to develop adult plumage; during this time, they may be difficult to identify. In contrast, young terns (once they have shed their down) resemble the adults.

but are usually seen singly or in pairs – the avocet and the oystercatcher are examples, as are many other long-legged, long-billed waders.

Behaviour is also a help in identification. For example, the straight-billed dowitcher has a feeding action like a sewing machine. Sanderlings, as their name suggests, patter back and forth on sandy beaches, and neither enter the water nor venture into the dune grass higher up on the beach. On the other hand, the mixed flocks of small sandpipers and plovers often rest on the sand, but they feed in muddy areas. Skimmers (black-and-white relatives of terns) feed by skimming along the water with their large red beaks open, scooping up prey.

In spring, the presence of shorebirds in breeding plumage simplifies identification. Then, it is easy to spot the strikingly marked black-bellied plover, the much smaller dunlin with a black belly patch, the stocky little knot with its rusty breast.

In autumn you may spot the white wing-patches of a skua on its passage south. Skuas are pirates, forcing gulls and terns to disgorge their catches.

Not all the birds of the beach can be seen only during migration – some species are also summer residents. Piping and snowy plovers, both as pale as the sand itself, breed above the high-tide line. Upper beaches and dunes are nesting areas for gulls and terns. Herring gulls and great black-backed gulls, fierce predators on tern colonies, often nest near their victims.

Gulls and terns deserve a second look. Many people think all gulls look alike. Actually, there are obvious differences between species – comparative size, wing marks, banded or unbanded tail, dark or light mantle (plumage of back and upper wings) – that will be revealed by a closer examination. And the same holds true for the flashing, diving terns, with their slender bodies and long wings.

Herring gull

Gulls are strong fliers, with a slow, regular beat of their broad wings; their tails are square or rounded. They often soar on thermals (warm air), or ride air currents created by ships, or glide low over water.

Common tern

Terns are graceful fliers. Their wings are long and narrow, their tails more or less deeply forked. Terns often hover with rapidly beating wings and bills pointed down. They rarely soar or glide.

 PHOTO TIPS
Capturing bird behaviour on film

If you approach slowly and quietly, birds of the shore will often go about their business – thus providing you with many opportunities to record their various life-styles. (Photography is often the way a birdwatcher starts recognising birds.)
• Shorebirds move quickly. You need a very fast lens or very good luck – or both. Come prepared to take many photographs (inevitably, some shots will not be in focus).
• A flock of shorebirds makes an excellent subject. The photograph below illustrates two aspects of sanderling behaviour: they tend to keep by themselves, and often face in one direction – into the wind.
• Courtship behaviour is a difficult but rewarding subject. You may be lucky enough, for example, to film a tern presenting its mate with a small fish.
• Be careful about intruding when shorebirds have eggs or very young chicks. If you want to take a photograph, use a telephoto lens.
• Preening, feeding, and fighting are other activities to look for when you have a camera on the seashore.

Shadows and reflections of sanderlings at rest make a pleasing pattern of light and dark. A telephoto lens is necessary for capturing a flock of skittish shorebirds on film.

Inhabitants of the sand

As waves wash the shore and then retreat back to the sea, the hard-packed beach resembles a freshly swept pavement – clean and flat, except for an occasional hole or hump in the sand. But if you know what to look for, the seemingly empty stretch of sand is crammed with life. And if you are fast enough, you may even be able to catch some of the residents.

As any child who has ever made sand castles can tell you, moist sand is an excellent building material – it holds its shape well. Most inhabitants of the sandy shore take advantage of this, and excavate homes for themselves.

Where are all the residents of the sand?

The next time you watch a wave sweep over a beach, look for tell-tale signs. As the thin sheet of water goes back down the beach, tiny bumps appear in the sand. If, as soon as a bump appears, you quickly scoop out a double handful of sand, you may pick up the animal that is responsible for the bump. You can tell whether you have caught it if you feel a tickling on your hands as you hold the sand. Do not be afraid – this is just a little animal, perhaps a shy masked crab, trying to escape danger by digging deeper. If you carefully sift the sand between your hands you may actually see the crab, which may not be much larger than a grasshopper. If you do not get the crab in the first scoop of sand, stop trying. No matter how fast you dig, it will always dig faster.

Masked crabs move up and down the beach with the tides, thus staying at the water's edge. They feed by digging just below the surface of the sand; their antennae project into the film of backwash and filter out minute marine plants and animals. Sometimes these exposed antennae reveal a crab's hiding place in the sand.

Most beaches have a line of rubble – pebbles, shells and debris – that is tumbled up and down the beach with the waves. In this debris you may notice a shell that seems mysteriously to defy the rush of the water, often moving against the current. Take a closer look at such a shell; you may discover that, unlike the other shells, it has an occupant. Its inhabitant is a hermit crab, a "squatter" that moved in after the original owner vacated the shell. If you are patient, you may see two eye-stalks emerge as the crab peers out. It is safe to pick up hermit crabs if they are relatively small.

The same shell often provides house and home for other creatures. On the outside there may be a colony of hydroids – tiny animals related to coral polyps – or perhaps a much bigger brown-striped anemone. Indoors, the crab sometimes has worms and barnacles as guests.

Further up the beach, just above the top range of the waves, you may notice holes that are about the size a mouse might make. The owners of these holes – called porcelain crabs – scurry furtively near the mouths of their burrows. They are camouflaged by their sandy colour to the point where they seem to vanish. And their holes also seem to disappear around midday, when the animals temporarily seal themselves in for a brief "siesta". The best time for watching porcelain crabs is at night, when they emerge in large numbers to feed. You may even catch a platoon in the beam of a torch.

In addition to the many species of crabs on a beach, there are ghost shrimps, which construct complicated burrows there. Cockles bury themselves in the sand, projecting their siphons into the waters of a rising tide. Lugworms reveal their presence by castings left in the sand outside their burrows. Sometimes, too, there are visitors from the sea – horseshoe crabs (which are not crabs but relatives of the scorpions), sea turtles and seals. These animals, which breed on the shore, arrive in vast numbers – and the result is an impressive sight for any human visitors who are there at the right time.

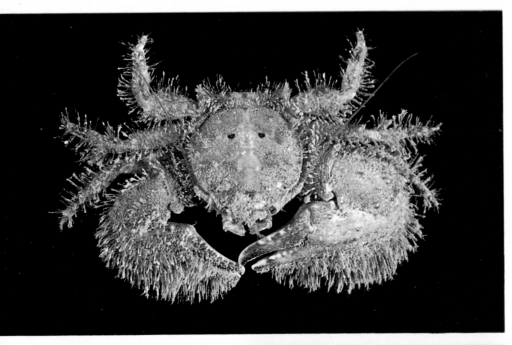

With body raised high, a hairy porcelain crab surveys its surroundings, ready to take evasive action. Its bulbous eyes swivel around and enable it to spot an enemy approaching from any quarter. Scuttling sideways, the crab moves with amazing speed, vanishing into its burrow – it is seldom captured, even on film. Its body is about 1 in. across.

The hermit crab borrows the armour of other animals – mainly empty shells. As it grows, the hermit crab must seek a larger home. When it finds a suitable shell, a quick transfer takes place. The crab is most vulnerable at this time because its own body defences are weak. (Its soft abdominal membrane affords no protection from enemies.)

As waves ride up the beach, they form thin layers that retain a separate identity to a remarkable degree. The cross-hatched pattern on the sand is made by the backwash of the waves. If you look closely, you will see there are also small, rounded breathing holes made by sand-dwellers.

Burrowing animals hidden beneath the surface

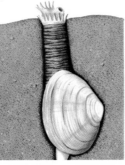

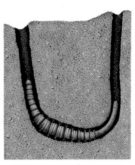

Masked crabs move with the tide, and feed with antennae above the sand.

Ghost shrimps constantly sift the sand for food with their flattened appendages.

Soft-shell clams draw in food and air through long, flexible tubes (siphons).

Lugworms, like earthworms, digest organic matter in the soft mud they excavate.

Porcelain crabs dig holes in dry sand, but return to water to wet their gills.

125

The shifting of sandy shores

Sandy beaches are constantly moving. The next time you are on a beach, simply stand at the water's edge and wait. Soon your toes – then perhaps both feet – will be covered by sand. The waves keep the sand in continual motion, with the result that some of it slips out from under your feet, starting at the edges, and you may sink slightly. At the same time, you will find small deposits building up on the top of your feet. On most large beaches, countless tons of sand are moved along this way in a single day.

To discover which way the sand is moving, watch the waves as they wash up on the beach. Keep your eyes on some small object (perhaps a shell or bit of seaweed) to see in which direction it is being carried. The motion is not just upwards; it is also sideways.

You will also probably notice that some of the water in each wave sinks into the sand rather than flowing back into the sea. As the water disappears, it deposits its floating cargo – bits of shells, grains of sand, pieces of seaweed and driftwood. Some water seeps out of the sand and runs back to the sea in tiny rivulets. But little sand is transported this way.

In addition to sand, the waves deposit pebbles and, if the waves are strong enough, even large rocks. Look at the slope of a beach on your next visit. Generally, the steeper the slope, the larger and more violent were the waves that brought the sand.

Since most waves run obliquely to the coast, their effect is to shift sand, pebbles and rocks along the shore. Breakwaters are built to tame the waves and prevent beaches shifting elsewhere. You can see how effective they are: on one side of a breakwater, sand and pebbles are usually higher than on the other.

The force of waves is amazing. A gale striking the coast of Scotland once swept away a concrete breakwater weighing 2,600 tons. On the eastern coast of North America, storm-driven waves sent a 135 lb. rock flying through the roof of a 91 ft high lighthouse. Such tremendous forces are constantly pounding rocky coasts, converting rock into fragments, and eventually into sand.

Most sand originates inland, produced by the weathering and erosion of rocks. Pebbles and sand are transported by rivers and may be carried far out to sea by the current. But this sand may still find its way to the beach. Currents dredge up and can deposit sand from as deep as 50 ft beneath the surface. On many coasts, there are continental shelves (the submerged edges of continents) that are relatively shallow. In such places, river-borne sand may be dropped, only to be picked up again, and sometimes become part of a beach.

Most sandy beaches in the temperate zones are light brown or grey, shading into white. Generally, the coarse, light-coloured sand is pulverised granite; fine grey sand is from basalt. In the tropics, the beaches are more varied. For example, on one side of Tahiti the beaches are a brilliant white – the sand originated in the adjacent coral reefs. On the other side of the island the beaches are jet black – the sand was derived from lava beds.

A beach may even be supplied with sand by wind blowing from a desert. For example, the prevailing winds over the Sahara carry sand to the Mediterranean region. Although the powerful wind carries the sand to the sea, it is the waves that do most of the work of gathering the sand into beaches.

Another beach phenomenon to look for is the way that waves pile up particles and sort them out. The larger pieces, such as pebbles, are not carried as far up the beach as the finer ones. On a California beach, thousands of tin cans were once washed ashore. The waves neatly sorted the cans, with the largest at the bottom of the beach and the smallest at the top.

On shores where a sandy beach exists at the edge of rocks, high storm waves may wash nearly all of the sand out beyond the surf. But during calm weather, smaller waves may re-deposit the sand, clean and fresh, as if it had just been laundered.

NATURE OBSERVER
Walking dunes, miniature deltas, and sand close-ups

A beach holiday is full of opportunities to try out sand experiments.

• Dunes are ideal places to observe the movement of sand, because dunes really do walk. A large dune may move forward by as much as 20 ft a year; small dunes move even faster. (The diagram below shows how you can gauge this movement.)

• Look for an area of walking dunes where sand is beginning to cover the bases of bushes and trees. Eventually, the sand will smother the plants. The dead trunks will later be uncovered, sand-polished by the wind. These relics make interesting photographs.

• Where grass grows over the dunes, look for circular marks etched in the sand as the wind swings the tough grass blades. This, too, is a good subject for photographs.

• Watch how the receding water cuts channels in the beach and deposits sand and gravel, forming miniature deltas. Here is a chance to play dam-builder. You can divert or stop the flow of water and alter the shape of a delta by moving several of the stones.

• Digging in moist sand is also appealing, especially to youngsters, but beach-goers of all ages can enjoy building elaborate sand castles. Sand sculpture has enjoyed a wide popularity in recent years. Marvellous dragons and innovative architectural forms have won prizes in a number of contests.

• When you dig on the lower beach, you reach water quickly; digging on the upper beach, you have to go far deeper. The depth of the hole will give an approximation of the height of the beach above water level.

• Pieces of "beach glass" are artificial sand treasures – actually, they are fragments of bottles, polished smooth by years of jostling with sand and pebbles in the surf. Beach glass comes in different colours, with blue the most prized.

• A close-up study of sand will reveal many kinds of particles. Use a magnifying glass and see if you can pick out individual grains of quartz or shell. Ruby-red specks may be bits of garnet. A magnet will allow you to collect particles of iron ore.

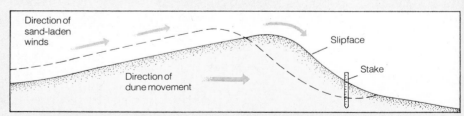

In a simple demonstration, you can see for yourself how fast sand travels – even how an entire dune moves along. Choose a moderately breezy day and a small dune. Place a stake on the sheltered side of the dune, a few inches from the crest. Soon you will notice that the grains of sand are moving up the windward side and accumulating at the crest. There, the wind combines with the weight of accumulated sand to push it down the steep front, or slipface. Thus the whole mass moves closer and closer to your stake. In this way prevailing winds from the sea move dunes gradually inland.

An aerial view of the tip of Cape Cod on America's north-east coast gives a good idea of its structure. Rocky deposits laid down by glaciers some 30,000 years ago formed the basis of the Cape. A similar peninsula has been formed by waves pounding against Britain's Norfolk coast at Scolt Head. Vegetation holds the sand in some sections, but there are long stretches of bare sand, and many places where the sea can invade.

A miniature river system on a sandy, stone-dotted beach mimics the braided flow of some large rivers. (This could be an aerial view of a full-scale river.) The overlapping pattern develops only when water flows down a sloping bed, bearing a load of coarse sediment. In certain places, the water drops its load and the channels widen and grow shallow. Then they divide and join, repeatedly, until the tide washes everything flat again.

Variegated grains of sand on a beach include polished bits of white shell and many fragments of quartz and other rocks, torn from nearby surf-battered cliffs. This photograph was taken from a distance of about 2 in., using a close-up lens attachment.

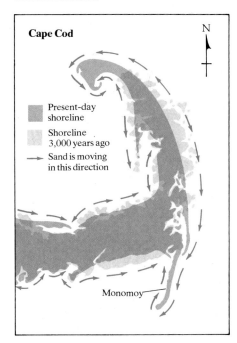

Cape Cod

N

Present-day shoreline

Shoreline 3,000 years ago

Sand is moving in this direction

Monomoy

The crooked elbow of Cape Cod began to take shape many thousands of years ago, when increasing amounts of sand were deposited at the end of a curving spit. The ocean currents that carried this burden are still at work, constantly swinging around Monomoy, building up and washing away shoals, sand bars and beaches as they go.

Dune plants that stabilise beaches

To the casual eye, sand dunes behind a water-washed beach may seem somewhat untidy. But this beach backdrop, with its scattering of vegetation, is worth a second look.

Most dunes are born of small accumulations of debris, or perhaps a piece of driftwood. Blocked by this insignificant obstruction, the ocean winds that cross the beach lose much of their force and drop any sand they may have picked up. A little mound forms, enlarges into a hillock and eventually into a dune. Some dunes grow eventually to a height of more than 100 ft.

Dunes are tough going for would-be climbers, whose feet sink into the sand. They are also inhospitable to many plants and animals. Consider the deterrents – strong wind, salty spray, hot sun, and the probability of being overwhelmed by drifting sand. Many seeds wafted into the dunes by the wind manage to sprout, only to perish quickly.

But certain plants – beach grasses – are adapted to this difficult area. They sprout readily and send numerous runners into the sand. Though such plants may look fragile, they are durable and tenacious. They have an ability to grow back to the surface if their leaves are buried, to bend with the wind, and to survive drought, heat and cold.

Beach grasses knit together a network of roots and stems, and the dune acquires a degree of permanence. (Beach grasses, especially a species known as marram grass, are often planted for the express purpose of stabilising a dune area.) The sparse vegetation, serving as a windbreak, traps additional wind-blown sand, and the dune keeps growing. Though the grasses may look insignificant, these plants are the dune's defence against being blown away.

Beach grasses are pioneer plants – they create an environment more attractive to other species of plants, and thus encourage colonisation by animals. Slowly, the dune changes character. Rest harrow trails along the sand, adding brilliant flecks of rose and purple when it flowers. Sea holly, an ashy grey plant native to Europe and now a common resident of North American dunes, also creeps along the sand. Shrubs take hold, including such species as privet or myrtle (evergreens with wax-covered fruits, which are used in making scented candles). Eventually, the dune may be transformed into a woodland. If you walk away from the sea, cutting across ridges of dunes, you may traverse all these plant stages, until you finally reach the trees.

To protect the dunes at a delicate stage of their development, visitors are sometimes asked to keep away. But most seaside resorts with dunes welcome careful visitors. On a fresh sunny day their hollows make ideal sites for sunbathing, sheltered from the wind yet open to the sky. Parking is often provided near by.

In some coastal areas, you may encounter another beach phenomenon – the development of a barrier beach. As waves shift the sand to offshore shallows, a sand bar begins to rise. After many years, it may be high enough to show above the water. At first, the sand bar appears and disappears, as storm-driven waves wash over it and seasonal currents displace the accumulated sand. Eventually, these forces cut channels between segments of the bar, and water surges in and out of the protected area between the bar and the shore. In effect, the rise of the sand bar creates a lagoon between itself and the mainland. As the barrier beach becomes more stable, dunes form, plants become established, and the whole drama is repeated.

Densely matted roots of dune grass and marram help to stabilise spreading dunes. These pioneer plants are highly resistant to violent winds, strong sunlight and salty spray, but despite this protection, dunes are still vulnerable. Vehicles should stay on established roads.

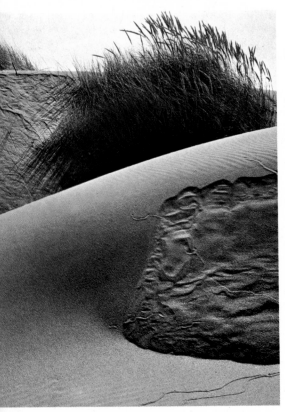

Sturdy clumps of beach grass struggle to hold down these dunes, where the constant wind cuts away at the surface of shifting sands.

Above high-tide line on a beach, vetch hugs the ground and traps blown sand with its leaves and blossoms.

Five stages in the life history of a sand dune

This series of profiles shows the growth of a new dune and the role of plants in both the establishment and protection of a dune. At the start, winds and waves deposit sand on a mainland beach or on a newly emerged sand bar. Dunes follow a fairly predictable pattern of development. In time, there will be primary and secondary dunes (named not for their order of formation, but for their position relative to the ocean). They act as a defence against assaults of wind and spray. They can also be a dangerous place for children.

A dune begins when sand is blown inland by strong winds and accumulates. Here, a sand-bar beach between the ocean and a bay is relatively barren at first.

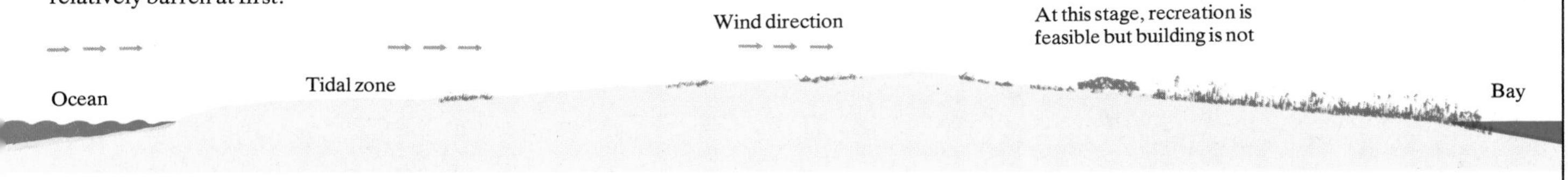

Wind direction

At this stage, recreation is feasible but building is not

Ocean

Tidal zone

Bay

Dune build-up starts where small clumps of beach grass and other plants arrest the wind-blown sand. This eventually becomes the secondary dune. Shrubs grow behind it.

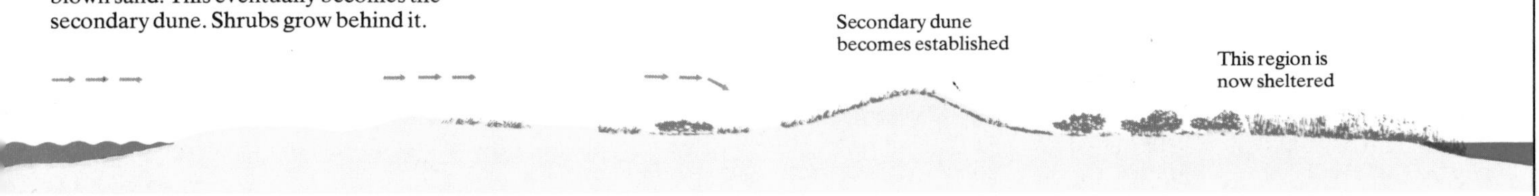

Secondary dune becomes established

This region is now sheltered

As beach grass grows towards the sea a primary dune forms in front of the secondary dune. Behind the secondary dune, a thicket of privet and woodbine springs up.

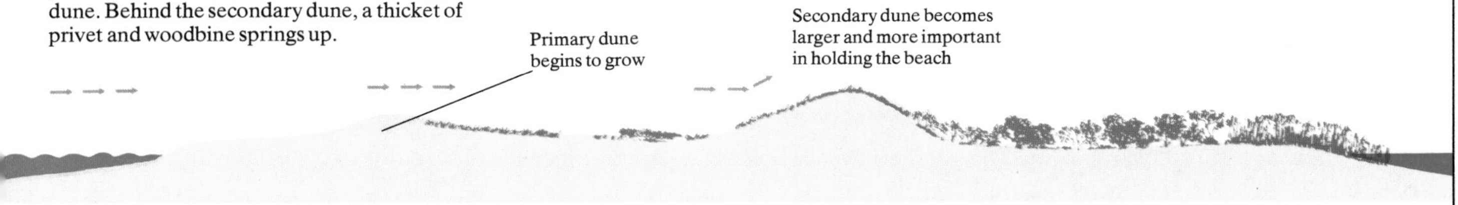

Primary dune begins to grow

Secondary dune becomes larger and more important in holding the beach

In the sheltered duneslack or trough between the dunes, shrubby growth joins the grasses. Pines and other conifers begin to climb up the back slope of the secondary dune.

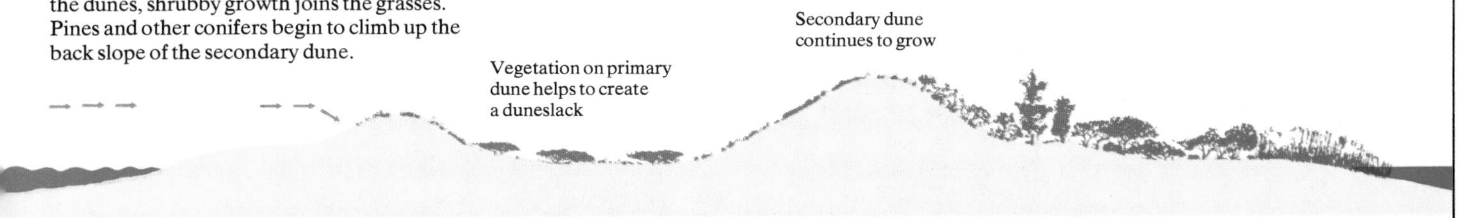

Vegetation on primary dune helps to create a duneslack

Secondary dune continues to grow

The stabilised secondary dune now has tall trees and dense shrubs. The plant cover increases in the trough, and beach grass invades the tidal zone.

Trough is now suitable for picnicking and camping

This region is eligible for some building

Marshy region encourages wildlife

Salt marsh: a living powerhouse

Marshy shores look inviting from a distance, but they are best appreciated from a small boat or from higher, more solid ground. Close approach is deterred by tall, tough grasses. The muddy flats require heavy rubber boots, and there is often a pungent odour that is less than inviting. Consequently, few people have first-hand knowledge of the rich life forms of a marsh – a region with more wildlife than any other type of coast.

Unlike the waters of other shores, those of a salt marsh are usually placid. The plants and animals do not have to withstand a pounding surf or surging sea for any length of time. In fact, a salt marsh will form only in a bay or quiet estuary where the shore is protected from coastal currents. Only there can silt, clay, and plant and animal debris collect and form a muddy bottom – the base of a salt marsh. Even the tides are relatively gentle, ebbing and flowing along meandering channels through the reeds.

Occasionally, of course, storms do sweep a salt marsh. At such times, a marsh serves as a natural breakwater – the resilient plants bend and sway as they absorb the impact of high winds and crashing waves. The result is that areas inland from the marsh are sheltered from the fury of stormy seas.

Grasses are the dominant plants in a salt marsh. Tall grasses and reeds grow along the edges of tidal channels. Characteristically, these sturdy plants are both salt-tolerant and adapted to occasional freshwater runoff from the land. Within the embankments of these tall plants, short grasses and other low-growing plants fill the flat stretches.

Where the marsh borders solid land the ground usually rises gently, and the vegetation changes. Short grasses blend with the taller sedges – these are plants that thrive in salty mud but cannot tolerate immersion in sea water for any length of time. Still further back, seaside golden rod and rose mallow bloom in late summer.

The plant production of a typical salt marsh is enormous. It exceeds the plant material produced by a wheat field of equal area. It has been estimated that sugar cane is the only crop that can out-produce a salt marsh in sheer volume of plant material.

Marsh vegetation provides a food base for a large and diverse community of animals. The first to catch your eye – perhaps even before you see the marsh itself – may be gulls and terns flying over the marsh. You may also notice a marsh harrier diving swiftly to catch a water vole swimming for the muddy bank. Numerous other birds stay concealed in the grasses, taking flight only when you venture too close.

Scuttling from one clump of reed to the next go muskrats, mammals well adapted to water-life, while sleek otters patrol the channels in pursuit of fish shoals.

But even the bare mud, exposed by low tide, contains a wealth of animal life. Marine biologists have estimated that an acre of marsh mud may contain as many as 82,000 individuals of a single species of worm. These and many other mud-dwellers live by filtering tiny plants and animals and bits of decaying matter from the water. These creatures, along with millions of bacteria, process immense quantities of food. What they consume ultimately fertilises the mud, and gives the marsh its great vitality.

A frequently overlooked asset of a marsh is its capacity to produce oxygen, and to filter impurities from the air and water. This may seem like a paradox, if you consider the heavy odour usually associated with a marsh. Nevertheless, a salt marsh on the outskirts of a city improves the air quality for local inhabitants, as well as providing interest for nature lovers.

Key to marsh animals

1. Yellow wagtail
2. Muskrat
3. Marsh harrier
4. Otter
5. Water rail
6. Grey heron
7. Reed warbler with nest
8. Cockles
9. Shore crab
10. Swan mussels
11. Black tern

Early on a summer morning, a salt marsh is a hive of activity. Its dense growth of salt-tolerant weeds provides a congenial environment for many kinds of wildlife. Cockles and swan mussels are embedded in the mud waiting for food that the rising tide will bring. A shore crab leaves its burrow in search of breakfast.

Standing in the shallows a grey heron awaits the glint in the water that tells it to start catching fish. Three young reed warblers beg for food from their harassed parent, clinging to a reed, while nearby a black tern sits on its nest at the water's edge. Across the little creek a water rail treads daintily on the mud, looking for worms and shrimp-like creatures among the Norfolk reed, through which it can slip like an eel. Overhead a yellow wagtail captures a dragonfly on the wing, while further up the creek a sleek otter returns home from fishing. Had they spotted the marsh harrier on the skyline, the smaller birds would be taking cover, like the muskrat swimming towards its nearby nest. Beyond the marsh lies the North Sea, with its fierce gales and icy currents. But here the wildlife cycle goes on undisturbed by such harsh conditions and virtually free from human interference, provided the marsh is not polluted by oil-tar and chemical waste.

The land-building mangroves

Some shores are built by trees. The unique mangroves grow in places where other trees and shrubs cannot survive – in the wet, salty world of tide-washed tropical and subtropical seas. Along such coasts, mangroves have created virtual jungles on stilts.

Most trees produce seeds that do not sprout immediately, even if they are planted. But one of several mangrove species, the red mangrove, produces exceptional seeds – they sprout while they are still attached to the branch. A root bursts through the fruit and forms a long, dagger-like point that may reach 9 in. in length. When the seed finally detaches itself from the branch, it falls, often planting itself upright in the soft, muddy bottom.

A mangrove seedling floats horizontally in the water, like a well-designed canoe. This explains how mangroves spread, from coastline to coastline. The seedling can float for months, unaffected by salt water, scorching sun, and battering waves – and even continue to grow. Its sharp root tip turns downwards; if the seedling strikes land, it quickly sends roots into the soil. New roots emerge in tiers that extend out and downwards from the trunk, forming arches (called prop roots) that resemble umbrella stays. The prop roots may send up new trunks where they touch the ground. Red mangroves are so well braced that they can usually survive hurricanes that flatten other trees.

In 20 or 30 years, the red mangrove reaches its maximum height (about 30 ft). The profusion of prop roots and new tree trunks forms a dense, interlacing mesh that traps sediment, plants and debris. Soon a swamp is formed at the edge of the sea. Gradually, as more mangroves sprout up, new land is created. Every year, the land edges a few more inches into the sea.

Some kinds of mangroves, including the black mangrove, do not have prop roots, but send roots up from beneath the soggy ground. These "air roots", which may be 1 ft or more high, absorb oxygen from the air when the underground roots are covered.

There is a definite sequence to the seaward march of a mangrove swamp. In the Florida Keys of the United States, where mangroves have built vast areas of new land and new islands, the youngest and smallest red mangroves grow next to the water. Their roots are usually submerged, except during the lowest tides. Behind them, washed only by high tide, are the taller black mangroves, which grow to 70 ft. Their thick branches and dark dense foliage form a nearly solid canopy.

Trees and other plants more typical of the land grow behind the mangroves, but in the swamps, mangroves usually crowd out other vegetation. Numerous animals depend on mangroves for protection and support. Oysters attach themselves to the prop roots, where they are covered by high tides. At night these oyster beds are raided by raccoons. Fiddler crabs burrow in the mud between the roots; starfish move slowly over the muddy surface. High up in the dense canopy, large colonies of pelicans and herons may roost and nest.

These may spell danger for the whole life-system. Bird droppings (guano) are highly active chemically, and if the bird colony gets too numerous the guano will scorch the mangrove leaves until all the trees die. But even as one thicket succumbs, another may be beginning where a single seedling has been washed up.

Where a few inches of soil make a world of difference

Wherever mangroves grow, there are zones of plant life as the soil level changes. In time, soil accumulates around the roots and eventually builds a foundation for other mangrove species. The diagram (right) shows the zones of vegetation that occur in the Florida Everglades, starting with a red mangrove community at the edge of the sea. Such areas may extend as far as 60 miles inland. Where the mangrove flourishes along tropical shores of the Atlantic it usually occupies a relatively narrow strip of land. The coastlines of India and South-east Asia have wider and denser mangrove jungles.

Red mangroves are the first to colonise a narrow margin of shallow, relatively quiet waters. Their underwater roots trap sediments and debris, thus building up soil. Black mangroves grow further up; their roots form a dense mat.

At a slightly higher elevation, white mangroves and gumbo-limbos thrive in brackish water (a mixture of sea water with fresh water from inland sources).

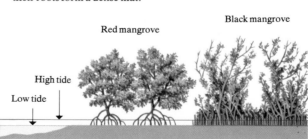

Red mangrove

Black mangrove

White mangrove

High tide

Low tide

A community of young roseate spoonbills (above) was probably born in this lush vegetation. They venture forth daily and return to roost here at night. Their plumage changes from white to pink as the birds mature. Notice the arching roots that are characteristic of red mangroves.

A coastal prairie in the United States (left). This panoramic view shows saw grass and mangroves in the foreground. As the land fills in, it takes on the appearance you can see in the background – a transition from low-growing shrubs to tall trees. Eventually all the water will disappear.

An underwater view of mangroves (right) shows how their prop roots jut downwards. Some of the roots will penetrate the soil. A spiny sea urchin rocks in the sun-dappled waters.

Gumbo-limbo

Hardwood hammocks are elevated islands of dry land. Freshwater ponds help sustain tall trees such as the cabbage palmetto.

Sweet bay

Saw grass

Cabbage palmetto

At the highest level, sandy soil supports a scattered growth of slash pine and low-growing saw palmetto. The soil is formed of underlying coral and limestone.

Saw palmetto

Slash pine

CHAPTER FIVE

Grasslands and meadows

In ancient times, grasses fostered many civilisations, even giving rise to such inventions as calendars and currency.

Fields and pastures are often described as heartlands. This is no mere figure of speech; it is a reflection of the fact that our daily bread comes from grasses. Early civilisations developed where crops grew readily. The floods that made the Nile Valley fertile were predicted from one year to the next through the laborious recording of events (in the main, the stars provided guidance – and astronomy was born as a science). In time, calendars came into being. The surpluses of crops brought commerce to a higher level, beyond simple barter. Record-keeping, numbering systems and currency all owe a debt to grasses.

How old are the grasses? No one knows for sure. The first fossils go back about 26 million years, far less than the fossils of mosses and ferns, and many species of trees. The fossil record shows that the grasses of antiquity were amazingly similar to present-day species. So, too, were the grasslands themselves – occupying broad, flat plains.

The fact that early grasses have endured to the present in relatively stable forms does not mean that grasses are simple. Rather, they have retained the early, successful forms, and have also diversified – spontaneously crossbreeding and forming new strains. Early ancestors of modern corn crops – such as wheat, barley, rice and maize – were first grown by Stone Age man.

Mankind has taken advantage of the flexibility of grasses and, by selective breeding, has developed better producing strains. Dwarf wheat, which has dramatically increased food production in many parts of the world, is one recent example. Corn has even been grown with ears at uniform height, for easy harvesting.

Grassland scents are the pollen of countless, tiny grass flowers. The ribbed stems of grasses bend before the wind and rise again; their rubbing creates a rustling sound – an eerie music that, once heard, cannot be remembered without a pang of nostalgia.

Steppes, prairies and pampas

No matter what grasslands are called – prairies, steppes, downs, savannah, veldt or pampas – they all have several things in common. They are usually situated on level or gently rolling plains, and are swept by nearly incessant winds. Grasslands are relatively dry, at least for part of the year. The similarities are reflected in the names: savannah is the Spanish word for plain; pampa, the Indian word for flat area.

The world's largest grasslands are the steppes of Europe and Asia. They once stretched in an unbroken expanse from the deep green meadows of the Danube Valley eastwards nearly to the Pacific. Like most grasslands, the steppes have been largely converted to agriculture. It was on the steppes near the Caspian Sea that the horse was first domesticated. Livestock now graze where herds of wild animals once roamed. Domesticated grasses – for instance, wheat and barley – have replaced native species. But enough remnants of original grasslands are left to allow you to discover what these immense worlds were like before they were "tamed".

The prairies of North America were named by French explorers in the 16th century – the word prairie means meadow in French. Prairies receive more rain than many other grasslands, mostly in the spring and early summer. In fact, rainfall seems to determine where each type of grass grows on the prairie. Tall grasses, such as the 8 ft big bluestem, flourish in the east (near the Great Lakes), where rainfall is greatest. Further west, the mid-grasses, such as little bluestem and western wheat grass, take over. Still further west, in the arid region near the Rockies, the grasses are short – blue grama, buffalo grass and others. The enormous herds of buffalo (actually bison) that once roamed North America were not restricted to the short-grass regions. These large, shaggy beasts grazed from the Rockies to the Atlantic seaboard. Alongside them lived packs of wolves, herds of antelope, cottontail rabbits and other burrowing animals by the million, and huge flocks of birds.

The pampas of South America are among the flattest grasslands in the world. They are like a tabletop, perched between the foothills of the Andes on the west and the Atlantic Ocean on the east. Near the ocean, the pampas receive abundant rain, and make up the agricultural heartland of Argentina. But the western pampas, blocked from moisture-bearing winds by the Andes, are dry and mostly barren. Sometimes air masses from the two regions collide near Buenos Aires, producing violent rainstorms known as pamperos.

The word savannah is used to describe tropical grasslands on several continents, including South America (near the Amazon) and Australia (in the north). But to many people, East Africa is *the* savannah, a region famous for its spectacular herds of wild animals. There, a great variety of mammals shares a relatively restricted amount of vegetation. For example, zebras usually eat only the coarse tops of grasses; wildebeest and topi (two kinds of antelope) eat the leafy middle stems; gazelles eat the young shoots.

The grasslands of South Africa are usually called veldt – also spelled veld, but pronounced felt – a Dutch word for field. Although there is no clear distinction between the veldt of southern Africa and the savannah further north, the veldt is usually drier and covered with various species of red grass. The animal inhabitants are similar – wildebeest, giraffes, elephants, lions and cheetahs. In some cases, however, they may be of different species.

At the edge of the Argentine pampas, a stream from nearby hills waters the sparse growth. Elsewhere on the pampas, vast pastures, which stretch unbroken from horizon to horizon, sustain huge herds of beef cattle. Gradually, they are being fenced off for agriculture.

PHOTO TIPS
Meadow patterns

To capture a field of flowers (as in the photograph below), use a tripod. Set your camera for a small lens opening, and check your light meter for an accurate reading. Your picture will be sharp from the foreground to infinity. But if you use a long exposure beware of the wind blowing the flowers.
• For a different effect, you can focus on a few nearby blossoms and let the rest – in both the foreground and background – become fuzzy.
• Take one exposure in sunlight and one in the bright, shadowless light of a passing cloud.

The bison of North America (left) are ideal prairie-dwellers. Insulated by their shaggy coats, they can endure extremes of weather. These bulls are grazing in Yellowstone National Park; sagebrush covers the hills.

In the late afternoon, waterbuck leave their resting places in the shade to graze on the African savannah (above). These heavily built antelope have long, coarse hair; only the males bear the curved, ridged horns.

In remarkable profusion, daisies and hawkweeds bloom, framed by the deep green of a June meadow. Grasses can also be photographed successfully like this.

Breadbaskets of the world

How is the world to feed more people? A look at this map shows two kinds of food-producing regions – farmlands and grazing lands. These fertile areas occupy far less space on the globe than is generally supposed, and they have built-in limitations. Although a few places in the world have produced bountiful crops almost every year since time immemorial – the Nile Valley, for example – many of the world's vast grasslands are marginal regions. During wet years they may be successfully farmed, but during dry years, the land can only be grazed.

Land is at the mercy of climate, which may – without apparent cause – change from favourable to unfavourable (and back) over decades and centuries. This map is a reflection of current conditions; it neither shows how the world was in ancient times nor forecasts the future.

Mankind has been slow to recognise the limitations of the land. Even now, the rain forests of Brazil are being cut down for farming, in the hope that crops will grow with the wild abundance of native vegetation. Unfortunately, the soil that supports tropical forests will not sustain agriculture for any length of time. Nutrients are leached out of the soil by heavy rains, and food crops (which exhaust the soil) eventually fail.

Grazing animals are often deplored as a wasteful means of food production. So they may be if they occupy rich arable land. But when they subsist on grassland that cannot support crops, they play an essential role in feeding the world.

Most of the land that feeds the world is planted with cereals – domesticated grasses that are grown 'or their edible seeds. Other food crops include tubers, such as potatoes. But current interest centres on legumes, such as soya beans, which are rich in protein. As world demand for protein grows, the richer countries will probably have to eat legumes as a substitute for part of the meat and fish they are accustomed to.

The grasslands of North America are the world's greatest wheat-producing areas. Their rich harvests often supplement those of less fertile countries.

HAWAIIAN ISLANDS

Sugar cane, a grass native to the South Pacific, is an important crop of the Hawaiian Islands.

Discovery of the New World made possible the exchange of many crops. Corn, potatoes and peanuts were added to European diets, and grains and livestock were brought to the Americas.

Potatoes were first cultivated in South America, carried to Europe, then brought to North America by the English colonists.

The pampas of Argentina are rich grazing lands for cattle. These broad plains also support a large wheat crop.

Ploughed lands versus grazing lands

Arable lands, or farmlands, are areas best suited for growing food crops. Climate and soil determine which plants will do well.

Grazing lands, or pastures, are used for livestock. The grasses are resilient enough to withstand grazing and trampling.

Non-agricultural lands include such areas as tropical rain forests, broad-leaved and coniferous forests, deserts and tundra.

Plants that provide food for man and livestock

Maize, grown all over the world, is called corn by Americans. The names often cause confusion.

Oats are known primarily as a cereal grain, and can be grown successfully even in poor soil.

Soya beans are an important source of protein. Like all legumes, they extract nitrogen from the air.

Barley, perhaps the hardiest of grains, thrives in cool climates and is mainly feed for livestock.

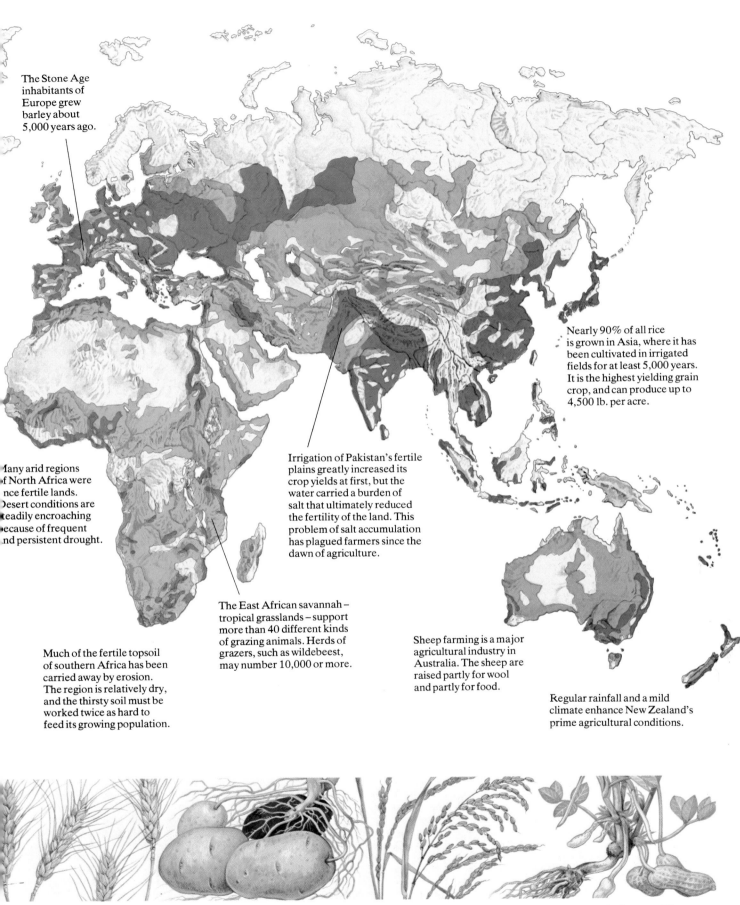

The Stone Age inhabitants of Europe grew barley about 5,000 years ago.

Many arid regions of North Africa were once fertile lands. Desert conditions are steadily encroaching because of frequent and persistent drought.

Much of the fertile topsoil of southern Africa has been carried away by erosion. The region is relatively dry, and the thirsty soil must be worked twice as hard to feed its growing population.

Irrigation of Pakistan's fertile plains greatly increased its crop yields at first, but the water carried a burden of salt that ultimately reduced the fertility of the land. This problem of salt accumulation has plagued farmers since the dawn of agriculture.

Nearly 90% of all rice is grown in Asia, where it has been cultivated in irrigated fields for at least 5,000 years. It is the highest yielding grain crop, and can produce up to 4,500 lb. per acre.

The East African savannah – tropical grasslands – support more than 40 different kinds of grazing animals. Herds of grazers, such as wildebeest, may number 10,000 or more.

Sheep farming is a major agricultural industry in Australia. The sheep are raised partly for wool and partly for food.

Regular rainfall and a mild climate enhance New Zealand's prime agricultural conditions.

Wheat is possibly the most widely grown grain. Note the resemblance of its stalk to that of barley (left).

Potatoes are tubers, which are food-storing roots. They are starchy and give quick energy.

Rice is a staple food in the diet of more than half the world, and is grown in warm, moist climates.

Peanuts are also legumes. They "plant" themselves by pushing their seed pods into the ground.

The story of soil

When the earth's molten crust first began to cool, there was no soil. It was a nightmare time, unlike anything we now know, with countless volcanoes giving off molten rock and steam As the world cooled, the steam condensed into liquid. The volcanoes continued to erupt, and titanic storms swept the earth. Rain sizzled on the scorching surface of the rock like a drop of water on a hot iron – turning to steam again, but at the same time causing the rock to crack and crumble. The debris caused by this means (a process known as weathering) was lifeless.

According to scientific theory, it was not until millions of years later that land plants began to grow on crumbled rock. Like some mosses and algae of today, these early, rootless plants required no soil. Their internal chemistry produced acids that broke down rock and made it available as a source of nutrients. These plants prospered for countless centuries, capturing energy from the sun. The debris of dead plants is rich because of the residue of energy within it. Once captured, the sun's vitality can be recycled.

Thus soil is not just an aggregation of rock particles, but a mixture of rock and once-living materials. Today, except on rocky outcrops and beneath ice caps, most of the earth's dry land is covered with 1 ft or more of soil.

Soil that has recently formed from plant debris and crumbled rock is different from old, established deposits. Climate – especially rain – works on the soil, separating it into layers called horizons. The three main layers, starting at the surface, are topsoil, subsoil and loose rock. Soils are classified by the depth and contents of each horizon.

Humus is the dark-coloured, decaying material in the topsoil (or "A" horizon), which is the basis for the soil's fertility. Beneath this is the subsoil, or "B" horizon, impoverished in humus but rich in materials that rainwater has washed down from the topsoil. (This sorting by water is called leaching.) The hard-pan you sometimes hit in this layer when you dig in your garden is washed-down clay that has been compacted into a solid mass. Loose rock forms the "C" horizon, and is soil in the making. This is underlaid by bedrock.

Soil particles are graded in size from sand (the largest), to silt (which is smaller), to clay (which can be powdery when dry). The bits of soil you see when you crumble dirt between your fingers are made of different kinds of particles joined together in varying amounts. It is the character of this mixture of soil particles

that determines the ease with which roots, air and water move through the soil. Loam, for example, includes all three kinds of particles (sand, silt and clay) in varying quantities.

Strictly speaking, soil is dead. But every handful contains a whole world of living matter. A single ounce of healthy soil houses between 30 million and 1,500 million bacteria and up to 30 million fungi, not to mention the countless smaller viruses. Without such microscopic organisms, consuming dead plants and animals and transforming them into plant food,

crops could be grown only by artificial feeding.

As for the bigger forms of life, scientists calculated that in one sample acre of British soil there were living 1,000 million nematodes (roundworms), a million earthworms, and a hundred shrews – not to mention a multitude of ants, beetles, millipedes, centipedes, slugs, snails, spiders, mites and an occasional field mouse. Some 40 tons of plants and animals live in the topsoil of a typically healthy acre, with more life deeper down. All in all, there is no such thing as plain dirt.

Are moles mathematically minded?
This strange question arises because they almost always change tunnelling direction with a 90 degree turn. No one knows why. It is a point to ponder while the little animal "cultivates" your lawn.

Worms turn earth into rich topsoil by eating dead leaves and grasses, and leaving behind fertilising waste products. Worms also drain soil by creating channels: rain soaks into them rather than running off. A single worm processes ½ lb. of soil a year, providing circulation from surface to depths.

Profiles of four common soil types and the vegetation they support

If you look at a river bank, road cutting, or other exposed section of soil, you can see that the soil is divided into layers, called horizons. Soil horizons develop over a period of time, as water transports minerals from the upper region and carries them downwards (this process is called leaching). According to a recent classification, there are about a dozen main types of soil, each with the same basic arrangement of layers (see diagram below). Four of the types are shown (right). Both climate and vegetation can influence the soil: for example, heavy rains in northern coniferous forests extract acids from fallen needles, which makes the earth acidic. In turn, the soil influences the vegetation – an important factor in determining what plants will grow where.

Grassland soil has no sharp divisions between its upper layers; they blend into one another in this type of soil. This soil is the moist, fertile earth of maize-growing areas and grassy plains.

Chernozem (the Russian word for black earth) has a dark layer of humus at the surface; the deeper, light-coloured band contains calcium. Wheat grows well in this soil.

Close-up of soil horizons

The depth of a particular horizon is highly variable.

The "A" horizon is the topsoil, which has more animal life, more humus, and greater changes in moisture and temperature than the other layers.

The "B" horizon (subsoil) gets minerals that have been washed downwards by rainwater. Clay often collects in this layer.

The "C" horizon contains loose and weathered rock, and is often the parent material of the soil above.

The "R" horizon is made of bedrock – solid rock that has not been eroded.

Grey-brown podzolic soil underlies the temperate broad-leaf forest. Podzol means "ash-beneath", and refers to the light-coloured, washed-out layer just beneath the topsoil.

Podzol is the name of the soil that supports northern coniferous forests. Because podzol is acidic, lacks topsoil, and generally requires large amounts of fertiliser, it is not good for farming.

HOW TO
Test your soil

The prosperity of a number of plants depends on the degree of alkalinity or acidity in the soil in which they grow. The degree of alkalinity or acidity is expressed as a number on a pH scale, with a neutral rating at the middle (7), where most plants do fairly well. If you suspect that your gardening is being adversely affected by too much of one or the other extreme, here is how to test your soil.
• Buy a few strips of litmus paper from a chemist. Press the litmus paper against damp soil. Repeat the procedure in several places in your garden. If the paper stays blue, your soil is either alkaline (called "sweet" soil) or neutral.
• If the litmus paper turns reddish-pink, however, your soil is predominantly acid. (An acidic pH would explain why you have not been able to grow vigorous peas, beans or lettuce plants.) You can either grow acid-loving plants such as azaleas, rhododendrons or mountain laurels, or you can add lime to change the chemical balance in the soil, making it more hospitable for other kinds of plants.
• But there is a catch: you will have to add lime every year to get good results. There is an old European farming proverb that says, "Lime makes rich fathers and poor sons". This means that although the initial effect of lime is to accelerate plant growth, ultimately the other nutrients in the soil are exhausted, and even additional lime will not help.
• The temporary nature of any change in either acid or alkaline balance can be traced to the character of the soil: it is wedded to the parent rock and to the climate. It is really better to go along with nature rather than fight it. If you move house you may not be able to go on growing the same plants. Ask your neighbours what does well locally.

Grasses are supremely flexible

The roots of grasses are more intricate than the stalk of the plant above ground. A relatively simple demonstration shows just how extensive and complex their roots are. Botanists grew winter rye in a box containing 2 cu. ft of soil. In a four month period, the slender plants grew 20 in. tall. Then the scientists carefully teased out the root system and measured it. The main roots reached a total of 378 miles in length and the minute root hairs 6,000 miles – an average daily growth of some 3 miles of roots and 50 miles of root hairs. The total surface area of the roots was estimated at nearly 7,000 sq. ft.

Prodigious root growth is only one amazing aspect of grasses. They, more than any other group of plants, contain nutrients accessible and palatable to man, domesticated livestock, and innumerable species of wild animals.

Grasses have a wider range than any other family of flowering plants. They grow on the continent of Antarctica, on wind-blown mountain peaks, and on equatorial deserts. A few even grow partially underwater in marshes and bogs. About the only places most grasses will not grow – as you may have noticed if you have trees in your garden – is where there is deep shade, such as in dense forests.

There are about 3,500 species of grass, some of them hardly resembling the familiar plants of field and lawn. They include wheat, oats, barley and maize, sugar cane, bamboo and rushes, the latter used for thatching and making mats.

Most grasses have hollow stems with solid joints; all have leaves with parallel veins. The lower part of each leaf, called the sheath, is like a tube split along one side and wrapped around the stem. The upper part of the leaf is the blade; leaves occur alternately on one side of the stem, then the other. When a grass plant is cut or grazed, it generally recovers quickly. New leaves originate from a growing point at or below the ground.

Grasses utilise the wind to fertilise their flowers – no bees or other insects are needed. The flowers of most grasses are small and inconspicuous, and grow in small clusters called spikelets, each containing many flowers. The blossoms do not have petals, which are the structures that attract insects to other flowers. Instead, they have tiny capsules (like hinged sea shells) that enclose the inner parts of the flowers. Each set of capsules protects a feathery pistil, which is the female part, and stamens, which produce the pollen (usually each has three stamens).

Each grass flower opens only once in its life, and then for only about an hour. Wheat is known to open its flowers for a mere 15 minutes. Botanists believe that a particular combination of temperature, humidity and sunlight causes the capsule

How to look at a grass plant

The uniform structure of grasses makes them easy to recognise. Grasses have ribbon-like leaves, or blades, and round, jointed stems. (Sedges, which resemble coarse grasses, have triangular stems.) Except at the joints, called nodes, most grass stems are hollow; maize and sugar cane, which have solid stems, are exceptions. Grasses spread slowly by seeds, and rapidly by means of rhizomes or stolons (see below).

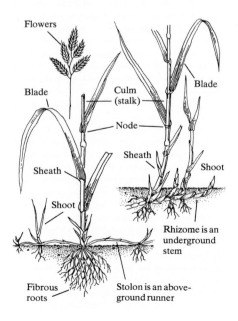

Flowers
Blade
Culm (stalk)
Node
Blade
Sheath
Sheath
Shoot
Shoot
Rhizome is an underground stem
Fibrous roots
Stolon is an above-ground runner

Grasses taller than man were encountered by the covered-wagon pioneers on the prairies of America. Tough roots bound the sod so firmly that early settlers used it to build their houses. Here, tall Indian grass – a prairie species – and fruiting sumac ripen on a Nebraska farm.

to spring apart and briefly expose the flower.

Most grass flowers open early in the morning (one exception is oats, which open in the early afternoon). The stamens quickly elongate, sometimes doubling their length in ten minutes, and release innumerable pollen grains. As a safeguard against self-pollination, the pistils may not emerge until after the pollen is discharged. They can then catch pollen from another plant. Thus the grasses ensure that they will benefit from a constant exchange of genetic materials.

Like pollen, grass seeds are carried by the wind – some have even been collected from the air by a plane flying at 5,000 ft. This means that grasses are constantly sending out "colonists". Sometimes they arrive in an area just in time to halt erosion of topsoil – in the wake of flooding or a mudslide. Just as often, the seeds were at the site, awaiting favourable conditions.

HOW TO
Grow a better lawn

For the best possible effect, mow your lawn frequently. During periods of the most rapid growth, the grass may need cutting as often as twice a week. Set mower blades to medium height. Also rake the lawn frequently.

• Once a year, in spring, fertilise your lawn, using several ounces per square yard. Your local gardening shop or nurseryman will recommend a suitable type of fertiliser.

• If you are starting with bare ground, the soil will need some preparation – removing stones and adding fertiliser. Grading may be necessary to create an even surface that slopes away from your house, thus protecting the foundations from dampness.

• Whether you are beginning a lawn or re-seeding an established lawn, your choice of seeds has much to do with the success of the planting. Choose a variety of grass suited to your soil and local climate. Again, a gardening shop or nursery in the neighbourhood can advise you on this.

• The best times for sowing are from mid-March to early May, and from mid-August to October. Unless your garden is exceptionally large, sow the seeds by hand, using about 2 oz. of seeds per square yard. Then rake the area, or sprinkle a light coating of soil over the seeds.

• Frequent weeding and watering are especially important for a young lawn.

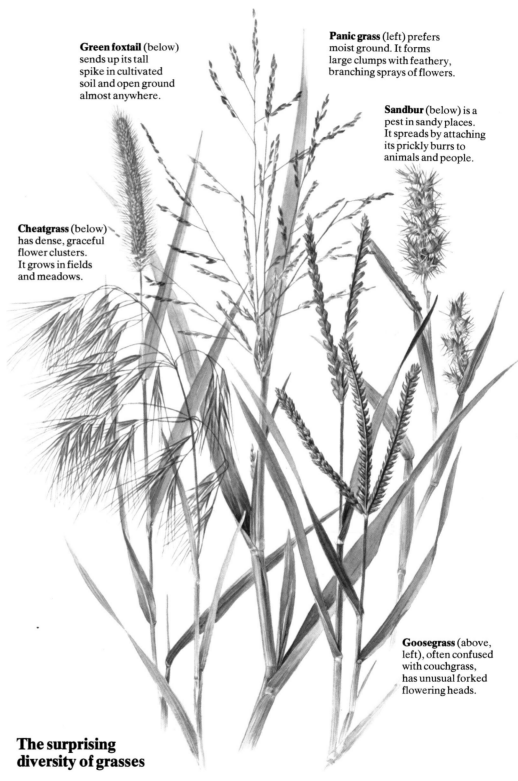

Green foxtail (below) sends up its tall spike in cultivated soil and open ground almost anywhere.

Panic grass (left) prefers moist ground. It forms large clumps with feathery, branching sprays of flowers.

Sandbur (below) is a pest in sandy places. It spreads by attaching its prickly burrs to animals and people.

Cheatgrass (below) has dense, graceful flower clusters. It grows in fields and meadows.

Goosegrass (above, left), often confused with couchgrass, has unusual forked flowering heads.

The surprising diversity of grasses

Grasses are some of the most successful plants in the world – they will sprout and take root in any neglected nook or crevice. The five species above thrive on building sites, roadsides, abandoned fields, and other city and country wastelands. Because their seeds are carried by the wind and by birds, they will appear where they are not wanted. These unappreciated members of the grass family are weeded out when they invade lawns, gardens and other cultivated regions. But in a barren environment, they perform a vital function, holding soil and preventing erosion. They add a touch of beauty wherever they appear.

How grasses compete with trees

Rainfall is the most obvious factor in determining whether grasses or trees will dominate a particular area – most trees require more water than grasses. In some areas, there is about the right amount for either. Here competition is keen, but the advantages are usually with the grasses. Before man interfered they were so successful that about a quarter of the earth's land surface was under grass of one sort or another.

For a start, grasses are better equipped to withstand fire. Archaeologists have unearthed ancient charred plants that tell us there have been fires since vegetation first appeared on land. They were probably started by volcanoes or by lightning. Today, as you read this page, some 1,800 thunderstorms are sweeping across the earth, and within the next 20 minutes, about 60,000 lightning bolts will strike.

Fires are most common in early spring, before plants turn green, and in autumn when much of the vegetation dies. After the flames pass, the soil is black with ash and charred stubble. The growing tissues of trees – especially saplings – are often destroyed, but the growing point of grasses, near or below ground level, is less affected by fire.

Soon after the burning, a rebirth occurs that is one of the most amazing in nature. The blackened earth absorbs the heat of the sun. In the African grasslands, temperatures on burned ground can be 22°C (40°F) hotter than on an unburned area. This encourages the germination of certain seeds. Grass seeds, borne on the wind, are universally present and swift to sprout.

Burned or not, grasses have the further advantage of an extremely well-established root system. The dense network of roots infiltrates the soil so thoroughly that you have to cut a sod with a blade or tear it apart, if you wish to move it. (This tough binding is what made the sod-block houses of the early American prairie settlers so durable.) When, after a life of perhaps 20 years, a grass plant dies, the roots from surrounding plants quickly fill in the vacancies, sometimes following the pathways of the decaying roots.

Wind is also a decisive factor in the contest between trees and grasses. Grasses are able to bend in the wind, and their blades are slender and resilient. The branches of trees are more rigid and may break in the wind. The leaves of trees are often broad, and their attachment to the tree may be less flexible than the jointed stalks of grass.

But more important is the fact that all plants must lose moisture through their

exposed surfaces, and a broad leaf results in greater evaporation. As the wind constantly carries off water, the tree draws moisture up from its roots – roots that are nowhere near as extensive (in proportion to the size of the plant) as those of grasses. When the tree cannot replenish the water, the leaves wilt and become less capable of producing nutrients; a downward cycle begins, and the tree may die.

What kills trees actually aids grasses. They thrive in this windy world. Paradise, for the 19th-century English poet Algernon Swinburne, was "Where air might wash and long leaves cover me, Where tides of grass break into foam of flowers, Or where the wind's feet shine along the sea." The wind is much more than a movement of air. It is one of the immense forces that has helped to shape the world over countless centuries.

Many animals feast at fire fronts. The kori bustard above patrols an African savannah in the path of a blaze. Small animals that escape the fire may run into this predator.

A wall of flames sweeps across the grasslands in Zambia, forcing all the animals to flee for their lives. Most birds can fly away; some animals take refuge underground. Insects have the greatest losses, but their eggs survive.

Trees protect as well as being beautiful. A screen of trees breaks the force of the wind. This is beneficial in many ways – a windbreak can lessen fuel bills, improve the quality and quantity of crops, and create shelter for livestock. Farmers planning a windbreak collect information about the kinds of trees that are recommended for the climate and soil in the area. They choose slow-growing species with a maximum height that will not overshadow the house too much. If there is already a row of shrubs on the windward side of the house, it is possible to intersperse the shrubs with conifers and flowering trees. It is also possible to make the windbreak look attractive by including, say, cherries for spring bloom, oaks and maples for autumn colour and spruces and firs for winter greenery.

Thick shelterbelts of trees form wind barriers around this prairie farm. Trees can protect adjacent areas for a distance roughly 20 times their height. For example, a row of trees approximately 75 ft high will protect a strip of land some 1,500 ft long. In cutting down the wind flow, two or three rows of trees are more effective than only a single row.

A solid barrier – a stockade fence or a tree with dense foliage – blocks wind flow and causes areas of turbulence on either side. This decreases a windbreak's efficiency.

A rail fence or a widely branching tree with sparse foliage filters the wind. It reduces wind speed and force without creating turbulent eddies that may damage nearby vegetation.

Grazers great and small

The world's fastest animals live on grasslands, where hiding places are scarce and running is often the only way to elude enemies. In fact, speed is a requirement for predators, too, in their pursuit of prey. The holder of the animal land-speed record – the cheetah, which can run at up to 70 mph over a short distance – lives on the African grasslands. The runners-up, the gazelles, which are often the cheetah's prey, can reach 60 mph. The third-place holder is the 50 mph ostrich, which also lives on the African plains.

In Britain, both the roe deer and the red deer can reach speeds of up to 40 mph, but the roe deer has greater staying power. The much smaller hare, however, can run at up to 45 mph in short spurts.

The red kangaroo of Australia's dry central grasslands is not exceptionally speedy (its maximum speed is only about 30 mph), but its "strides" are actually giant hops on long, muscular back legs. An "old man" red bounds along in a series of 25 ft leaps that may be 6 ft off the ground, holding its small front legs as if in prayer and stretching out its strong, heavy tail for balance. These high leaps also enable the red and other kangaroos to keep a lookout above the grass for considerable distances. The tail, which is a formidable club, serves as a rudder, enabling the kangaroo to change direction quickly even when it is bounding along at top speed.

The fastest wild animal of the South American pampas is the ostrich-like rhea, a long-legged and flightless bird. Rheas usually form flocks of about 50 birds. During the breeding season, the male collects a harem. He prepares a nest by pulling up grass with his bill and creating an open zone around a shallow depression. All the females lay eggs in this nest, and the male incubates the eggs – sometimes as many as 50 at a time.

Like rheas and kangaroos, which gather in groups called mobs, many grassland animals form herds. On the grasslands, there is safety in numbers. The greater the number of sentries, the greater the chance of detecting an enemy. Herd members fleeing in all directions often distract a would-be predator.

Many grassland herds regularly migrate hundreds of miles to follow the food supply. As the rainy season in Africa's Serengeti Plain ends around March, immense herds of wildebeest form and move westwards where the grass is greener, mating during their trek. The herds return east with the rains, in October, and calving begins on the lush, rainy-season grass.

Wildebeest are ruminants – animals with four-chambered stomachs – as are many large grazers such as gazelles, giraffes and zebras (as well as domestic cattle). This complicated but efficient stomach allows ruminants to digest large quantities of tough, low-quality vegetation. It lets them eat and run.

As a ruminant eats, the food goes first to the rumen (the word from which these animals were named). There the food is fermented, as bacteria break down the tough parts of the plants. The food is later regurgitated and chewed as cud. Swallowed once more, the food then passes through the rest of the digestive system.

Grassland animals much smaller than ruminants also live in large groups. Burrowers such as North American prairie dogs and gophers, South American guinea pigs and cavies, Australian wombats and kangaroo rats, African hyraxes and meerkats, and Eurasian hamsters and susliks live in "towns" of 1,000 or more individuals.

If you have ever had a pet rodent (such as a gerbil), you know what vigorous diggers these animals are. Susliks, which resemble some types of marmots, riddle Eurasian grasslands with burrows up to 8 ft deep. In digging out their storerooms, sleeping chambers, passageways and escape routes, the susliks bring up quantities of rich earth. Scientists believe that this continual tillage helps to maintain soil fertility. Although the diggers are small as individuals, their numbers are so great that without them the world's grasslands would be vastly different.

Flightless rheas (above), the largest New World birds, travel in small flocks over the pampas. They feed on grass, grain and insects, and are very fleet and wary. Once numerous, these ostrich-like birds are now becoming scarce.

Australia's grazing animals are the kangaroos (above right). They thrive on the scanty, spiny grasses of the semi-arid plains and, when in need of water, dig holes in dry river beds. This benefits birds and other animals.

Ever on the alert for predators, the suslik – a ground squirrel of eastern Europe and Asia – basks in the sun (right). Susliks eat seeds, roots, bulbs and insects, and seem to cover the dry grasslands with their many burrows.

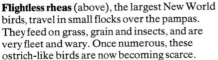

Multitudes of migrating wildebeest, up to 50,000 in a single herd, roam the East African plains seeking new pastures. These bulky antelope thrive on the sparse grasslands. As a large herd of wildebeest grazes, the grass is kept short, green and succulent; with a small herd it becomes too tall and dry to serve as food. This may be the reason that wildebeest move across the plains in such vast numbers.

Pronghorn antelope are unique to the plains and scrublands of western North America. Not true antelope, they have horns that are shed every year, like the antlers of deer. Pronghorns are among the world's fastest mammals – they can reach 60 mph in short bursts of speed. In summer, they travel in small groups, feeding on grasses, weeds and shrubs, but in winter they converge into large herds.

What is a food chain?

Every living thing depends on the sun. But only green plants, which make food by photosynthesis, can use the sun's energy directly. A plant-eater, such as a grasshopper on your lawn, gets a share of the sun by eating plants. Shrews and other insect-eaters obtain energy by eating grasshoppers. An owl may eat a shrew, thus acquiring the food originally produced by plants.

When a plant or animal dies, its tissues are still useful to the living world. Vultures and other scavengers eat some of the material; the rest is broken down by bacteria and fungi, and then returned to the soil, where plants take advantage of it in their growth.

Decomposing tissue is called *organic* because it contains carbon compounds found only in things that are living or were once alive.

The transfer of food from plants through a series of animals is known as a food chain. The various levels of consumption – the links in the chain – have been identified, but actually the word *chain* is something of an over-simplification. *Web* is really better, for it gets closer to a true picture – prey-predator relationships are neither limited nor predictable, but are often haphazard. For example, insects are usually eaten by small insectivores. But they are also consumed (sometimes accidentally) by everything from grazing animals to hefty carnivores such as bears.

There is endless interlocking of the many different consumption patterns in the natural world – thus the expression "food web" is often used by ecologists, and sometimes they use the word "network".

Regardless of the name used, the levels of consumption correspond to the transfer of energy. In each stage, there is loss of

The sun powers the energy cycle for plants and animals

In this representation of an energy cycle (food chain) on an African savannah, energy from the sun is absorbed by the plants and then transferred to many plant-eating animals. The various animal participants – from ant to vulture – eat and, in turn, are food for others. In reality, a food chain is more complex than is shown here. For example, many carnivores are also part-time scavengers. There are also a number of species at any one level of the food chain.

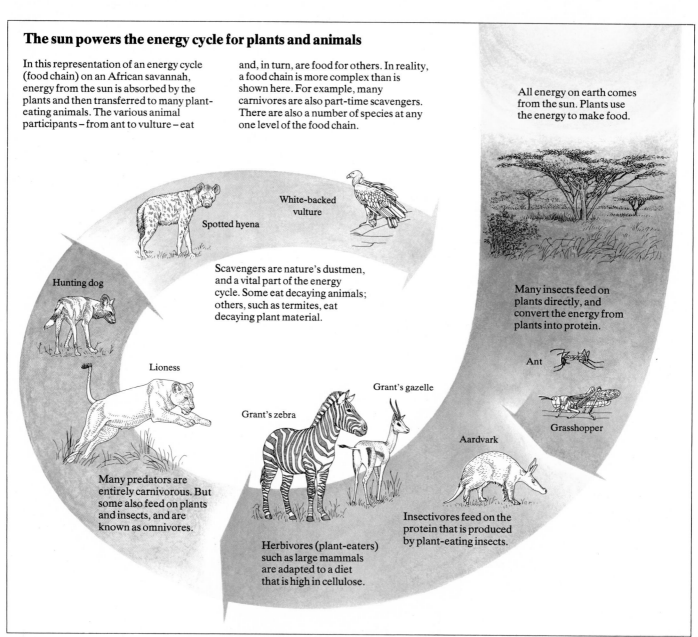

All energy on earth comes from the sun. Plants use the energy to make food.

White-backed vulture

Spotted hyena

Scavengers are nature's dustmen, and a vital part of the energy cycle. Some eat decaying animals; others, such as termites, eat decaying plant material.

Many insects feed on plants directly, and convert the energy from plants into protein.

Hunting dog

Ant

Lioness

Grant's gazelle

Grant's zebra

Grasshopper

Aardvark

Many predators are entirely carnivorous. But some also feed on plants and insects, and are known as omnivores.

Insectivores feed on the protein that is produced by plant-eating insects.

Herbivores (plant-eaters) such as large mammals are adapted to a diet that is high in cellulose.

energy (usually in the form of heat). For example, the grasses and other plants on an open plain use only an estimated 10% of the solar energy that strikes their leaves.

When plants (called producers) are eaten by certain insects, rodents and grazing animals (all herbivores), they, too, acquire only a fraction of the energy that was lodged in the plant. Much of what they get is lost because it is not digestible, and what they do get is quickly used up in body processes – chewing, running from enemies, and so forth. Only a small proportion of the original energy is stored in the tissues of the herbivores.

Consumers on the next level eat vegetarian animals. Hawks, owls, moles, weasels, ferrets and others are called secondary consumers. Animals that prey on secondary consumers are tertiary consumers, and these include foxes, eagles and wolves. They, like all the others, use only a small amount of the energy stored in their prey.

This pattern produces a pyramidal picture. The greatest amount of energy and number of individuals occur at the first level – the plants, which comprise more than 95% of all living tissue. For example, on the South American pampas, it takes about 1,000 lb. of grass to feed 100 lb. of guinea pigs (which amounts to about 100 animals). These will feed a 10 lb. maned wolf, which, if eaten by a jaguar, would allow the jaguar to gain only about 1 lb. of body weight.

But again, food chains or webs are seldom simple, and a species does not always occupy the same feeding level. For example, sometimes a golden eagle is a secondary consumer (when it eats planteating mice and geese), and sometimes a third-order consumer (when it eats foxes and hawks). And it may be a scavenger (when it eats carrion).

Any description of food chains is complicated by the fact that although there is always a *loss of energy* when food is transferred from one level to another, there may also be a *concentration* of certain substances.

This was dramatically brought to light when scientists discovered that pesticides build up in the tissues of animals far removed from the place where the chemicals were used. Nor is there anything simple about the ways that this kind of build-up occurs.

An animal may produce tissuebuilding proteins that can be used by others or cancel its role in the food chain by being inedible, possibly even toxic.

Closing the gap, a cheetah is ready to attack a gazelle. Actually, prey and predator are more evenly matched than they seem to be. The cheetah is fast, but tires easily; the gazelle has stamina. To elude a predator, a gazelle must be able to recognise an enemy and to gauge how far away it is before beginning to flee.

Neither prey nor predator, a rhino is a plant-eater. The black rhino (left) is a browser, feeding on leaves and twigs; the white rhino – really grey – is a grazer, cropping grass with its wide muzzle. The white gets its name from a Dutch word, *wijd* – meaning "broad".

 NATURE OBSERVER
Rank among feeders – who eats first?

Animals do not waste energy in ceaseless warfare – many of their battles are settled in advance by the development of "rank". For example, in a study of five kinds of vultures in Africa, it was discovered that the different species approached a carcase in a definite order.

• Vultures are often the animals that lead other species to a kill. All eyes are upon them. A cheetah, which is a swift predator, may be driven from its kill by the arrival of more powerful predators, such as a pack of hunting dogs or even a few hyenas. These usually yield to a prowling lioness. In films and photographs of the African plains, you

may notice that while one species feeds, others wait around the kill.

• You can observe rank among feeding animals in your own home, if you feed more than one pet at the same time. Whether two dogs, two cats, a cat and a dog, or another combination, usually one gets first choice. And if you have a bird-table outside your window, you can observe rank among your local birds. For example, jays invariably assert their claims above those of sparrows. A squirrel is probably the only animal that will take on a jay – but even this plucky little mammal will avoid a pair of jays competing for the same meal.

Predators: the misunderstood species

If you saw a hawk swooping down on a mouse or rabbit – an event that is particularly visible on grassland – you might assume that the animal on the ground was living on borrowed time. Predators seem to have the upper hand. Some birds of prey can scan an entire valley in a matter of minutes, spot a mouse at vast distances, and dive at speeds exceeding 100 mph. Owls can even detect small, scurrying animals in the dark by the tiny sounds they make.

What chance has a mouse, rabbit or squirrel against such "super-hunters"? Surprisingly, the odds favour the meek. Studies of hunting birds reveal that, in general, they miss their prey as often as they catch it.

Birds that capture other birds on the wing have an even worse batting average. For example, certain falcon species (such as merlins) are likely to fail 95 times out of 100 attempts.

Predators are not always successful because prey species have evolved defences against them. For example, many small mammals have acute hearing and can react swiftly to approaching predators. Some take a zigzag path to dodge their attackers, or run into a burrow.

With the resources of predator and prey so evenly matched, the question changes: how do predators keep from starving? Like other animals, predators conserve their energy. Generally, they do not waste their time attacking healthy, mature animals. They look for easy kills – the sick, young or old. One study of wolves on Alaska's Mount McKinley showed that full-grown wild sheep were almost immune to attack. A similar study of cougars indicated that even these formidable predators usually attacked the most vulnerable prey.

Predators that hunt strong animals run the risk of becoming victims themselves. A lion that attacks a zebra or giraffe may be killed by sharp, flailing hoofs. An osprey unable to withdraw its talons from too large a fish may be pulled underwater and drowned.

The diet of a predator is generally quite varied. Coyotes will attack deer, but in the absence of large prey, a coyote will hunt mice and other small animals. Small prey, in fact, makes up the greater part of a coyote's diet.

If even these creatures prove elusive, a coyote will eat carrion. The line between predators and scavengers is not always clearly drawn – some animals hunt for themselves, but also steal the kills of other predators.

Some predators resort to plants for food. Coyotes are known to eat a wide variety of plants. Bears consume large amounts of vegetation, as well as prey. Pioneering naturalist John Muir said of the grizzly bear: "To him almost everything is food, except granite."

For a long time, people have believed that predators controlled the numbers of prey animals. Thus many predators have been killed in the hope that this would mean more game for human hunters. But the facts do not give full support to the idea.

For example, on the Serengeti Plain in Africa, the immense herds of wildebeest are preyed upon by lions, leopards, cheetahs, hyenas and hunting dogs. But not even these many enemies have a significant effect on their numbers. The most important cause of death among wildebeest is the separation of calves from their mothers. The effect of a drought is much more deadly than the combined forces of the many predators.

In isolated situations, predators do play an extremely important role in regulating the prey population – as when wolves and moose are confined to a single, relatively small island. But in general, predators simply do not live up to their bad reputations.

What future for the restless, far-ranging tiger?

The different life-styles of the two largest members of the cat family – tigers and lions – help to explain why lions are generally faring better than tigers. Tigers are solitary hunters that need about 10 sq. miles of living space to seek their natural prey – deer, antelope, buffaloes and smaller mammals. Lions, on the other hand, need less room. They live in prides and hunt co-operatively. Unlike the restless, roaming tigers, lions are great sleepers. If well fed, they will sleep for 22 of the 24 hours in a day, and so are less of a threat to man. A tiger has only itself to depend upon (except when a mother rears her cubs), and its habit is to wander ceaselessly. In recent years, human encroachment on tiger habitat has reduced its range and killed off its natural prey; the tiger has turned to domesticated animals for food. This brings retaliation from farmers, and the tiger is pressed even further. In general, tigers do well in zoos, which are becoming their last refuge. Their future is clearly in human hands.

The adaptable coyote of North America is the centre of controversy. Sheep ranchers regard it as a killer that should be exterminated. Many conservation groups defend its right to live, and point out that it has a role in controlling rodent pests. Meanwhile, the coyote is not only surviving, it is actually extending its range. Some have taken up residence in steep, wooded areas in the city of Los Angeles. In Europe, foxes too have begun to move into the wooded suburbs of towns.

Young burrowing owls (above) cram the entrance to their den, awaiting the return of a parent with food. These owls are valued by farmers for their insect and rodent-eating habits. The young may fall prey to skunks or snakes. Oddly enough, the owl's chief defence is a hissing sound – an almost perfect imitation of a snake.

The meerkats of southern Africa (left) live in colonies on the grasslands. They are relatives of the Asian mongoose, and have a similar, almost domesticated status in many homes – they are excellent mousers. In the wild, meerkats eat mostly insects, spiders and plant materials.

Birds of the grasslands

The grasslands of the world are rich in flowering plants that produce seeds, and in insects that feed on them. One estimate puts the insect population on an acre of grassland in midsummer at 10 million. This abundance of insect and vegetable food attracts many kinds of birds to grassy pastures, meadows and croplands.

Grassland birds are an asset to the farmer because they are voracious eaters of insect eggs and caterpillars, and innumerable beetles, grasshoppers and other insects. European lapwings, for example, often follow a plough or tractor, snatching up grubs. Birds are not an unmixed blessing for agriculture – wood pigeons and migrating geese are notorious crop raiders – but on balance, the many species of grassland birds are definitely an aid to farming.

Birds that breed in the grasslands share certain patterns of behaviour. Almost all indulge in spectacular courtship rituals; these may be dances, fights or song flights. Unlike forest birds, many grassland birds, such as bobolinks and meadowlarks, sing on the wing, or from roadside wires or fence posts. At least half of these birds build partially domed or concealed nests protected by arching grasses, which they enter by scurrying through the vegetation like little mice.

The champion dancers of the bird world are the 14 species of cranes; in Asia, the common and sarus cranes; in North America, the sandhill and whooping cranes; in Africa, the crowned cranes; and in Australia, the brolgas all perform their circling, bowing, and leaping routines on open plains.

A more aggressive kind of courtship ritual is that of the ruff (named for the male's extraordinary breeding adornment). These European sandpipers nest in damp meadows and display on grassy mounds. Such parade grounds are known as leks. Dominant males have small territories on the leks, which they defend pugnaciously. Fierce fights alternate with the raising of neck ruffs and ear tufts. No two males look alike; ruffs and body plumage may be black, white, brown or reddish in any combination of colours. Females, called reeves, resemble the more typical sandpipers.

The sharp-tailed grouse and prairie chicken also stage fantastic shows on their dancing grounds. The males inflate brightly coloured air sacs on their necks, patter their feet (a motion copied by plains Indians in their dances), and utter loud, booming sounds.

Even more spectacular is the courtship display of the great bustard, a rare resident of the central European grasslands. It is one of the heaviest land birds capable of flight.

The male bustard turns himself into a snowy-white ball of feathers by exposing his fluffy undertail and wing coverts. Inflating his throat pouch to the size of a football, he utters deep, hollow, moaning sounds to attract a female.

Celebrated in literature, the song flight of the Old World skylark is pure poetry. Spiralling up into the sky, the bird warbles continuously, then hovers and descends. Other larks on other continents make similar song flights to attract a mate and mark their territory.

A remnant of vanished prairies, this European field is gay with wildflowers and busy with breeding birds. Not all the wildlife depicted here would be visible at the same time of year, but all these birds and plants live in this habitat at one time or another. Here, a covey of partridges take flight, while a lapwing, which also nests in the grass, stands pensively by the track. Perched on a branch, a yellowhammer ignores the predatory magpie flying by. On the fence post a spotted flycatcher competes with the meadow's champion singer, the skylark, standing on a rock below with its tail among the daisies. The blue-headed, blue-rumped fieldfare looks for a meal of insects from the cross-bar of the fence, while a wheatear searches for seeds among the brambles. The splendid goldfinch clings to a thistle; later he will use thistledown to weave his nest.

Key to birds of the grasslands

1. Partridge
2. Magpie
3. Yellowhammer
4. Spotted flycatcher
5. Lapwing
6. Fieldfare
7. Goldfinch
8. Wheatear
9. Skylark

Flowers in abundance

Human beings are the main reason that grassland flowers are so widespread. Land that has not been cultivated – heathlands untouched by the plough – may have clover, sunflowers and others. But they never put on a show like the carpets of Queen Anne's lace, daisies, marguerites and dandelions which bloom exuberantly in fields that were formerly tilled.

In agriculture, often the first thing a farmer does is clear off existing vegetation. This produces a highly artificial situation that is an open invitation to colonisation by seeds in the vicinity.

In a way, this sums up the farmer's prime concern – how to encourage one particular crop and exclude all other plants. With centuries of experience, farmers have learned to do just that – to grow certain species of plants selectively.

But throughout the history of agriculture, another recurring problem has been harder to solve – exhaustion of the soil. A field that will produce good crops for several years eventually uses up the nutrients in the soil, and crop yields drop.

An ancient remedy still in use is crop rotation (where the type of crop is changed from year to year); another is allowing a field to lie unused so that the soil can recuperate.

A fallow field is inviting to the great opportunists of the plant world – the familiar roadside plants that spring up on cleared land. They produce a super-abundance of seeds that are spread worldwide by wind, animals and man. For example, Queen Anne's lace (wild carrot) originated in the Middle East and travelled around the globe.

Such pioneer plants are tough competitors and grow well in dry, sunny conditions typical of grasslands. The first species will grow rapidly – for example, couch grass, ragwort and sorrel. In quick succession, plantain, goldenrod and other species appear.

At this time, there is a great bustle in the fields, with insects and rodents tunnelling in the soil, and incidentally aerating and bringing up nutrients. Eventually, the soil recovers its fertility, and the farmer may clear it again. Or, to accelerate and control the "recovery" of the land, he may plant red clover, which restores nitrogen to the soil and can be grazed while it is doing its work.

A flowering meadow is colourful with

Lacy discs of wild carrot and marguerites overshadow smaller blossoms in a meadow (above). The carrots we eat are hybrids of several wild species.

The red clover in the field on the right is not a weed; it has been planted in order to restore nitrogen to the soil. This will result in a more fertile field – and also a crop of honey.

blossoms of red, pink, orange, yellow, blue, purple and white. Despite the array of hues, nearly all the flowers belong to the same family of plants – the composites. To appreciate the intricate nature of a composite, first look at a flower that is not one – say, a buttercup.

In its centre is a single, protruding stigma, surrounded by pollen-bearing anthers, which are themselves surrounded by colourful petals.

Compare this pattern with that of a thistle flower. A thistle "blossom" is actually a dense cluster of tiny flowers – hence the term composite. In this type of composite, each unit looks like a miniature flower – a floret or disk flower. They have male and female reproductive parts, but no petals.

A typical composite flower, however, has a more elaborate pattern. Take the daisy, for example. The yellow centre is a tight cluster of disk flowers, surrounded by white petals. The petals are actually ray flowers, but they function as ordinary petals do – as an attractant, bringing insects to the centre where the disk flowers are located, and where seeds are produced.

There is yet another kind of composite, which is strange indeed. The dandelion is the most widespread example. It has no pollen-producing parts, but is composed solely of female ray flowers, and no pollen is required to fertilise the plants and produce seeds.

⚠ HIKING AND CAMPING
⚠ The surprising variety of edible weeds

Have you ever tried adding nutritious and tasty weeds to your menu? The leaves of violets have four times as much vitamin C as oranges; chicory leaves are an excellent source of calcium and vitamin A.

• Young dandelion leaves add zest to a salad of mixed greens. The mustard family provides a choice of greens for a mixed salad – watercress, winter cress and garlic mustard, to name a few. Mustard greens are best in the spring when young and tender; later in the year, their seeds are excellent as seasonings.

• Weeds to use as steamed vegetables or in soups and stews include chickweed, milk thistle, hops, common sorrel, and even stinging nettles. Wild onion leaves and bulbs will add flavour.

• Delicious teas can be brewed from the leaves of chamomile and various wild mints; the dried flowers of heather; and rose hips, which are especially rich in vitamin C.

• Wild plants should never be eaten unless you have positively identified them – there are many helpful guides to wild foods. And like all new foods, they should be tried in moderation at first. When you are camping is a good time to try them.

Elderberry blossoms add flavour to fritters and pancakes. Fruits make good preserves.

Cleavers, a common plant in thickets, is excellent if it is cooked like spinach.

Lawn chamomile makes a refreshing tea if you steep its flower in water.

Common sorrel makes a delicious steamed vegetable – or thickens soups.

The orderly pattern of sunflower seeds

One of nature's most fascinating shapes is the spiral. The heads of composite flowers, such as the sunflower (right), are often spirals; note how the seeds at the centre form two sets of spiral rows. Usually you can see one of these sets right away, but the other may require a closer look. If you count the spirals in each set (see diagram below), you will arrive at two special numbers – both part of the Fibonacci series, named after a 13th-century Italian mathematician. This series begins with the number 1; 1 plus 1 equals 2; 1 plus 2 equals 3; 2 plus 3 equals 5; 3 plus 5 equals 8; and so on. In other words, each number in this series is the sum of the two preceding numbers.

The diagram (right) represents the arrangement of seeds in a ripened sunflower of average size. The two rows of spirals are indicated by the black and white lines; they spiral out in opposite directions from the centre. The 34 black lines form a clockwise spiral; the 21 white lines, a counterclockwise spiral. Both are Fibonacci numbers.

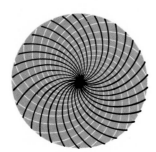

Goldenrod: a golden invitation

Every summer and autumn, a temporary world comes into being in grasslands and meadows. Beginning as early as July in parts of Europe, a tide of golden flowers sweeps across the fields. To humans, the change may seem no more than a pleasant indication of the changing seasons, but to countless animals, a billowing field of goldenrod represents a new and ideal environment in which to live and reproduce.

Though the appearance of goldenrod

Ragwort, not goldenrod, is the culprit when hay fever strikes in late summer. But because goldenrod grows near and has more conspicuous flowers, it usually gets the blame.

flowers is often quite sudden (they seem to come from nowhere), the plants have been there all along. Even in winter the brown stems are visible, sticking up through the snow. Goldenrod is a perennial – most of the plant dies during the winter; the roots survive and produce bright green shoots in the spring. During the summer, the new shoots grow tall alongside the old, dead stems, until the green prevails.

To see the flowers of goldenrod properly, look at them from three different viewpoints. From far away, the golden blossoms look like graceful plumes on top of slender stems. If you approach more closely, you will see that each plume is made up of individual flower heads arranged along spike-like stems. If you look still more closely, perhaps with a magnifying glass, you will see that each flower head is made up of small, individual florets.

It is often difficult to tell just what kind of goldenrod you are looking at. There are more than 100 species in the United States alone (goldenrod grows across North America and in parts of South America, Europe and Asia); the different species cross readily, forming new varieties. However, if there is a delicious aniseed-like aroma wafting up from a field of goldenrod, it is probable that the plants are the species called sweet goldenrod. Its leaves make a savoury tea.

In Britain, goldenrod is found, though only rarely, in the south-east. In addition to the wild plant, a cultivated species sometimes "escapes" from a garden and spreads on open ground. It flowers from August to October, a month or so later than the wild variety.

But other eyes are on the goldenrod.

As soon as the blossoms appear, so do hordes of insects that feed on their nectar and pollen. Butterflies flit from one plume to another, like children in a sweet shop. Heavy-bodied beetles fly clumsily to the flowers, giving the impression that they are bumping into the blossoms by accident. An abundance of bees and flies crawl among the florets.

Some predators in America use goldenrod as a hunting ground. One is the ambush bug, a small insect with irregular projections along its back and sides. It feeds on almost anything it can catch – it can even overpower an insect several times its size. There is also an interesting example of camouflage: the crab spider's yellow colour blends perfectly with the flowers. This spider, which looks and moves sideways like a crab, does not spin a web. It catches prey by lurking on the flowers until a butterfly or other potential victim alights – then it pounces.

After their brief moment of glory, the goldenrod flowers begin to wither: their leaves turn brown. Most of the animals move to other areas. The crab spider may scuttle over to, say, a purple flower. Though at first the yellow spider looks out of place, gradually it changes colour to match its new home. On a white flower, it turns white.

Many of the insects survive the winter in the same way as the roots of goldenrod – below the surface of the soil. Others die, but leave eggs that hatch in spring. Several insects leave offspring in the goldenrod itself. One of these is the goldenrod gall fly. Its larvae are lodged in ball-like lumps, called galls, that are visible on goldenrod stems. Like the brown goldenrod itself, the galls are a reminder – and a promise – of next year's spring.

COLLECTOR'S TIPS
Common flowers versus rarities

Some plants are as limited in their range and number as are rare animals. The rarity of a particular flower may be quite natural – in other words, lady's slipper and similar species have probably never been common. It is interesting to discover (using a reference book) which of the common flowers that fill fields and line roads are native species, and which are aliens – that is, from another part of the world.

● Some rare wild flowers are protected by law in Britain now. But in any case obey signs that forbid picking flowers; many parks prohibit removal of even common

plants. Be sure to obtain permission before gathering from private property.

● Even when flowers are abundant, pick only a few of each kind, leaving the rest to reproduce. It may be time to restore the old custom of taking only one of each.

● Cut blossoms instead of breaking them off, and do not uproot the whole plant. The best way to collect flowers is on film.

● If an area is about to be cleared for roads, it is permissible – and desirable – to move any plants, common or rare. In this case, try to move them to where the growing conditions are similar.

A waning summer's landscape is warmed by the glow of goldenrod, which towers over a sprinkling of small white asters. Some herbalists use an infusion of goldenrod leaves and flowers as a pain-reliever; the plant also produces a yellow dye. Goldenrod nectar is a favourite food of bees, which often can be found buzzing about. Bees mix this nectar with that from nearby asters, and make a splendid honey.

Marching on long legs across golden florets, a soldier beetle seeks out the pollen-bearing parts of the blossoms. Though the adults eat pollen, the young prey on other larvae.

Gently poised with folded wings, a copper butterfly unfurls its long proboscis, which will be inserted in the flower tube to draw up nectar. Near by, a bee collects pollen.

As yellow as the goldenrod, a crab spider lies in wait for its minute prey. When on blossoms of another colour, the spider will change its camouflage to match the new setting.

The essential work of bees

The mining bee is a solitary insect – it does not live in colonies. Named for its digging habit, this bee deposits its eggs in underground tunnels, along with a food supply of nectar and pollen.

Dusted with pollen, a honeybee concentrates on gathering nectar, oblivious of its important role as a pollinator of vegetables and other food crops. Honeybees are social insects and live in colonies.

The busiest bee is the bumblebee, which visits twice as many flowers in the same time as other bees. Most are larger and more colourful than honeybees.

Something for nothing is rare in this world, but every year we humans have a multi-million-pound job performed for us virtually free of charge. The job is pollination, and it is done mostly by bees and a host of other insects. Without their tireless work, we would not have most fruits and many other foods – not to mention honey.

Before a plant can produce fruit or seeds, it has to produce flowers – and flowers must be pollinated. That is, pollen must be transferred from the male part to the female part, where fertilisation takes place. Though many important plants, such as grasses, are pollinated by the wind, numerous others "enlist" the aid of insects.

One of the fascinating discoveries of botanists has been the way insects and flowering plants have evolved together, one influencing the other over millions of years. During this long evolutionary process, the partners have developed mutually beneficial working arrangements. In some cases, plant and pollinator are absolutely dependent on one another – if the plant dies out, so will the pollinator, and vice versa.

For most pollinators, the rewards are pollen and nectar, which is produced within the flower. Plants have evolved a variety of signals that help bees and other pollinators find their way to these desirable substances.

Both attract insects by their sweet odour. Bright colours help to advertise the flowers. The petals of some blossoms are modified so they provide "landing fields" and guiding patterns, which lead insects to the right places.

Unlike pollen, nectar is purely an attractant and is not directly involved in reproduction. Most insect-pollinated flowers have special glands that secrete

SAFETY AND SURVIVAL
How to avoid stings

Many bees and wasps build their colonies in early spring, and are therefore fewer in number at that time. But by autumn, a single colony of bees may have as many as 3,000 individuals. Thus, the chances of being stung will increase as the summer advances. Both gardens and fields of wildflowers are likely to have bees and wasps, since flowers are their food source.
• Insects are attracted by bright colours.

Khaki is an ideal outdoor clothing fabric – not only is it pale in colour, but it also has a tightly woven texture that is not readily penetrated by an insect's sting.
• Do not wear perfume, scented lotion or hair spray. These smells will attract stinging and biting insects.
• If a bee or wasp flies into your car, stop slowly and open all windows. A stationary or slow-moving vehicle will give the insect an opportunity to leave.
• If you are in a field and are attacked by several bees from a disturbed nest, run through a wooded or shaded area, where

the leaves and branches will hinder their direct and speedy pursuit.
• Wasps are attracted by food; many species feed their larvae on the remains of picnics.
• The best sting antidotes are A for B and V for W: in other words, ammonia for bee stings, vinegar for wasp stings.
• Some people are more sensitive to stings than others. If someone is stung and has a strong reaction, do not underestimate the seriousness of the situation; get medical help for the person as soon as possible – stings can occasionally be fatal.

nectar. As a child, you may have sampled the nectar of honeysuckle by pinching off and sucking the lower part of the blossom. (You can make an artificial nectar by dissolving a small amount of sugar in a shallow dish of water. Put the dish outdoors in the sunshine, and see what insects will come.)

Bees, especially the species called honeybees, are important pollinators. Honeybees are social insects, highly organised into castes, which have specialised duties. Colonies of wild bees often live in hollow trees. Domesticated bee colonies are housed in a hive, usually a box-like structure.

All the work of the colony is done by female worker bees. Only one caste, the foragers, collects nectar; these bees carry it inside their bodies in a special crop, and feed it to other members of the colony. To obtain a full load of nectar, a forager may have to visit thousands of flowers.

Honey is derived from nectar. The nectar is aerated in the bees' mouths, a process that evaporates much of the water. The addition of digestive juices completes the transformation into honey. Worker bees seal the honey into the hexagonal cells of beeswax that make up the honeycomb. Stored honey will be used later as food for the bees – unless a human bee-keeper removes the comb first. Solitary species, such as yellow-faced and carpenter bees, do not live in colonies, but nevertheless they gather nectar and make honey.

In collecting nectar, bees brush by the flower's pollen-producing parts. The golden powder is sticky and adheres to the bees' hairy bodies. Some of it is dislodged and pollinates the same or a different flower.

The rest is carried back to the hive in the bees' pollen baskets – small depressions surrounded by bristles on their hind legs. If you watch a bee at work, you may be able to see such bee bread, as the pollen is called, on its body.

The pollen, an important food for bees, is stored in the hive. A typical bee colony may consume about 50 lb. of pollen a year; collecting this amount would require some 2 million trips.

White clover is a favourite with honeybees. This is because the bees can easily remove the nectar from its relatively small blossoms. Red clover, on the other hand, gives them more difficulty – occasionally the bees' tongues do not quite reach the nectar. Clover honey is one of the most subtle-tasting popular varieties.

Bees and flowers adapted to one another

The construction of some flowers, such as certain orchids, determines the way a bee enters and departs. It is, in fact, a system that ensures pollination. Intent on gathering nectar, the bee follows lines and grooves, called honey guides, that lead to the nectar. The bee cannot extract nectar without being dusted with pollen. When it visits another flower, pollen is left behind, and cross-pollination results.

The lower lip of this flower is a landing platform for a bee that is seeking nectar.

The bee's weight depresses the lower petal, swinging the pollen-covered anther down.

As the bee leaves, it brushes against the anther, getting a liberal coating of pollen.

The beauty of butterflies and moths

A flowering meadow is a splendid place to watch butterflies. Unconcealed by foliage, the butterflies flit about near the tops of plants, just at or below eye level. Here, in temperate latitudes in midsummer, you will see the greatest numbers of butterflies.

Settle down in the middle of a meadow. At first, let your eyes wander, taking in the blazing colours of blossom and butterfly, the scents of field and flower. Then select a particular nearby butterfly – just one, for a start. It takes some concentration to do this, for you will see numerous other butterflies out of the corner of your eye. Note the size, shape, colour and any speckles or eyespots (large dots of colour on the wings). These features can help you to identify the species. But whether you have a guidebook or not, watch how the butterfly alights on a flower, and how it sips nectar. It uses its long tongue (proboscis) as a straw.

When a butterfly lands it usually folds its wings, concealing all but the relatively drab undersides. But, if disturbed, a butterfly may suddenly spread its wings, revealing brilliantly coloured patterns on the upper surface. A burst of bright colour may startle a pursuer long enough for the butterfly to escape.

Butterflies and their close relatives, the moths, have other defences. The eyespots may actually frighten a would-be predator. Other wing patterns may make the less-vulnerable tail look like the head. One of the most surprising defences belongs to certain species of moths that are preyed upon by bats. Bats send out high-frequency squeaks, somewhat like sonar, that help them locate prey. But these particular moths take evasive action when they "hear" the high-frequency sounds. If the signal from the bat is strong (which means that the bat is near), the moth zigzags through the air; if the signal is weak, the moth dives and takes cover.

Butterflies and moths play a significant role in pollinating flowering plants (though they are not as important as bees). These insects obtain food – the sugar-rich nectar – and pick up pollen in the process.

There are butterfly flowers, and other flowers that attract moths. It is usually easy to distinguish between the two. Most moths are nocturnal. Moth flowers typically have a strong fragrance and are light in colour; thus they are readily perceived in the dim evening light. Another characteristic of moth flowers is that they often hang downward, easily reached by hovering moths.

The copper butterfly will drive off most other butterflies – regardless of size. It is not intimidated by larger animals, even humans. It sips nectar through its straw-like proboscis. The copper is identified by its bright colour and dark spots (the colour varies). Coppers are seen in open areas such as marshes, roadsides and meadows.

A moth at rest is often very well camouflaged. The pattern of brown and green on the forewings of this small New Guinean species – an arctiid, or footman, moth – makes it resemble a drying leaf. It might be overlooked by a lizard or a bird. There are more than 6,000 species of these arctiid moths, which are distributed world-wide from the Alps to the tropics.

When Charles Darwin, the British naturalist, visited Madagascar in 1862, he noticed a large orchid with the pollen and nectar-producing parts a full 10 in. deep inside the tip of the blossom. He knew that many orchids were pollinated by moths, and so he predicted that some day a moth would be discovered with a 10 in. proboscis. Eventually, such a moth was found.

The silk-worm, which has clothed the rich and the beautiful through the centuries, is the caterpillar of a moth. The silk is the cocoon it weaves round its body.

Butterflies do not hover when they feed, but actually land on a blossom. Butterfly flowers are upright, which provides a stable landing platform. Butterflies, which are usually active during the day, are attracted to blossoms by both scent and colour, and butterfly flowers tend to be orange or red. There is even an orange-flowered species of milkweed called butterfly weed – a veritable magnet for these beautiful insects.

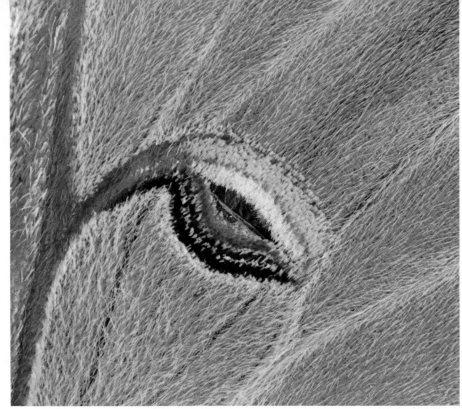

Uncanny eye-like spots – one on each forewing (above) and also on the underside – are the luna moth's defence. A flash of these bold markings may confuse a predator and gain time for the moth to escape. The feathery texture on this moth's wing is typical of many moth species.

A microscopic view of delicate wings

The colours on butterflies and moths are produced by overlapping scales, shown here through an electron microscope. The colours result from two types of scales. In one, the presence of pigments causes colour. In the other, a layered structure, without pigments, creates an illusion of colour. Iridescence occurs when light hits cells at different angles, transmitting, perhaps, now a shimmer of purple, now one of green.

The wing of a South American castniid moth shows finely structured, overlapping scales arranged in an irregular pattern.

Light bouncing off tiny ridges on the scales of an Asian swallowtail butterfly creates these beautifully blended colours.

Man versus insect

In the never-ending battle against disease and pests, scientists are starting to turn the clock back – by using nature's own control techniques. Instead of chemical poisons which may contaminate crops, they are using the pest's own natural enemies or treating and releasing the pests themselves.

In one experiment, male cattle flies were sterilised by radiation, then dropped over grasslands to find mates. When they mated with the females, the hope was that the eggs would be infertile, and the females would not be able to mate again. The effectiveness of this strategy was demonstrated by the decline in infected cattle over one eight-year period, from 50,000 to 150 head of cattle.

This method of using one living thing to manage another is called biological control – biocontrol, for short. Animal populations in nature are balanced in this way, through predation, parasitism and diseases, as well as food supply and climate. Biocontrol, as practised by man, is not new. As far back as 1,000 years ago, the Chinese used ants to attack insect pests on fruit trees. One of the first modern experiments was in 1888, when Australian ladybirds were imported to prey on scale insects infesting Californian fruit trees. It went so well that by 1890 the scale insect was no longer a problem.

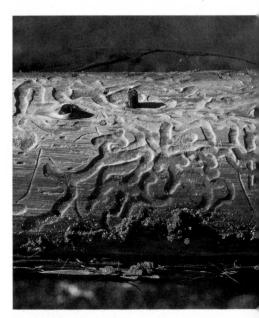

These etchings in wood were made by larvae of a metallic beetle while the tree was alive. Feeding on sapwood, the larvae gnawed broad channels and killed the tree. When the bark dropped off, the damage was revealed.

The life history of an industrious pest

An iridescent Japanese beetle, seen here making lacework of an alder leaf, is an alien species which has invaded America. It eats the leaves, flowers and fruit of some 300 kinds of trees and shrubs. Because it is an alien in the US, it has few natural enemies – except the starling. Like many other insects, Japanese beetles pass through various stages of development (see below). Efforts to control Japanese beetles take advantage of the fact that they are most vulnerable at the larval stage. Spores of the bacteria that feed on the larvae are injected into the ground. There they infect the larvae and kill them before they can mature.

Japanese beetle egg

Larva

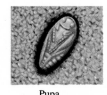
Pupa

Adult

Biocontrols became more important after the Second World War, when the disadvantages of chemical pesticides such as DDT became obvious. Although they were often necessary to protect crops and to prevent outbreaks of disease, chemical pesticides build up dangerously in the environment and kill beneficial animals as well as pests.

One of the most successful biocontrols has been to "enlist" a pest's natural enemy as an ally. A good example is the mosquito fish, a North American species that feeds on mosquito larvae. In 1905, the fish were released into Hawaiian ponds and streams to help control mosquitoes. The results were so successful that the species has been introduced into South America, Europe, Asia and New Zealand. In fact, the species may now be the most wide-ranging freshwater fish in the world.

The search for a natural adversary may lead around the world. After combing Europe and Asia, scientists found a wasp in Iran that served as a parasite of certain insects that are notorious pests on Californian olive trees. However, the Iranian wasp did not do well in the new climate, and another search turned up a Pakistani wasp that was better suited to the New World.

The Japanese beetle has been successfully controlled in some places by spraying crops with bacteria that cause milky-spore disease. Though these bacteria are deadly to the beetles, they are harmless to other animals. Experiments are also being made with viruses in the hope that an epidemic, like the influenza that killed millions of people in 1918, can be made to kill pests without harming useful creatures.

One weapon was discovered when certain laboratory insects died before reaching maturity. Those that succumbed lived in cages that were lined with American newspapers, such as *The New York Times:* the survivors' cages were lined with copies of the London *Times.* The premature deaths were traced to chemicals found in American balsam fir trees used in the paper pulp, but not found in European trees. Similar chemicals are now used as sprays to prevent insects from developing normally, or to make them emerge from cocoons at an unfavourable time.

But even the best biocontrols are not perfect. There have been renewed outbreaks of cattle flies (biocontrols always leave a few remnants unharmed). Such controls also tend to work slowly. Scientists look on them as only one tool against harmful insects. Combined with carefully handled chemical insecticides, biocontrols offer a hope that we can protect ourselves and our crops without causing damage to our environment.

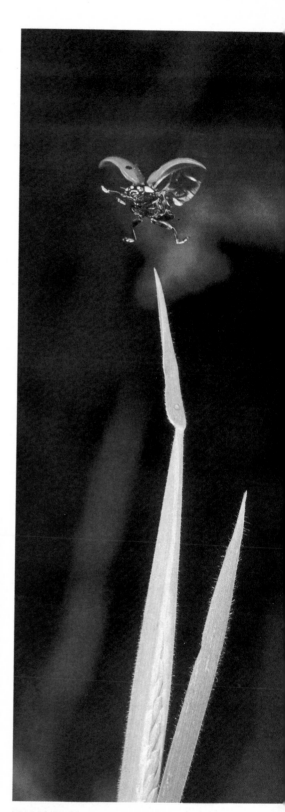

The praying mantis gets its name from its characteristic posture when at rest. Blending with the surrounding foliage, it waits with spiny forelegs raised; any unsuspecting insect is quickly captured and devoured. Because it feeds on beetles, caterpillars and other insects, the mantis is considered beneficial. In America, these predatory insects can be bought and released in the garden to help control insects that damage plants.

A ladybird, with orange wing-covers raised, is about to alight. This little beetle eats so many different destructive pests that it is sometimes introduced into orchards to help protect the trees from infestation.

How farmers manage water and soil

Small gullies and muddy streaks – which appear after rains – are warning signals of further erosion. Water will widen and deepen these channels.

Seeding the gully with ryegrass is good first aid. The roots will hold the soil even if the grass dies. Later on, a more permanent ground-cover is planted.

Water-carrying ditches, especially along roads, too often turn into ugly and dangerous pits. They may undermine paths and roads.

Filling a ditch with small stones will not impede the drainage, but it will lessen erosion of the soil. The ditch will also look better.

Animals such as otters sometimes make a slide in a grassy bank. Or damage may take place because of construction.

Flat stones can be stacked in the slideway, starting with bigger rocks at the bottom of the bank. Care has to be taken to make the construction stable.

Human beings tend to think of soil and water as separate entities (and, of course, they are); but all over the surface of the earth, the two are almost inseparable. Vapour in the air condenses around particles of dust; thus rain brings tiny bits of soil down to earth. Water dissolves many substances, and transports others. When rivers are dammed, to impound water or to generate hydro-electric power, the affinity of soil and water is sometimes overlooked. For example, the Aswan Dam in Egypt is silting up so quickly that it may soon become virtually useless. Meanwhile, the once-fertile Nile Valley is deprived of much of its annual renewal, which came in the form of silt-bearing flood waters.

The Aswan Dam example reveals the paradoxical nature of flooding – it is sometimes beneficial, sometimes catastrophic. In one instance, fertile soil may be deposited, but in other places, topsoil may be carried away, impoverishing the land. The loss of topsoil, which supports food crops, is regarded by some experts as the most serious of all depletions of our natural resources. As one scientist said; "If the soil disappears, so do we."

Usually, the longer water flows over the land, the more soil it picks up – and the harder it is to manage swelling streams. The water of a tiny rivulet on a high grassland generally carries very little soil, and it is readily controlled. But in the lowlands, where numerous streams may come together, the waters change character. There they may become destroyers, like a

herd of wild animals on a rampage. Effective flood control and soil conservation must take place upstream. And in recent years progress has been made along these lines. Once farmers used to bury tiles in their fields to hasten the run-off of heavy rains. Nowadays, many farmers do all they can to detain water. If water soaks into subsoil, it becomes part of the water table, which is an underground reservoir.

Contour farming is an important form of soil conservation. That is, fields are ploughed and planted following the natural contours of the ground. The furrows run across a slope rather than up and down. In effect, this forms a multitude of small dams. Often different crops are grown along the contours in relatively thin bands, so that when one crop is harvested a nearby strip will still protect the slope against wind and rain erosion.

Grasses have been enlisted in the work of slowing run-off and soaking up rain. Their extensive root systems capture tremendous amounts of water. On a hillside where drainage channels are planted with grasses, the grass is not cut. As water flows, the bending grasses form a blanket that prevents erosion.

Grasses are now used as a bed for other crops. Corn or some other grain is set into the grassy beds in narrow slits – in other words, the land is not cleared at all. Some grasses (chosen because they do not compete with the main crop) improve soil structure and help keep weeds out. Terracing, too, is an important means of controlling water. (See facing page.)

Once a eucalyptus forest, this area in Victoria, Australia, was cleared for pastureland (most likely for sheep). The animals grazed the land to the point where its protective cover of grass was destroyed. The occasional heavy downpours of rain in this otherwise dry region washed away the topsoil. Deep gullies formed, and now the land is a desert.

Elevated rice terraces (above), characteristic of the Philippines and other parts of Asia, are an ancient form of farming. Terracing permits even steep hillsides to be used in regions where level land is scarce. The terraces are built so that water from a ridge above will spill on to those below. In parts of Europe grapes are grown on terraces.

Using the contours of the land

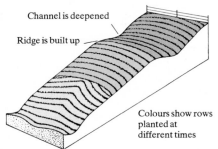

Channel is deepened

Ridge is built up

Colours show rows planted at different times

This diagram illustrates how terraces are created on gently sloping terrain. Farmers make ditches (channels), and use the soil to create ridges. This artificial landscape helps to hold water and stem erosion.

Contouring and strip farming, combined in this Pennsylvania valley (left), are ideal conservation techniques. In contour farming, the crops are planted along lines that follow the curvature of the land; rain does not run off quickly, but remains in the ditches and is gradually absorbed. In strip farming, different kinds of crops are planted in alternating bands so that during ploughing or harvesting, adjacent land has some plant cover.

Wonder crops and wild plants

In guarded vaults at an American installation in Colorado, there are treasures that are among the most valuable assets to life on this planet. The contents of these vaults (maintained at a constant temperature and humidity) are not precious metals or rare medicines. In fact, you could undoubtedly find some of these same treasures in your own garden. They are seeds.

Gradually, as more and more land has been taken over by agriculture, cities and roads, countless wild plants have been displaced. Some species have died out entirely. The Colorado seed-storage system is just one effort to keep alive as many genetic strains as possible. The vaults hold seeds from around the world, including the seeds not only of endangered species, but also of plants that are not in current use. For there are fashions in agriculture, as in every other human activity.

Most of our present-day food crops – such as rice and barley – came from wild ancestors, and apparently were easily cultivated by early farmers. Two of the world's most important plants, maize and wheat, are products of natural cross-breeding. Plant scientists have bred these and many other crops to achieve greater productivity. (The "miracle rice" of recent years is another example.) Two strains of any plant species are sometimes crossed to increase yield or nutrient content. Other crosses have given us crops that are particularly resistant to drought, or to insect pests.

So successful were these hybrids that they were planted on a continent-wide basis. Only after doing this a few times did scientists and farmers discover that there were hazards attending these successes. The corn blight of 1970 was just such a harsh lesson. This leaf virus reduced the US maize crop by some 15%. The epidemic could not be halted because so many plants of the same strain had been planted on adjacent farms. Field after field was afflicted. Fortunately, plant breeders had many other types available to replace the decimated strain. Present farming now encourages diversity.

Seeds are of great interest at present because agricultural specialists believe that technology – which has increased harvests in the past – cannot go much further in increasing production. For example, fertilisers are expensive, and farm machinery is already extremely efficient. The experts must look elsewhere. Until now, farmers have had great success with relatively few species of plants. Some species have never been tested for their food potential.

There are interesting options available to plant breeders. For example, maize is now being bred to take greater advantage of the energy from the sun. Usually, the leaves of a sweet-corn plant grow opposite to one another. Now, a strain is being developed where the leaves grow all around – giving the plant more exposure to sunlight. Eventually, there should be more growth per plant.

Another development has been to breed maize that can flourish in the sparse sunlight of a British summer.

The most amazing wonder crop may come from new "fused-plant" experiments, using genetic materials from two entirely different plant species. One proposed species may be "pomatoes", plants that would produce tomatoes above ground and potatoes below. Another visionary plant is called "soycorn", and would do much the same thing – grow more food in less space. Whatever the direction agriculture takes, the fundamental need is to preserve as many genetic strains of plants as possible. We never know when we will need them.

Maize began as an ordinary grass

Centuries before Columbus landed in the New World, Indians in the Western Hemisphere were growing primitive maize. Most likely, their maize resembled a grass called teosinte, which is shown right. The natural cross-pollination among wild grasses, probably including teosinte, produced several varieties of maize (called corn in America). When Europeans arrived in the New World, Indians were growing all the main types of maize we have today – sweet, pop, flour, dent and flint. The tremendous change in maize is shown below. Teosinte (between the fingers at the left of the photo) has about nine kernels. Teosinte still grows wild, and is also cultivated for fodder in parts of the United States, Mexico and Central America. An ancient type of South American popcorn (in the hand at right) has many more kernels. Multicoloured Indian maize is next in size. The all-yellow modern hybrid in the background is the longest ear of maize that breeders have yet been able to develop. A single ear of this type may contain about 1,000 large kernels.

Techniques for photographing plants and animals on a farm

Farms and the fields around them are excellent places for photographing animals. But many of the best subjects are camera-shy and fast shutter speeds are needed to catch them in a good pose. Telephoto lenses allow a photographer to take pictures without getting too close and scaring the animal away. If you have a single-lens reflex camera, an extension tube will open up a new world of intriguing close-ups of insects and plants.

● Even grasses swaying in the wind can be captured on film. Use a shutter speed of 1/125th or faster, to freeze the action.

● Try isolating a few grass stems by using a large aperture and letting the foreground or background soften. Only the selected stems need to be in sharp focus.

Strong backlighting from the mid-morning sun created the deep shadows and contours of this pastoral scene (above). Sheep are on a steep hillside above the photographer, and the sunlight is parallel to the slope. A polarising filter was used to deepen the tones and enhance the halos.

Clarity of texture is evident in this portrait of golden grain (upper right), photographed under the light of a noonday sun. To achieve this effect, use the smallest aperture and wait for a moment of stillness.

To get a silhouette, try for an uncluttered background. Early morning and late afternoon are favourable; the light is relatively horizontal. Photographed from a higher level, the horse (right) has been silhouetted against the grass. A slight underexposure increases density and contrast.

CHAPTER SIX

Lakes and rivers

The wonderful thing about water is that it can be recycled endlessly. Most of the present-day supply is millions of years old.

There is probably no such thing as pure water. Even when water is created artificially in a laboratory from hydrogen and oxygen, it must be stored in something, and water will dissolve a slight amount of whatever holds it. Water is rightfully called the universal solvent. When you drink a glass of water, you are also drinking a few harmless molecules of dissolved glass.

Few physical facts have greater significance for all living things than this ability of water to dissolve and transport materials. Water is the main ingredient of life-supporting substances – in the blood-streams of animals and in the vein systems of plants. It is indeed the medium of life.

Water begins picking up "passengers" when it falls as rain – it dissolves gases in the air and carries tiny particles too. As water flows over land on its way to the sea, it picks up a trace of almost everything it touches, particularly salts. Thus a river may already be somewhat salty by the time it reaches the sea.

But most fresh water on land is not in lakes and rivers; it is hidden underground in vast reservoirs collectively called the water table. It has always been clear that springs and wells were part of an underground water supply. But rivers and streams, too, are supplied by the water table, as are countless fertile fields, meadows and forests. By its very nature, the water table is hard to survey. Over countless centuries, water has seeped where it could, sometimes blocked, sometimes travelling along underground channels. Far more water is needed to replenish these reservoirs than is supplied by even a long winter's rainfall. Therefore, like so many other resources, water must be drawn upon carefully, so that it may last.

Lively, noisy and handsome, a flurry of ducks takes off from a lake. Green-headed male mallards stand out in contrast with the less colourful females of the species. Mallards, pintails, wigeons and many other waterfowl stop off in hundreds of waterways along their migration route. For them, protection of every pond, lake and marsh is of vital importance.

Beautiful freshwater worlds

By far the most abundant substance on the surface of our planet is water. Surprisingly, only a tiny fraction – about one five-thousandth – of this water is fresh water that we can drink. Nevertheless, it is this "drop in the bucket" that keeps us – and all other land animals – alive.

It is hard for us to grasp just how small a share of the world's water is fresh. The supply seems unlimited. Yet, if all the water in all the rivers, lakes, ponds, swamps and puddles were distributed evenly over the surface of the earth, it would reach a depth of little more than 1 ft. By contrast, the sea water contained in the oceans of the world would be more than $1\frac{1}{2}$ miles deep.

There is one great difference between the water in most rivers and lakes and that in the oceans of the world – salt. Most fresh water contains only a slight amount of salt, which is mainly sodium chloride.

"Water is the driver of nature," Leonardo da Vinci once wrote. Without the evaporation of water from the sea, its fall as rain or snow, and its return to the sea via the world's network of rivers, there would be no weather. Without the water cycle, much of the world would become too hot, too dry, or too cold to support life.

Although the relative amount of water in the rivers of the world at any one time is minute, immense quantities pass through them annually. The Amazon, the world's largest river, discharges some 3,000 cu. miles of water a year – about one-fifth of all the water that runs off the land. The flow is so great that it creates a freshwater "river" in the sea that stretches beyond the sight of land.

The water in lakes moves slowly or not at all. Filling in depressions in the land, they contain nearly all of the fresh water easily obtained by man. Much of this water is tapped by man to irrigate crops, but industry also uses large quantities – the manufacture of 1 ton of steel, paper or woollen cloth requires from 250 to 600 tons of fresh water.

It is easy to appreciate the importance of a large lake as a freshwater reservoir, but another significant role is invisible. Lakes are some of the world's greatest evaporators. Only about one-third of the water that falls on land flows back directly to the sea. Much of the remainder is evaporated from lakes back into the air, then carried by the wind to new sites where it falls again as rain or snow. Marshes, swamps and other wetlands perform yet another role in the world's water cycle: they are places where water readily soaks into the earth. This replenishes the store of underground water that supplies wells, springs, and contributes to many of our purest streams.

The many faces of water – rivers, marshes, swamps, bogs, lakes and ponds – are all so different, they hardly seem to lead one into another. For example, marshes are usually well-lighted because trees do not grow within them. But bogs and swamps, which support trees, have a dark aspect – to some people, they are mysterious; to others, they seem forbidding, almost dismal.

For sheer picture-postcard beauty, few bodies of water can rival the sparkle of a mountain lake, or the quiet, silvery-blue of such a lake as Geneva in Switzerland. And nowhere in the world are they more picturesque than in Britain. In its relatively small compass, for instance, the English Lake District includes the barren, stony grandeur of Wastwater, the tree-girt magnificence of Derwentwater and the shy beauty of Grasmere. And what visitor would ever forget the Scottish lochs or the bare crags rising sheer over the Welsh lakes?

Lakes not only show off their own features but also reflect the things around them – sky, clouds, perhaps an entire mountain. Thus they get the reputation of romantic moodiness. No wonder that poets have loved them through the centuries.

In a clear sky they glimmer happily. If thunderstorms gather overhead, the lakes take on the dark anger of the sky, or they may blaze with fire from the reflection of a spectacular sunset.

 PHOTO TIPS
Water in action

Rushing water is a challenge: how can you catch its elusive, fluid quality on film? First, go where the action is, to a thundering waterfall or to the headlong tumble of white-water rapids.

• When you have found water that is "alive", your choice of effects may be determined by what your camera can do; if it has adjustable shutter speeds, you can get a crisp, stop-action quality to the flowing water. Use a fast shutter speed, such as 1/250th of a second or faster, which will "freeze" the water, as in the photo, right. For an ethereal, veil-like effect, as in the waterfall on the facing page, use a shutter speed of 1/60th or slower – and a tripod or other support to prevent camera movement.

• Still waters, which are easier to photograph, can be enhanced by picking up sparkling highlights (as in the marsh photo, upper right). A lens hood is needed to stop extraneous light striking the lens and causing flares.

Marshes such as the Coto Doñana in Spain (above) shelter a wealth of wildlife – including animals as large as deer. Although marshes were once believed to give off noxious gases, we now know they produce tremendous quantities of oxygen.

The rushing waters of Eagle Creek (above) feed Lake Tahoe, high in the American Rockies. Tahoe is one of the few crystalline lakes in the world – which means that its waters are cold, clear, and relatively devoid of plant and animal life.

Visiting a quiet, lazy, limpid stretch of mountain stream like this one on the left, it is hard to remember that its idyllic waters are part of a larger system. Collectively, many such streams add up to wide rivers that tumble into the ocean.

171

Network of lakes and rivers

On archaeological evidence, many of mankind's first cities were situated on rivers. Notable among them were cities on the Tigris and Euphrates in the Middle East, and on the Indus River in India. Rivers invited settlement not just for the drinking and irrigation water available, but because they provided arteries for trade.

If you follow any river on a map – whether showing ancient or modern times – you will find an impressive roster of cities. Vienna, Budapest and Belgrade are located on the Danube. Minneapolis-St Paul, St Louis and Memphis are major inland ports on the Mississippi River.

Although the 20th century is commonly regarded as the age of cars, lorries and aircraft, riverboats (barges and tugs) remain significant vehicles of commerce. In many nations, rivers carry more freight than all the highways, railways and ocean transports combined. The Ohio River, for example, carries more tonnage than does the Panama Canal.

This is surprising when you consider that lakes and rivers contain a negligible share of the world's water – only about 0.01%. At that, few rivers provide clear passage for their entire length. Systems of canals and locks have been constructed to bypass rapids and connect navigable rivers. Today, you can sail on inland waters all the way from Amsterdam near the North Sea to Marseilles on the Mediterranean. In the United States, you can go by inland and intercoastal waterways from Texas to New York City.

When locks are used, such as those that help link the Great Lakes with the Atlantic, the system is one of creating small, self-contained "lakes". A ship enters a chamber, both ends are blocked, and the water level is changed; then one end is opened and the ship continues along. The one navigational challenge that has never truly been bypassed is a giant waterfall, such as Murchison Falls in Africa (now called Kabalega), which prevented exploration of the upper Nile. In fact, the many waterfalls and rapids of the Nile kept the river's source a major geographical mystery for centuries – the upper gorge of the Blue Nile was not mapped until the 1960s.

All too often we have misused lakes and rivers as sewers and dumps for chemical waste, poisoning the water and killing vegetable and animal life. Recently governments and industry have been co-operating world-wide to clean up fouled waters. In some British rivers salmon are back for the first time in decades, but much remains to be done.

Many rivers in Alaska and the Yukon (such as the Klondike) were important sources of gold

The Columbia River is of vital importance to salmon, which swim upstream against strong currents to reach their spawning grounds

The Colorado River, which carved the Grand Canyon, is the major source of water for the south-west

Lake Nicaragua, largest lake in Central America, has been proposed as an alternative to the Panama Canal. But the region is plagued by earthquakes

The five Great Lakes of North America, together with the St Lawrence River, form an inland waterway from the Atlantic to the mid-west

The Mississippi links network of rivers that drain the middle reg of the United States

The Amazon, the world's largest river, is about 4,000 miles long. Although it originates high in the Andes, the Amazon flows through such profuse tropical jungles that some areas are still inaccessible to man

Lake Titicaca, the highest navigable lake in the world, is 12,500 ft above sea level

The entire Plata Rive is really an estuary, which means it is an arm of the sea

Waterfalls – where rivers drop dramatically

Water plummeting thousands of feet is perhaps one of the most spectacular of all natural wonders. Height alone, however, does not determine the fame of a waterfall – some are notable for their volume of water, width or pattern of flow. The volume of water flowing over Niagara is about 212,000 cu. ft a second. Angel Falls, the world's highest, descends in two steep falls. A succession of falls along the same stream-bed, such as Iguaçu, is called a cascade.

1. NIAGARA'S HORSESHOE FALLS
176 ft high
Niagara River, Canada-US

2. ANGEL FALLS
3,212 ft high
Churún River, Venezuela

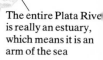

3. IGUAÇU FALLS
269 ft high
Iguaçu River, Brazil-Argentina

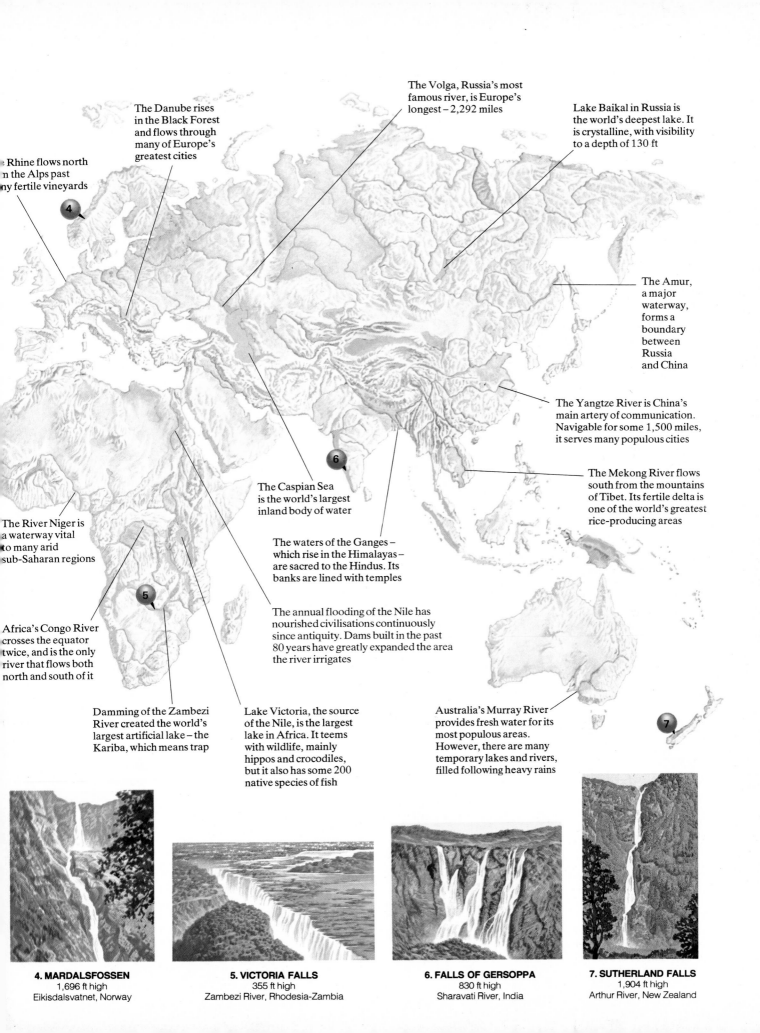

The Volga, Russia's most famous river, is Europe's longest – 2,292 miles

The Danube rises in the Black Forest and flows through many of Europe's greatest cities

Lake Baikal in Russia is the world's deepest lake. It is crystalline, with visibility to a depth of 130 ft

Rhine flows north n the Alps past ny fertile vineyards

The Amur, a major waterway, forms a boundary between Russia and China

The Yangtze River is China's main artery of communication. Navigable for some 1,500 miles, it serves many populous cities

The Mekong River flows south from the mountains of Tibet. Its fertile delta is one of the world's greatest rice-producing areas

The River Niger is a waterway vital to many arid sub-Saharan regions

The Caspian Sea is the world's largest inland body of water

The waters of the Ganges – which rise in the Himalayas – are sacred to the Hindus. Its banks are lined with temples

Africa's Congo River crosses the equator twice, and is the only river that flows both north and south of it

The annual flooding of the Nile has nourished civilisations continuously since antiquity. Dams built in the past 80 years have greatly expanded the area the river irrigates

Damming of the Zambezi River created the world's largest artificial lake – the Kariba, which means trap

Lake Victoria, the source of the Nile, is the largest lake in Africa. It teems with wildlife, mainly hippos and crocodiles, but it also has some 200 native species of fish

Australia's Murray River provides fresh water for its most populous areas. However, there are many temporary lakes and rivers, filled following heavy rains

4. MARDALSFOSSEN
1,696 ft high
Eikisdalsvatnet, Norway

5. VICTORIA FALLS
355 ft high
Zambezi River, Rhodesia-Zambia

6. FALLS OF GERSOPPA
830 ft high
Sharavati River, India

7. SUTHERLAND FALLS
1,904 ft high
Arthur River, New Zealand

The why's and where's of lakes

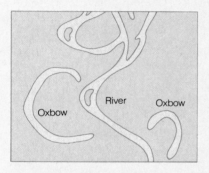
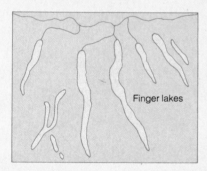
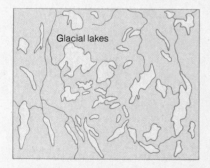
A lake's shape often tells a great deal about its origins. If you see a narrow, comma-shaped lake in low country, near the bend in a river, the chances are that the lake is an oxbow. This kind of lake is formed when a meandering river changes its course, and part of the river – a loop – is left behind. The oxbow becomes even more isolated from the river as evaporation lowers its level. But it may continue to exist for a long time.

Some lakes are souvenirs of immense glaciers from the Ice Ages. Where a glacier covered level land, it frequently scoured out shallow lake beds – in Finland, parts of Scandinavia, and in central southern Canada and the northern United States there are tens of thousands of such small glacial lakes.

Glaciers that were confined to valleys leave a different imprint. As they moved, they carried immense loads of rubble in the ice. When the ice melted, the rubble was left as a dam, and a lake formed behind it. Many of the mountain lakes of Norway and Sweden are typical of such dammed valleys.

Some lakes develop rapidly. The round, high-walled lakes of many mountainous regions lie in a basin created when a volcano blew its top, or when the top of the volcano collapsed. Some of these lakes, such as America's Crater Lake, are a result of a volcanic explosion followed by a subsequent collapse.

The oldest and deepest lakes in the world were formed when huge blocks in the earth's crust sank. Lake Baikal in Asia and Lake Tanganyika in Africa were formed in this way some 25 million years ago, making them hundreds of times older than the majority of lakes. There are several lakes with a larger surface area than Baikal, but none holds more water. Baikal is more than 1 mile deep – by far the deepest lake in the world. Lake Tanganyika is the second deepest – 4,700 ft.

Surprisingly, some lakes are no deeper than a mud puddle and no older than a few hours. These are the playa lakes, which form in flat areas in dry regions after a rare rainstorm. In America's Black Rock Desert, a playa lake of some 400 to 500 sq. miles – but only a few inches deep – develops nearly every winter, then disappears.

Man-made lakes rival the largest natural ones, but perhaps the world's most devoted lake-builder is the beaver of Eurasia and North America. Some beaver dams may be 12 ft high and 1,800 ft long, containing hundreds of tons of logs, mud and rocks. After population declines caused by trapping, these animals are being re-introduced into many areas as a conservation measure; they help to control run-off and stem erosion. As one conservationist said: "Beavers will build you a £5,000 dam for nothing."

However, beavers breed prolifically. There are now about 3 million in the United States and 5 million in Canada.

Crater Lake, in the north-western American state of Oregon, was formed when a volcano exploded and collapsed. This lake, which has no inlet or outlet, is the deepest in the United States.

Preparing for winter, a beaver carries an aspen branch back to the lodge – a prized addition to its underwater food cache.

A beaver dam requires constant repair. Dams are strengthened with mud and stones; soil and leaves trapped by the dam reinforce the structure.

Engineering feats of a beaver colony

A beaver colony has up to a dozen individuals, including the parents and offspring from two litters. (Each litter usually consists of four kits.) When the young are about two years old, they leave the colony and seek a mate. Beavers are renowned for their ability to build and maintain a dam; they also construct a well-engineered lodge, which has several underwater entrances. In addition, beavers build canals, which allow these aquatic animals to haul food (they eat bark) from distant places. When the food supply is exhausted, the beavers will move elsewhere and establish a new colony.

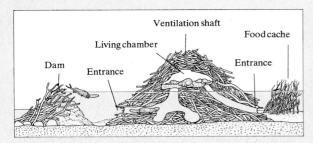

Dam, lodge and food cache are close to one another. In autumn, beavers may enlarge their living chamber – or even add a room.

This abandoned beaver dam in Alaska still shows its basic design – a graceful curve. The dam is widest at the bottom, where water pressure is greatest.

Insulated by snow and frozen mud, a beaver lodge keeps its inhabitants warm in winter. (Sometimes you can even detect steam rising through the ventilation shaft.) Beneath the ice at the surface of the pond, the beavers swim to and from their food cache. Air pockets under the ice provide oxygen. The beaver's warm, water-repellent coat is shown (right).

Lakes transformed by time

As soon as a lake is created, natural forces begin to fill it in. Though the process may take only a few years, or as long as several centuries, every lake – no matter how deep or wide – is destined to become dry land.

A lake is born when water fills a depression in the land. Usually, the first community to thrive in the young lake is minute, drifting water plants and animals, called plankton. They do well because what they need is already present – sunlight, minerals and other nutrients dissolved in the water. The plant plankton convert these ingredients into food, and are themselves "grazed" upon by animal plankton.

During its youth, the lake's waters are often a brilliant, transparent blue. This indicates that the water does not yet contain much life. However, the plankton usually increase their numbers and soon support many larger animals, including mussels, insects, fish and birds. These attract other animals.

As generations of animals succeed one another, some plant and animal remains are recycled by scavengers, but some debris accumulates on the bottom. Thus the bottom is built up, perhaps a foot or two a century; gradually, the lake becomes shallower.

The thick debris on the lake floor provides food and shelter for an increasing number of bottom-dwellers, including worms, snails and terrapins. Many of the later settlers replace the original pioneers. Perch, for example, may be among the lake's first residents, but they require a clean lake floor for their eggs. As plants and debris accumulate, the perch give way to fish that are better adapted to the changing conditions. Generally, the older a lake is, the more diverse its plant and animal life.

Submerged water plants begin to take root in parts of the lake where the bottom is built up to within about 20 ft of the surface. They slow the currents and accelerate the accumulation of silt and detritus. Plants also encroach from the shore. Reedmace, bulrushes and bur-reeds thrive near the water's edge. Further from the land, pondweed, arrowhead and water

The inevitable filling-in of lakes and ponds

A new pond begins to fill with life almost as soon as it forms. The pioneer species include microscopic plants and animals known as plankton. The wind and also the feathers and feet of waterfowl are the means by which seeds of plants and eggs of animals are brought to the pond.

In a young pond, the increasing growth of small aquatic plants and animals supports larger species, such as catfish and terrapins; a green heron hunts from the bank. Plant and animal debris forms a fertile layer at the bottom in which reedmace and water lilies take root.

A mature pond teems with life. Zones of aquatic vegetation run parallel to the edge, encroaching on the water. Sedges invade the marshy shore, where a bittern eyes a swimming frog. At the margin, the thickening layers are penetrated by earthworms, which aerate the damp soil.

A filled-in pond provides a habitat for land plants and animals. The moist, fertile soil promotes the growth of trees – one day, a forest may flourish here. All ponds eventually become dry land. How long a pond lasts depends on its initial size, water supply and the local climate.

lilies reach the surface from depths up to about 5 ft. The roots trap sediment and decaying plant matter, gradually building new soil and making the lake smaller. Marshy shores and patches of floating algae are signs that the lake has reached old age.

The life-span of a lake depends upon its size and surroundings. Of course, the larger of two similar lakes will last the longer. Lakes in the tropics generally age more quickly because plants can grow all year round.

Other local conditions may cancel the effect of climate. If the soil surrounding the lake is rich in plant nutrients, these will probably be carried into the lake by streams. This speeds up the lake's plant growth and its ageing. Some lakes seem to age more slowly because their surroundings are rich in salts that inhibit plant growth. As a rule, salt lakes are usually in dry climates, and will evaporate more quickly than their freshwater counterparts.

Cities and industries have had an impact on the life cycles of lakes. Materials dumped into lakes often accelerate the growth of plankton. The results are paradoxical – so much prosperity among species at the surface can (and often does) take up too much oxygen, suffocating species, such as game fish. Eventually, even the plankton may die, leaving only bacteria to release foul-smelling gases.

A spreading border of sedges and lilies will eventually transform this placid pond into a marshy meadow. In more northern places, where the growing season is short, the gradual transformation will take place more slowly than in the longer summers further south.

When alkaline lakes dry up, they become deserts. Lake Elmenteita in Kenya has a high salt content, which promotes the growth of algae. Vast flocks of greater flamingos gather in the shallow waters and feed on this rich nutrient "soup". Note how barren the land is in the foreground.

Life on a lily pad

The quiet beauty of a water lily is appealing to the human eye. But to myriads of insects, the plant is a refuge and a source of food.

If you sit quietly at the edge of a pond in summer, you may occasionally hear a distinct popping sound. The noise comes from the water, but what is making it? No frogs, birds, water voles or other animals are to be seen – only water lilies on the pond surface. If you watch the water lilies closely, at the next pop you may see circles of waves spreading from one of the lily pads.

Now perhaps the mystery can be solved. Get close to the lilies and look beneath the surface of the water. You will probably see a small, shallow-water fish, such as a perch or carp, lurking under the lily pads. Suddenly, it may dart forwards and take an audible nip at the leaf.

The fish may be eating the leaf, but more likely it is eating something attached to the leaf. Such floating green rafts provide a veritable feast for fish. Dozens of different kinds of creatures – including water mites, aphids, caterpillars, worms, and even small freshwater snails – live on the undersides and stems of lily pads. These islands are also nurseries for various animals that lay their eggs there, such as beetles, caddisflies and snails.

A lily pad offers several advantages to its residents. It provides them with a place of attachment so they do not drift at the mercy of the currents or sink to the bottom. The pads keep them at the surface of the pond, where there is plenty of sunlight and where the water is oxygenated by wave action. The air spaces in the stems of the plants enable animals to breathe, though a resident may be several feet below the surface.

The great diving beetle is an example of a pond-dweller that is very much at home among the lilies. A rather large, metallic black beetle, equipped with powerful jaws, it swims among the stems, pouncing on any unsuspecting prey, even a small fish or frog. This "tiger" of the pond occasionally rises to the surface for a fresh supply of air, which it obtains by tilting its body so that it can pump in a supply under its wing covers.

To produce a family, the female pierces a lily stem in which she lays her eggs. In a few days these hatch into elongated larvae that crawl about among the plants.

As a larva grows, it sheds its outer skin from time to time until it is ready to become a pupa, which takes about three years.

For a long time no one had found a pupa, until Hugh Main, a British naturalist, tried an experiment. He kept some larvae in an aquarium that had a bank of earth to imitate the pondside. A larva crawled out, buried itself in the soil, and turned into a pupa. Some three weeks later it hatched into an adult, which then entered the water and became the first diving beetle pupa to be observed by a scientist.

Among the lily stems are many other pond dwellers: snails, tadpoles, fish fry and mosquito larvae which are caught by the beetle larvae. Like the parents, the larvae also have strong jaws and need to rise to the surface occasionally for fresh air.

Although designed for life in water, the great diving beetle can also fly and moves from pond to pond.

As you look at the bottom of a lily pad, notice the bubble-like air cells that help to keep it afloat. The bottom surface clings to the water; the top is waxy and water-repellent. These textures on the top and bottom of the leaves help to hold them upright, even when the water level changes.

Most lily pads can be measured in inches, but the pads of some tropical water lilies may grow to a diameter of 6 ft. On their undersides, these pads have large air cells that resemble an ice-cube tray; their edges are upturned – hence the common name, water platter.

The purple gallinule, a native of warm coastal waters in North America, has long toes that enable it to patter across mats of lily pads. It forages for snails and other small prey. Here, an adult (right) finds a bountiful supply of food for a young gallinule (in brown plumage).

Assembling and caring for a pond aquarium

Here is how to establish your own indoor miniature pond, complete with plants, insects and even microscopic animals.
- A standard 5 gallon or 10 gallon tank is ideal. To allow for air circulation, you will need a fine-mesh cover, or a piece of glass, raised at the corners with pieces of cork.

- If possible, put the tank in a place with a constant temperature (about 18°C, 65°F). Avoid direct exposure to the sun.
- You can use pond water, but remember that a pint weighs a pound. An easier supply is tap water. Let it sit a few days to allow the chlorine to escape.

- Buy sand in an aquarium shop. Rinse it thoroughly to remove dust. Spread the sand in a layer, graded from 1 to 2 in. (Debris will collect at the lowest point. To remove wastes, use a dip tube.)
- To catch small creatures, you will need several pieces of equipment (see below).

Equipment for collecting

A magnifying glass and tweezers make examination easier.

A kitchen sieve can serve as a dip net. Attach a long handle if necessary.

Use small jars to carry your catch. Punch air holes in the lids.

One way to trap insects is to use a piece of mesh attached to two sticks.

To dredge for tiny plants, make a net of fine-mesh cloth, wired to a hoop.

Supplying your aquarium

Your first trip to a local pond should be for plants. These can be supplemented by any pet shop that stocks aquarium supplies.

Plants are important because they provide oxygen for a well-balanced tank.
- When adding water, pour it slowly to avoid dislodging the plants.
- Spring and summer are the best

seasons for collecting small plants and animals. Fish usually do better if caught in autumn. Remember that some fish eat others.
- Animals adapted to fast-moving water will not survive long in a pond aquarium.

Microscopic life

A hydra looks like a plant and moves about by somersaulting – foot over tentacles

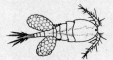

The cyclops is a tiny crustacean that often clings to plants. This female has egg sacs

Daphnia, a transparent water flea, feeds on algae and pond debris

Dragonfly nymphs do not resemble the adults (they live in water and do not fly). Nymphs must be fed insects or bits of meat

Vallisneria is a favourite food for aquatic life. Place such large plants against one wall of the aquarium; anchor them with stones

Whirligig beetles skim the surface, making tiny ripples; their divided eyes let them see above and below the water at the same time

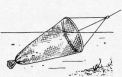

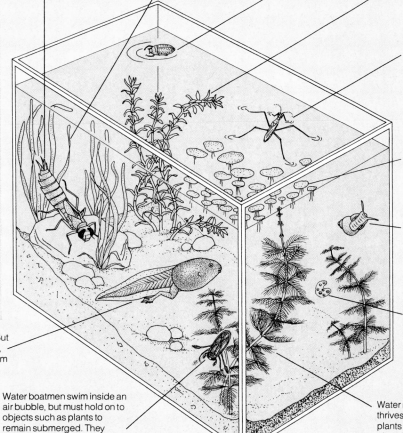

Elodea (waterweed) does well in aquariums. Like other plants, it absorbs carbon dioxide and gives off much-needed oxygen

Pond skaters "dimple" the surface of the water with their long spider-like legs. They feed on insects such as back swimmers

Duckweed floating on the water can be decorative; but if it covers the surface, remove some, so that light reaches other plants

Snails glide along on the inside of the glass, cleaning it as they go. You can watch their movement as they feed

Clusters of snail eggs are sometimes seen on the wall of an aquarium

A tadpole is a plant-eater. But when it develops into a frog, remove it from your aquarium – otherwise it will eat the smaller animals

Water boatmen swim inside an air bubble, but must hold on to objects such as plants to remain submerged. They feed on waste matter

Water milfoil, a fern-like plant, thrives in aquariums. Such plants provide food and a place for insects to lay eggs

The dynamic world of a pond

There are millions of ponds throughout the world, and each one is unique. They share the common events of birth, growth, maturity, decline and, ultimately, filling in. Nevertheless, their individual histories are so varied, and their numbers are so great, that pond study is one of the aspects of nature that offer great scope to amateur naturalists.

Pick a pond, preferably one near where you live that you can visit often. When and how was it formed? Sometimes the date and circumstances are known precisely. Local records may reveal the date of, for instance, an air raid in which a crater was made that later became a pond. In farm country, too, many ponds are created under conservation programmes.

You can usually work out a pond's general age. There is a variety of evidence

– a newly formed pond will have certain pioneer species of plants and animals. Windborne seeds arrive at once and germinate around the edge of the pond. There is a fringe of plants, rather than a thicket. Flying insects such as water beetles take advantage of the opportunity and lay eggs.

Water birds are quick to investigate a new pond. On their feet and feathers they carry a cargo from ponds elsewhere – the eggs, spores and seeds of numerous plants and animals. Colonising a pond is not a miracle. It is only a matter of time before a whole range of representative pond species arrive.

Then there is a period of adjustment. All the plants and animals settle down, influenced by one another and by the special conditions of the particular

pond – its depth, exposure to sunlight (or shade from nearby trees), and whether its waters are replenished by springs, streams or rain. General climate and the kind of basin – whether rocky or sandy – are also factors.

Gradually a pond matures. A pond's prime of life can be defined as that time when the greatest variety of species co-exist. To the practised eye, a pond is swarming with life and activity. Distinct zones of vegetation can be seen. The cover provided by thick vegetation invites bigger animals – water voles, water snakes and terrapins. Reedmace and water lilies thrive, and vegetation begins to show in the middle of the pond.

Ponds start to die when the accumulation of sediment and debris fills the bottom, and when plants encroach on the

margins. As the pond becomes smaller, fewer aquatic species of animals can live there. Death or emigration of various species means less food for their predators. As its resources are depleted, the pond world narrows.

Next comes stagnation. New groups of animals and plants take over. The pleasure for the amateur naturalist is in knowing one pond well, watching the whole development take place, or in discovering that your pond is thousands of years old – even a legacy from the Ice Age. It is probable that you know a pond, and it is also probable that it has not really been studied yet. If you are prepared to spend the time in making a detailed study of it, you will be following in the footsteps of the old-time naturalists, who knew their own world intimately.

NATURE OBSERVER
Pond-watching throughout the year

Whether you enjoy the diversity of pond life, or have a special interest in birds, plants, insects, amphibians, fish or reptiles, the seasons will have a great influence on what you can see.
- The edges of ponds are richest in both plant and animal species; they can be most conveniently explored from shore. Wear wellington boots or old plimsolls.
- Pond activity is greatest in spring. Large frogs and tree frogs are so noisy at this season – with their hooting and trilling – that you can even find an otherwise concealed pond by following their sounds. These amphibians are now mating and laying their eggs. Adult dragonflies and damselflies emerge from wingless aquatic larvae called nymphs. Ducks, coots, rails and wading birds nest along the shores; herons roost in trees near the pond.
- In summer, pond tortoises and water

snakes hatch. Copepods and daphnia swarm in warm surface water, and pond skaters and water beetles are numerous. (You may find a male water beetle carrying the female's eggs on his back.) Herons are busily fishing to supply their young. Downy ducklings and coots swim among the lily pads. Frogs can be seen sunning themselves on logs and rocks near the pond.
- Autumn is a less-active season in the pond. Many amphibians and reptiles begin their long winter sleep. The pond may be visited by a migrating osprey in search of fish, or a water vole adding mussel shells to a growing pile near its nest.
- In winter, a snow-covered pond is a good place to look for animal tracks, but be sure to stay off thin ice. At this time, some fish are active but comparatively sluggish under the ice.

The intricate relationships among pond animals

Certain groupings, or communities, of animals appear again and again in nature. Ponds are prime examples of such communities. In each pond, the particular species may be different, but the "job openings" – the niches – will be filled by equivalent animals that play the same

role in the community. In the woodland pond shown at left, the species are European. Given a similar climate and water, a pond of the same size and age on any other continent will support a community of animals that are remarkably similar in their life styles.

Key to pond animals

1. A grey heron waits to feast off a pond fish.

2. A mallard drake is a colourful pond resident. The female is drab coloured.

3. The kingfisher eyes the pond for a passing fish, which it will quickly catch with its large, strong beak.

4. The Emperor dragonfly always rests with wings outspread. Females lay their eggs on water plants.

5. The terrapin lives in swamps and along the edges of lakes, mainly in southern Europe.

6. The common edible frog, whose hind legs are considered a delicacy, consumes great quantities of water insects.

7. The catfish is a bottom-dweller which searches out food with its sensitive whiskers, or barbels.

8. The whirligig beetle is easy to identify because its name describes its motion.

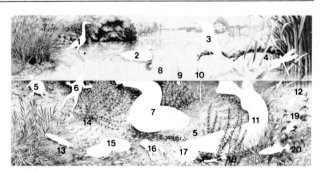

9. The water boatman swims upside-down, using its long hind legs like a pair of oars.

10. The water stick insect often looks like a twig hanging below the surface.

11. The pike is a swift hunting fish which lurks, well camouflaged, among the reeds.

12. A diving beetle traps air under its wings; this enables it to remain submerged.

13. The newt, like other salamanders, sheds its skin from time to time as it grows.

14. Tadpoles grow from eggs to adult frogs at varying rates, depending on the species.

15. Freshwater mussels often live buried in the bottom.

16. The crayfish is active mostly at night; it feeds on plants, fish and insects.

17. Tubifex (red tube-dwelling worms) live in colonies in mud tubes, waving their bodies to catch food.

18. Caddisfly larvae live in curious egg cases fashioned from twigs, leaves or pebbles.

19. The pond snail glides about on a muscular foot.

20. The red-throated male stickleback builds a nest for its mate's eggs, then guards the nest when they hatch.

The still waters of marshes and swamps

The difference between a marsh and a swamp eludes many people. Both may seem extremely humid and their waters stagnant. If a current is to be seen in either place, it is likely to be slow-moving. But the two habitats are as different as a prairie and a forest. In fact, a freshwater marsh resembles a wet prairie, while a swamp can be compared to a wet woodland; a marsh is dominated by grass, a swamp by trees.

Besides grasses, typical marsh vegetation includes reedmace and sedges. Reedmace, also called the bulrush, is unmistakable. But to distinguish between grasses and sedges, roll their stems between your fingers – grass stems are round, sedges triangular. One common marsh sedge, papyrus, has been used by man for cen-

turies, and gave paper its name. The Egyptians used papyrus as early as 3500 BC.

Most marsh plants have extremely dense root systems, which trap silt and debris. In some places, the interlacing roots form firm tussocks that rise above the water level and can be used as stepping stones. But take care: the roots also form false bottoms that only *look* like dry land.

If water currents are present and strong enough to keep a marsh swept clean, it may remain a marsh for centuries. Some marshes bordering the Nile are believed to have existed since the time of the pharaohs. But if the accumulation of debris continues, the marsh becomes progressively shallower, and shrubs and trees (cypresses, mangroves, red maples

and others) take root. Sometimes the marsh becomes a swamp. The surface of a swamp is much more uneven than that of a marsh – patches of relatively dry and solid land may be surrounded by small areas of open water.

Often linked by time, marshes and swamps are stages in the processes that slowly convert a body of water into dry land. Such a changing landscape is found at the edges of many lakes, ponds, or slow-moving rivers. The open water gives way to a marsh, which may become a wooded swamp bordered by forest. Often marshes and swamps are intermingled. Much of the Florida Everglades, in America, for example, consists of extensive marshes surrounding swampy wooded "islands" called hammocks.

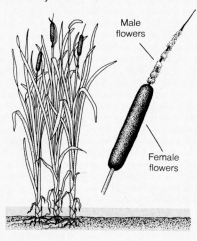

Male flowers

Female flowers

Notice the marked zonation of the vegetation in this marshy lake. In the foreground are brown-tipped sedges. Two mats of floating water pennywort are separated by a growth of rushes. Waving in the background, a lush forest of reeds indicates shallower water.

Although marshes and swamps seem uninviting to human visitors, they are havens for wildlife – especially snails, which feed on the plentiful supply of decaying plant material. Many species of reptiles – terrapins, snakes, and lizards – seem to love these quiet wetlands, which also provide resting places for a wealth of waterfowl. Large land animals, such as deer, also venture into swamps on "bridges" of firm ground.

Transitional zones between land and water, marshes and swamps are places where you can see aquatic and land animals living side by side.

Remember, however, that a marsh and a swamp have one thing in common: they are both dangerous places. Unless you are with a guide, stick to established paths.

Tall, feathery papyrus borders the extensive swamps along the upper Nile basin in Uganda. Wild date palms root in more solid soil.

Terrapins, sunning themselves on a log, are extremely shy of human beings. A slight disturbance will send them diving out of sight.

Tall tupelos rise from the still, brown waters of a Mississippi deep-water swamp. Like the bald cypress, which also grows here, the swamp tupelo has a buttressed trunk, gnarled knees, and an extensive root system that effectively supports it in the soft, water-saturated mud.

183

Bogs: where plants eat animals

In a northern bog, a diminutive green tree frog perches on a cluster of blueberries and basks in the sun. Frogs are among the few permanent residents of this environment.

In some parts of the world, a human intruder walking on wet, spongy soil at the edge of a pond or forest feels the ground quake and sees trees as far as 25 ft away begin to sway with every step. Both these events are announcements that the traveller has entered the special world of a bog. Like marshes and swamps, bogs are wetlands that often result from the natural filling-in of ponds and lakes.

Marshes and swamps grow from the bottom up as debris accumulates on the floor of a body of water. A bog grows in the opposite direction as well – from the top down.

Several kinds of plants at the water's edge, particularly bog-bean, send out floating "runners" along the surface of the water. In North America, the water willow (which is not really a willow) makes a "pontoon bridge" out from shore. When the tips of this plant's arching branches touch the water, they form a spongy, air-filled pad from which new branches grow.

A floating network of plants forms a mat at the edge of the water. This mat is usually filled in and thickened by sphagnum moss, sedges and grasses. This float-ing "garden" may eventually cover the whole body of water.

Many of these mats become sturdy enough to support a person or even several people. But anyone exploring a bog should proceed with caution. There is always the chance of breaking through a thin place and falling into water of unknown depth.

The bright green carpet is sphagnum moss, the dominant plant in most bogs. Of course, bogs, marshes and swamps often blend into one another so subtly it is hard to tell where one begins and another stops. Bog waters are low in minerals and extremely acidic. They also are low in dissolved oxygen because the mossy mat covers the water and prevents contact with the air.

The high acidity and limited oxygen and minerals slow the rate of decay in a bog. Plants, animals and even people that have fallen into bogs have been preserved like mummies for centuries.

The lack of certain kinds of nutrients in bog soils has caused some bog plants, such as the pitcher plants, sundews, Venus's-flytraps and butterworts, to evolve a

Zones of vegetation that build a boggy shore

Bogs are widely distributed over cold, damp northern regions. Whether they occur in Europe, Asia or North America, all bogs share certain characteristics. They occupy steep-sided, water-filled basins with poor drainage. They have cushion-like mounds of mosses and shrubby plants. They contain an accumulation of partially decayed plant material called peat. Like lakes and ponds, any open water in a bog is ringed by zones of vegetation.

These zones are not always clearly defined owing to the flourishing growth of sphagnum moss, which fills in the spaces between shrubs and other plants with a sponge-like, velvety carpet. The water-retaining sphagnum creeps into the more solid area surrounding the bog. The only trees that can establish themselves must be able to tolerate having their roots bathed with rainwater and seeping acidic water; black spruce is one example.

Scattered clumps of coniferous trees – larch and spruce – anchor the soil and add their debris of needles and cones to the accumulation of peat.

Yellow water lilies colonise the deep areas at the centre of the bog.

A border of sedge floats on a water-saturated bed of peat, formed over the years from decaying roots, stems and leaves.

Low evergreen shrubs, such as bog rosemary and bog myrtle, take root in soil that builds up on the peat. This peat is formed from sphagnum moss.

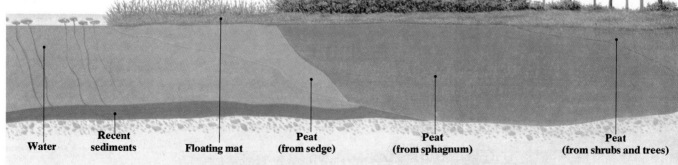

Water   Recent sediments   Floating mat   Peat (from sedge)   Peat (from sphagnum)   Peat (from shrubs and trees)

bizarre way of acquiring the missing sub-stances. They trap insects. Many botanists believe that such carnivorous plants are acquiring nitrogen by this means.

Decay in a bog proceeds so slowly that there is usually a great deal of partially decayed plant material, called peat, which settles on the bottom. You may have used dried peat as potting material for house plants or in your garden – and therefore know that peat holds water extremely well. Sphagnum can hold 20 times its weight of water, but it is low in nutrients, and little will grow in it without fertiliser.

When the peat and living moss around the edges of a bog dry out somewhat, certain species of plants become estab-lished (such as heathers and bog myrtles). Eventually, trees take root. Thus, if you look at a mature bog from high ground, it has the appearance of a target – a "bull's-eye" of open water, surrounded by con-centric rings of moss, moss and sedges, shrubs, and finally trees.

Gradually the bog becomes dry land, but because of the special conditions created by moss, bogs have a longer life than most other wetlands.

A climax forest of spruce and fir surrounds the bog. In some warmer areas, a climax forest may be made up of maple and birch trees.

Humus   **Weathered rock**   **Bedrock**

Sensitive hairs on each leaf-blade of the Venus's-flytrap, found in America, operate like triggers. When an insect, such as this fly, touches a hair, the halves close, trapping the victim. Exactly how the plant extracts nutrients from its prey is not yet understood.

Leathery leaves of a pitcher plant are lined with downward-pointing hairs. At the bottom of the leaf is a reservoir of water. If an insect enters the plant, it cannot escape – and drowns.

Sticky, translucent beads "decorate" the long wands of the thread-leaved sundew. Here, a blue-winged damselfly and a cabbage butterfly have been fatally ensnared by the plant.

Birds of the wetlands

Few habitats support more varied bird populations than the swamps, marshes, bogs, ponds and sloughs of the wetlands. One reason is well known to anyone who has ever watched a bird-bath. Water attracts birds. A majority of species – even those that do not live in wetlands – must travel to fresh water daily to drink.

But wetlands offer more than just a convenient water supply. They provide plentiful food, shelter, and protection from many predators. It is no accident that the world's main flyways (the traditional migration routes used by millions of birds every year) generally pass along large rivers and coastal regions, and over areas with shallow bodies of water. During the migration periods, it is not unusual to see patches of water nearly covered with birds.

Pond ducks, such as mallards and teal, usually feed at the surface of the water by snapping at floating food, meanwhile gabbling noisily. This raucous dabbling, which sends the water flying, looks comical to a human spectator, but it is actually very efficient – fine tooth-like projections around the rim of the ducks' bills sieve out tiny water plants and animals. Pond ducks also feed from the bottom in shallow water by tipping beak-down and paddling vigorously, with only their wriggling rumps showing.

A duck's short, widely spaced legs are fine for swimming and "tipping-up", but this arrangement is responsible for its typically awkward walk. The legs of stiff-tailed ducks, such as the North American ruddy ducks and Australian musk ducks, are placed so far back that they can walk only for short distances and rarely leave the water except to fly.

Some European ducks, such as the chestnut-headed pochards that are common in town parks, spend autumn and winter in western Europe but breed in Siberia and the east.

Diving ducks, such as goldeneyes and mergansers, often feed in deeper waters. They can dive as deep as 25 ft after their prey. The bills of the mergansers are pointed, with a hook-shaped tip and backward-pointing "teeth" that hold captured fish.

Perhaps the oddest method of feeding is that used by the small shorebirds called phalaropes. They stir up food in shallow water by spinning rapidly or swimming in close circles. Swans and ducks achieve the same effect by turning rapidly and paddling with their broad feet. Often food turned up by a stirrer attracts other birds, and a water "parade" begins – a crazily spinning bird followed by dabblers.

Long-legged wading birds use other methods to capture their prey. Snowy egrets stir up food with their feet. Cranes, storks and herons often "still-hunt" – they simply wait in the cover of abundant water plants for a small fish or frog to come within range of their lightning-quick, pointed beaks.

You can tell where a wading bird hunts by the length of its legs. Predictably, small, short-legged sandpipers hunt at the water's edge; other species, such as cranes and grey herons, hunt in deeper water.

If you frighten the birds as you approach a marsh or pond, you will undoubtedly notice striking differences in the way they take flight. Pond ducks, sometimes called puddle-jumpers, can leap into the air from land or water. Many diving ducks and other wetland birds require a long "runway" – up to 650 ft – and a few cannot take off from land at all. Some of these birds, including grebes and loons, dive when startled, rather than trying to fly.

Some wetland birds with young that cannot fly or dive will take their offspring to hiding places before fleeing. But grebes have what may be an even better method. Like swans, these small, duck-like birds often carry their young on their backs. Young grebes hold on tight to the parents' feathers with their bills. The adult birds can then dive with their young safely on board.

A black-winged stilt, a bird of wet meadows and shallow waters, prepares to fold its long legs and brood its four camouflaged eggs.

Ready to strike at prey, a young heron displays its hunting instinct. Later, its striped plumage will give way to rich cinnamon around the crested head and short neck. In some regions, almost every pond and wooded stream will have resident herons.

Largest of the swan species, a trumpeter convoys her flotilla of downy two-week-old cygnets through a floating sea of duckweed. Once nearly extinct, trumpeter swans are breeding in increasing numbers on the marsh-bordered lakes of the western United States and Canada.

 BIRDWATCHING TIPS

How to tell the difference between geese and ducks

Ducks and geese, together with swans, belong to an order of birds known as waterfowl. There are about 150 species in this order – most of them ducks. Both ducks and geese usually have short tails and legs; their feet are webbed. Bills tend to be flattened, with edges that help strain food. The young can swim and walk within a few hours after hatching. Gregarious by nature, ducks and geese form large flocks, especially during migration. Here is how to tell the geese from the ducks:

Male and female geese have identical plumage

- Large birds with long necks, geese are good walkers.
- Geese, which moult only once a year, look the same at all times of the year.
- Nests are placed in hollows on grassy or marshy ground.
- Geese usually feed on land, grazing on grass and grain; brant, a sea-going species, feed on eelgrass. Though geese are powerful swimmers, they do not dive.
- Geese are strong fliers. They often form precise V's or long, irregular lines. They are quite noisy in flight.

Canada goose

Male ducks are more colourful than females of the species

- Small, plump birds with short necks, ducks have stubby legs and walk clumsily.
- Ducks moult body feathers twice a year. Most kinds have two plumages – breeding and non-breeding. Males in eclipse (non-breeding) plumage look like females.
- Ducks nest in various sites – some even in tree holes.
- All ducks can dive. Some species dive to obtain fish; others eat molluscs or aquatic plants.
- In flight, most ducks form loose flocks.

Female mallard

Male mallard

Where the fish are

We humans, as land-dwellers, tend to think of what lies beneath the surface of lakes and rivers as one big, wet, homogeneous world. But to freshwater fish, that watery world is as diverse as our own.

Some species of fish live only in clear, leaping mountain streams; others inhabit only slow, muddy, lowland rivers. Some fish patrol the wind-tossed surface of lakes; others prowl the less-disturbed bottom. Certain species can live in one particular lake or river and nowhere else on earth. And – as any successful fisherman can tell you – many fish move back and forth between "neighbourhoods", depending on season and time of day.

Most freshwater fish are border-dwellers. They prefer to live and feed where one type of environment borders another. Thus, many fish may be found at the edge of a weed bed, near a drop-off on the bottom, where a stream enters a lake, or where fast and slow-moving waters meet in a river.

Why are fish so choosy? Biologists believe it is mainly because the life processes of each species of freshwater fish function best at a particular temperature and salinity. Fish seek out areas where the most favourable conditions prevail. Temperature is also an important reason why fish are found at different levels as the seasons change. The cool temperature many species prefer exists as far up as the surface in spring and autumn. In summer, the sun warms the surface, and fish go deeper. In winter, if surface temperatures drop below freezing, the fish move down.

The water-quality requirements of some species confine them to specific areas. Trout, dace and minnows are characteristic of swift upland streams. Warmer, muddier and saltier lowland rivers and lakes usually contain carp, catfish, perch and barbel. Sea bass, dogfish and some kinds of flounder prefer estuarine rivers, where salt water mixes with fresh. The only sizeable bodies of water without fish are those where temperature and salinity reach their extremes – in hot springs and salt lakes.

Some fish, notably salmon and eels, spend part of their lives in fresh water and part in the ocean. Salmon spawn in fresh water; eels in mid-ocean.

Sometimes you can tell where a fish lives just by looking at it. Streamlined, torpedo-shaped fish, such as trout, are usually from fast-moving streams. A flattened fish like a bream could not live there; it would be swept away the first time it turned sideways into the current. But in its customary pools, lakes, or sluggish streams, the bream can slip freely through the vegetation. A fish with "feelers", or barbels, around its mouth (such as a catfish) is usually from a muddy river or lake; the barbels help it locate food in murky water.

By far the greatest variety of freshwater fish live in tropical rivers and lakes. The Amazon River system alone contains about 2,000 species – from miniature catfish to giant arapaimas weighing several hundred pounds. Some of the most notorious residents of the Amazon are the piranhas. These ferocious fish rarely grow longer than 2 ft and usually feed on smaller fish, but they go into a frenzy at the taste of blood. A school of piranhas can consume an animal as large as a cow in a few minutes.

One tropical fish – an African species of lungfish – holds the record for staying alive without food or water longer than any other vertebrate. When rivers dry up, lungfish form cases of mucus and mud around their bodies; these balls dry as hard as bricks. Experimental specimens have lived in this condition for more than seven years and become active again when reintroduced to water.

Life in slow-moving waters

Most fish of lakes and slow-moving lowland rivers spend their entire lives in the quiet waters of their surroundings. Unlike fish of fast-flowing rivers, they are seldom strong swimmers. They range from lethargic carp to lightning-swift northern pike.

Perch spawn at night in spring, laying jelly-like ropes of eggs as long as 7 ft. The young hatch a week later.

Fish of brackish waters

The brackish waters of bays, estuaries and marshes are transition zones for migratory fish. Here they adjust to the change from salt water to fresh. However, some species live their entire lives within this environment.

Newly hatched Atlantic salmon subsist on the yolk sacs attached to their bodies. (Notice the empty "cases", and the eggs ready to hatch.)

Pacific species are notable because the adults die after spawning; Atlantic salmon recover from the journey and spawn again.

Fish of cold, swift streams

The cold, rushing waters of mountain streams are the preferred habitat for some species of fish. These fish are usually muscular, adapted to swimming in – and against – swift currents.

Salmon migrate from the ocean to the freshwater streams of their birth when the time comes to spawn. Young salmon find their own way from the stream to the sea.

Brook trout, a favourite of fishermen, thrive in cold mountain streams. They are often grown in hatcheries.

Smallmouth bass breed in rocky shallows or near sunken logs. They are mainly predatory, feeding on other fish and on amphibians.

The burbot is a cod, a freshwater member of its family. This fish is active only at dawn and dusk.

Carp are found mostly in warm, weedy backwaters. They feed on insect larvae, crustaceans and aquatic vegetation.

The northern pike is a large predatory fish that lurks along shores of quiet waters, particularly in oxbow lakes.

European eels range widely along the Atlantic shore. The eels spend most of their lives upstream or in brackish waters, but spawn in the sea.

Atlantic sturgeon, now uncommon, have been sought for centuries for both their flesh and unshed eggs – used for caviar. Like salmon, sturgeon are sea-dwellers that spawn in the fresh water of rivers.

HIKING AND CAMPING
Fishing through ice

In northern regions where lakes and ponds freeze in winter, ice fishing is popular. Many fish – among them perch, barbel, catfish and carp – survive the winter by living at the bottom of these lakes.

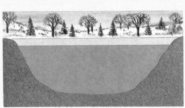

In summer, a lake or pond is warmest at the top, coolest at the bottom. Fish seek the temperature and feeding conditions that suit them best.

In winter, the surface may be iced-over. Temperature stratification disappears, and the location of fish is less predictable. Cold makes fish less active.

In a severe winter, or if you go on holiday in northern Europe, you may want to try ice fishing yourself. Local people will usually provide helpful information about the best spots for it, and will also warn you of hazardous places. But even with the best of advice every fisherman needs to stay on the alert against thin spots in the ice. It is unsafe to be on a lake alone and never let children go ice fishing on their own.

● Equipment can be simple and inexpensive. The first requirement is a chisel to cut holes in the ice. This is extended into a "spud", a pole with the chisel attached firmly to one end. A skimmer is also needed to scoop out bits of floating ice: a kitchen sieve will serve the purpose. To carry his bait, the fisherman must have a pail, but the sieve will double as a dip-net for the bait. A sledge is useful for carting the gear, including several fishing lines and a vacuum flask of something hot. The sledge will also serve as a place to sit and to attach a windbreak.

● An easy way to find a good fishing spot is to use a hole left by someone else, even if it is slightly blocked. It is easier to clean out ice than to open a new hole.

● Bait should be changed frequently. Mealworms, grubs and minnows are good bait. Where the water is deep, try using a small, shiny spoon as a weighted lure.

The wonder of waterfalls

Many of the world's waterfalls are so big that it is nearly impossible to see them at one glance. The highest one on earth, for example – Angel Falls in Venezuela – is best seen from the air. Plane passengers see the Rio Churún leap from Devil's Mountain and plummet 3,212 ft, barely making contact with the sheer face of the mountain. The existence of the waterfall was unknown to the outside world until it was spotted by an American aviator-adventurer, James Angel, who first saw it in 1935.

The poet Ralph Waldo Emerson wrote that "frugal nature" gave waterfalls only one sound, and anyone venturing near a great waterfall will learn what that sound is – thunder. The noise seems to wrap itself around you like a heavy blanket. It is no wonder sound is often reflected in the names of waterfalls. Niagara Falls derives its name from an Indian word meaning "thundering waters".

The original name for Victoria Falls in Africa was Mosi-oa-tunya – "the smoke that thunders". At Victoria Falls, during the rainy season, hundreds of thousands of tons of water crash to the bottom each minute. When the water hits the floor of the chasm, it is estimated to be moving at over 100 mph. Here, after its plunge, the foaming water flows into a vast canyon (in this case 45 miles long and hundreds of feet deep), which creates an impressive "echo chamber" for the roar of the waterfall.

The spray and fog produced by the rampaging waters are so dense that David Livingstone, the first European to see Victoria Falls, wrote, "These columns of watery smoke . . . give the impression that the yawning gulf might resemble a bottomless pit."

Yet one of the pleasures of seeing a waterfall is that even a small cascade can be beautiful or inspiring. Some of the most famous and best-loved falls are comparatively small ones, located in all parts of the world – the glens of the Scottish Highlands, the tumbling sprays beside Norway's majestic fjords.

The wild waters of Virginia Falls in Canada's Northwest Territories are parted by an immense limestone spire. The pillar towers above a 300 ft drop in the South Nahanni River. Notice the layering of the rock, which reveals that this outcrop was once part of the canyon wall.

Britain's highest waterfall is in the Scottish Highlands. It is Eas Coul Aulin, which rises to a height of 658 ft.

Although human beings are drawn to waterfalls as by a magnet, the appeal is aesthetic, even spiritual. For animals, waterfalls are inhospitable. But there are a few species that manage to live with the tremendous pressures. Some kinds of insect hang on to the rocks, and small birds called dippers choose waterfalls for their homes.

Fish generally avoid waterfalls. But salmon descend streams on the coasts of many countries in temperate latitudes when they are young to live in the ocean, and return by the same routes when they are adults, ready to reproduce. Often a salmon will travel hundreds of miles upstream, leaping over countless waterfalls and rapids.

These powerful fish are capable of jumping 8-10 ft in the air. The damming of rivers has interfered with the life cycle of these animals but, nowadays, fish ladders – a series of stepped waterfalls – are often constructed alongside dams, enabling the fish to return home.

This silky, shimmering veil of water is one of many falls in North America's Cascade Range. The water drops in a slender stream, providing a gentle spray that encourages plant growth.

 NATURE OBSERVER
Specialised lives in streams and torrents

People walking in the country who are lucky enough to see a dipper beside a rushing stream may not believe their eyes when they see it fly directly into a waterfall. The bird frequently nests behind such a falling curtain of water, rearing its young in this unlikely spot. The dipper can search for food in the water, swimming with its stubby wings or "walking" along the bottom of a stream. It searches for caddisfly larvae and other insects attached to rocks.

Insects adapted to rushing water

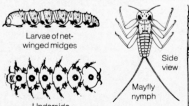

Larvae of net-winged midges

Underside

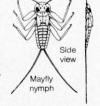

Side view

Mayfly nymph

Young net-winged midges (flies) have suction pads that grasp rocks firmly.

Mayfly nymphs have very flat bodies. Their shape prevents them from being swept away by currents.

The cutting power of water

One of the best ways to appreciate the massive power of water is to stand at the edge of a canyon that was cut by water. How can anything as seemingly pliant as water have such an impact on solid rock? Actually, it is not water alone that does the cutting. Water in rivers and streams is often slightly acid in content (the acid is picked up from the ground over which it travels). This acid eats away at rock – particularly limestone. And, as water flows over the land, fine particles of clay, sand and rock are picked up and carried along. Each part of this burden, no matter how small, is capable of scratching, scraping and grinding off bits and pieces of rock.

The faster water moves, the more it can carry and the faster it cuts. According to the laws of physics, when a stream doubles its speed, the size of particles it can carry increases 64 times. During a torrential rainstorm in California, a train jumped the track in the Tehachapi Mountains and plunged into a flooded stream. The locomotive and tender were carried half a mile downstream and buried under a deep layer of dirt and debris.

The heaviest loads of streams are rolled and skipped along the bottom of the stream bed, and this is where most cutting takes place. Fast-moving waters usually cut steep-walled canyons, rather than wide valleys.

The speed of a river is usually determined by its slope. Thus, mountain streams, where the slopes are steep, are usually faster and cut deeper than streams in the flatlands. The Rhine, for example, has cut its broad valley across the gently rolling countryside of West Germany, France and Holland, creating lush farmlands and a vital trade route. By contrast, Britain's River Avon, which drops fast and steeply from the Cotswolds to the sea, is cutting a deep, narrow valley, whose deepest point is the dramatic Clifton Gorge in Bristol.

Throughout the world, there are zones where the underlying rock structure creates a row of waterfalls, called a fall line. If a river flows from hard to soft rock, the soft rock will be worn down more quickly. A step may be cut and a waterfall created.

One of the most distinctive fall lines runs near the eastern coast of the United States, where the hard crystalline rocks of the Appalachians meet the softer sedimentary rocks of the coastal plain. The line is marked by important cities including Philadelphia, Baltimore and Washington. A similar fall line – the Craven fault – runs across Yorkshire in England. Cities were often built on these fall lines, sometimes because they were barriers to settlers trying to move up the rivers. Another reason for city growth was that falling water could generate power for industries.

The hard rock of many fall-line waterfalls lies over softer rock. Eventually, the turbulent water at the base of the waterfalls undercuts the overhanging hard rock, which breaks off. This process is causing the Niagara Falls to retreat upstream at the rate of about 4 ft a year.

Rivers have traditionally attracted people, tending to bring them together rather than separating them, in spite of waterfalls (an easy human solution was the building of bridges). However, very deep canyons cut by rivers have been effective barriers to many kinds of wildlife. For example, the Grand Canyon is a boundary between two distinct biological provinces, each with many different species. Certain snakes and squirrels on the north side differ markedly from close relatives to the south.

In some parts of the world, like Borneo, rivers are still the main transport routes. In Europe the Rhine and the Danube are still major highways, though less vital than in days before roads.

When a waterfall flows over extremely hard rock, as happens often in Scotland and Norway, erosion will occur very slowly and the falls may remain a step-like cascade for centuries.

Deer Creek is a small, spring-fed tributary that flows into the Colorado River, upstream of the Grand Canyon in America. This part of the gorge drops into a plunge basin, then glides along for a short stretch before dropping again. Notice the rocky debris caused by the cutting action of the water.

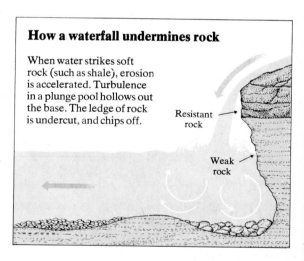

How a waterfall undermines rock

When water strikes soft rock (such as shale), erosion is accelerated. Turbulence in a plunge pool hollows out the base. The ledge of rock is undercut, and chips off.

Resistant rock

Weak rock

Pierced by shafts of sunlight, this cathedral-like gorge (right) in Oregon invites exploration of its depths. Powerful forces formed the channel, but now this section of Oneonta Creek is level and relatively placid. Alder and maple, moss and sword fern, cling tenaciously to the steep walls.

The journey of rivers from source to sea

"Where do rivers come from?" seems a simple enough question. It is obvious that rain supplies rivers, but this is more an offhand answer than a real account of what is involved. Less than half the water now flowing to the sea came directly from the run-off of rain. Most of the water comes from ground supplies, and from melting snow and ice. In northern Europe, and in mountains further south, such water is produced all year round from snow banks, whenever the temperatures rise, especially in early spring.

Thus, no matter how impressive lakes and rivers may seem, they represent only a small part of the water that is present on earth. Most freshwater supplies are contained in polar ice caps and glaciers, or stored beneath the surface of the land in the water table.

For practical purposes, human beings make a distinction between fresh water (because we need it in this condition) and the salt water of the oceans, but both supplies are part of a global picture – called the hydrologic cycle. Oceans contain by far the greatest amount of water, but there is a constant interchange between the two types. The sun evaporates water from every kind of surface – oceans (leaving the salt behind), lakes and ponds, and even bird-baths in your garden. You can see vapour when it forms clouds. But eventually the vapour condenses and returns to the land as dew, mist, rain and snow.

One seldom-considered part of the water cycle is living organisms – mainly plants. They use and give off tremendous amounts of water, often quite rapidly. But they also retain large quantities for the length of their lives. Only when a plant dies and dries out is the water put back into circulation.

This painting shows the roles and changing appearances of water as it travels over the land. Scientists have tracked much of what happens, but there is still a good deal to be learned.

What happens when water sinks underground, becoming a subterranean river? (Cave exploration is hazardous for this very reason – so little is known of the underground landscape. No one knows when or how forcefully an underground flood will occur.)

Many millions of tons of water move daily from one part of the planet to another. Sometimes water is gaseous, sometimes liquid; sometimes it is held as ice. In whatever form, water on the move is full of fascinating stories.

The source of a river is usually a glacier or mountain spring. Canyons carved by rushing streams carry rocks and other large particles. The steeper the canyon, the faster the stream flows and the greater its load of particles.

Melting snows and rains create many small, interlaced brooks. Some will vanish during dry weather, leaving mossy traces. In wet weather they reappear, often in the same channels.

This waterfall was created when the river encountered a layer of hard rock. Some waterfalls also spill from the streams of hanging valleys.

Plunge pools are often formed by the grinding action of a waterfall.

The darker underground portion of this illustration indicates the water table. This saturated zone has a contour of its own, and does not follow the contour of the surface terrain. This is because rocks have different capacities for holding water. The water can remain underground for hundreds of years, but surfaces again, feeding rivers and lakes.

Marshes are another type of terminal for rivers. Here, the fresh water may mingle with salt water from the sea, creating a unique habitat.

Merging tributaries form a larger stream, which may feed into a lake (a depression in the land that was perhaps gouged out by an ancient glacier). To some extent the inflow of water will govern the spillover at the opposite side of the lake, into the broader river below it.

A gathering of storm clouds is part of the ceaseless cycling of water. Evaporation from lakes, rivers and seas all contribute to the formation of such clouds. Rains release the stored moisture and renew the cycle.

As a river reaches the level plains, it slows down and becomes sluggish; its meanderings often leave pockets of water, thus creating swamps.

Deserts are highly eroded areas with sparse vegetation, where even a trickling stream can carve canyons.

When a meandering river changes course, a loop may be stranded, forming a lake called an oxbow.

A lighthouse perched on a rocky promontory is often a ship's major safeguard against treacherous fogs. Because of temperature differences between land and sea, fogs often occur in coastal areas.

The sandy shore is pierced by many small channels, through which fresh and salt-water flow.

A delta is formed as silt accumulates at the mouth of a river. The pattern of branching is highly variable.

Downwards, ever downwards

If you follow a brook downwards far enough, you will see it join a larger stream. Follow this, and you will find that other tributaries, like the first brook, contribute to the main stream, making it wider and more forceful. When it is broad or deep enough to be an established part of the landscape, the stream may be shown on maps and given a name. When several streams of this size join forces, the resulting stream may be called a river – although there is no particular size a channel must attain to earn this title. For example, in arid regions in the south of Europe, a stream you could jump across may be referred to as a river, while in the lush valleys of Scandinavia, something ten times as wide may qualify only as a stream.

The upper edges of river catch basins are called watersheds. We are just beginning to understand that human action close to these dividing lines – such as diverting water for irrigation or discarding pollutants – affects the entire system. For example, industrial wastes dumped into the upper Rhine can cause damage to the water quality all the way to the ocean. True, rivers have a remarkable ability to cleanse themselves by various natural filtering systems – not just passage through sand and gravel, but by the action of tiny organisms that convert wastes into available nutrients. However, there are limits to this capability.

Most of the small, upland streams you might encounter will feed into the same larger waterway. But in some areas, streams that are relatively close together may have vastly different destinations, as, for example, on North America's Continental Divide, which runs along the Rocky Mountains. Most streams on the western side eventually drain into the Pacific, while those on the other side flow into the Atlantic or the Gulf of Mexico. Theoretically, you could stand on such a dividing line and pour water that will reach either of two oceans, a continent apart. The point is, all rivulets and rivers, by whatever name, are part of a larger network.

Some political boundaries are set by rivers and streams. For example, the Rhine separates part of West Germany from France. The Danube marks some of the frontier between Romania and Bulgaria. But river borders present problems: the rivers (and waterfalls) have a habit of changing course. In some places, America's Mississippi has moved miles since it was originally surveyed in 1765. Frequently, the moving river changed the borders between states.

In South America, the border between Argentina and Chile is the line where the waters of the Andes divide, part running down towards the South Atlantic and part towards the Pacific. The British monarch is the agreed arbiter and, every few years, a team of British surveyors goes out to revise the boundary as contours change.

Yellow monkey flowers flourish in a seepage area on a cool mountainside. Countless trickles such as this ultimately make a river.

Bright autumn leaves lodge on a tiny island in a tumbling stream. Leafy debris, branches and soil collect behind a natural rock dam. Seeds sprout in the newly created habitat; insects wing their way to the island. Such "clutter" adds complexity and beauty to the stream.

No part of a watershed – whether brook or river – travels in a straight line. It follows the contours of the land. A stream may loop or make a sharp turn. In many areas, there are characteristic drainage patterns – often resembling the branches of a tree or the rungs on a ladder. The more curves there are in a stream bed, the slower the water flows. Thus loops and detours have the effect of moderating the force of spring floods. Such small backwaters also hold pockets of life – known as micro-environments – which contain communities of plants and animals. When human beings attempt to "tame" a river by damming or straightening it, there may be a change in the river that reduces its vitality. Instead of supporting a rich wildlife community, it becomes a sterile ditch.

It is a far better practice to dam and reforest (and also cleanse water) upstream than to allow the sum total of neglect to strike the lowlands. When floods do come, as they inevitably will, damage can be avoided by recognising the nature of the land; certain places – such as floodplains – will never be safe for building, only for farming and for parks.

NATURE OBSERVER
Patterns of stream drainage are affected by terrain

When you are in an aeroplane – particularly if you are flying low in clear weather – you can sometimes see how rivers relate to the terrain. (You can also see this on some maps.) Stream patterns vary greatly, and the rocky bed has much to do with the way that water flows. Here are three of the most common drainage systems: dendritic (which means branching, or tree-like), trellis, and radial patterns:

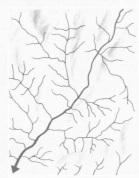 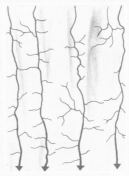 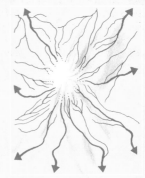

Dendritic patterns develop mostly in regions underlaid by granite or basaltic rock.

Trellis drainage is common among folded mountains, where streams follow valleys.

Radial patterns are typical of hilltops, where water flows from a central point.

The winding Firehole River in Wyoming, USA, is a fisherman's delight. Trout do well here, despite the river's source – hot springs.

Early spring rains overflow the rock-piled banks of a dry-region river. Though the rushing waters whirl away some of the soil, trees that line the banks – sycamores, willows and other water-loving species – help prevent soil erosion. Such trees are often planted along waterways.

197

Lowland rivers and deltas

Meandering rivers and oxbow lakes characterise this floodplain in central Alaska. Notice the deposits of sand and other sediments on some curves. These deposits indicate an uneven flow – slower and shallower on the sandy stretches, faster and deeper on the opposite shores.

Sprawling over a vast area, the Waitaki river in New Zealand seems to lose its identity in the maze of sand bars, spits and islands that divert its waters. This random appearance of streams and sediments, here close to the sea, is an indication of extremely flat terrain.

In *Life on the Mississippi*, Mark Twain, a one-time river pilot, tells about a group of fellow pilots who organised a system for reporting the daily changes in the river's channel. Today, a century later, rivermen use radio, radar and depth finders for the same purpose. Although it has been dredged and dammed, the "fickle" Mississippi is still changing.

The Mississippi is wide and sluggish in its lower reaches because it flows through a broad, flat valley. At some points, this river drops only about an inch per mile. The lowlands that border many large rivers (the Nile, Niger or Yangtze, for example) are often only a few feet higher than the river itself. These valley floors, or floodplains, are a part of the river channel and are subject to frequent inundations.

For much of their length these slow-moving rivers deposit more material than they pick up. These deposits may develop into sand bars, shoals, and banks, but such shallows can be washed away almost overnight. Sand bars may divert the current to the opposite bank, where erosion is then increased. This process causes the river bed to migrate slowly over the floodplain. If the river is navigable, its channel must not only be monitored, but also dredged from time to time. In any case, the channels are frequently marked with lights and buoys, and river charts are revised regularly.

In the early 19th century Admiral Nelson used to put into the estuary of the River Dee. Now the estuary, some 12 miles long and 5½ miles wide at the mouth, has degenerated into mudflats because the flatness of the Cheshire Plain reduces the pace of the river to a crawl.

Most of the sediment and other material dropped by a river falls out along its banks where the current is slowest. These deposits frequently build natural dykes, sometimes 10 to 20 ft higher than the floodplain. Many lowland rivers – ranging from the Mississippi to the Hwang Ho in China – have such natural walls. Eventually, these deposits prevent tributary streams from entering the river. The blocked streams may form lakes, or run parallel to the main stream for great distances. Such streams are called yazoos in the United States, after the Yazoo River, which meanders next to the Mississippi for about 100 miles before joining it.

Although serene and scenic most of the time, lowland rivers change drastically after spring thaws and thunderstorms. A swollen river may flood an entire valley from wall to wall with a sheet of water. For example, a section of Cincinnatti, on

America's Ohio River, was once covered by flood waters to a depth of 80 ft. In more recent times, floods in Italy have jeopardised art treasures of incalculable value, notably in Florence.

At the mouth of a river, soil that is not carried away by ocean currents may be dropped, creating a new platform of land. In the 5th century BC, the Greek historian Herodotus named such formations deltas, after the triangular capital letter of the Greek alphabet. But only a few deltas are actually triangular. They may resemble open fans or hands with spread fingers, forming branching rivers.

The volume of soil dropped in a lowland delta is demonstrated by the speed with which a delta may grow. For 800 years, the Po Valley delta in Italy advanced seawards at a rate of from 80 to 200 ft a year. The town of Adria, a seaport during Roman times, now lies approximately 14 miles inland.

Deltas are not always solid accumulations of sediment. Instead, lakes may develop within their arms. An example is the famous Zuider Zee, near the mouth of the Rhine. This delta lake has been transformed by the Dutch; cut off from the sea, several regions have been closed by dykes, and the excess water has been pumped out.

Because of the deposits of rich soil, such reclaimed areas become fertile farmland. The most extensive reclamation in the world is in the Netherlands.

The Netherlands: a nation that triumphed over powerful seas

Several rivers empty into the North Sea in the Netherlands – including the Rhine, the Meuse and the Scheldt. The resulting deltas have become more extensive with the years, as the silt carried by the rivers accumulated in the shallows of the North Sea. Delta regions are generally ideal for farming because they are fed by fresh water from inland, and because the land there is frequently enriched by deposits of topsoil. No other nation in the world has made more extensive use of deltas. The massive engineering feat that closed off the Zuider Zee resulted in a great gain of farmland and, later, in space for both residential and industrial development. There are many smaller projects throughout the country. But the present one, the Delta Project in the south-western part, is intended more for flood control than for land reclamation. Flooding is a danger both from the rivers and the sea. Many islands and peninsulas have also been linked by bridges and roads.

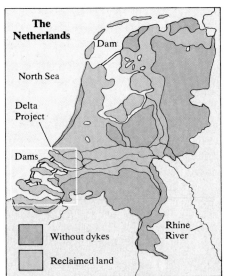

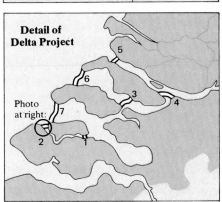

The lower map shows the order in which the Delta Project dams were built. Gates relieve the pressures of river currents and ocean tides.

To close the Veerse Gat (part of the delta of the Scheldt), immense blocks of concrete – called caissons – were pulled into place by tugboats and sunk on underwater foundations. Finally, at the turn of the tide, steel gates were lowered, thus blocking out the sea.

CHAPTER SEVEN

Deserts
and arid lands

*Like oceans, deserts become more perilous
as you cross them. Those not born to
the rigours of deserts are safest at the edges*

The deserts, like the continental shelves, are rich sources of oil. They also have extensive deposits of phosphates and other minerals. Consequently, deserts throughout the world attract prospectors. These modern explorers venture into the "forbidding" desert environment by truck or aircraft – usually loaded with supplies in case they get lost, and, in any event, capable of radio contact with the outside world. Occasionally they are confronted by the sight of native children, nonchalantly leading a goat or camel across the trackless waste with their meagre (but adequate) supplies tied in a small bundle. Of all human beings, only a few hardy peoples have been able to survive in the desert. Nomadic Bedouins, Mongol herdsmen, American Indians and Australian Aborigines are among the few peoples whose social customs, and even physical attributes, have enabled them to live well there. These desert peoples – as much as the plant and animal inhabitants – throw light on just what the word *adaptation* really means. They are all truly at home on arid lands. They do not find deserts "hostile" or "searing", for such descriptions are an outsider's way of looking at this world. In fact, a cactus or a pack rat would find life nearly impossible in a well-watered, shaded woodland or meadow.

The reason a desert is *not* deserted is that many forms of life have adapted to the extreme conditions. You might even find the desert bursting with life – a procession of animals at a waterhole, or a profusion of wildflowers budding after a rare shower.

*In the aftermath of heavy rains, brilliant poppies and lupins
spring from the ground in astonishing abundance. In a
matter of days, they prosper, set seed, then vanish. When
drought returns to this American desert, only a few sturdy plants
will remain, with the tall cactus standing like a sentinel.*

The many faces of deserts

Shimmering mountains of sand rolling on endlessly for as far as the eye can see – this is the picture most people have of the world's deserts. Yet the Sahara, which contains more sand than any other desert, is sandy over only about 10% of its total surface. Like most deserts, the Sahara has hard, flat "desert pavement" cut by twisting chasms, stark mountains and boulder-strewn hills, with their pinnacles of weirdly sculptured rock.

The Sahara is the largest desert in the world, covering an area almost the size of the United States. It is mostly a barren plain covered with rocks and gravel, and crossed by dry stream beds. Such deserts are usually called hamada types, after the Arabic word for rocky desert. Another African desert, the Kalahari, and the immense Australian deserts are almost entirely hamada. By contrast, deserts in North and South America contain small hamada areas within their vast limits.

Perhaps the oddest features of the Sahara, and of many other hamada deserts, are sections of flat pavement, called billiard-table deserts. Some of these are actually bedrock that has been swept bare by driving winds. More often, the pavement is a crust of minerals; these accumulated on the soil surface whenever rainwater evaporated, the way a hard scale may form on the inside of a kettle. Some of these pavements are up to 40 ft thick, and those of the Australian deserts are believed to be several million years old.

Rocky deserts are raw material for sandy deserts. Particles are chipped from the rocks by strong winds and infrequent rains, and these may collect in dunes. This is why rocky and sandy deserts are often found next to one another. Frequently, windstorms carry the sand far beyond the borders of the desert where it originated. Winds from the Sahara, for example, may carry dust and sand across the Mediterranean Sea.

There is now world-wide concern that most deserts, especially the Sahara, are spreading into once-fertile regions.

Most of the deserts in the Americas differ markedly from those in the Eastern Hemisphere. The Great American Desert in Utah and Nevada, for example, is a series of gaunt mountains and hills separated by wide, level basins called bolsons. At the edge of a bolson, where deep mountain canyons stop abruptly, immense fans of rocky material often form. These distinctive fans are debris brought by occasional rains.

However, many desert formations have sharp edges. You may have noticed this in photographs of deserts, or seen it yourself when you travelled. In such places, the desert features have not been smoothed down by the steady workings of running water. Also, the angularity of a desert is exposed to view by the absence of vegetation.

Desert rocks resemble one another in their reddish or greyish "paint". This hue is called desert patina, or varnish. The paint-like effect is a coating of metal oxides that have accumulated on desert surfaces. The varnish is believed to be the result of light desert dew that dissolves substances from the soil surface, and then evaporates. It is thought that at least 2,000 years are required for the thin coating to accumulate because it is found only on desert ruins known to be this old or older. Thus, on some deserts, you are seeing the colour of time.

Clusters of cacti typify many North American deserts. This dense concentration (above) is cholla, perhaps the prickliest of all cacti.

These bleak, ancient slabs of rock (right) are in Argentina's Monte. Parts of this desert contain rocks that are believed to be more than 150 million years old – older than the Andes.

The golden dunes of the Sahara are among the most spectacular in the world. Here, the wind creates sculptures that are both softly contoured and razor-sharp. The enormous dunes in the distance provide a dramatic contrast with the delicately etched ripples in the foreground.

Sun-loving lizards, such as the wall and green lizard, that live among rocks and ruins around the Mediterranean, are familiar to holiday visitors. Although often well camouflaged and very lively, they can be approached slowly and quietly. Or, better still, make yourself comfortable beside rocks where you have noticed lizards and wait for one to appear. Have your camera ready in advance, check the light meter and use a filter to minimise glare. A good shot that can be enlarged will give you a chance to study these creatures.

This Australian blue-tongued skink has been caught by a photographer in its threat display. Some skinks, either short-legged or legless, are found in southern Europe.

From desert lake to salt flat

In 1833, in one of the most desolate, mountainous reaches of the Sahara, a French officer, Lieutenant Brenans, clambered into the cool shade of a cavernous gorge. As his eyes became adjusted to the dim light, the young officer was astonished by paintings on the walls. In one of the driest places on earth, the rocks were covered with pictures of creatures from rainy tropical regions – rhinoceroses, hippopotamuses and elephants, some of them even spouting water.

For years, scientists believed that the world's large deserts had always been dry. Yet prehistoric paintings, such as those discovered by Brenans, argued against this idea. Gradually – sometimes in the most unexpected ways – new evidence has given us a different view. Geologists know that sand is made mainly by water, not by wind. For example, the expansion and contraction of water during temperature changes crack rock; it is crumbled further as water carries off small pieces. Sand is the end product of centuries of abrasion. So the most obvious clue to the former presence of water on or near deserts is the sand itself.

Grooves in exposed bedrock in the Sahara have been identified as glacial in origin. This is clear evidence that water must have been present in abundance. A further curious fact is that the distinctive red soils of the Australian deserts were probably the products of humid tropical conditions in the past.

When deserts were opened up for commercial exploitation, they provided even more conclusive evidence of the fact that deserts have changed. Vast oil and natural gas supplies lie beneath many deserts – and these come only from ancient sea deposits and, to a lesser extent, swamp vegetation.

The story of these transitions has meaning today because we are able to see the continuing process in various parts of the world. The case history of America's Great Salt Lake has been well documented. Millions of years ago, the region was covered with a freshwater lake of nearly 20,000 sq. miles – about 20 times the size of the present Great Salt Lake. Many rivers flowed into it, and the lake itself drained into the ocean through the Snake and Columbia rivers.

As the world's climate warmed, evaporation reduced the supply of water to the lake. (Former shorelines can be seen on neighbouring mountainsides, where the surf cut beaches and terraces.) When the water dropped below the drainage outlets, the only way it could leave the great basin was through evaporation.

As the water continued to evaporate, the lake shrank, and the original, relatively small amounts of salt carried down by many streams from mountains and uplands became increasingly concentrated. The salt flats that border the present shoreline were once deposits at the bottom of the lake.

Such deposits of minerals are widespread throughout the world. White Sands in New Mexico, USA, is the largest area of gypsum in the world. The gleaming sands are piled up in dunes that reflect the desert sun with almost unbearable intensity. Many areas that were once regarded as wastelands are now understood to be treasure troves of minerals, some used in industries such as building. Regardless of its modern uses, salt is important to mankind.

Although lakes and flatlands with high salt concentrations are inhospitable to life, salt is absolutely essential to the human body. Before the invention of refrigeration, it offered the only way of preserving meat for times when game was scarce. Thus, from time immemorial, expeditions have travelled long distances to obtain salt. Until a few years ago, salt was transported by caravans of up to 2,000 camels from salt swamps in North Africa 450 miles to Timbuktu.

LIVING WITH NATURE
Crossing a desert

Even deserts that have modern roads across them have their hazards. In Australia and other parts of the world where there are vast distances between settlements, motorists crossing a desert have learned to take the following special precautions:
- The driver will make sure that the car has been serviced before leaving and is equipped with tools and spare parts.
- He will carry a supply of water for the passengers and the radiator. A first-aid kit, including remedies for sunburn, spare sunglasses, a mirror for signalling during daylight and flares for night-time are also advisable. Blankets are useful for the cold desert night.
- If a car breaks down in the desert, the occupants are always advised to stay close to it and await help rather than trying to strike out across the desert.
- The occupants are also advised to limit their exertions so as to conserve body moisture and to keep their clothes on to reduce water loss and minimise sunburn.

Laguna Colorada (colourful lake) is a shallow basin in the Bolivian Andes. Red algae tint its salty water. At 13,500 ft, the lake is the home of a rare species of flamingo. It is just a matter of time before the lake dries up and becomes a desolate, salt-rich plain.

This region of Death Valley in California is called Dante's View. From here a visitor can see the lowest point on the continent of North America. The name was derived from the dire experiences of gold prospectors, who searched for treasure, but found an inferno instead.

Drastic changes in a salt lake

The Great Salt Lake in Utah (below) receives 90% of its water from rivers that feed into the southern part. When an old railway crossing was replaced by a new, nearly solid trestle, the lake was effectively dammed. The northern arm became saltier as its water evaporated and was not replaced; the southern arm became more and more diluted by river water. Rich salt deposits can be extracted from the north more readily, but this region is likely to dry up faster, and become a salt flat.

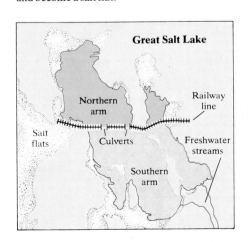

Great Salt Lake

Northern arm

Railway line

Salt flats

Culverts

Freshwater streams

Southern arm

The Devil's Golf Course is the lowest part of Death Valley. Water with a high salt content flows down to this area, then evaporates. The jagged forms are salt, deposited over centuries.

205

Where water is scarce

In many people's minds, deserts and the equator seem to go together. But if you look at the map, you will see that only a relatively small desert region – the Somali-Chalbi, in eastern Africa – actually touches the equator. In the equatorial region, generally, the sun strikes the earth most directly, and the heat is greatest. Water vaporises at the surface of the sea. When this warm, moist air rises and strikes the cold upper atmosphere, the vapour condenses and drops to earth in the form of torrential tropical rains.

Winds from the equatorial region continue their travels, but they are now almost completely devoid of moisture. As they sweep over the land, they pick up any available surface water. It is this wind pattern that maintains arid conditions in deserts such as the Sahara.

Some deserts, such as the Gobi and Takla-Makan in central Asia, are dry simply because they are so far from any large body of water. In other places, moisture-bearing winds are blocked by mountains. For example, the western coast of the Americas is swept by damp winds from the Pacific. But as the air strikes the coastal mountains, it rises to higher, cooler altitudes, and the moisture condenses as rain or snow. By the time the winds reach the opposite (eastern) side of the mountains, the air contains little vapour. Thus, the American deserts and scrublands that are blocked from moisture by mountains are called rain-shadow deserts.

Swift evaporation accounts for some desert areas. They may receive as much rain as a grassland, but the moisture evaporates too quickly to support grassland vegetation. Sometimes the total annual rain and snowfall may be high, but if it comes in only one or two big storms a year, the area is dry the rest of the time. Many marginal regions are deserts for a few years, and then become grasslands – only to revert to desert conditions as the climate fluctuates. Nomadic peoples living at the edges of the desert accelerate the process by grazing their livestock, denuding the land then moving on. Eventually, this see-sawing may stop – usually at the desert stage. That is, the area becomes a permanent desert.

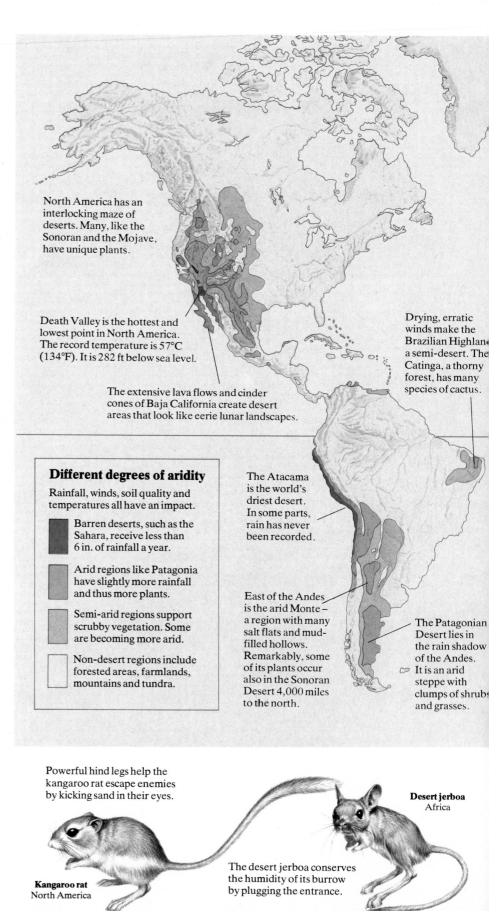

North America has an interlocking maze of deserts. Many, like the Sonoran and the Mojave, have unique plants.

Death Valley is the hottest and lowest point in North America. The record temperature is 57°C (134°F). It is 282 ft below sea level.

The extensive lava flows and cinder cones of Baja California create desert areas that look like eerie lunar landscapes.

Drying, erratic winds make the Brazilian Highlands a semi-desert. The Catinga, a thorny forest, has many species of cactus.

The Atacama is the world's driest desert. In some parts, rain has never been recorded.

East of the Andes is the arid Monte – a region with many salt flats and mud-filled hollows. Remarkably, some of its plants occur also in the Sonoran Desert 4,000 miles to the north.

The Patagonian Desert lies in the rain shadow of the Andes. It is an arid steppe with clumps of shrubs and grasses.

Different degrees of aridity

Rainfall, winds, soil quality and temperatures all have an impact.

- Barren deserts, such as the Sahara, receive less than 6 in. of rainfall a year.
- Arid regions like Patagonia have slightly more rainfall and thus more plants.
- Semi-arid regions support scrubby vegetation. Some are becoming more arid.
- Non-desert regions include forested areas, farmlands, mountains and tundra.

Small, nocturnal desert animals

Almost every desert has its native species of rodents. In spite of their fragile appearance, they are well-adapted to a hot, dry habitat. Most are nocturnal, escaping the heat of day in deep burrows. One surprising adaptation is an ability to get along without drinking water. The marsupial mouse, which resembles a rodent, but is not one, has a similar life style.

Powerful hind legs help the kangaroo rat escape enemies by kicking sand in their eyes.

Kangaroo rat
North America

Desert jerboa
Africa

The desert jerboa conserves the humidity of its burrow by plugging the entrance.

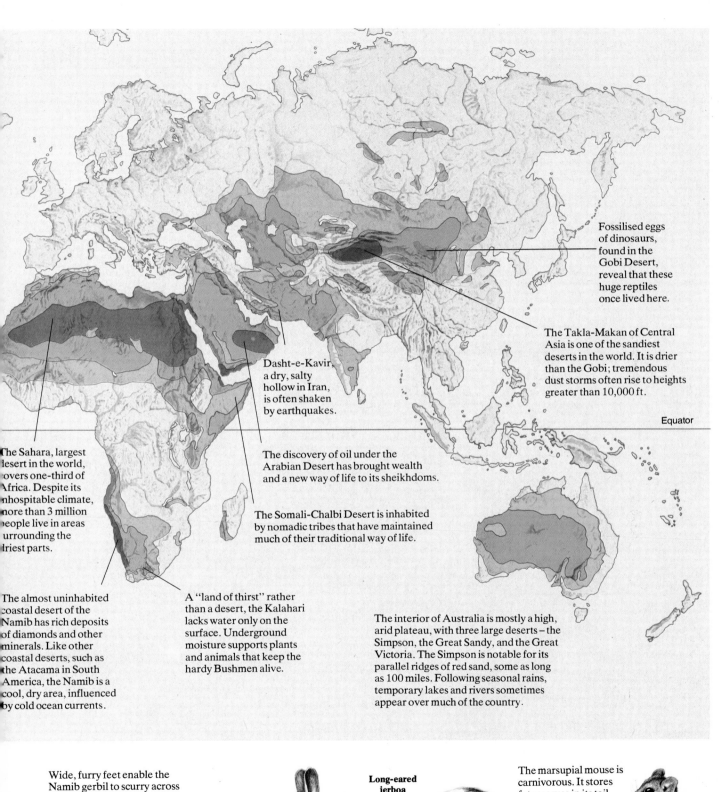

Fossilised eggs of dinosaurs, found in the Gobi Desert, reveal that these huge reptiles once lived here.

The Takla-Makan of Central Asia is one of the sandiest deserts in the world. It is drier than the Gobi; tremendous dust storms often rise to heights greater than 10,000 ft.

Dasht-e-Kavir, a dry, salty hollow in Iran, is often shaken by earthquakes.

Equator

The Sahara, largest desert in the world, covers one-third of Africa. Despite its inhospitable climate, more than 3 million people live in areas surrounding the driest parts.

The discovery of oil under the Arabian Desert has brought wealth and a new way of life to its sheikhdoms.

The Somali-Chalbi Desert is inhabited by nomadic tribes that have maintained much of their traditional way of life.

The almost uninhabited coastal desert of the Namib has rich deposits of diamonds and other minerals. Like other coastal deserts, such as the Atacama in South America, the Namib is a cool, dry area, influenced by cold ocean currents.

A "land of thirst" rather than a desert, the Kalahari lacks water only on the surface. Underground moisture supports plants and animals that keep the hardy Bushmen alive.

The interior of Australia is mostly a high, arid plateau, with three large deserts – the Simpson, the Great Sandy, and the Great Victoria. The Simpson is notable for its parallel ridges of red sand, some as long as 100 miles. Following seasonal rains, temporary lakes and rivers sometimes appear over much of the country.

Wide, furry feet enable the Namib gerbil to scurry across dry sand at amazing speeds.

Namib gerbil
South-west Africa

Long-eared jerboa
Asia

The marsupial mouse is carnivorous. It stores fat reserves in its tail.

Fat-tailed marsupial mouse
Australia

The large ears of this jerboa help alert it to the faintest sound of danger.

Vast desert lands of Africa

If you ever visit the Sahara, listen for Raoul, the invisible drummer. Winds sweeping across the desert create an eerie, rumbling sound. It may be caused by strong winds buffeting the eardrum. But many natives believe it is caused by Raoul, a drummer that no one has ever seen.

A sandstorm on the Sahara is an awe-inspiring sight. As the wind picks up speed, a dark wall of sand approaches with alarming rapidity. In a few minutes, the blazing desert sky may become as black as the darkest night – a particular danger to travellers who happen to be there at the time. Flyers have reported that the darkness may extend upwards for several thousand feet.

Travellers familiar with the desert usually wait out a severe sandstorm, even if it lasts several days. Those caught out in the open lie down on the ground, sheltering in a depression or behind a rock or other obstruction that blocks the stinging sands. Search parties cannot be sent out until the storm is over.

Tales of sandstorms burying people are mainly fictional, but the wind-borne sand can blast the paint off a car or aeroplane, and turn a windscreen into a piece of frosted glass. The sandblasting effect is most pronounced near the ground, where the heaviest particles strike. Centuries of such abrasion have eroded desert rocks into mushroom-shaped pedestals and other bizarre forms. Sometimes the sand bores completely through the rock, creating uneven windows.

In some parts of the Sahara and the Kalahari (an arid region in southern Africa) the wind has excavated so much soil over the years that immense depressions, called blowouts or pans, have formed. On the Kalahari, the pans may be miles long and 50 ft below the level of the surrounding plain. Sometimes the wind is a boon to archaeologists; it unearths long-forgotten ruins.

Part of the Kalahari is a wildlife reserve called the Kalahari-Gemsbok National Park. This is a good place to see animals during the southern winter. Certain areas of the Kalahari have acacia trees, shrubs and grasses, which support plant-eaters, including gemsbok, springbok, hartebeest

and other antelopes. Roads in the park have been built along the two water-courses. There is seldom any inconvenience to traffic since they have been filled with water only once or twice in the past century.

Though the Namib borders the Kalahari, it bears little resemblance to its neighbour. The Namib is a narrow desert, stretching some 1,200 miles along Africa's south-western coast. The western edge of the Namib (the part next to the sea) is cool – temperatures are usually about 10–15°C (50–60°F). Coastal breezes create a blanket of cool, moist air, and skies are often foggy.

The Namib is an extreme desert. Though it has large areas covered by slowly moving dunes, a large part of this desert is completely without soil or sand; the surface is solid bedrock, swept clean of any particles by the winds. Like other coastal deserts (such as the Atacama, in South America), it is almost rainless,

Man-made craters called soufs are a unique system of irrigation that has been constructed on the deserts of Algeria. These pockets allow palms to reach water that flows underground. To prevent the craters from refilling with sand, the banks are packed with fallen palm leaves.

208

despite the presence of heavy fog. The sporadic rains are usually brief showers, dropping only about ½ in. of moisture each year in the driest parts. A few small, succulent plants manage to survive on the moisture furnished by the fog. But the Namib is mainly devoid of vegetation, a quality reflected in its name, which means "place where there is nothing". The word "nothing" refers only to life: big reserves of diamonds are said to await discovery in this forbidding land.

 NATURE OBSERVER
Reading sand dunes

Dunes have very definite shapes and patterns, which generally indicate the direction of the wind. Below are three common types of dune formations.

Transverse dunes are marked by ridges that form at right-angles to the direction of wind. They are found mostly in areas of moderate breezes where tiny sand particles are blown about into wave-like shapes.

Crescent-shaped dunes, called barchans, are formed by strong winds. Sand builds up around obstacles, with the tips pointing in the direction of the wind.

Star-shaped dunes are variations on the barchan type. Such shapes build where the wind comes from various directions. The net result is a stable formation.

A family of hartebeest (top) plods across the plains of the Kalahari. These normally friendly antelope seldom use their horns in combat.

Smallest of foxes, the fennec (centre) is an inhabitant of Africa's most arid regions. Its large ears enable it to locate insects moving underground; the ears are also a means of radiating excess heat.

The ostrich (right) can outrun most predators. Its height enables it to spot an enemy from a great distance. The ostrich is a sentinel for many other species – when it runs, others do too.

The amazing Australian Outback

Imagine that you are standing 1,000 ft above the desert floor, on the summit of one of the most unusual geological formations in the world – Ayers Rock, in central Australia. Shaped like a giant pre-historic creature, the rock measures more than 5 miles around its base. Yet this great outcrop is just the tip of a larger sandstone hill, even as the greater part of an iceberg lies below sea level.

Stretching in every direction as far as the eye can see, endless plains of red sand are interrupted only by other sandstone outcrops. This is the Australian Outback – the largest desert area outside the Sahara. There is great variety in Outback deserts. One kind is the gibber desert. Gibbers (an Aboriginal word) are flat, red stones, frequently composed of an iron-rich substance called laterite and polished by the sand-bearing winds. Where gibbers cover the soil, they deter many plants from sprouting.

A map of this continent can be misleading. More than 200 lakes and rivers dot the Outback; the largest of these, Lake Eyre, covers some 3,600 sq. miles and measures about 90 miles long. But these "bodies of water" are rarely filled. Some are remnants from the wetter climatic conditions that prevailed thousands of years ago. Others require a "gulley washer" – the desert receives a soaking rain, the rivers go on a rampage, and muddy waters flow on to the sun-baked land. Floodwaters fill Lake Eyre about twice a century.

When the infrequent and unpredictable rains do occur, the results are dramatic and colourful: the vegetation turns a luxuriant green, and new plants sprout in places where there were none. The Outback is vibrant with life – but within a matter of days, unless there is more rain, the grass turns brown and the flowers disappear.

Some water-filled basins, however, are less transitory (Nelly's Hole, near Ayers Rock, is an example). These waterholes are perhaps the best places to look for animals of the Outback. A patient visitor may see kangaroos (of which Australia has about 50 species), marsupial mice, lizards and snakes. Australia has a higher proportion of venomous snakes than any other country, and many of these are found in the Outback. But the majority of poisonous species are small and not dangerous to man; their venom affects only prey.

Birds are present in abundance in the Outback, most of them adjusting their life cycle to the timing of the rains. Some 60 species, including the large and flightless emu, have been observed near Ayers Rock. Visitors may see large flocks of zebra finches – the zebra part of the name deriving from the banded, black-and-white tail. Pigeons (the wild kinds, such as the plumed pigeon) are common in some places, as are parrots – though the rarest and most mysterious Outback bird is the species known as the night parrot (few other parrots are nocturnal, and this one may even be extinct).

Ayers Rock in the Outback is ancient sandstone, far older than the landscape over which it looms. Marked vertical grooves – a result of erosion – reveal that Ayers Rock was tipped sideways when the upthrust occurred. You can get an idea of the overwhelming effect of this monolith in the photo at right, where a man is dwarfed by the huge entrance to one of the many caves. In different lights, the rock changes colour – from rich brown to dark red to steel grey.

According to the legends of the Aborigines (the first people to inhabit Australia), the deserts of the Outback were created by their ancestors during "dream time". Ayers Rock is especially significant to the Aborigines. Its caves are decorated with paintings that depict great events and ceremonies in the lives of ancient Aborigines. Paintings and names of places at Ayers Rock also immortalise the animal inhabitants – the rock python, marsupial mole (a subterranean animal that emerges only during rain or overcast weather), and the spiny-cheeked honey-eater. It was not just to please the eye that the artists drew them, but as part of the ritual with which the Aborigines contacted and appeased the forces of nature in the vast Outback.

Many-trunked mulga trees (right), a species of acacia, cover large areas of Australia's arid interior. Mulgas do not have true leaves. Their scanty foliage, which is an adaptation to a dry habitat, consists of expanded leaf stalks.

A dingo trots across a sun-cracked stretch of the Outback, searching for rodents and other small prey. The dingo was probably brought to Australia by early Aborigines.

The swift-running sand goanna is found throughout Australia. This insect-eating lizard may grow up to 4 ft and is able both to swim and to climb trees.

Galahs are on the increase in Australia. These birds, also called rose-breasted cockatoos, devour huge amounts of seed.

211

North American deserts and canyons

Spectacular canyons are distinctive features of North American deserts. Some of these great geological formations – for example, the Grand Canyon and the knife-sharp chasms and pinnacles of Bryce Canyon – are world-famous. But if you travel anywhere in the region generally referred to as the Great American Desert, you are likely to come upon smaller, no less intriguing, formations. The reason that such canyons exist is that this region of North America has been moving upwards for millions of years. Rivers, such as the Colorado, continue to cut the land as it is uplifted, creating narrow, steep-walled ravines. Britain's Cheddar Gorge was formed in the same way.

The Great American Desert sweeps thousands of miles from deep in Oregon, across most of Nevada and Utah, through Arizona, and far below the Mexican border. "Tongues" of desert extend north-wards again into New Mexico and Texas. This vast arid zone, about twice the combined size of France and Spain, is actually many deserts in one, though some are only small pockets of sand or lava wedged between mountain ranges. Compared to deserts elsewhere, the North American desert has relatively plentiful vegetation.

By far the largest desert in North America is the Great Basin, which nearly fills the gap between the Sierra Nevadas and the Rocky Mountains (and contains the Great Salt Lake). This high plateau is sparsely covered with desert vegetation, mainly sagebrush. In places, the monotonous landscape is broken by huge sand dunes, some almost golden and others brilliant coral-red. If you think you have seen them already, you are probably right. These areas have been used repeatedly as locations for Wild West films.

Nowhere is the Great Basin more colourful than in the region called Four Corners, where the states of Utah, Colorado, New Mexico and Arizona meet. Vivid purples, reds and yellows tint the Painted Desert (the colours result mainly from deposits of iron-bearing minerals). In the Four Corners area, monumental mesas and buttes – high, isolated, flat-topped remnants of rock layers from the past – project above the lowlands. Petrified Forest National Park is here, strewn with fossil logs that gleam with the hues of onyx, agate, jasper and other minerals.

Near Death Valley – the lowest, driest and hottest spot in North America – sagebrush gives way to one of the most startling plants on any desert. This is the Joshua tree, which produces leaves only at the tips of its branches. These odd-looking trees signal the approach to the Mojave Desert. More than a century ago, similar trees seemed to motion with outstretched arms, reminding Mormon settlers of a prophet beckoning them across the desert, and they named the plant after the Old Testament leader.

The Joshua tree grows on hills, scorched in summer and chilly in winter. Transplant it lower down and it does not flourish – unless occasionally put into a large refrigerator and kept nearly frozen for a couple of months.

As you travel south, the vegetation becomes stranger still. You know you are in the Arizona Desert when you see saguaro, a tall, branching cactus. The Chihuahan Desert, which is nearly as large as the Great Basin Desert, extends from Mexico into the neighbouring parts of the United States. Its eastern regions are desolate lands mostly covered with mesquite and yucca, but to the west, prickly pear and other cacti appear. The Sonoran Desert, which lies mostly south of the Mexican border, has many giant saguaros and other tree-like cacti, as well as a great variety of other succulent plants. Few experts agree entirely on the names and boundaries of these various deserts, because they merge into each other.

LIVING WITH NATURE
Building a solar still

Experienced travellers can extract drinking water from desert plants and seemingly dry soil by using a solar still. The only equipment they need is a waterproof sheet and a container to catch the water.

• A hole is dug 3 ft across and 2 ft deep and the container is put in the centre. Any available desert plants are put in the hole and mashed flat against the ground.
• The sheet is spread over the hole, its edges anchored with stones. Then a fist-sized rock is placed in the centre of the sheet, so it will sag towards the container but not touch either the ground or the plants.
• The travellers then sit in the shade and wait for water to collect.

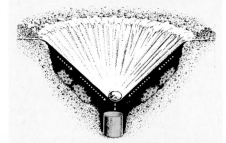

The sun heats the soil and the vegetation beneath a sheet in this solar still. Moisture condenses on the underside of the sheet, which is cooled by the outside air. The water drips downward into the container.

Snow on the desert is not unusual. An inch or two falls every year on most North American deserts. Snow is more beneficial than rain because it melts slowly and sinks into the ground.

These shifting sands in New Mexico are composed of grains of gypsum, which accounts for their startling whiteness. The sand is washed down from surrounding mountains into this basin. Notice the sharp borderline where the scrubby vegetation is losing ground to the advancing dunes.

The brilliant russet spires of Bryce Canyon, Utah, were stained by iron deposits, as the forces of erosion whittled away at the land.

Sunset at Joshua Tree National Monument in California silhouettes these curious plants. They are not really trees, but a giant species of yucca.

Desert contrasts: day to night

If you visited the same area of a desert at 3 p.m. and again at 3 a.m., you might not believe you were in the same place. Few regions on earth vary as much from day to night. In the afternoon, you need sunglasses and a broad-brimmed hat – the temperatures may soar to above 38°C (100°F) under a blazing sun. At night, when temperatures often drop below the freezing mark, you would do well to have a winter jacket. The reason for the drop in temperature is that desert air contains little heat-retaining moisture. Thus, the heat of the day is not held over at night.

As you might expect, these dramatic variations in the environment cause great changes in animal behaviour. Birds are the only conspicuous animals seen in the early morning. As the heat of the day intensifies, most animals take cover – even lizards, which are perhaps the hardiest of all desert-dwellers. They prefer to spend the hottest hours hiding in the shade of plants or in burrows.

The first time you visit a desert at night, you will probably be impressed by the darkness of its cloudless skies. (You may become aware – possibly for the first time – of the role clouds often play in providing some night-time illumination. Frequently, in other regions, light from below the horizon is reflected by clouds and produces a soft, diffused glow.) If the moon is visible,

Daily parade in the desert

During the day, at any time, birds are the most easily seen of desert animals. In this Arizona desert scene, a Gila woodpecker pauses at its nest hole in a giant saguaro. Another nest hole houses a dozing elf owl. The Harris's hawk, carrying a lizard in its talons, heads for an untidy stick nest. Also carrying a lizard is a roadrunner - an odd-looking member of the cuckoo family. The cactus wren, perched on a bristling cholla, is impervious to spines. Plumed Gambel's quail share the waterhole with peccaries. Lizards bask, but the jackrabbit seeks shade.

Animals seen by day

1. Cactus wren
2. Harris's hawk
3. Elf owl
4. Gila woodpecker
5. Collared peccaries
6. Gambel's quail
7. Antelope jackrabbit
8. Tarantula
9. Roadrunner
10. Desert horned lizards

or if the stars are particularly bright, you may catch a glimpse of animal activity.

The night-time is well supplied with small, furry mammals – mostly rodents such as mice, rats and gerbils. As night falls, they emerge from their burrows, where the insulating soil protects them from the heat of the day. It is not surprising that these animals are active at night in deserts – that is their habit in other environments, too. What is notable is that many larger desert animals are more nocturnal than they are in other places such as forest and field. As the sun sinks below the horizon, foxes, badgers and deer come out, searching for food and water.

Most desert snakes and predatory birds, such as owls, also take advantage of the cool darkness. They often hunt by waiting for prey to come within striking distance, and many nights they wait in vain. But with any luck they will carry home one of the amphibians – frogs, toads and salamanders – that have adapted themselves to this peculiar environment.

Compared with other natural regions with their far richer vegetation, deserts are sparsely populated, except around waterholes. Those who know the dangers are careful not to visit the holes at night unless they are wearing thick-soled high boots as a protection against poisonous snakes or scorpions.

The night guard takes over

In the cool of evening, mammals and some reptiles take over the desert. The pool attracts mule deer, a hog-nosed skunk, and a Gila monster (one of the world's two species of poisonous lizards). A desert tortoise has ambled out of its underground burrow for water. Poised to strike, a diamondback rattlesnake eyes a desert wood rat on a prickly pear. The ringtail preys on small rodents, such as the pocket mouse behind the saguaro. A long-nosed bat seeks nectar in a night-blooming cactus. And the sparrow-size elf owl comes out to feed.

Animals seen by night

11. Long-nosed bat
12. Elf owl
13. Mule deer
14. Ringtail
15. Desert wood rat
16. Gila monster
17. Hog-nosed skunk
18. Diamondback rattlesnake
19. Desert tortoise
20. Desert pocket mouse

Waterholes and oases

An eland quenches its thirst while zebras wait their turn. This bulky antelope is surprisingly agile, and can leap as high as 8 ft. Waterholes such as this are a boon to the animals of the Namib Desert – a barren, practically rainless strip along the south-western coast of Africa.

In some deserts, regulations require travellers to equip themselves with a rope of a specified length before setting out. It can make the difference between survival and disaster. Sometimes thirsty travellers have come upon a well, but were unable to reach the water. Other regulations may require travellers to report at each source of water (in the Sahara, these may be about 100 miles apart). If travellers are not heard from in 24 hours, a search party is sent out. The reason is simple: under extreme desert conditions, a human being dehydrates rapidly.

In addition to isolated wells, many deserts have natural waterholes by which the traveller must plan his route like a ship sailing from port to port. Better still is an oasis, a moist, fertile region. The word oasis was applied by the ancient Greeks to one particularly fertile spot in the Libyan desert (part of the Sahara). A waterhole does not have lush vegetation around it. It may be less permanent than an oasis and even dry at certain seasons. Some oases are not much bigger than an average garden; others may cover an entire valley. A river flowing through desert may create ribbon-like oases along its banks. The Nile Valley is the largest oasis of this kind in the world, bringing fertility to a strip of desert nearly 2,000 miles long.

PHOTO TIPS
Photographing animals by night – where and how

To take photographs of wild creatures by night it is essential to discover beforehand where they are likely to appear. An ideal spot in dry weather is a pond or stream, which all sorts of animals are obliged to visit. When water is plentiful the entrances of burrows or thickets make good targets. So do known owl-roosts or places where footprints indicate animal traffic.

• Stay as far away from your target as possible in order not to frighten the animals. Put the camera on a tripod and use either a telephoto lens or a long shutter-release attachment to keep your distance. Of course you will need a flash.

• Bring a torch to check camera settings in the dark, a seat and sandwiches to keep yourself comfortable. A raincoat, too, may come in useful. You may have to wait quite a while for success.

An American photographer framed this night picture between tree trunks. Two coyotes are caught as they pad to a stream.

An oasis is an unforgettable sight. Few contrasts in nature are as striking. Wherever water is present, the barren desert bursts into vegetation. This is especially true where the water irrigates plantations of date palms, citrus fruits, vegetable crops and cereal grains. Such oases sustain many animals, both domestic and wild, that are rarely found elsewhere in the desert.

Where does an oasis get its water? Since desert rains are few and brief, the source is invariably distant – as much as 500 miles away. Sometimes an underground channel rises to the surface in the desert. On a number of deserts, the groundwater follows the gravelly deposits beneath a dry river bed; slanting underground tunnels that were dug generations ago are still tapping these sources. In the Nile oasis, water is still brought up by means of the *shadoof*, an ancient system consisting of a bucket and rope at the end of a pivoted pole.

In rocky areas, the water may burst spontaneously through the desert floor. Such natural springs are common in the oases of both the Australian and Saharan deserts. Where the desert is sandy, the wind may help in uncovering a water supply. As it slowly piles up the sand into dunes, it occasionally exposes the water table. A spring or waterhole may then break through. For a time, plants and animals may take advantage of this natural oasis, but the waterhole is soon covered again by the wind. Eventually, another sand dune may smother the temporary oasis and the wildlife will disappear beneath the arid wilderness.

The geology of an oasis

The water that feeds many oases travels for great distances underground through porous layers of rock. Its path turns up where a break, or fault, in the rock creates a conduit to the surface. Such geological formations produce either gentle springs or gushing artesian wells.

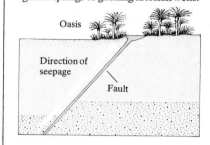

A lush island of green, the Tunisian oasis of Gabès is located on the eastern fringe of the Sahara. This fertile agricultural area, which boasts some 300,000 date palms, is watered by the Oued Gabès. (Oued or wadi is the Arabic word for a stream that dries up for part of the year.)

When the rains come

The desert is one place where you can stand outside during a rainstorm and not get wet. On many deserts, thunderclouds churn up and rumble, lightning flashes and it rains – but in the hot, dry desert air the rain evaporates before it hits the ground. You may even be able to see rain falling in the sky and still not get wet. Desert rainstorms are probably the most localised in the world. Rain may fall beside the road you are driving on, yet not a drop will strike your windscreen. Or you may be travelling a sunlit road and suddenly run into an area where rain is pouring. The wet part of the road begins as abruptly as if the water had been poured from a giant watering can.

On parts of the Sahara, no moisture at all has fallen for about ten years, but most deserts get at least some rain annually. As a rule, the less rain a desert gets, the more unpredictable its storms will be. When they do arrive, the desert may get its entire annual rainfall in a single cloudburst.

Deserts such as the Kalahari generally receive rains at certain seasons of the year.

A desert rainstorm is often spectacular. It may pour so heavily that dry stream beds suddenly become roaring torrents – the raging stream often rips out bridges and roads, and uproots trees. Soon after the storm has passed, the water soaks in and the streams return to their former placid condition. Only a crop of suddenly emerged plants records the coming of the rains; and they soon die.

Storm clouds over the Kalahari Desert in south-western Africa herald the arrival of autumn (which is in March in the Southern Hemisphere).

Unlike many deserts, much of the Kalahari has fairly good plant cover – grasses and acacia trees, which depend on this short rainy season.

Water sometimes collects in immense shallow lakes that may temporarily cover several square miles.

Dried-up gullies or "washes", which are common in deserts – they are called wadis in the Arabian deserts, arroyos in the United States – are no place to be during a rainstorm. They often appear to be a mere dip in the road. These gullies are dry nearly all year round, but sometimes storms create thick, muddy rivers – mixtures of water and sediment in which boulders may be carried along. These rivers of mud can bulldoze banks and stream beds.

Campers new to dry conditions may not recognise the hazards of setting up a camp in what looks like a peaceful, sheltered area. In a matter of moments, a cloudburst far away can flood a gully, sweeping everything in its path. The hazard is impossible to predict – clear conditions locally are no guarantee of safety. And at night, when there may not even be the warning of clouds on the far horizon, the result can be catastrophic. Whenever you camp, hike, or just ramble in a desert, stay alert to the situation – be sure you are never in a low-lying gully that could suddenly fill up and overwhelm you.

In other areas, seeping storm water may slowly remove underground sediment, leaving a series of large channels. These channels have created fantastic natural arches and bridges that stand revealed when most of the roof has fallen away. The giant arching formations in many deserts were bored out by running water and not by the wind.

The feel of the soil underfoot reveals one reason for desert flash floods. Unlike soil in a forest, desert soil is not mixed and tunnelled by earthworms, or covered with decaying leaves. As a result, some parts of a desert are underlaid by a layer of compacted soil, and rain does not soak into the ground as it would in a garden.

Desert storms sometimes go on for a few days, and may be accompanied by strong winds and hailstones. Within an hour, a desert floor may be carpeted with hailstones, which melt as quickly as they appeared. After a rain, the burning desert heat may be replaced by freezing cold. On some deserts, such as the Mojave, snow may fall, creating a beautiful, if somewhat incongruous, scene. This is another reason (beyond the daily temperature changes) why travellers to a desert should be prepared for cold as well as hot conditions.

Even in normal circumstances, a desert that is sweltering hot by day can become very chilly soon after the sun goes down.

Desert rainstorms are often violent. The rain does not soak into the rocky or compacted soil, but goes on a rampage down gullies that were dry a few minutes earlier. If the water is in a sandy region, however, as here, it may soak into the ground and quickly disappear.

NATURE OBSERVER
Mirages: when you seem to see water

Mirages are often thought of as peculiar to the desert, but strange optical effects may also occur over the ocean and in very cold regions. You have probably seen many mirages – those "wet spots" that appear on roads on sunny days, but disappear as you approach. Ocean and cold-air illusions generally appear to loom high above the horizon in an upright position. Desert images look like lakes or ponds. Occasionally, a palm tree or a caravan will appear to be elongated or upside-down.

A shimmering lake seems to be in front of the trees on a dry plain in Tanzania. The water is a mirage. Some mirages make a distant object appear much closer than it really is.

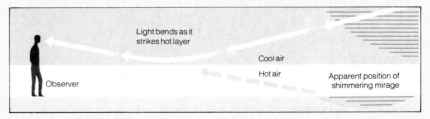

Mirages occur when light passes through two layers of air with different temperatures. The desert sun heats the sand, which in turn heats the air just above it. The hot air bends light rays and reflects the sky. For an observer, the different air masses act like a mirror.

219

Deserts that bloom like magic

After rains soak a desert, wildflowers take over the barren land. Yet if you lived on this same desert and watered the soil faithfully, very few flowers would grow. Most desert wildflowers sprout only after a certain amount of rain has fallen, within a certain length of time, and during a certain season. Even if the proper amount of water reaches the seeds by soaking through the soil, they will remain dormant; the water has to be in the form of rain. Such seeds, in effect, have a built-in rain gauge, clock and calendar. Some of them even have a "yardstick". They must be carried a certain distance by a stream before they will sprout.

How can seeds tell what is going on around them? The seed coatings of many desert plants have a substance that inhibits sprouting and must be washed away before the seeds can germinate. If too little rain falls, or if the water reaches the seeds by soaking through the soil, the inhibiting chemical remains. Laboratory experiments have shown that some desert wildflowers can tell how much rain falls to within half an inch. If the rain comes in spurts, even though it might be the right quantity, the seeds will not sprout – the seeds replace their inhibitory coating of chemicals during dry spells.

The seeds of many desert plants also seem to know the season. Usually, the seeds of winter-sprouting species will not sprout after a summer rain; likewise, many summer-sprouting flowers are unaffected by winter rains. Greenhouse experiments have revealed that summer seeds require warm temperatures as well as the proper amount of rain in order to germinate, while winter seeds require cool temperatures. Amazingly, less than 5°C (10°F) separates the "correct" temperatures for some species of so-called summer and winter plants.

The smoke tree, named after its smoke-like clusters of flowers, grows along the banks of stream beds that are usually dry. This desert plant has a curious distribution; frequently, the young trees are some 50–100 yds downstream from the parent plant. Scientists have discovered that it is the bruising action of the floodwaters in the stream bed that triggers germination. If the seeds are not washed far enough, their coating remains resistant and prevents germination. If they are swept downstream for too great a distance, the seeds may be so bruised that they never germinate.

Over millions of years, desert plants have become finely tuned to their environment. It is easy to see the survival value of these adaptations. If seeds germinated after a light rain, the soil would not retain enough moisture to support their growth. It would be disastrous for summer-sprouting flowers to germinate in winter. And a young tree growing 50 yds away from its well-rooted parent will have a better chance of survival in such barren terrain than if it had to compete for food and water close to its mother-tree.

Desert plants that can reproduce quickly, while moisture is sufficient, have an advantage in the desert. One of the record-holders for speed is a North African desert plant. It sprouts, flowers and produces mature seeds within only about a week to ten days. Such fast-blooming plants, called ephemerals (from the Greek for "lasting a day"), turn some desert regions into flower gardens overnight. Even if you know the reason for this amazing transformation, the sudden bloom of a desert still seems to have been brought about by magic.

When rain falls on the desert, courtship begins

Many desert birds are opportunists – they start to breed whenever and wherever rain falls. Even before the rain stops, these birds will be busily courting and building their nests. Following heavy rain, there will be an increase in plant growth and numbers of insects – food for young birds. Often the rained-on area is only a narrow strip. In neighbouring dry areas, the same species of birds may not breed for several seasons. This opportunism is called adventitious breeding and occurs among many desert birds, ranging from ostriches to tiny zebra finches.

Scaled quail

The tiny, lively sprites below are called variegated wrens, but in fact they are close relatives of European warblers. In dry areas of eastern Australia, they flit about in small parties. These birds nest soon after a rain, at any time of the year.

Scurrying denizens of the Arizona desert, scaled quail feed on seeds and succulent plants. They usually nest after June rains, but may breed into September if rains are late in coming.

Variegated wrens (male and female)

Vulturine guineafowl

Gregarious birds of the East African scrub, vulturine guineafowl may breed in either of the two annual rainy seasons. These stately, strikingly marked creatures get their name from their bare, vulture-like heads.

Flaming cups of desert mallow (left) light up the rocky slopes of ranges near Death Valley, California. Smaller desert flowers crowd around the base of this handsome perennial.

In favourable years, trumpet-shaped flowers of purple mat brighten areas of Death Valley. In dry years, the plants may put out almost no leaves and perhaps a single blossom.

An inch of winter rain may be enough to trigger a profusion of spring flowers. On the left, yellow evening primroses cover the sand near Lake Mojave, in Nevada.

Clumps of daisy-like flowers (above) carpet the reddish soil outside Alice Springs in Australia. The scattered mulga trees were killed by prolonged drought.

221

Plants adapted to the desert

The cactus is a plant without leaves. In most plants, leaves are the site of photosynthesis, the "factories" where the sun's energy is used to make food. Why then do cacti and many other desert plants lack leaves?

Though leaves help a plant, they can also do it some harm. Their microscopic openings allow gases – including water vapour – to enter and escape. During a single summer day, a large tree may lose several tons of water. Usually, this is not a problem for plants, but in the desert, water loss can be deadly.

For most of the year, the ocotillo, a common North American species, is a thorny bundle of brown, wand-like branches, each 10–20 ft long. Soon after the spring rains – if they come – brilliant red flowers emerge from the end of the wands (they give the plant another of its common names – candlewood). Within a few days, leaves emerge from the stems; their small size minimises water loss. By early summer, the leaves have fallen.

Like the ocotillo, the creosote bush (its Spanish name means "little stinker") has small leaves that remain on the plant for only a short time. But the creosote bush has an even better trick than the ocotillo – in a severe drought it loses twigs and branches too. In addition, the creosote bush poisons neighbouring plants – a substance secreted by its roots kills nearby seedlings which might compete with it for water. Creosote bushes often grow evenly spaced, as if they were planted in an orderly fashion by human beings. The spacing is a living record of the climate; the heavier the rains were in preceding years, the closer together the bushes grow because the moisture washes the root poison deeper into the soil. (Liquid creosote, the familiar wood preservative, is made mainly from coal tar, not from these shrubs.)

Many plants in the crassula family (one member, the jade plant, is a common house plant) have leaves with a night life,

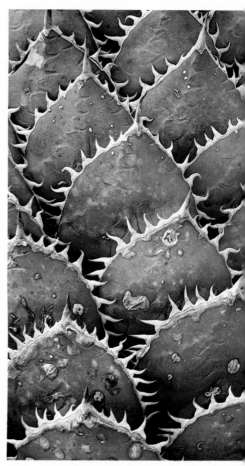

Awesome teeth that resemble cactus spines (above) border the leaves of a yucca. Native to North American deserts, yuccas belong to the lily family; Spanish bayonet is one example.

This is ocotillo at its finest, with leafy stems topped by scarlet blossoms (left). Ocotillo, smoke trees, paloverde, and a number of other desert species shed their leaves during dry periods. Since plants lose water through their leaves, this helps them to conserve moisture.

so to speak. At night, they take up gases from the air. During the day, the leaf openings close, thereby preventing water loss.

Cacti have spines, not leaves. Because the spines have no openings, water loss is not a problem. In addition, the spines are believed to provide some shade for the cacti and to trap an insulating layer of air. And of course the spines also serve as a deterrent to plant-eaters.

A cactus's outer skin is a tough, waxy coating that further protects the plant from water loss, almost as if it were covered with Cellophane. Photosynthesis takes place in the stem of the cactus, which also stores water. A fully grown saguaro cactus, the Nelson's Column of the desert, will contain about 8 tons of water.

Botanists classify cacti in a group of plants called succulents, which are juicy and retain water. The moisture in many succulents takes the form of a gummy sap. (The plant can nevertheless be used as a water supply for thirsty travellers, if the pulpy interior is pulverised.) The sap may dry out if the plant is wounded, creating a plastic-like "bandage" that lessens water loss. Long after a cactus is dead and gone, these cup-like formations – called desert shoes by some Indians – may remain on the desert floor.

A coating of salt gives the Australian saltbush its greyish pallor. Notice the regular spacing among the bushes, which lessens competition for water. By absorbing salt these plants improve the soil.

Feathery white blooms are the only clue that these South African "pebbles" are actually plants. The colour and pattern of these living stones may help conceal them from the eyes of hungry or thirsty animals. Living stones make interesting house plants – but be sure not to overwater.

 HOW TO
Grow a cactus garden

A collection of cacti is a personal thing – *you* choose the species, the container and the arrangement of the plants.

• Many garden centres have a good selection of cacti. You can buy more unusual species from specialised mail-order firms. Or obtain cuttings from a friend's plants. In the case of cacti, cuttings are actually "breakings"; many species produce shoots at the base, which are easily broken off. Let the cuttings dry for a few days before placing them in soil. This will lessen the chance of a fungus infection. Once established they are hardy.

• Cacti are notorious for their ability to defend themselves with their spines. The easiest way to handle them is with a piece of newspaper folded into a "collar".

• Use a shallow clay container and sandy soil. (Buy the soil at a garden-supply shop.) To landscape the cactus garden, include a few stones or bits of wood.

• Cacti need lots of sun but infrequent watering. In fact, one of the joys of a cactus garden is that these plants will do quite well without much care at all. Nevertheless, they need an occasional watering.

To give your cactus garden a natural look, choose plants of varied shape, texture and hue. This garden includes one cactus-like species (the Haworthia) that is actually a member of the lily family

Bunny ears
(*Opuntia microdasys*)

Old man cactus
(*Cephalocereus senilis*)

Lady finger
(*Mammillaria elongata*)

Golden barrel cactus
(*Echinocactus grusonii*)

Haworthia
(*Haworthia fasciata*)

Bishop's cap
(*Astrophytum myriostigma*)

Animals at home in a hot, dry world

If a caravan is lost in the desert (perhaps in the aftermath of a blinding sandstorm), the leader may simply turn his camels loose and follow them. If there is water to be found, the camels will find it – some of these "ships of the desert" can smell water as far away as 30 miles. It is difficult to estimate how many times this capability has saved human lives over the approximately 3,000 years since desert peoples began using camels as beasts of burden.

Over the years, the camel has come to symbolise the desert. Indeed, it is completely at home there. Along with the burros of the North American deserts, camels are the only domesticated animals that can live in such harsh conditions. Their coarse, yellowish hair – which appears mangy to the uninformed observer – is a good insulator against both the heat of the day and the chill of the night. A camel's nostrils have special valves that shut out sand and dust. Long hairs around the ears and long eyelashes – which give the animal an incongruously sophisticated expression – serve the same purpose.

The camel has soft, pliable hooves, which resemble leather-covered cushions and prevent the animal from sinking into soft sand. Thick calluses protect the camel's knees whenever it sits or kneels. The animal has a leathery mouth and tongue that let it make a meal of thorn trees and fibrous shrubs; in fact, a camel will eat these thorny desert plants even when there is plenty of grass near by. It picks the foliage with its versatile split lip, almost the way an elephant uses its trunk. The lip also aids the animal in spitting – a feat it performs at remarkable ranges and with impressive accuracy, when anything incurs its displeasure. Visitors to zoos (where camels are a popular attraction) have sometimes learned about this the hard way.

The camel's most renowned feat is its ability to carry several hundred pounds of baggage over the burning sand, going for four or five days without water. This is not a matter of storing water in its hump. The camel's hump contains fat. Instead, extremely efficient kidneys help a camel to conserve water. Like other mammals, such as the horse, it sweats as a means of cooling off. However, unlike a horse, a camel loses very little moisture in this way.

Even more remarkable desert mammals are the many small rodents that never drink water at all but extract or produce water from their food. This characteristic is confined to the male of the species (pack rat, gerbil or kangaroo rat); the females need water when they are nursing their young. Appropriately, the breeding period coincides with the brief rainy period on the desert.

Surprisingly, some amphibians, such as the spadefoot toad, can also live in the desert. This smooth-skinned creature takes its name from the scale-like spur on each rear foot, used for digging into the ground. As the ground begins to dry out, the spadefoot digs into the soil and secretes a protective, gelatine-like envelope around itself. This means of waiting out a dry spell is called aestivation – a sort of dry-weather hibernation, when the body processes slow down.

Like other amphibians, a spadefoot lays its eggs in water. Thus, a rainfall is needed – and a good one – to move the spadefoot out of its protective location. But once a puddle has been formed, it suddenly returns to active life – after a sleep of eight or nine months – and races through courtship and mating. The development of this species from eggs to tadpoles to adults is swift – it may take place in only 12 days.

A camel like this African dromedary may lose 200 lb. while crossing a desert. But as soon as it arrives at an oasis, the camel is capable of rapidly drinking some 30 gallons of water.

The spadefoot toad is capable of a remarkable disappearing act. Equipped with back feet designed for digging, it can burrow so rapidly when scared, that it seems to be sinking into the ground it is standing on.

The migration of a butterfly seems strange because the insect appears to be so fragile. Nevertheless, a number of species have elaborate life-cycles that include travelling over great distances. The European painted lady is extraordinary for its journey across the Mediterranean Sea. Both the Sahara and the British Isles have members of this species. Some individuals reach as far north as Finland. They have even been seen fluttering through the Alps at very high altitudes. The American painted lady is also a migrator.

 HOW TO
Take care of pet hamsters and gerbils

Gerbils and hamsters are animals native to arid regions of Africa, Asia and Europe. Though they are both rodents (gnawing animals), they rarely bite or scratch when handled gently.

• Plastic or wire cages designed for small mammals are available from pet shops, or you can make your own. The cage should include an exercise wheel. Both species are active at night. .

• Keep an inch or two of dry, clean sawdust on the floor of the cage and change it twice a week.

• Put the cage on a shelf or table away from draught and direct sunlight.

• Gerbils and hamsters require little water, but it must be available when needed. Place a water bottle in the cage (this, too, can be purchased at a pet shop). Wash the bottle and change the water as needed.

• You can feed these pets on bird-seed and sunflower seeds, commercial rodent foods, unsugared breakfast cereals or salad scraps.

• Like all rodents, hamsters and gerbils must gnaw frequently or their teeth will grow too long. Give them wood scraps and cardboard for "teething".

• Keep males and females in separate cages unless you want them to breed.

• Gerbils, which mate for life, will live compatibly with their babies. Male hamsters will attack their young, so remove the male from the cage before an impending birth.

Golden hamsters are friendly with owners, reserved with strangers. A "bribe" of sunflower seeds or a piece of carrot sometimes helps as an introduction.

Gerbils (left) retain their desert-adapted way of life – they store food wherever they can in their cages. In spite of these caches, the animals rarely overeat.

CHAPTER EIGHT

Weather
and astronomy

*We tend to think of weather as a daytime
phenomenon, and of astronomy as
possible only at night. This is an illusion,
caused mainly by the atmosphere.*

W e rarely think of ourselves as "bottom-dwellers" living beneath a vast sea, but this is exactly our situation. The blanket
of air above us – the mixture of gases called the atmosphere – acts like
a fluid. It is often compared with water, which also exerts increasing
pressure at greater depths. At sea level, the weight of the atmosphere
is about 15 lb. per square inch. Of course, we are so accustomed to
this weight, we seldom notice it.

But even a slight change in altitude, such as a ride in a lift, can
cause our ears to pop, as the air pressure within the ear adjusts to the
pressure outside. Aeroplanes are pressurised because of the requirements of the human body. Like bottom-dwellers in the ocean, human
beings cannot leave the atmosphere without being "fish out of
water". Thus astronauts have to wear pressurised suits when they
travel in outer space, where there is no atmosphere.

The atmosphere has a profound influence on what we see. Just
as a drinking straw appears bent when you see it in a glass of water, so
the atmosphere also bends images. This is what allows you to see the
sun for a few minutes after it has actually gone below the horizon. The
twinkling of stars is another effect in the atmosphere, not a result of
the behaviour of the stars themselves. For centuries, the atmosphere
hampered the study of astronomy. Now, from spacecraft, we have an
unencumbered view of the universe.

*Seen from a spacecraft, the outlines of planet earth's continents
appear as reddish masses against a blue sea. The swirls of
white are clouds. These veils of condensed water give some idea
of just how thin the atmospheric layer actually is, relative to
the globe itself. Paradoxically, it is only at night, when the
rays of the sun cease to dazzle our eyes with light striking the
atmosphere, that we can see to the star-strewn universe beyond.*

Watching sky spectaculars

In the mid-1880s, people in widely scattered parts of the world began to notice that their sunsets were unnaturally red, a condition that lasted for several years. The cause was the greatest volcanic eruption in modern times – that of Krakatoa, in Indonesia, in 1883. The gigantic explosion shot a billowing column of smoke and debris 33 miles into the atmosphere. It was the dust from this explosion that coloured the sunsets.

As in other spectacular displays in the atmosphere, it is not the air itself that creates the effect, but minute particles. In Krakatoa, it was volcanic dust; in other instances, it may be moisture. For example, the setting sun is much more impressive when there are clouds present. Water droplets in the clouds reflect the last rays of the sun and give then infinite nuances of colour, form and shading.

But why are sunsets red? This too is due largely to impurities in the atmosphere. Sunlight is made up of different wavelengths of light. You can see this when light shines through a prism, and the various colours (red, orange, yellow, green, blue and violet) are separated into a spectrum. Like radio waves, these colours have different wavelengths, the red being the longest and the blue and violet the shortest. Dust and water droplets in the air always absorb or deflect more of the shorter blue waves than of the longer reds. At dusk the sunlight reaches us slantwise through the atmosphere and its rays have to pass through much more cloud and dust than during the day. As a result much of the blue light gets lost and we see mainly the red rays with their better penetration.

At midday, when the sun is overhead, the effect is different. Now the rays reach us the shortest way through the atmosphere and the blue light penetrates much better, bringing the brilliance of high-noon sunshine. The scattering of blue light as it passes through the atmosphere gives the impression of blue skies.

The scattering of light is also responsible for another beautiful phenomenon – twilight. Night would fall like a light being turned out, if it were not for the atmosphere and its impurities. Particles scatter light from the sky and reflect them into the earth's shadow, causing the soft, gentle rays of twilight to linger after sunset.

Water sometimes forms a natural prism, as you may know from seeing an array of colours when sunlight shines through a glass of water. Droplets in the air do the same thing, if the sun strikes them at a particular angle the result is a rainbow. To see a rainbow, you have to have the sun at your back.

Water in the form of ice particles in a cloud will also act as a prism. This creates a halo around the sun or moon. Sometimes, the light of the sky is so bright that you can see only the more visible colours of the spectrum (usually red, orange or yellow). The Zuni Indians of North America believed that when the sun was "in his tepee" (that is, inside a halo), rain would follow – and often this is, in fact, the case.

Perhaps the most impressive of all sky spectaculars is the northern lights, or Aurora Borealis. Curtains, streamers, trails, flashes and pinpoints of coloured light seem to dance across the night sky. Auroras originate on the sun. Solar winds emit vast quantities of electrically charged particles. The particles that reach the vicinity of the earth are deflected by the earth's magnetic shield. Though some enter the belts, most are sent spinning toward the poles. As the charged particles fall earthwards near the poles, they bombard the gases there. Energy is given off as light, producing a spectacle that perplexed men through the ages.

Who is not awed when nature sets out a lavish sunset display? Vast clouds pile up, shift, change hue and then vanish. Few of us are up early enough to see the equally vivid sunrise panorama. This was taken at 5.30 a.m.

PHOTO TIPS
Rainbows are the highlights of a rainy day

Look for rainbows on days when rainy spells alternate with sunshine. You might even see a double bow, like this one. In a single bow, the red is always on top; the second, fainter, bow reverses the order of the colours. Have your camera ready because a rainbow is often short-lived. Over expose slightly.

This cold-weather cousin of the rainbow occurred when the sun went behind a screen of high-altitude, cirrocumulus clouds. Ice crystals separated the sunlight into colours, but the effect is scattered.

The Aurora Borealis means northern dawn: the Southern Hemisphere equivalent is Aurora Australis. These ghostly lights, which change in colour, intensity and form, are most clearly seen in polar regions.

The ways of winds

Our knowledge of prevailing winds was established in folk wisdom by mariners and farmers long before there was any theory to account for the ways winds behave. We now know that all winds are caused by unequal air temperatures and pressures, and the rotation of the earth. But the best-known winds were the "trades", which are the most persistent and dependable in the world. In fact, the name trade – as applied to winds – comes from a Middle English word meaning track or path. During the days of the sailing ships, every captain knew these oceanic "paths", and travelled them carrying cargoes from the Old World to the New, from Europe to the Orient.

The Northern and Southern Hemispheres are separated at the equator by low-pressure areas of light wind or dead calm. These areas – called doldrums – were troublesome to early navigation because the winds are mostly updraughts from evaporation, not the kinds of gusts that fill the sails and push ships onwards.

But it is your own local winds that are likely to occupy your attention. On all coasts, there is a regular day-night pulsing of winds, because land and sea absorb heat and cool off at different rates. Cooler, denser air from the sea blows inland during the heat of the day; the reverse takes place at night.

Some mountain and valley winds also change daily. The side of a mountain facing the sun heats up more quickly than the valley, causing a breeze to climb the slope. At night, cold air will pour down, cooling the valley once again.

Such naturally occurring air patterns are now recognised as significant to the health of towns and cities. In the early 1950s, in the city of Stuttgart in southern Germany, local officials became concerned over the poor quality of the air. Stuttgart is located in a valley, where air tended to become stagnant. Increased population, as well as industrialisation, threatened to make air quality even worse. Climatologists were called in and quickly located the channels where cool, oxygen-rich air flowed into the city each night. They also identified which places – tree-clad hillsides – should be preserved in their natural state. Many measures were taken to enhance an already existing wind pattern that supplied the city with air. The success of this project provides a good example for other cities that are similarly situated.

There are many famous local winds, such as the monsoons that blow off the Indian Ocean. When they fail, the farmlands of Pakistan and India are parched and starvation threatens. If they bring too much water thousands die in floods. The mistral, which blows cold over southern France, can wreck crops and vineyards. Typhoons bring havoc to East Asia, tearing ships from their moorings and inundating the countryside.

But the most dreaded wind of all is the tornado, commonly called the twister because of its spiralling funnel shape. It usually strikes on hot summer days and is a small but intense storm. During this storm wind speeds can reach 300 mph.

Its dangers are impossible to overestimate. Just two of the many appalling examples of tornado tragedy occurred in America, the main twister country, this century. On April 11, 1965, a tornado, consisting of at least 37 whirlwinds, hit six states, killing 271 people, with over £160 million worth of damage.

An earlier, even worse, tornado system killed 689 people on March 18, 1925.

Violently swaying palms (above) are frequently the signal of an approaching tropical storm. Such high winds can build up into hurricanes. The main ingredients of a hurricane are warm, moist air and driving winds. Hurricanes form mostly in the Caribbean and Gulf of Mexico, and often occur during the late summer.

Funnel-shaped clouds of winds, called tornadoes or twisters, form so quickly that they are sometimes not detected until fully grown. They are the result of a rapid collision between warm and cold air masses. These rotary winds often leave a path of destruction. Twisters are most common in the plains states of North America, where there are vast, flat stretches of land without hill barriers.

HOW TO
Participate in the ancient sport of flying a kite

People have been using kites to play with the wind for several thousand years, especially in the Orient. Some of the most popular types are shown here. Most kites are inexpensive to buy, but they can also be made in your home. If you build one yourself, you will need precise dimensions, so get a book from the library or buy an inexpensive paperback on the subject.

• The tail of a kite aids in control. It can be lengthened, trimmed or weighted, on a trial-and-error basis.

• Pick a good open area for flying kites – a place such as a beach – away from trees, buildings, and especially electric power lines and low-flying aircraft. Never fly a kite when there is a chance of lightning.

• Benjamin Franklin's famous experiment of capturing lightning with a kite was dangerous and should not be copied.

• Choose a day with a good steady breeze. No kite will fly well without a wind – or with strong gusts.

• Do not give up easily. Once you get your kite above the tricky ground wind the high winds will make it soar.

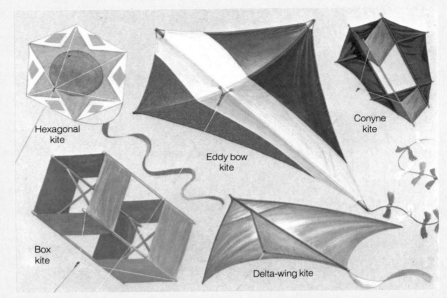

A reel is needed to bring in your kite. A spool can be adapted, perhaps with offset handles, for winding the line. A fishing rod with a large-capacity reel will also work well.

Flat kites require a tail for stability. On the Eddy and other bowed kites, it is optional. Conyne and

In a good breeze, you can launch a kite alone. Toss or snap it into the wind by the string. In a light

box kites are steady in strong winds, high winds make deltas flex their wings.

wind, a helper can hold it and then toss it up, while you pull, or run towards the wind.

Regional wind patterns and what causes them

In many regions of the globe, there are patterns of winds so persistent and predictable that they have their own names. Some are renowned world-wide. Their causes are not completely known, but it is believed that the type of terrain – such as the location of valleys relative to high mountains – is an important factor. Temperature differences and the rotation of the earth also contribute to the formation of these winds, which greatly affect climate.

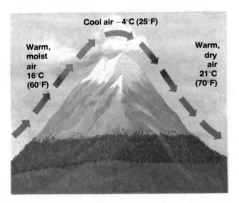

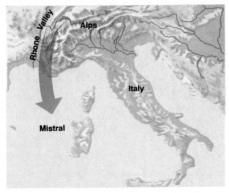

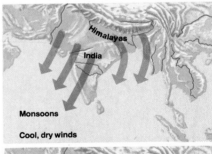

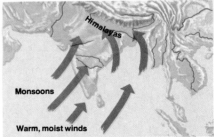

Mountain winds all operate on the same principle. As warm air rises on the side of a mountain, it cools and loses its moisture as rain or snow. The dry air rushing down the opposite side gains momentum, which heats the air. The foehns of the Alps and the chinooks of the Rockies are mountain winds.

Valley winds include the mistral of southern France. Drawn by a low-pressure system above the Mediterranean Sea, this cold, dry wind rushes down the Alps and through the Rhone Valley at speeds of up to 60 mph. Many local streets in such regions are built in an east-west direction, to serve as a buffer.

Seasonal winds, such as monsoons of India, occur because land warms and cools more quickly than water, creating differences in air pressure and temperature. During summer, warm, moisture-laden winds are drawn off the sea, resulting in the notorious torrential rains. In winter, cool, dry winds blow from the land.

A guide to cloud identification

When you exhale into cold air, the puff you see is actually a small cloud. It disappears too quickly to be studied, but it is of exactly the same material as the formations that tower in the sky. Large or small, clouds are fascinating not only because they can be beautiful, but also because they often indicate coming changes in the weather.

The source of clouds is water that evaporates into the air from the surfaces of oceans, lakes and rivers. The leaves of plants also give off vapour – a single acre of corn can transpire more than 300,000 gallons in one season. Millions of tons of water rise from the earth every day, but we do not see it happening because vapour is invisible.

Clouds form when water vapour cools enough to condense. You can see this condensation effect on a cold glass or window-pane. When moisture-laden air strikes it, tiny beads form. In a cloud, a droplet may start out microscopic.

As the water droplets ride air currents, one of three things may happen, depending on the temperature and wind. The droplets may re-evaporate, or rise and freeze into ice crystals, or they may collide and form larger drops that sometimes become heavy enough to fall as rain or sleet.

Will it rain? There are times when one look out of the window tells the story. If, for example, deep-grey clouds block the sun, rain is imminent. Most of the time weather prediction is more difficult, but there are three basic guidelines: decide which type of clouds are there, gauge how high they are, and note how fast they are changing.

There are three key cloud types: cirrus (wispy), cumulus (heaped-up) and stratus (layered). Two other words you should know are nimbus (meaning rain cloud) and alto (which refers to the middle regions of the sky). Classic combinations of these terms are shown in the illustrations on the right. The spelling variations are simple: when one of the names is used as a prefix, the ending changes to "o"; when used alone or at the end of a word, the spelling is "us".

Clouds are always on the move, constantly forming new combinations. So when you look out of your window, you will usually see several types that may overlap. Cloud names provide a shorthand system for discussing their dominant characteristics.

Clouds are classed by altitude: high, medium or low. But checking the altitude of a cloud formation is easier said than done, even for experienced cloudwatchers. It is difficult to gauge distance without a basis for comparison, such as a mountain. It helps to know that clouds do not form above a height of about 50,000 ft, where the stratosphere begins. All moisture has already been extracted before the air rises to this frigid zone.

The rate of change in cloud formations may be overlooked by amateur weather forecasters because, very often, a single look at the sky *does* give an adequate weather prediction. But what if the sky does not seem to reveal anything specific? A series of observations can help.

If clouds are accumulating or dispersing, if they are changing from high to medium altitude, or from light to dark, the comparison tells you what you need to know. With practice you will acquire skill in forecasting the weather. But remember that the British Isles are surrounded with widely different weather-creating regions, which make firm predictions extremely difficult, even for the experts – as we know from some of their forecasts.

High clouds
20,000 to 50,000 ft

High clouds tend to be thin ones, for there is little moisture in the air. In polar regions, clouds develop only up to a height of about 25,000 ft.

Middle clouds
7,000 to 20,000 ft

Clouds are transient, changing in shape and colour as they move from one level to another. Altostratus clouds often turn into nimbostratus forms.

Low clouds
from ground to 7,000 ft

Certain types of clouds are more typical of one time of year than another. Look for cumulus clouds on a bright summer day.

5. CUMULONIMBUS
(heaped-up, dark rain cloud)

SAFETY AND SURVIVAL
Following clouds to find land

If you are ever lost at sea, watch for patches of fleecy-looking clouds on the horizon. They can lead you to safety as they have been leading lost seamen since the days of early navigators.
• You can identify such clouds by their woolly appearance and seeming immobility. They are usually not directly above the island but a little off to the side.

Clouds form above islands because of moisture carried in the rising air to cooler temperatures above. In the tropics, some of these clouds have distinctive colours reflected from the sand or perhaps the shallow waters surrounding the land.
• Overhanging clouds can also warn against dangerous hidden rocks and coral reefs at the approach to an island.

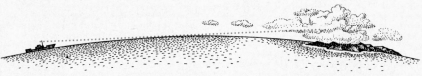

1. CIRRUS
(curl-like)

2. CIRROCUMULUS
(curl-like, heaped-up)

3. ALTOSTRATUS
(middle, layered)

4. ALTOCUMULUS
(middle, heaped-up)

6. CUMULUS
(heaped-up)

7. NIMBOSTRATUS
(dark rain cloud, layered)

8. STRATUS
(layered)

1. Cirrus clouds are long, wispy fibres of ice crystals, sometimes called "mares' tails".

2. Cirrocumulus clouds, like cirrus formations, foretell fair weather.

3. Altostratus clouds are striped, like frosted glass. Light rain probable.

4. Altocumulus clouds form puffy patches or parallel bands. Rain possible.

5. Cumulonimbus thunderclouds have anvil tops and ragged, storm-laden bases.

6. Cumulus clouds are fleecy. Fair weather ahead – unless the puffs begin to pile up.

7. Nimbostratus clouds are rumpled, dark sheets that produce steady rain or snow.

8. Stratus clouds are low – like fog – but do not touch ground. May produce a drizzle.

How we forecast weather

Consider the complexity of weather forecasting. The area of study is vast, and there are many factors at work, some of them invisible – such as temperature and atmospheric pressure. Radiation from the sun is the source of weather, and is relatively constant.

Clouds affect the amount of solar energy that strikes portions of the earth – a heavy cloud cover may obstruct light and heat locally. Heat is absorbed unequally over different types of regions, such as deserts, oceans and green pastures, and over places at different distances from the equator. This creates air masses of different temperatures.

An air mass can be considered a moving parcel of gases, all of a particular temperature and humidity. The leading edge of an air mass is called a front. Cold air from, for example, a polar region, may come into an area and meet warm air. Weather forecasters, who are called meteorologists, represent this boundary by a heavy line with sharp points on one side, which show the direction of the front (see illustration right). Warm fronts are also indicated by heavy lines, but with rounded projections in the direction of the front. A line with sharp and rounded pro-jections on different sides indicates a stationary front – a stalemate in the weather.

Cold air is heavier than warm air and holds less moisture. When a cold front invades a region of warm air, it usually does so not as a wall but as a wedge. This cannot be seen in the two-dimensional weather maps that are shown on television or in the newspapers. The contoured lines on weather maps, called isobars, are not fronts; they indicate the presence of pressure boundaries. All along any particular isobar, the barometric pressures are the same. Many people notice the similarity between isobars on a weather map and the contour lines that show elevation on a topographical map. The isobars give the "contours" of the weather, which change hourly.

Weather is monitored in several ways – from weather stations on land, weather ships, balloons, and also from earth satellites that send back photographs of the atmospheric conditions.

Speed is of the essence in accurate forecasting, and many readings are taken at regular intervals daily. The information is relayed by computers to various centres – especially to ones in the presumed path of a weather system.

Most weather systems have a predictable *general* direction, dictated by the spin of the earth. The atmosphere responds to the rotation of the earth and to the heat of the sun by producing bands of prevailing

Probing the atmosphere

For accurate weather forecasting, a larger picture is needed than any that can be seen by a single human observer. The diagram on the right represents bands of winds (marked by clouds), all swirling at different altitudes. In this case, clouds are spinning in towards a low-pressure area. Cold air, with a cold front (towards the lower part of the diagram), is heading towards a warm front. High above, the swift jet stream exerts its strong influence.

Satellites orbit the earth 24 hours a day, and relay pictures back to weather stations.

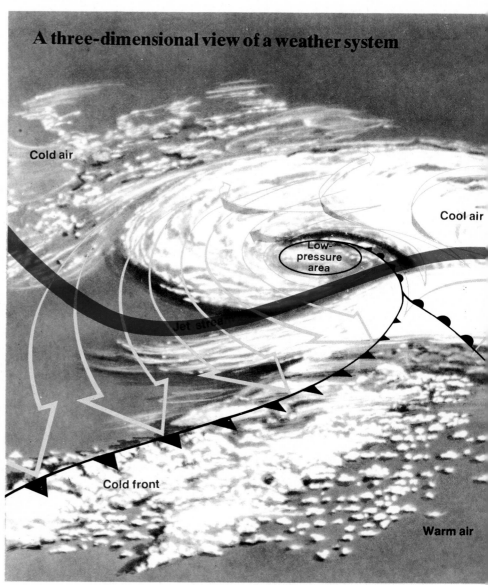

A three-dimensional view of a weather system

Cold air

Cool air

Low-pressure area

Jet stream

Cold front

Warm air

winds. Thus the meteorologist knows the likely path of a weather system.

In West Europe the weather usually – but not always – arrives from across the Atlantic, travelling generally eastwards. The Atlantic weather chart is all-important, therefore.

There are two kinds of forecasting – local and long-range. The long-range approach, which brings us to the study of climate and predictions for years and even decades ahead, has significance for everyone because climate affects the food supply.

Locally, we may get rain when we were promised sunshine. But forecasts are more often right than wrong, and are becoming more accurate every year.

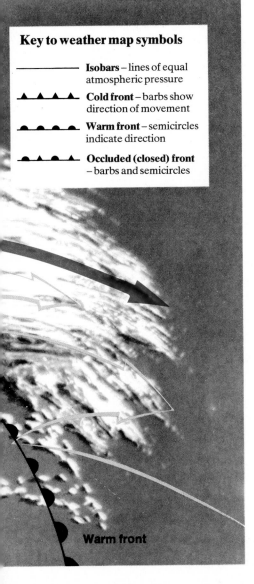

Key to weather map symbols

— **Isobars** – lines of equal atmospheric pressure

▲▲▲▲ **Cold front** – barbs show direction of movement

●●●● **Warm front** – semicircles indicate direction

▲●▲● **Occluded (closed) front** – barbs and semicircles

Warm front

Cities are warmer than the countryside

The temperature difference between a city and the surrounding countryside is often most noticeable when you travel out from the city centre into the suburbs. This is especially true during summer. There are several reasons for this: city buildings are larger and more numerous, and are mostly built of concrete. There are miles of streets and pavements with few trees and grassy areas. The pavements and buildings absorb more of the sun's heat and retain it much longer. Also, much of the fuel and electricity that is used to keep the city functioning is expelled into the air as heat.

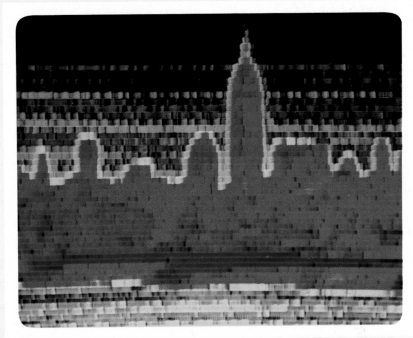

This thermogram, or heat picture, of the New York skyline, shows the different temperatures in the buildings and in the skies above. Red indicates great heat retention; blue shows cooler regions. Urban areas tend to retain the daytime heat throughout the night.

Why weather conditions vary from place to place

The temperature of an air mass is influenced by the terrain over which it passes. Cities give off heat 24 hours a day, driving cooling winds upwards. During the day, farmlands also give off heat, but cool rapidly as soon as the sun goes down. Rivers and woods – always cooler – act as channels for cold air. Thus, all year round, each type of terrain has more "extreme" weather conditions than the forecasters predicted; but the difference itself tends to be predictable.

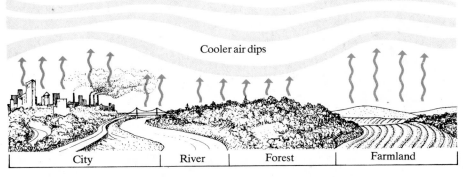

Cooler air dips

City   River   Forest   Farmland

Fog is a low-lying cloud

Fog is the name we give to a cloud that forms near the ground or drops down and touches the land or sea. The ideal conditions for fog-formation are the presence of moisture, a gentle breeze and two different temperatures – warm and cold. For example, cool breezes passing over the warm waters of a swamp will create fog, as will warm air over a cold stretch of sea. The breeze distributes the fog.

Fog is welcome in some situations. A vineyard, where the plants are particularly vulnerable to damage from frost, may gain a measure of protection from fog. In fact, Soviet meteorologists have developed a means of making artificial fog, which extends the productivity of some kinds of farming. In many places that do not receive much rainfall, fog supplies appreciable amounts of water. In some parts of the Hawaiian Islands, fog may drop some 10–12 in. of moisture on to the vegetation in a single month. During the dry season, cloud forests – high peaks near the tropics that are permanently shrouded in clouds – retain their lush vegetation, watered by the fog.

Fog ranges from an asset to an inconvenience (as when a flight arrival is delayed at an airport), to an extreme hazard (in the case when fog suddenly envelops a highway, and it is dangerous even to pull off the road). The water droplets in a fog measure anywhere from 2 to 50 microns (about one-thousandth of an inch), but a more common way of looking at fog is in terms of visibility. If your field of vision is obscured during the daytime to a distance of about 400 yds, it is accurate to call the conditions foggy. At night, fogs are harder to define – though not to identify!

The increase in air pollution has turned the combination of fog and dust particles into grimy, tear-producing smog. This combination is worse than either moisture or dust by itself, because smog is more stable than a blanket of fog alone. The sun can "burn off" fog rapidly; if anything, the sun makes smog worse.

It seems strange that anything as gentle and often beautiful as fog should become dangerous. But so it has, as traffic-accident and air-pollution figures show. In the disastrous smog that enveloped London in December, 1952, an estimated 4,000 people were killed by the foul air.

Smog is caused by two main forms of air pollution. The old-fashioned "pea-soupers" in Britain came from bituminous coal inefficiently burned in factories and millions of homes. The smoke combined with water droplets in misty air to become smog.

While city authorities have been coping with this menace by creating smoke-less zones and imposing smoke regulations on industry, another smog-maker has developed. Year after year ever more cars and lorries have thronged the streets, discharging hydrocarbon gases. Exhaust smog has become a serious problem, particularly in Los Angeles.

These problems have stirred planners; greater attention is now being paid to existing weather patterns in determining the location of airports, roads and even entire communities. Ideally, any of these should be upwind of industrial installations (and not in the path of accidental emissions of polluting particles). Plateaux are ideal places for airports – if above the fog belt, and below any usual cloud cover.

Once we learn to cope with such problems, we may find ourselves actually welcoming fog, for the picturesque veil that it lends to the landscape.

Fog creeps stealthily inland from the waters of Lake Wanaka, New Zealand. The heavy, moisture-laden air seems to follow the contours of the hills, as it infiltrates the patch of woodland below. When the morning sun strikes, the fog will swiftly evaporate.

NATURE OBSERVER
Using a barometer for local forecasting

Barometers measure atmospheric pressure – the weight of the blanket of air that covers the earth. The words fair, stormy and change, printed on the face of a barometer, are more traditional than accurate. What is important is any change in the reading and any change in the direction of the wind. It is broadly true that fair weather comes with a veering wind (one shifting along the same course as the sun) and bad weather with a backing wind (one shifting against the sun).
● If the barometer is fairly high, but showing a decided fall when tapped, unsettled weather is approaching, especially if the wind is backing to south or south-east. If the barometer is low, but rises when tapped, expect clear skies and sunshine if the wind has veered between south and north-west. A rapid rise means the improvement will be only temporary.
● Professional weathermen use a mercury barometer, in which the weight of the atmosphere pushes a column of mercury about 30 in. up a tube. Home barometers, like those shown here, contain no mercury, though they still read in "inches of mercury" Known as aneroid barometers, they are activated by metal bellows, which expand or contract with the changing pressure.
● Because heat and cold affect the reading, mount your barometer away from draughts and heat sources, such as fireplaces and radiators on the wall.
● Set your barometer to your elevation above sea level. Adjust the dial to the same reading with the set screw.
● Tap the dial lightly whenever you take a reading, to "unstick" the moving parts.

Home barometers are often in a panel with temperature and humidity instruments (below), which also help you forecast.

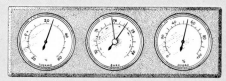

Countryfolk and the weather

Before weather forecasts were available on television and in the newspapers, countryfolk predicted the weather mainly by observation of clouds and wind direction. They knew from long experience, for instance, that ragged clouds blowing up from behind a certain hill meant a coming storm.

Many of their old saws and jingles also served as useful guides. Perhaps the most reliable of them is the well known

Red sky at night is the shepherd's delight.
Red sky at morning is the shepherd's warning.

Although not infallible, this is a good rough guide. In fact sunset forecasts can be extended to other colours. Yellow often heralds gales within 36 hours; green can mean showers; copper, thunder; grey, rain; and dark blue with sharply outlined clouds, unsettled weather.

Another folk-saying with a basis in fact concerns the halo round the moon.

The bigger the ring the nearer the rain.

This is true. The halo, a faint ring, red-tinged on the inside and yellow outside, is caused by moonlight shining through thin clouds of ice-crystals – and these usually mean that rain is on its way. But do not confuse the halo with a corona, a series of rings round the moon, seen when it shines through thicker clouds of water droplets. A corona, which has red on the outside of its rings, does not regularly precede rain.

However, many of the country sayings are unreliable. One of the best known and most fallacious is the myth that rain on St Swithin's Day (July 15) means rain for the next 40 days. Equally untrue is the saying that fine weather on St Paul's Day (January 25) foretells a good harvest, while rain and snow augur famine.

Still unproven are the traditional country tokens of good weather to come: swallows flying high, spiders weaving long webs and cuckoos cuckooing.

Coniferous trees, faintly seen behind a spray of daisies, are actually water-collectors. The fog condenses on their needles, and the water seeps downwards.

237

The amazing properties of water

The film on the surface of water is one of nature's strangest habitats. Some plants and animals – such as duckweed and pond skaters (long-legged aquatic insects) – are supported on top, like the leaves above. Just beneath the surface, there is a vastly different world. Aquatic animals, like the water-boatman insect (right), walk on the underside. If a small inhabitant of either world is caught on the wrong side of the film, it may perish because it does not have the power to rise (or dive) home.

Fire produces water. You can watch this happen at a campfire, where a film of water forms on rocks that surround the flames. Whenever a substance containing hydrogen (and carbon) burns, the hydrogen unites with oxygen from the air, forming the familiar molecule of water, H_2O. (Although it is a well-known fact that water is often a by-product of combustion, the actual quantity of water produced by this means is small.)

Water is a unique substance. H_2O does not behave like any other molecule. For example, both hydrogen and oxygen are very light gases that float in the air. Even when they are combined, one might think they would still float. Why is H_2O a liquid, and not a gas, at moderate temperatures? Not until the dawn of nuclear physics was it possible to solve water's mysteries. Physicists learned that when two hydrogen atoms combine with one atom of oxygen, the shape of the resulting molecule is like the head of a toy bear. The oxygen is its head, and the two hydrogen atoms are the ears. The hydrogen atoms have positive electrical charges, the oxygen atom has a negative charge.

Because of the relationship of the atoms (called chemical bonds), the top of the water molecule, or its "head", is positively charged and the "chin" is negatively charged. Thus the molecule H_2O is like a tiny bar magnet. Opposite charges attract, and so the positive "ears" readily hook up with the negative "chin" of another water molecule. This forms a chain of H_2O molecules. Water is not really H_2O; it is H_2O-H_2O-H_2O-H_2O – and so on. The length of this chain depends on many factors, but under typical conditions, the chain may contain about 40 H_2O molecules.

Early theories about water molecules showed the hydrogen atoms hooked up with the oxygen symmetrically, so that the "ears" were on exactly opposite sides of the "head". It was not until the position of the "ears" was understood (that is, the position of the chemical bonds) that scientists could account for water's strange behaviour. For example, nearly all other substances contract when they are cooled. Water contracts only until it begins to freeze, and then it expands – as, for example, when ice cubes become dome-shaped in a refrigerator. As water freezes, the chains of H_2O do not fit together compactly. Thus water is less dense as a solid (ice) than it is as a liquid – which is unlike the behaviour of nearly every other substance.

Another interesting property of water

is the way it forms a strong film at its surface. This is what enables some aquatic insects to walk on water or to attach themselves to it from below, as mosquito larvae do. This same characteristic also causes drops of water to take a rounded shape when hanging from a leaf or falling through the air.

Water makes things wet. Wetness is a tactile impression of an object; roughly speaking, the physical effect is one of attraction. If you look closely at a glass of water, you will see the water clinging to the inside of the glass and rising slightly at the edge. This is because hydrogen in the water is attracted to oxygen in the glass. The rising is halted when the weight of the water is in balance with the force of attraction to the glass.

The hydrogen in water is attracted to most substances. Thus just about everything will dissolve in water. And water has been the chief architect of our landscape. It is the vehicle of life for plants and animals. Among the first data sought by scientists in their investigation of the planets is evidence of water. Were it not for water's remarkable properties, the earth would be barren of life. And if it is not present on a planet, or a planet's moon, there can be no question of any life existing there.

Contrary to popular opinion, water drops are not usually drop-shaped. Surface tension acts like a tight "skin", which tends to make the drop as compact as possible. Since the sphere is the most compact of forms, most drops are nearly spherical, whether falling through the air as rain (right, above) or clinging to a blade of grass after the rain has fallen.

 HOW TO
Investigate the way water behaves

• One of water's most impressive properties is strength – it can support an object that is both heavier and denser than itself.

• Cut a small square of tissue paper and put a needle or razor blade on it. Gently float the paper and its cargo on water in a small container. The tissue will slowly sink and leave the needle or razor blade supported by the water's surface tension, which forms as a film on the water.

• The wetness of water is largely a result of surface tension. Add a drop of wetting agent, such as a dishwashing detergent, to the water. This will greatly decrease the surface tension, and the needle or razor blade will quickly sink to the bottom.

• Put a transparent drinking straw in a glass of water. If you look at the straw closely, you will see that the water inside has flowed uphill slightly. This "climbing" property is called capillary action. Place a sugar cube on a teaspoon, and slowly submerge the spoon in a cup of coffee, tea or other coloured water. Hold the spoon steady as soon as the liquid touches the sugar. Note that the water rises in the sugar cube. It rises higher than in the straw because the spaces between the grains of sugar are smaller than the inside of the straw. In a tree, water can flow upwards more than 300 ft because of capillary action.

• Hold two small, bare wires against a torch battery, one at each end. Bend the wires so they are close together but not touching. Submerge the wires in water. Water conducts electricity, which will split some of the water molecules. After a few moments bubbles of gas will begin to form on the wires – hydrogen on the negative wire, and oxygen on the positive.

• Oil and water do not mix. You can see this whenever you make a salad dressing with olive oil and vinegar (which is mostly water). The two will quickly separate, with the oil on top. Oil is the reason why waterfowl are able to land in water without getting soaked. They have oil glands (usually near their tails) that secrete a waterproofing substance. Preening helps distribute this water-repellent.

Snow, frost and hail

When you look at photographs of snowflakes, notice how faithful they are to one pattern – they are all hexagonal. Until one flake collides with another, or is jarred and damaged, or melts, it is six-sided; and each snowflake is unique in its configuration, within this hexagonal plan.

Such hexagonal patterns have a fascination for everyone who deals with snow and ice, whether in glaciers or forming on the wings of aeroplanes at high altitudes. It is difficult for an amateur naturalist to get a good look at an individual snowflake,

for each flake is extremely small and fragile. (The array of nine snowflakes on the right was photographed by a man who spent years in pursuit of the hobby.) The fine detail may disappear even as you come close, melting just from the heat of your breath. Nevertheless, with luck and a powerful magnifying glass, you may be able to see the fine details.

Flakes that fall like fat coins may contain as many as 100 individual snowflakes, each much altered by collisions with one another. They may make good snowballs (if they are not too soggy – which is to say, close to melting), but they will not lend themselves to the study of their origins.

An easier subject for examination is frost. One of the unusual properties of water is its ability to change directly from a gas (water vapour) into a solid (ice) without going through the familiar liquid stage. When liquid water freezes, it may develop into sleet or hail. But when water *vapour* freezes (a process called sublimation), the results are often lightweight and diaphanous – the snow that melts so quickly, and the frost that forms on windows and has the look of delicate etchings. Perhaps the easiest place to see and enjoy the effects of frost is in your own garden. As the ground cools, usually at nightfall, moisture in the air settles on leaves and turns immediately to tiny ice crystals that look like confectioner's sugar. All around the edges of blades of grass, but mainly on the undersides of leaves and branches, there is a powdering of frost, sometimes

light, sometimes heavy. Frost is more durable than snowflakes, and if you are careful not to melt the crystals with handling (or with your breath), you can get a good look at frost.

Hail is another form of frozen water. Sleet was once known as "soft hail". This precipitation, which is simply frozen drops of rain, is common in winter; but in the summer, it usually melts before reaching the ground. Hailstones are more complex. They may start out as flecks of sleet, but they get driven upwards on turbulent wind currents, acquiring a watery coating on the way. When they reach chillier air, this coating freezes. Still tossed around, they pick up another coat of water and in its turn this freezes. Thus hailstones are built up, layer on layer, sometimes reaching the size of golf balls, before their sheer weight brings them down to earth.

Even when they are the size of peas, hailstones can be alarming to people caught in a downpour. In the French wine-producing regions hail of any size is dreaded, as it can ruin the grape harvest over a wide area.

All of the forms of frozen water – snow, sleet and hail – may have more changes to undergo once they reach the earth. The accumulations may melt almost at once, or refreeze again and again, or become compacted. Sometimes, powdery snows on mountain slopes are buried by later snows. Crushed by the growing weight above, they are gradually transformed into hard ice that eventually lies, ancient and glass-like, at the bottom of a glacier.

A bison in America's Yellowstone Park marches across the frozen surface of a pond. The air is foggy with moisture, the trees are dusted with snow. Drinking water has to be obtained from pools of thawed ice.

A sudden drop in temperature crystallises the morning dew on a clump of wild strawberries. If you happen to see this, use a magnifying glass to examine the glittering fringe of ice.

When water freezes, exquisite shapes develop

In 1880, a 15-year-old farm boy in Vermont, USA, was given a microscope for Christmas – a gift that enabled him to see snowflakes in all their beautiful detail. For nearly 50 years thereafter, Wilson Bentley photographed the many forms of snow (a few are shown above). Bentley was not a scientist, just an enthusiastic amateur. The illustrations on the right show one current system used to classify shapes of ice crystals. But as you can see, the variations leave some room for discussion.

Varied forms of ice crystals

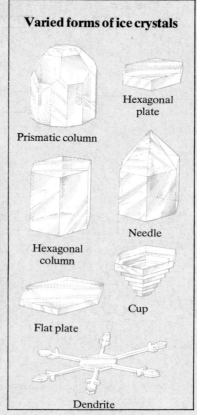

Prismatic column

Hexagonal plate

Hexagonal column

Needle

Flat plate

Cup

Dendrite

In a remarkable colour photograph, a spray of ice crystals lands on a winter pond in Vermont. Seconds later, the flakes melted.

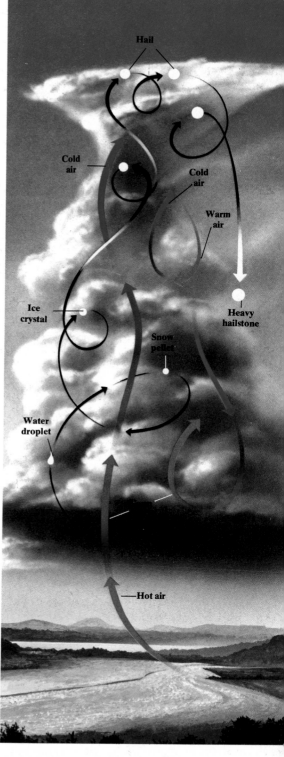

The build-up of a hailstone

One peculiarity of hailstones is that they form mainly in summer, rather than during the winter. As the diagram above indicates, the turbulent air within a thundercloud tosses water droplets, snow pellets and ice crystals in updraughts. When hail first forms – perhaps beginning as a frozen raindrop – it may fall to earth, or it may be thrown aloft again, and more moisture condenses around it. When it falls, the "stone" may be layered like an onion.

Birth of a thunderstorm

If you have ever been rained on at a picnic, you know how quickly a thunderstorm can develop. Under certain conditions, collisions between air masses of different temperatures speedily result in a thunderstorm – a turbulent shower of rain, hail, or (in a few cases) snow, each accompanied by thunder and lightning.

Some parts of the world, such as the tropics, are regularly drenched by thunderstorms. Panama, for example, may have about 200 such stormy days a year; France may have fewer than 25. Thunderstorms are most common in the middle of the afternoon, when the air near the ground is especially warm.

The first stage of a thunderstorm is the formation of an updraught, which lifts warm, moist air into the atmosphere. The air cools as it rises, causing the water vapour in it to condense, forming clouds. As updraughts continue, the clouds grow taller, extending higher into the atmosphere, where the temperatures are still colder. The microscopic water droplets in the clouds become larger and heavier. Some freeze into hail and snow, but usually melt before hitting the ground. When the drops are too heavy to be kept aloft by the updraughts, they fall. They are accompanied – and sometimes preceded – by downdraughts, so that cool, gusty winds near the ground are a warning that there may be a thunderstorm.

Surging air currents in the thunderhead create static electricity. Although this process is not completely understood, it is partially caused by friction and the breakup of the water. Positive charges develop near the top of the cloud, and negative charges cluster lower down. The negative charges attract positive charges in the ground. The air acts as an insulator between the opposing charges, preventing, for a while, the flow of electricity that would equalise the charges.

Lightning occurs when the charges build up enough voltage to overcome the insulation. (In some storms, the electricity may reach millions of volts.) Lightning may flash within the cloud, between different clouds, from cloud to ground, or from ground to cloud. On average, lightning strikes the earth about 100 times a second on every day of the year.

Most lightning occurs in two strokes. The first is an imperceptible "leader" of electrified air, which runs almost down to the ground. It is like a wire that establishes the pathway for the second stroke. As soon as the leader nears the ground, a "return stroke" leaps upwards along the path. This second stroke is the one you see and hear. It has a core of electrical energy surrounded by a tube of extremely hot air, which causes it to glow and expand explosively. This produces thunder. You can see the flash of lightning almost immediately, but it takes the sound of thunder about five seconds to travel 1 mile. Counting the seconds between the flash and the thunder and then dividing by five tells you approximately how many miles away the lightning is. (Often its distance will be a fraction of a mile.)

When lightning strikes so many miles away that the flash itself is not visible and all we can see is its reflection in the distant

A brilliant display of natural fireworks crashes and spits above the sleeping countryside in this picture which shows both cloud-to-cloud and cloud-to-ground bolts. Generally, lightning flashes occur one after the other but, as the intervals may be only fractions of a second, the eye – as well as the camera – sees them all at once, as crackling energy.

clouds, the phenomenon is known as sheet lightning. What people call forked lightning is a cloud-to-ground flash with many branches.

Lightning equalises the electrical imbalance within the storm cloud. Similarly, downdraughts created by precipitation equalise the temperatures of the hot and cold air. Rain cools the ground, and hot air no longer rises. Fair weather may quickly return – perhaps in time to save your picnic.

Lightning corrects an electrical imbalance

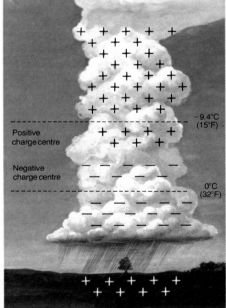

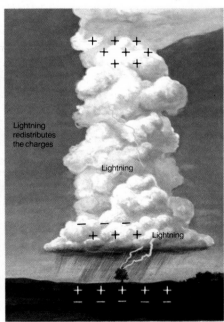

The positive and negative charges in a thundercloud (which become separated) are attracted to each other like the particles in a magnet. They are prevented from coming together by air, which acts as an insulator.

When electrical charges in thunderclouds and on the ground become strong enough, they overcome the insulating barrier of the air. Positive and negative charges connect in a brilliant optical effect we call lightning.

The anatomy of a hurricane

Early inhabitants of the Caribbean named hurricanes after an evil god, Hurakán, who was believed to be the source of these destructive storms. Hurricanes often wreak havoc by dropping tons of water in a short time, producing massive floods, uprooting trees, and toppling houses. Hurricanes can also cause giant waves – up to 40 ft high – that inundate low-lying coasts and sometimes sweep away entire communities.

Numerous photographs from satellites show that the raging storm is a hollowed-out circle in shape. Concentric rings of puffy clouds, towering thunderheads, and heavy rains all spiral towards the centre. The circle may be 300 to 600 miles across, even though the area swept by high winds may be only about one-tenth as wide. Here, winds may reach a speed of 200 mph, dropping almost solid sheets of rain as they pass. The centre (eye) of the hurricane is relatively small – only about 25 miles wide – and is calm. Often there are no winds, clouds or rain in these areas.

Hurricanes are born over tropical seas, and have different names in different places – the Caribbean and South Atlantic storms are called hurricanes; in parts of Asia, typhoons; and in the South Pacific, cyclones. Although the paths of hurricanes may vary, they gradually veer away from the equator and pass into higher latitudes. Hurricanes usually move with the major prevailing winds. In the hurricane belt of the Northern Hemisphere, this is to the west.

Hurricanes are seasonal in the Atlantic. Most occur in late summer, though they may strike Mexico, the Caribbean and the south-eastern United States at any time from June to October. When the sun has warmed the surface of the sea to a temperature of 27°C (80°F) or higher, a hurricane may begin to develop. At such temperatures, millions of tons of water evaporate every day. The layers of air close to the ocean also absorb heat from the water. The warmed, moistened air begins to rise in a column. When this happens, the rotation of the earth twists the air anti-clockwise in the Northern Hemisphere, clockwise in the Southern Hemisphere. The rising column creates a suction force – an area of low pressure – at its centre, the same way that your boots

The tremendous force of vast, swirling winds

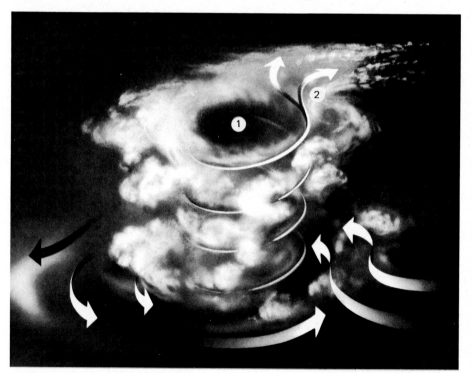

The hurricane system illustrated above has been greatly compressed to show the direction of the winds. Actual hurricanes, as seen from space, look like thin discs – even though they may be some 60,000 ft high. The calm eye of the storm (1) is the hub around which the winds (2) circulate. The storm system usually originates over water. It generally moves westwards at a steady pace of 15 mph; eastern coasts are usually harder hit than western shores. Recent satellite studies have provided new information about the amazing force of a hurricane's winds. Even a moderate-size hurricane can produce more energy than a nuclear explosion. In addition, hurricanes often spawn tornadoes, which may be more destructive in a small area because of the concentration of whirling winds.

Cross-section of a hurricane

1. The eye of the hurricane is often calm
2. High-speed winds exit at the storm's top
3. The eye-wall has the heaviest rains and winds
4. Rainbands spiral inwards toward the eye
5. The lowest clouds are about 500 ft high
6. The air flow pulls in more warm, moist air

cause suction when you try to pull your feet out of mud. If this low-pressure system (the twisting warm air) strengthens, it may become the eye of a hurricane.

As the air moves higher above the ocean, it cools. The moisture condenses and forms clouds around a low-pressure system, releasing heat in the process. A large hurricane may condense up to 20,000 million tons of water in a single day, and the heat produced in this way is tremendous.

The heat of a hurricane increases the updraught, which in turn attracts more moist air off the surface of the sea. As long as the hurricane is over warm water, it continues to draw in moist air. The spiralling winds grow stronger and stronger until, at a speed of about 75 mph, the storm is considered a hurricane.

Fortunately, hurricanes are short-lived, usually lasting only about a week. The storm's awesome power diminishes when it moves over land or cool water and

loses its fuel of warm, moist air. This explains why inland regions, such as central Europe, are spared the devastation of these storms.

One day it might be possible to control hurricanes by pumping water from beneath the tropical sea to cool the surface. But at present they can only be watched. Observer aircraft, mapping the movements of each hurricane to warn people and ships in its track, have probably saved thousands of lives.

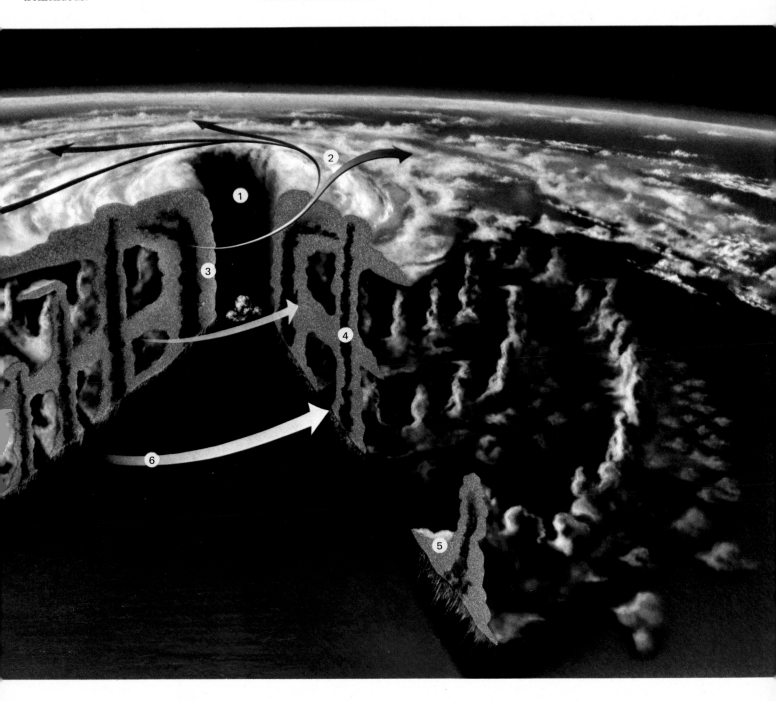

Where we are in the universe

Probably the simplest way to learn about astronomy is to postpone efforts to comprehend the figures involved. They really *are* astronomical, and just thinking about the basic unit of measurement – the light-year – is enough to send the mind reeling. (Light travels at 186,000 miles per second; a light-year is the distance light travels in one year, going at that speed.)

Another way to get into the subject is by reading science fiction; much of this literature is based on sound astronomy, and some of the better authors will give you a feeling for the effects of gravity, the varied distribution of the elements, and the immensity of space. Science fiction helps you to accept such astonishing ideas as the fact that light reaching us from distant stars was produced long before our solar system was even formed.

The scale of early discoveries in astronomy was limited by its uses – for example, as calendars to help farmers choose the times for planting seeds – and also by the capabilities of human eyesight. In many cultures, the heavens were of great religious significance, and the approach to astronomy was more reverent than analytical. The use of a telescope by Galileo in the early 17th century is often cited as the most important breakthrough in astronomy. Indeed, his drawings of the Moon are remarkable. But of almost equal importance in the development of astronomy was the precision of data-collecting made possible by photography. With photographs, two people could be certain they were discussing the same celestial topics; through time-lapse photography they could follow the movement of stars over long periods of time.

Over the centuries, we have learned that Earth is one of nine planets in orbit around a medium-sized star called the Sun. Earth is not remarkable – not the largest planet, nor the smallest, nor the hottest, nor the coldest. We are not the only planet to have a moon revolving around it. But Earth is probably the only planet in our solar system that has conditions favourable to the development of life.

We know, further, that our solar system itself is part of a larger group of stars, gases and dust called a galaxy; our particular galaxy is called the Milky Way. The name was originally given to the white streak running across the night sky. Now we know that the "milk" is formed by millions of distant stars in our own galaxy. Beyond lie millions of other galaxies.

As you can see from the illustration on the right, the solar system is located in one of the arms of the Milky Way. Because of the relatively slight tilt of the Earth on its axis (as it travels around the Sun), some parts of the Galaxy can be seen only in the Northern Hemisphere, and other parts only in the Southern Hemisphere.

Viewed from many light-years away, the Galaxy may look like a single star, a bright spot against the velvet black of outer space. It is not a really large galaxy, even though it is so big that it stretches the human imagination.

To observers here on Earth, the main part of our own galaxy appears as the glowing Milky Way in the night sky. It is formed by a huge number of distant stars. All the apparently bigger stars visible to the naked eye are also in our own galaxy. If we were to view the Galaxy from afar (right), it would appear as a disc with arms spiralling out from the centre. The Sun and its planets are in one arm (see inset).

The Sun is a star, the centre of our solar system. The textured effect on the surface of the Sun is created by hot gases welling up. At the top of this picture, a solar flare erupts outwards.

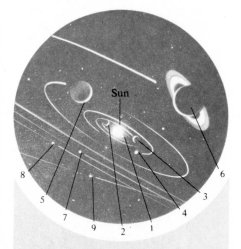

Nine planets revolve around the Sun, travelling in elliptical orbits. They are numbered here in the order of their distance from the Sun. Jupiter (number 5) is the largest, although from this perspective, Saturn (6) appears bigger. Pluto, known as the outermost planet, has an orbit at an angle to the others. At times, Pluto crosses Neptune's path, making Neptune the outermost planet.

1. Mercury	4. Mars	7. Uranus
2. Venus	5. Jupiter	8. Neptune
3. Earth	6. Saturn	9. Pluto

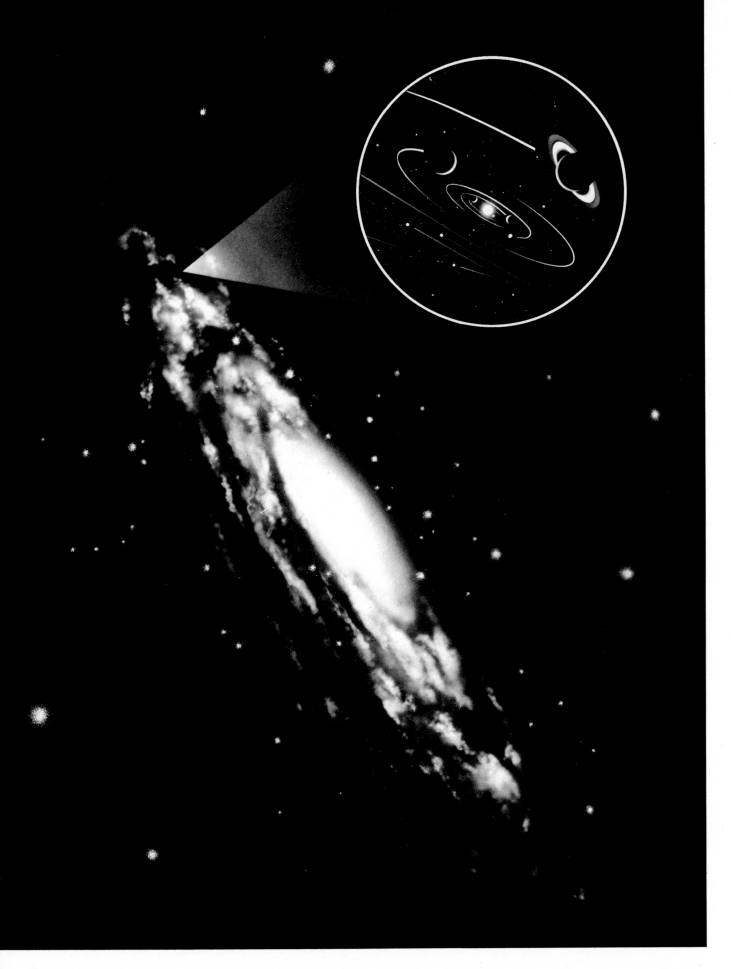

Star-gazing in your own garden

Familiarise yourself with a chart of the heavens *before* you go out to look at the sky. Star charts are available in natural history magazines, periodicals that specialise in astronomy and some newspapers. Each month, these charts are slightly different, because of the Earth's movement around the Sun. For stargazing, you can also use a movable star wheel or planisphere like the one shown below, which can be adjusted to the sky for any time of year and for any time of night.

Star charts simplify the sky. Instead of showing all the stars (some 2,000 may be visible on a clear night), they include only the major ones. The Moon and planets are not on such charts because they move too quickly across the heavens.

Usually, some of the stars on a chart have been drawn larger than the others. Locate these first – they are the brightest stars. In most cities, star-gazing is greatly simplified – lights block out all but the brightest stars, which is why urban areas are especially good for amateur astronomers. For the same reason, beginners do best without telescopes or binoculars,

which pick up the fainter stars and confuse rather than help the observer.

Fortunately for beginners, the stars are not distributed evenly in the sky. This gives you more "landmarks". To the ancients, stars seemed to form into groups, called constellations, and modern star charts still depict these groupings. Though their shapes may bear little resemblance to their names, constellations are often easier to locate than individual stars. For example, the Plough, part of the Great Bear (Ursa Major), is a well-known landmark in the northern sky. This constellation will help you to find Polaris, or the North Star. Since it looks nothing like a modern plough, imagine it rather as a child's pushcart. The front of the pushcart points upwards to Polaris. If you follow the curving handle of the Plough, you will find another bright star, called Arcturus, in the constellation Boötes.

Certain stars, such as Arcturus, are easy to locate in a particular region of the sky because of their colour. The colour of a star is one of its characteristics (that is, it remains the same for centuries). Scientists have discovered that colour tells some-

thing about the temperature of a star – the hottest stars are blue-white (Spica is a good example), and the colder ones (such as Arcturus) tend to be reddish-orange. "Cold" in this sense is a relative term; a star with a comparatively low temperature is nevertheless extremely hot – at least 1090°C (2000°F).

The important thing to remember about star-gazing is that there is no hurry – the stars will still be visible the next clear night. Do not try to find all the constellations or prominent stars in one evening. Give yourself time to let the wonders of astronomy come to you, just as light does from the stars.

Only as your interest deepens is it worth buying a telescope.

All star charts, such as the one on the right, function in a similar way. When held above your head in the correct north-south orientation, the stars on the map match those in the sky at a particular time. (This map is for the late evening hours in May.) The red line is the ecliptic – the Sun's path in the sky. The blue line is the celestial equator.

NATURE OBSERVER
How to get your bearings in the night sky

Star-gazing is a portable hobby – all you need to start is a sky map with the major constellations printed on it. There are two types of maps – star charts, which are often printed in natural history magazines and apply to a particular month, and star

wheels, which are adjustable for any time of the year. Whatever kind of map you obtain, read it indoors, where you can see it clearly, before trying to use it outdoors.
● Some sky maps are luminous and can be read in the dark. For others, you may need

to use a dim torch, or one with red Cellophane covering the glass. This makes it easier for your eyes to adjust to the change from light to darkness.
● Choose a clear, moonless night, and a place that is free of obstructions.

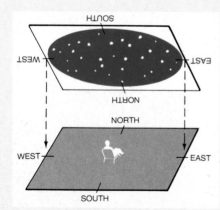

In matching a sky map to your own location, you will have to overcome a lifelong habit of holding reading material below eye level. You and the map should be positioned as in the diagram above. This may seem awkward at first, but it will soon become automatic.

The advantage of a movable star wheel over a star map is that once you have set the wheel to the appropriate date and time, the cardboard or plastic "mask" on the wheel will block out any part of the sky that will not be visible at that particular time.

Landmarks in your own garden can make it easier to become familiar with the direction in which the constellations move. The silhouette of a house or garage will give you something against which to gauge the speed of stars and planets. Relax in a garden chair.

The northern sky at night

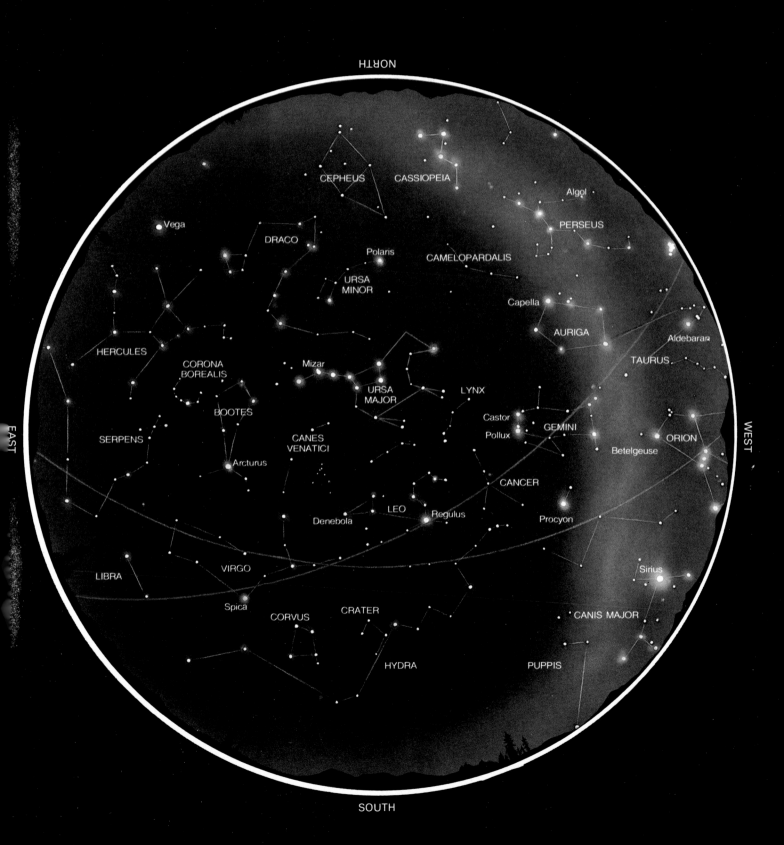

As Earth moves, other stars come into view

Why certain stars seem to rise and set

Beginners at star-gazing are sometimes puzzled when a particular constellation is not where it appears on a star chart. What has to be taken into account is the fact that the sky changes from hour to hour, because of the rotation of the Earth. The easiest way to understand this change is to visualise the sky as a huge celestial dome, with the stars attached to it. (This is the method used in planetariums.) In this view, the Earth appears as a flat disc, bounded by the horizon – the limit of the observer's sight.

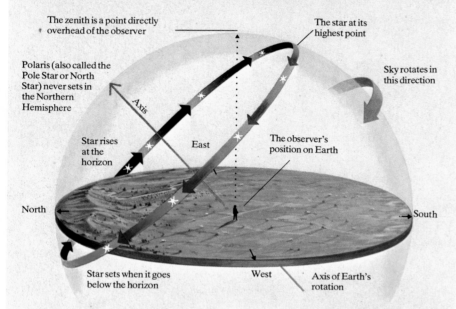

The zenith is a point directly overhead of the observer

The star at its highest point

Polaris (also called the Pole Star or North Star) never sets in the Northern Hemisphere

Sky rotates in this direction

Axis

Star rises at the horizon

East

The observer's position on Earth

North

South

Star sets when it goes below the horizon

West

Axis of Earth's rotation

During the night, the celestial dome rotates, and the stars are carried along. (This also happens during the day, but we cannot see it.) Only one star does not move – Polaris, which sits above the North Pole, at the tip of the axis on which the Earth rotates. Stars far from Polaris on the dome appear to rise above the eastern horizon to a point high in the sky, then drop to below the western horizon. The greater the distance a star is from Polaris, the less time it can be seen above the horizon.

The entire universe is in motion. But the stars are so distant from the Earth that their relationship to one another seems fixed. Their position in our sky *does* change; however, this is more an effect of the Earth's movements than anything else.

The Earth rotates on its axis every 24 hours. During this time, different stars come into view. Sunrise occurs when our nearest star, the Sun, rises above the horizon; sunset, when it drops below. Similarly, as the evening progresses, certain stars rise in the east and set in the west. For example, in early July, in the constellation Virgo, a bright star called Spica is visible only until midnight, when it falls below the horizon.

The stars seem to circle around a fixed point in the sky. In the Northern Hemisphere, this point is Polaris, the North Star. Constellations that appear near this star are visible the entire night; they include Cassiopeia, Draco (the Dragon), and the Plough (which is actually part of a slightly larger grouping called Ursa Major, or the Great Bear). Near the Pole, where there is prolonged darkness during the winter, such constellations are visible for the entire 24 hour cycle. But because they appear to be circling around Polaris, they do not always look the same – witness the change in Cassiopeia, from the shape of the letter M to a W, and back again (see the diagrams below).

The other motion that affects our perception of the heavens is a result of the Earth's elliptical orbit around the Sun. The Earth is tilted $23\frac{1}{2}°$ away from the

Following two constellations that circle Polaris every 24 hours

In most regions of the Northern Hemisphere, certain constellations never set – in other words, they are visible as long as there is darkness. These constellations are in the part of the sky near Polaris (the North Star), and are known as the circumpolar constellations; they include Cassiopeia and the Plough. As the hours pass, these constellations slowly revolve around Polaris and take on a different appearance – the Plough flips over (as you can see in the sequence on the right). If you look at the sky once an hour for several hours, you can see some of the sequence (though you may come in on the middle of it). But to see all of it, you need a 24 hour period of darkness.

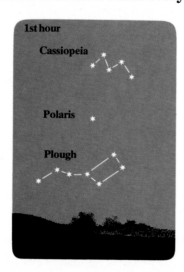

1st hour

Cassiopeia

Polaris

Plough

4th hour

8th hour

250

perpendicular to the plane of its orbit around the Sun. The seasons are a result of this tilt. To put it another way, if the Earth were not tilted on its axis, there would be no seasons on Earth. The slight tilt of the Earth may make astronomy difficult for beginners – but it introduces a far richer panorama of sights from outer space than would otherwise be visible.

Every night, the location of the constellations – at a particular hour – is slightly different. The constellations are actually in the same position, but are seen four minutes earlier than the night before. (In other words, if you were to photograph the Plough at 9.00 on a Friday night and at 8.56 on a Saturday night, its position would be identical in the two photographs.)

This four minute difference is not great, but it means that from one month to the next, there is about two hours' change in the skies. So, as the year progresses, a different group of stars appears. These may be stars that were above the horizon only during the day earlier in the year (and thus not visible), or only in the early-morning hours. For example, the constellation Leo is an important landmark in the spring sky; Orion is prominent in the winter. Many people attribute the bright skies of winter to the cold, clear weather, but this is only partially true. The winter stars are actually the brighter ones. Then, too, the portion of the sky that we see in winter is especially rich in stars.

A thought to remember as you gaze upwards into the night sky: the nearest star is 25,000,000 million miles away.

12th hour

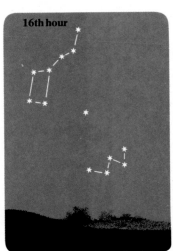

16th hour

20th hour

1st hour

Of stars, constellations and planets

Human perceptions are geared to our experiences here on Earth. If two objects appear to be the same size, it is natural to assume they are the same distance away. Only with the development of telescopes and radio-astronomy could scientists establish the locations of stars relative to the Earth. But even though we now know the true distances of stars, the human mind still thinks in traditional ways. For example, the stars in a constellation may seem quite close to one another, but they are usually far apart. Our eyes simply cannot perceive depth in outer space. Yet even astronomers use constellations as reference points in the sky – artificial and out-of-date though such configurations may be.

We have all observed that certain stars shine more brightly than others. Here, too, the element of distance comes into play. Some stars shine brightly in our sky because they are large and hot; others seem bright because they are relatively close to the Earth. The star Betelgeuse, which is located in the constellation Orion, produces much more light than does Sirius, in the constellation Canis Major (the Great Dog). But since Betelgeuse is nearly 100 times further from Earth, it seems fainter. (See the star chart on p. 249, to make your own comparison. Sirius is the brightest star in our night sky.)

Stars are nuclear furnaces, explosively giving off gases and light in huge quantities. In thinking about the behaviour of stars, we are again impeded by our own limited conceptions. It is difficult for our minds to comprehend the huge scale of the process, or the immensity of the time for which it continues.

Stars are born of dust and gases that collect in outer space. Influenced by its own gravity, the mass contracts and begins to radiate heat and light. In young stars, this happens because of a nuclear reaction under conditions of intense heat, which changes hydrogen into helium. This is the same process that occurs when a hydrogen bomb explodes, but in many stars it continues for millions of years with millions of tons of hydrogen being consumed every second. The release of energy in the form of heat and light is enormous. Scientists believe that when the hydrogen is finally used up, the star cools and expands, becoming a red giant or super-giant. (Betelgeuse is one example of a star at this relatively advanced stage of development.)

Some stars "die" at the red-giant stage. But the larger ones may recycle the helium, using this gas as fuel and changing it to carbon and oxygen in the process. If the star is large enough, these elements will also be recycled. Though it sounds unbelievable, the star may eventually develop an iron core. When most of a star's materials can no longer be used as fuel, a large star will contract, becoming what scientists call a white dwarf or a neutron star. Such stars are extremely small and

What is the zodiac?

Though the Earth moves around the Sun, it is the Sun that appears to change position from month to month. You can see this for yourself by looking at the sky just after sunset, or just before sunrise. Each month, the Sun sets (or rises) near a different constellation – one of the constellations in the zodiac. The zodiac was invented thousands of years ago by astronomers as a frame of reference for such movement and for the passage of the seasons. Modern astronomers no longer use the zodiac.

Zodiac means "circle of animals", though not all signs depict animals. Zodiac figures (on the wheel) were designed to include all the stars of a constellation, but do not form its outline.

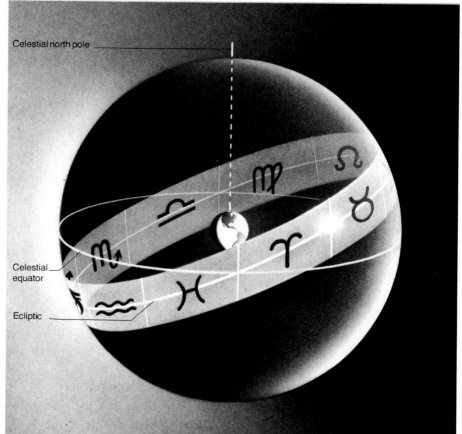

Imagine the sky as a huge globe, with the Earth at its centre. An extension of the Earth's axis points towards the celestial north pole. Similarly, the celestial equator is the extension of the Earth's equator. Constellations in the zodiac occur along a line called the ecliptic, which traces the Sun's yearly path in the sky. The Moon and planets follow this line.

dense, relative to other heavenly bodies; some can be detected only with special equipment. For example, if our Sun were to become a neutron star (it is about the right size to do so), it would contract from its present diameter of 864,000 miles to only 7 miles. Fortunately for mankind, it will be many millions of years before the Sun reaches old age.

Stars produce their own light; and planets shine with reflected light from the Sun. At least, that is the way most of us were taught to differentiate between stars and planets. It seems, however, that Jupiter is half a star, half a planet. Detailed measurements indicate that Jupiter emits more radiation than it receives from the Sun, and that its internal temperature is some six times as hot as the surface of the Sun. Jupiter is believed to be a star that failed – it never quite achieved the temperature required to light its nuclear furnaces. We have no direct evidence of how rare or common this phenomenon is.

The true distances of the seven stars in the Plough

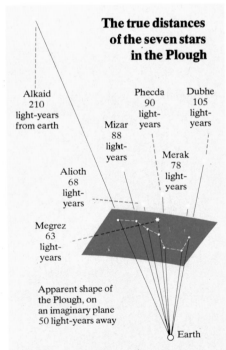

Alkaid
210
light-years
from earth

Phecda
90
light-years

Dubhe
105
light-years

Mizar
88
light-years

Merak
78
light-years

Alioth
68
light-years

Megrez
63
light-years

Apparent shape of the Plough, on an imaginary plane 50 light-years away

Earth

Though the stars themselves are real, the constellations are an invention of man. All the stars in a constellation appear to be associated with one another – but in reality they are light-years apart (a light-year is nearly 6 million million miles). The diagram above shows the actual distances between the Earth and stars of the Plough; the stars were named by Arab astronomers in ancient times.

The word planet means "wanderer"

From one month to the next, the planets shift position relative to one another and to the constellations. The Greeks noticed this long ago, and named these roaming celestial objects after their word for wanderer. Our solar system has nine planets. Each takes a different length of time to orbit the Sun, which is why they seem to shift position.

• To get to know the planets, locate them on a monthly star chart before you look for them in the sky. The number of visible planets varies from month to month; so does the time that each one rises and sets. Any planet you can see will always be near one of the constellations of the zodiac (see opposite).

• Some planets go through phases like those of the Moon, and their brightness changes drastically from month to month. Only five planets are ever visible to the naked eye. Mercury, the small planet closest to the Sun, is elusive; for all but a few weeks of the year it is hidden by the light of the Sun. Venus – the brightest object in the night-time sky (except for the Moon) – is sometimes a "morning star", sometimes an "evening star"; this is the planet nearest to the Earth. Mars is easy to spot because it has a reddish hue. Jupiter, the largest planet, is almost as dazzling as Venus. Saturn is the ringed planet. Uranus, Neptune and Pluto are usually not visible except through a telescope.

The rings of Saturn are a well-known feature of this planet, though without a telescope the planet is simply a bright "star". Saturn is the outermost planet visible to the naked eye. Because of this, it appears to move more slowly than the other planets against the backdrop of the sky.

This is Jupiter, photographed from a spacecraft. Near its centre, one of the planet's 14 moons casts a circular shadow; the Great Red Spot lies to the left. Jupiter is conspicuous for almost the entire year, but to see any of its moons you will need binoculars or a telescope.

Following the motion of the Moon

Because we have sent astronauts to the Moon, one might assume that the Moon is of greater significance in this day and age than in the past. The reverse is true. In old almanacs, the monthly illumination of the Moon was carefully logged; only when the Moon was shining could anyone hope to travel safely at night. Not only were the roads rutted and unpredictable, there was also no artificial illumination on either vehicles or highways.

The Moon, of course, does not really appear and disappear once a month – this only seems to happen because the Moon moves round the Earth. Moonlight is really the reflection of sunlight bouncing off the lunar surface. When the lighted side of the Moon faces the Earth, we see the so-called full Moon (really only half the Moon). When the shaded side is towards the Earth, it can be seen only in faintest outline (the so-called new Moon). These

A reddish halo round the Moon, seen beyond the haze (called the lunar corona), is a subject for meteorologists, not astronomers. It is caused by ice crystals in the atmosphere.

Changes, real and apparent

The Moon has two basic movements – it rotates, or spins, on its axis, and it revolves round the Earth. Because a complete rotation and a complete revolution take exactly the same time, we always see the same face of the Moon. (The red triangles in the diagrams on the right illustrate this point.) We see only the sunlit portion of the Moon, which, like the Earth, is only half of the sphere at any one time. The phases of the Moon – waxing and waning – are a result of the fact that not all the sunlit portion of the Moon can be seen throughout the lunar month.

This composite picture compares two views of the Moon, one taken approximately two weeks after the other. The Moon does not really change. Instead, because it has an elliptical orbit, its distance from the Earth changes; when close to us, it looks larger.

Moonrise over New York was captured by a photographer taking multiple exposures. (This view is southwards; the Moon always appears to rise in the east.) On this particular night, the Earth's shadow has fallen on the Moon, creating a partial lunar eclipse.

and other lunar phases are shown below.

The waxing and waning of the Moon are old and poetic terms from the days when little was known about the movements of the Moon. (Wax means grow, and this is what people believed was happening.) You can tell whether the Moon is waxing or waning by looking at the crescent. If the outer edge is towards the right, the Moon is waxing; if the outer edge is to the left, it is waning.

One of the surprising facts about the Moon is that we always see the same side. (It was not until Russia sent a spacecraft round the Moon that the other face was seen for the first time.) Like the Earth, the Moon rotates. But rather than rotating once a day (as does the Earth), the Moon turns only about once every 28 days. This is the same time that the Moon takes to orbit the Earth. Because the two movements happen to be synchronised there is

an illusion of stability in its positioning.

Like the Earth, which travels in an elliptical orbit around the Sun, the Moon has an elliptical orbit around the Earth. This means that once a month the Moon is especially close to the Earth (a situation called perigee) and it appears larger than usual; when furthest away (at apogee), the Moon looks considerably smaller. This is not to be confused with the situation where a full Moon seems to shrink as it rises during the night. One explanation for the illusion is that at the horizon the size of the Moon can be compared with buildings and trees, which make it look immense.

Even at its brightest, the Moon never produces anything remotely comparable to daylight. It gives us only 1/450,000 as much light as the Sun. So people who talk of reading by moonlight are paying tribute mainly to the remarkable adaptivity of their own eyesight.

In ancient times, the Moon's predictable phases led to its use as a calendar. However, no matter how one fiddles with the figures, there is no way to make lunar months (each about 28 days long) add up to a solar year (the time it takes for the Earth to orbit the Sun, returning to the same place). Because it is the Earth's relationship with the Sun that determines the seasons and governs farming, mankind had to discover some means of tracking the Sun. The circle of stones at Stonehenge on Salisbury Plain seems to have been used as a solar observatory.

The Moon's actual influence on Earth is not as a timekeeper but as a force on the oceans, creating the tides. The tides reflect the relationships of the Moon, Earth and Sun to one another. Tides exhibit their greatest variation when the three bodies are aligned, and the least when at right-angles (see p. 112).

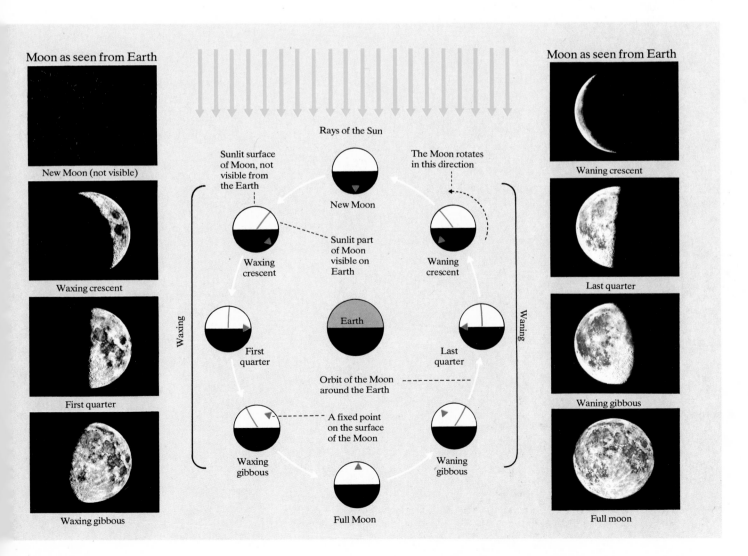

Moon as seen from Earth

New Moon (not visible)

Waxing crescent

First quarter

Waxing gibbous

Rays of the Sun

Sunlit surface of Moon, not visible from the Earth

New Moon

The Moon rotates in this direction

Sunlit part of Moon visible on Earth

Waxing crescent

Waning crescent

Earth

First quarter

Last quarter

Orbit of the Moon around the Earth

A fixed point on the surface of the Moon

Waxing gibbous

Waning gibbous

Full Moon

Waxing

Waning

Moon as seen from Earth

Waning crescent

Last quarter

Waning gibbous

Full moon

Visitors and invaders from space

This is Comet Bennett – a particularly bright comet that visited our solar system in 1970.

Comets have always seemed mysterious. Long ago, they were regarded with terror; now that the Earth has survived the close approach of numerous comets, scientists and amateur astronomers alike are delighted by the prospect of a comet coming towards us.

Part of the mystery associated with comets is their structure. According to a generally accepted theory, the head of a comet is a "dirty snowball" – a mixture of frozen gases (including water vapour) and dust. This part of a comet is relatively small, perhaps some 50 miles in diameter. In the early stages, while the comet is still at a great distance from the Sun, there is only a head. The tail develops later (composed of gases or dust), and may stretch for millions of miles. Slowly it becomes increasingly radiant and visible. Then, the light of the comet is masked by the greater brilliance of the Sun. As the comet con-tinues on its way, it may reappear on the other side of the Sun, or it may split in two, or it may disappear entirely.

Calculations of a comet's orbit round the Sun provide data on when – if ever – a comet will come close to the Earth again. Scientists may be able to determine whether a comet has been near to Earth before or is a new comet. Halley's Comet, shown at the top of the facing page, is an example of a comet that returns regularly within a relatively short period of time. Certain other comets keep returning at shorter and shorter time intervals.

Owing to their regular reappearance, comets have allowed historians to pin-point events of ancient times, chronicled only as "in the year of the great comet".

Though variations in behaviour of comets are of great interest to astronomers, they can be frustrating to the rest of the world. For example, in 1974, Comet Kohoutek disappointed many sky-watchers; it simply did not live up to expectations.

Although amateur astronomers often make discoveries, it is unlikely that a non-professional will spot a comet before the scientists, because so many comets cannot be seen by the naked eye. On average, nine comets, including some repeats, are recorded each year.

Because interest in astronomy is increasing, newspapers, news magazines, and natural history periodicals often print announcements about comets. Planetariums, too, can tell you the date and time that a particular comet is expected to be visible, and its location in the sky, relative to stars or planets. Frequently, comets are best seen at sunset, near the western horizon, or just before sunrise, near the eastern horizon.

Meteors may be the debris of comets – fragments produced during their orbit round the Sun. Many scientists believe that meteor showers occur when the Earth crosses the path of a comet (that is, where a comet has already passed by). Meteor showers are regular events during the year (see far right); at such times, numerous "shooting stars" streak across a particular region of the sky.

There are special terms for shooting stars. Far out in space, the debris is called a meteoroid. When it vaporises or glows in the Earth's atmosphere it is known as a meteor (or, if it is especially bright, a fireball). If the debris lands on Earth, it is called a meteorite. However, in spite of the many meteorites that land, few are large enough to produce noticeable craters.

A comet sweeps through our solar system, its tail always pointing away from the Sun. Unlike the planets, which stay within our solar system, some comets have orbits extending outside it.

Here, a comet is shown making a hairpin turn in its trip round the Sun. This illustration depicts the solar system from beyond Saturn; the Earth is the third planet from the Sun.

Halley's Comet was last seen in 1910, and is due back in 1986

As Halley's Comet neared the Sun on its last visit in 1910, its tail lengthened to some 150 million miles. Its closest approach to the Sun occurred in mid-May; after that, the tail shrank. In the 17th century, Edmund Halley, an English astronomer, first calculated the period of this comet. As comets go, this one has a short period – its next appearance will be in 1986.

April 26

May 2

May 4

May 15

May 28

June 3

June 11

Meteorites and meteor craters

This monster 34 ton meteorite was found in Greenland. It is now in New York on permanent exhibition at the American Museum of Natural History. Meteorites are immensely heavy for their size, as they are mostly metal. The rest of their parts boil away as the meteorite becomes white-hot during its dive into the Earth's atmosphere.

The impact of a crashing meteorite is believed to have produced this Australian crater, which measures more than 3 miles across; the crater's rim extends some 600 ft above the dry plain. Nearly 100 meteor craters have been identified in various parts of the world.

CHAPTER NINE

Geology and earth history

Geological events that took place millions of years ago are influencing our lives today – to an extent we are just beginning to realise.

I t is fun to be in on the start of something important. Suddenly, geology has become the super-star of sciences. After decades of quietly accumulating data about the earth and its history, geologists find themselves with a whole new body of information, and the far-reaching implications of a fundamental theory: the continents have apparently shifted their positions on the globe. The result is that every established fact (from geomagnetism to pole reversal) has to be re-examined. Does our present information confirm continental drift? Or does some obscure fact – as yet unappreciated – prove that they could *not* have moved as we now believe?

Not long ago, the theory of continental drift was ridiculed. Today, it is hard to challenge. What will the outcome be? No one knows for sure. One startling fact has emerged – in places where the earth is known to have shifted, there is a greater supply of valuable ores than elsewhere. Petroleum deposits, too, are connected with continental movements.

Those who first prodded the rocky surface of the earth were dealing with evidence they were unable to evaluate. The earth is so large and its surface movements so slow, that the connection between the two went undetected until recently. But now, with the development of sophisticated equipment, we can monitor the behaviour of a whole continent, even if it moves no more than an inch. We can predict earthquakes, although not to the precise time as yet.

Perhaps the "instrument" most important in this new world of geology is an open mind, which enables us to contemplate and to accept such fantastic things.

A natural bridge is surprising because it looks like something built by man. Such bridges were once believed to have been cut by wind; but in fact they were made long ago by underground rivers. This one – in what is now a semi-desert part of Utah in America – is a striking example of the work of water. The play of shadow and light dramatises the structure of the bridge.

Time: the master sculptor

We seldom see rocks being formed. Volcanic rocks are the exception – they are spewed out as molten material and quickly harden as they cool. The arrival of such rock (called igneous, meaning born of fire) may be localised in certain well-known places such as Mauna Loa in Hawaii. Or a volcanic eruption may be a sudden catastrophe, where concern for human lives overshadows the geological event. Another kind of rock, called sedimentary, builds up along the bottoms of lakes, rivers and seas, but in a less obvious way; compression of muddy deposits into rock is not visible. The third major kind of rock, metamorphic, is the result of extreme compression of the other two (igneous and sedimentary), and perhaps of other metamorphic rocks as well. Metamorphic rocks form under great heat and pressure, generally deep within the earth or inside mountains.

What we usually see is rock being dismantled. Bit by bit, rocks are cracked and carried off, usually by water and wind. As

A balancing rock is produced in a simple way – the surrounding material is just worn away. Here, in Arizona, USA, soft rocks have been completely eroded, leaving only a harder core.

The "perfect wave" sought by surfers has its 50 ft geological counterpart at Wave Rock, in

rocks weather, their origins may become clear. For example, many kinds of volcanic rock have distinctive seams, rope effects, hexagonal columns – the variety is great. If layering can be seen, the formation is probably of sedimentary origin. Sometimes the layers are flat, sometimes tilted, wavy, or even standing on end. The layers were originally laid down horizontally, but shifts in the earth's crust changed the position of the rocks.

The results of weathering are often so fantastic and intricate, they have the same appeal as sculpture. Many of the odd-looking rocks seen in Wild West films, for example, are largely a result of the composition of the rocks themselves. Some rocks have layers or veins of harder material. As the agents of weathering wear them away, the softer parts are eroded first, leaving the harder sections standing out like stone latticework. A rock transported from a distant place (perhaps an erratic boulder deposited by a passing glacier) may be harder than the stone on which it

rests. It may, in effect, form an umbrella for its foundation, and become stranded or elevated as the surrounding rock is eroded. Boulder-capped pinnacles or rocks on pedestals are signs of this process.

Probably the most bizarre formations are the balancing rocks, found in widely separated places all over the globe. Some of these rocks, like the Logan rocks in south-west England, seem about to fall over any minute. Yet what they demonstrate is how slow the weathering process actually is – they last much longer than you might expect. Some balancing rocks even sway when pushed.

Some of nature's most curious formations are the rounded holes you occasionally see in a rocky river bed. Such holes are caused by cavitation – the same process that produces bubbles around the propeller of a boat. When water is moved violently, some of it bursts into bubbles, which collapse rapidly and cause shock waves. The bubbles are like tiny hammer blows, and wear away the rock (or propeller). Sometimes, the hole is enlarged by smaller rocks that are swirled around, grinding the sides of the pothole like a natural pestle and mortar.

At first the centrifugal force of the water wears away the outside of the hole more quickly than the rest, leaving a cone of rock in the centre. But as the hole deepens, the centrifugal effect grows less powerful and the cone also wears away.

PHOTO TIPS
Sparkling stones

Water can bring out the intensity and richness of colour in stones. If the bright pebbles you find at the shore seem drab when you get them home, try putting them in water to see if they perk up. A sprinkling of water also adds a look of freshness in photographs of flowers and foliage.

Fragments of carnelian agate, found in a stream bed, were strewn on the bank and doused again before being photographed.

south-western Australia. Chemical weathering has produced streaks that add to the illusion.

Looking like candidates for a modern sculpture garden, these weathered boulders draw people

to South Australia's Kangaroo Island. They, too, were produced by natural forces.

The inside story of the earth

We think of the earth as having been thoroughly mapped. But this is true only of its surface. Mankind lives on the thin, outer skin of a huge globe; we are able to explore its exterior contours, but can only speculate on what lies beneath the surface. No person or unmanned exploratory probe has journeyed to the centre of the earth.

For thousands of years, most people thought that the interior of the earth was made up of the same kind of materials as the exterior – mostly rock. The evidence of lava flows suggested that it was molten in places, but no one had a clear picture of the extent of molten materials. Then, in the early 1900s, scientists began to monitor the shock waves of earthquakes. Timing the speed of the waves revealed much about "inner space". Waves travel faster through compact materials than they do through spongier regions. It became clear that the earth is composed of different layers.

Far from being like surface rock, the main constituents of the interior seem to be iron and nickel, which are not abundant on the outside. The different layers were named the crust, upper mantle, lower mantle, outer core and inner core. The arrangement of these layers was probably caused by a number of forces – including gravity, the earth's rotation and magnetism.

What you see in this illustration is a summary of many theories about parts of the earth we have never seen. The outer crust (shown in dark brown) is made up of separate blocks of granite-like rocks about 5 miles thick, which form the continents. These continental blocks rest on heavy basaltic rock (lighter brown), which is about 60 miles thick.

The crust "floats" on the upper mantle, a 400-mile-thick zone that is in constant motion. In places the inner turbulence is transmitted outwards, pushing up blister-like bulges beneath the crust. Sometimes the blisters break through, creating volcanoes.

The crust of the earth has been fractured into plates. Material flowing up from the mantle sometimes fuses to a plate, thus enlarging it. One place where this occurs is the East Pacific Rise. The opposite edge of the plate is sometimes pushed beneath another plate, which in turn is pushed up, as is happening in the Peru-Chile Trench, at the western edge of South America. This is called subduction. The great mountain ranges of the Andes and the Himalayas were both thrown up by subduction of colliding plates.

This cross-section slices the globe at an unusual angle in order to show many sites of geological activity.

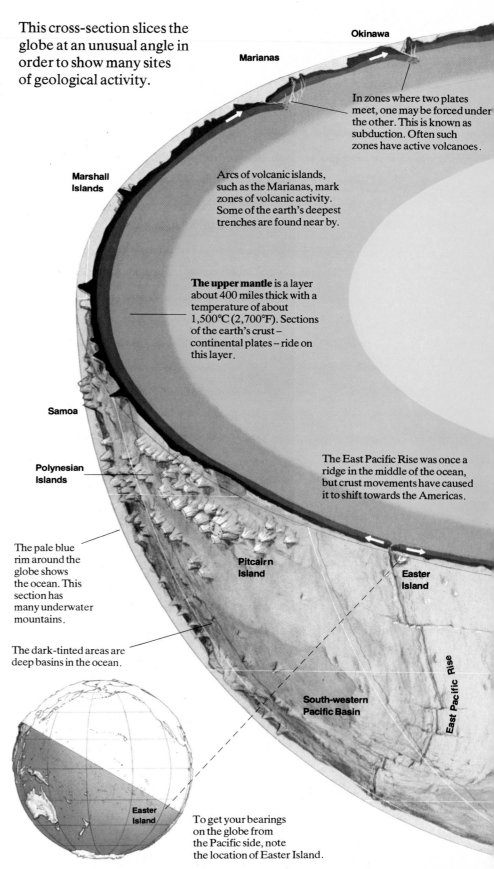

In zones where two plates meet, one may be forced under the other. This is known as subduction. Often such zones have active volcanoes.

Arcs of volcanic islands, such as the Marianas, mark zones of volcanic activity. Some of the earth's deepest trenches are found near by.

The upper mantle is a layer about 400 miles thick with a temperature of about 1,500°C (2,700°F). Sections of the earth's crust – continental plates – ride on this layer.

The East Pacific Rise was once a ridge in the middle of the ocean, but crust movements have caused it to shift towards the Americas.

The pale blue rim around the globe shows the ocean. This section has many underwater mountains.

The dark-tinted areas are deep basins in the ocean.

To get your bearings on the globe from the Pacific side, note the location of Easter Island.

Okinawa

Marianas

Marshall Islands

Samoa

Polynesian Islands

Pitcairn Island

Easter Island

South-western Pacific Basin

East Pacific Rise

Easter Island

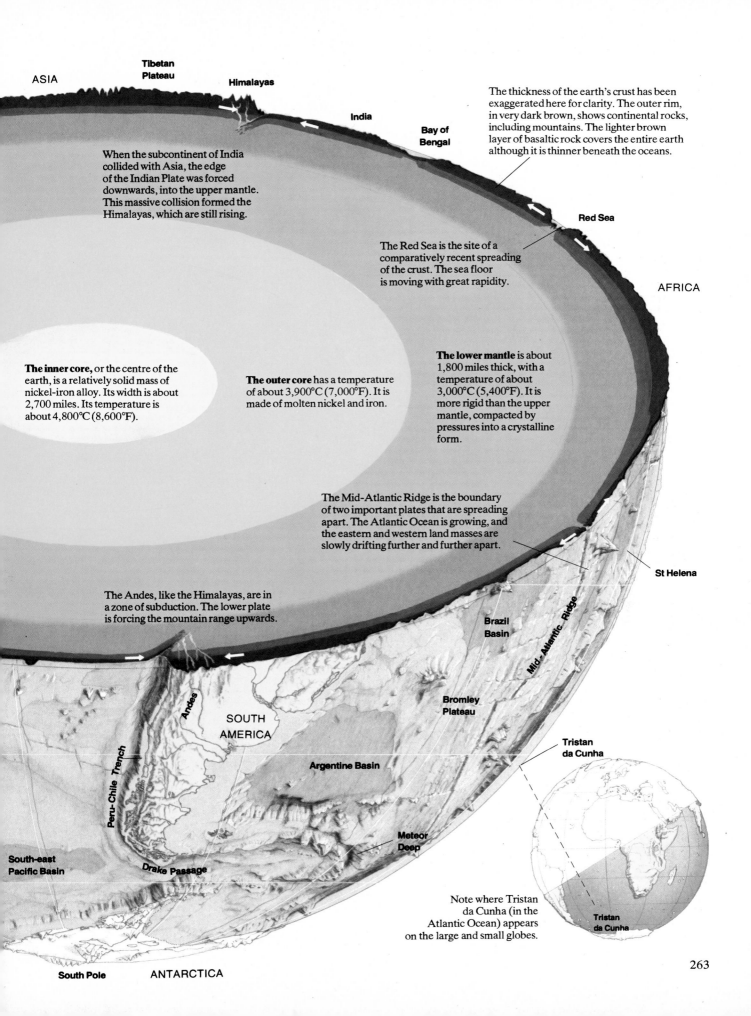

ASIA

Tibetan Plateau

Himalayas

India

Bay of Bengal

The thickness of the earth's crust has been exaggerated here for clarity. The outer rim, in very dark brown, shows continental rocks, including mountains. The lighter brown layer of basaltic rock covers the entire earth although it is thinner beneath the oceans.

When the subcontinent of India collided with Asia, the edge of the Indian Plate was forced downwards, into the upper mantle. This massive collision formed the Himalayas, which are still rising.

Red Sea

The Red Sea is the site of a comparatively recent spreading of the crust. The sea floor is moving with great rapidity.

AFRICA

The inner core, or the centre of the earth, is a relatively solid mass of nickel-iron alloy. Its width is about 2,700 miles. Its temperature is about 4,800°C (8,600°F).

The outer core has a temperature of about 3,900°C (7,000°F). It is made of molten nickel and iron.

The lower mantle is about 1,800 miles thick, with a temperature of about 3,000°C (5,400°F). It is more rigid than the upper mantle, compacted by pressures into a crystalline form.

The Mid-Atlantic Ridge is the boundary of two important plates that are spreading apart. The Atlantic Ocean is growing, and the eastern and western land masses are slowly drifting further and further apart.

St Helena

The Andes, like the Himalayas, are in a zone of subduction. The lower plate is forcing the mountain range upwards.

Brazil Basin

Mid-Atlantic Ridge

Andes

SOUTH AMERICA

Bromley Plateau

Tristan da Cunha

Peru-Chile Trench

Argentine Basin

Meteor Deep

South-east Pacific Basin

Drake Passage

Tristan da Cunha

Note where Tristan da Cunha (in the Atlantic Ocean) appears on the large and small globes.

South Pole **ANTARCTICA**

263

A theory that rides on immense plates

Continental drift took place over millions of years

Tantalising evidence of a relationship between the continents has existed for hundreds of years. But there was no way of learning more until relatively recent times.

According to the continental-drift theory, this is the way the world looked about 200 million years ago. The name given to the enormous ocean was Panthalassa; the name for the supercontinent was Pangaea. Lightly outlined on these theoretical drawings are the "seams" along which the great land mass is believed to have broken into fragments.

The first break was at the Sea of Tethys – separating Laurasia in the north from Gondwana in the south. This may have happened some 180 million years ago.

As fragmentation continued, each of the major continents became established, and the early formations (which are still theoretical, of course) lost identity.

Drifting involved not just separations, but collisions as well. About 60 million years ago, India is thought to have been separate, but heading for Asia.

The Atlantic Ocean, shown here at its present width, is believed to be growing wider. There is evidence that part of California is breaking off.

New York and London, now separated by some 3,500 miles, are slowly drifting further apart. South America was once joined to Africa, and the Pacific Ocean is about half as wide as it once was. If you had told this to anyone a few years ago, most people would have thought you were joking. Today, anyone with a general interest in geology knows that such a revolutionary idea has a basis in fact.

Basically, the theory is this: different parts of the earth's crust are moving in different directions. Most scientists agree that the hard crust is broken into about half a dozen major segments, or plates, and several smaller ones. These plates are slowly sliding on the upper mantle, a molten layer of the earth that lies beneath the crust. Some plates (which underlie the oceans, as well as continents and islands) are moving about 6 in. a year – a relatively fast speed, geologically speaking.

As you may have noticed, the facing coastlines of South America and Africa fit together like a jigsaw puzzle. For more than a century, scientists have speculated that the continents may once have been joined in a single supercontinent. But how could this have happened? What force was great enough to make them move?

Early in the 20th century, the German scientist Alfred Wegener went so far as to give a name to the theoretical supercontinent – Pangaea, from the Greek words meaning all lands. Wegener believed that Pangaea started to break up some 150 million years ago, when dinosaurs were the dominant life-forms on land. Slowly, the pieces began to drift to their present locations.

Wegener had supporting evidence for the continental-drift theory. Rock formations along the coast of Brazil are almost identical in composition and fossil deposits to those on the Gulf of Guinea in western Africa. Fossils of tropical life found on the continent of Antarctica were similar to those discovered in southern Africa. One possible interpretation for this was that, in the past, the whole world was warmer, and tropical conditions were widespread. Wegener saw these fossil deposits as support for his theory.

Even by snail standards, progress tends to be slow in these movements of plates. But in 150 million years a plate travelling at only one inch a year can move more than 2,000 miles. As some plates are known to travel much faster than this, there has been plenty of time for the movements described in Wegener's theory.

Technological advances in geology

have greatly extended our knowledge of the globe, just as the invention of the telescope opened new vistas for the science of astronomy, and the microscope for medicine. For example, some of the most convincing evidence supporting the continental-drift theory was uncovered in the 1950s and 1960s, when deep-sea drilling enabled scientists to study samples from the floors of different oceans. This is still being done with a drill that takes core samples. As the drill is pushed deeper, it fills with sediment and rock; the layers are brought up undisturbed, in the order in which they settled on the sea floor. This process makes it possible to establish the age of a deposit.

Evidence from core samples (along with many other clues) has made it clear that molten material rises from the earth's interior in rift valleys and along mid-ocean ridges. (This also occurs in a volcano, but volcanic eruptions are usually much more sporadic.) In these places, the new material is welded to the edges of the continental plates; in this way, the plates grow larger. At the same time, the opposite edge is pushed into a neighbouring plate.

The exposure of rock strata makes the Great Rift Valley in East Africa a source of interest to geologists. The upheavals have also been a boon to anthropologists tracing man's ancestry.

Crustal movement makes new rock and melts the old

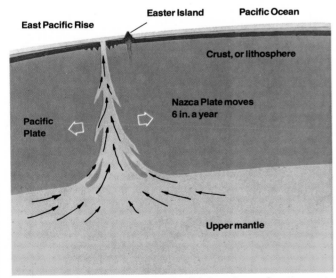

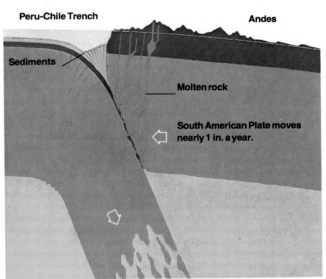

Plates separate at the East Pacific Rise. It is in such gaps that new crust is forming. The semi-fluid region below the crust is stirred by hot convection currents that force basalt up through any apertures.

Where one plate slips under another, in a process called subduction, the plate that goes under melts. The Nazca Plate, which is forming near Easter Island, is diving where it collides with South America.

265

When the crust erupts and shifts

Many millions of years ago, every part of the earth was influenced by volcanoes. Today, volcanic activity is much more limited – usually confined to fairly well-defined zones around the Pacific (called the Ring of Fire), areas along the mid-Atlantic Ridge, and parts of the Mediterranean and Caribbean seas.

Iceland, just 500 miles north of Scotland, is one of the world's most active volcanic areas. It has about 200 volcanoes. Between 1963 and 1967 a new one erupted and arose from the sea bed off the south-west coast, creating the island of Surtsey.

Earthquakes sometimes accompany volcanic activity – when the vent of a volcano becomes blocked and pressure increases, the earth may shake for miles around. But earthquakes often occur independently of volcanoes. The strain builds up in the earth with no outward sign, until suddenly the crust fractures, usually along a line of weakness. Two major fault belts together encircle the earth and 95% of all earthquakes occur along them. China, which has the world's worst record for earthquake deaths, stands on one of the belts.

A massive earthquake in the northern industrial area of Tangshan on July 28, 1976, is estimated to have killed 655,237 people and injured 779,000 – second only to the 830,000 killed in the worst recorded earthquake disaster at Shensi in 1556. However, not all earthquakes are disastrous. Any tremor in the earth's crust, no matter how slight, is an earthquake and you may well have lived through several without realising it.

Earthquakes are rated according to their intensity on the Richter Scale, named after an American seismologist. (Seismology is the study of earthquakes.) An earthquake rated as 1 on the scale is so minor that it is detectable only by instruments called seismographs. A tremor rated 2 might cause hanging objects to swing slightly. One rated 3 might cause rattling of objects on shelves, but would probably do little damage. The highest-rated earthquake recorded recently is the one that hit Alaska in 1964, rated at 8.9. China's 1976 earthquake was 8.2.

No spectacle on earth can match the seething fury of a volcanic eruption, such as the explosion of Volcán de Fuego (Volcano of Fire) in Guatemala. At 2.30 a.m. on October 14, 1974, the top of the mountain blew apart.

Eight hours later, when this picture was taken, clouds and volcanic ash were rising thousands of feet into the air. Such eruptions show the awesome heat and pressure below the earth's cool crust.

Most shifts in the earth's crust occur on the ocean floor. A wave created by such an earthquake is sometimes called a tidal wave; but because it has nothing to do with tides, scientists prefer to use the Japanese name, tsunami. They are also called seismic sea waves. By any name, such waves often cause heavy damage when they reach the shore. In 1896, one of the largest waves ever – about 100 ft high – battered miles of the Japanese coast and washed away about 10,000 houses. Although seismic sea waves travel at 400 to 500 mph, they are much slower than the tremors from the earthquakes that cause them. Thus, scientists can detect their location and size and give early warning.

Human activity can trigger an earth-quake. Seismic studies have shown that in some localities, pumping out water or petroleum from the earth (or pumping wastes in) can cause tremors. So can the construction of a dam; as a reservoir fills, the weight of the water puts stress on the rocks. In the future, geologists may be able to "defuse" a potentially disastrous earthquake by setting off a series of minor ones, thus relieving the strain. Realising the age-old dream of preventing earthquakes would be a great advantage on a planet where crustal activity is a fact of life. In the meantime it may prove possible to develop a warning system so that people can be evacuated from their homes before disaster strikes. Even an hour's advance notice would save many lives.

Catastrophic waves from an underwater earthquake

When an earthquake strikes the ocean floor, convulsions in the earth's crust may churn up giant waves, called tsunamis or seismic sea waves. The waves spread from the earthquake area in ever-widening circles, the way ripples do when you throw a pebble in a pond. In deep water, these waves are barely noticeable – they are only about 1 or 2 ft high and may measure 100 miles or more from crest to crest. However, when such waves approach a coastline, the friction of the shallow sea floor causes the waves to pile up, sometimes as high as 100 ft. Fortunately, a global monitoring system warns coastal areas hours before a tsunami strikes.

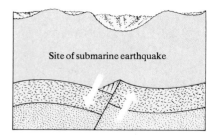

A typical tsunami results from a major submarine earthquake that occurs less than 30 miles beneath the sea floor.

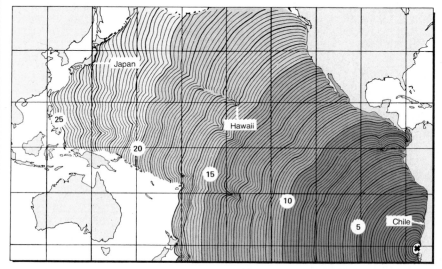

On May 24, 1960, a submarine earthquake near Chile produced a tsunami that spread over the Pacific as fast as a jet aircraft. Some 15 hours later the main wave crashed into Hawaii, 7,000 miles away, and in 25 hours it ravaged the eastern coast of Japan.

A minor fissure in the ground, such as the one that cracked this roadway in California, is produced by the same forces as those that cause major earthquakes. The ground may rise and fall in undulating waves, or in a more violent fashion. A giant tremor is often accompanied by a loud roar. The earth on either side of a fissure may move several yards, or it may become a gaping chasm. Such earthquakes can turn a tall building into a pile of rubble in a matter of minutes. In many earthquake-prone areas, the heights of buildings are regulated by law.

Hot springs and geysers

Iceland is, ironically, richer in hot springs than any other country in the world. It has alkaline "gushers" in about 250 places. Some have now been tapped to provide cheap earth-powered heating for the capital, Reykjavik. The biggest, called Deildartunguhver, throws out 55 gallons of boiling water every second. Among the most spectacular hot springs and geysers are those in Yellowstone Park in America. The first expedition to the mountain plateau in September 1870,

Quiescent for the moment, a hot spring lends itself to study. Note the mouth of the spring, and its elevation above the surrounding land.

gazed in awe at steam and water shooting hundreds of feet into the air. In New Zealand one record-setting geyser used to spout a column of water 1,500 ft high, and once lobbed a boulder weighing 150 lb. for a quarter of a mile.

If you have ever seen a hot spring or geyser, or even a photograph of one, you know that heat is an important factor; the steam makes that obvious. This heat is geothermal – earth heat. It is evidence that the interior of the earth is much hotter than the surface. Over most of the globe, the hot zones of the mantle lie miles beneath the surface; but in some places, the overlying crust is relatively thin. Such regions are usually associated with volcanic activity, and this is where hot springs and geysers are likely to occur.

Water is the other component of a geothermal area. Groundwater collects in cracks, where it is heated. When this water bubbles to the surface, it is called a hot spring. In some places the water does not have a chance to collect in the underground spaces, but is continually expelled as steam. These hissing openings are called fumaroles. A geyser is a hot spring with an underground structure that causes the build-up of steam; the pathway to the surface is crooked and has pockets where heat is trapped, steam collects, and pressure builds up. Periodically, the boiling water will emerge explosively in a geyser. The word geyser comes from an Icelandic word meaning to gush forth.

Each geyser has its own "style" of spouting. Some erupt regularly, almost on an hourly timetable; others spurt only at long, unpredictable intervals that may be reckoned in decades. One of the most regular of all geysers, Old Faithful in Yellowstone, erupts at intervals that range from half an hour to an hour-and-a-half. The world's largest geysers spout water as high as several hundred feet into the air. Other geysers are mere squirts, with water pushed only a few inches above ground.

Some plants can live in hot springs. The presence of blue-green algae may indicate even the temperature. (Such algae do not grow where the temperature is greater than 77°C (170°F)). The waters of hot springs and geysers carry large amounts of dissolved minerals, which also lend colour to the formations. As the hot, mineral-laden water reaches the surface, the water may evaporate. This often causes the dissolved minerals to drop and form a crater-like wall; where the water flows down a slope, ornate terraces may be created. Such deposits are often coloured yellow, pink or blue, depending on the particular minerals that were in the water.

Geothermal energy is sometimes used by man to generate electricity and heat buildings. It is also used by wildlife. For example, during winter bison can be seen grazing near thermal areas in Yellowstone; bears locate their dens near by; and ducks swim on the warm ponds when all other waters are frozen.

Steam clouds the air and mud oozes down the side of the "crater" as water at a temperature of more than 38°C (100°F) wells up.

A steaming fumarole resembles an inferno. Such hot-air vents, named after the Latin for smoke, hiss and sputter when hot gases (mainly water vapour) emerge from the earth's interior. The scorching heat prevents all but certain kinds of algae from growing near fumaroles.

Hot water rising under pressure

Heat and water are two obvious requirements of geysers, hot springs and fumaroles. But what cannot be seen are the fissures that extend downwards to the hot regions of the earth's interior. It is in these natural channels that water circulates and picks up heat.

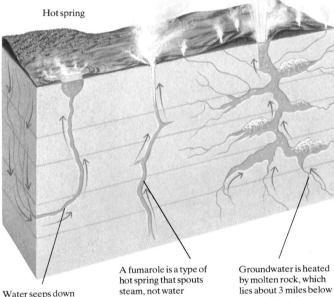

Geyser

Fumarole

Hot spring

Water seeps down and is recycled

A fumarole is a type of hot spring that spouts steam, not water

Groundwater is heated by molten rock, which lies about 3 miles below the earth's surface

Old Faithful geyser in Yellowstone National Park, USA, does not erupt at exact intervals. Nevertheless, it deserves its name – it has spouted about once an hour for as long as records have been kept.

The waters of a hot spring at Yellowstone's Mammoth Hot Springs run down sloping land. The heavy concentrations of minerals in the water account not just for the terraces, but for their colours as well.

Minerals: the building blocks of rocks

COLLECTOR'S TIPS
Hunting for rocks

Almost anywhere you see interesting rocks will do as a place to start this hobby – excavations, road and railway cuttings, quarries, cliffs, ravines and natural outcroppings. If you want to collect on private land, be sure to get permission first.

● The tools you will need are simple – a hammer (preferably one made for geologists), cold chisel, magnifying glass, heavy gloves and safety goggles (to protect your eyes from rock dust and larger pieces). You will also need paper and a knapsack, for wrapping and transporting your rock specimens.

● Use a small notebook to record the locations of your finds. For mineral identification, a reference book is necessary.

● Try to keep your samples small. If a piece is too large, shape it with your chisel or hammer. Remember that if you hit a rock too hard, you may end up with only a handful of dust.

● Label your finds individually (the larger your collection, the less you can trust this information to memory). Minerals can be extremely decorative, so plan to display them prominently.

● If you join a local club, you may have an opportunity to swap samples with other members.

One of the attractions of rock-hunting is the possibility that you will find something unusual. Here on a bed of quartz, is an extraordinary "sunburst" of white mica.

Walking on air is usually taken as a figure of speech, but in one sense it is literally true. Oxygen, the gas that makes up about 20% of the air, also makes up some 50% of the crust of the earth. It seems impossible that a substance we can neither see, taste, touch, nor smell is such an abundant substance in rock and soil. But this is indeed the case. Because oxygen combines readily with many other substances, it forms most of the earth's minerals – the building blocks of its rocky crust.

Geologists usually define a mineral as a naturally occurring, uniform solid that has never been part of any living thing. You probably eat at least one common mineral each day – salt. Most gems, ores, and many industrial raw materials are minerals. But there are so many minerals and so much disagreement about exactly what they are, that no one can state precisely how many kinds exist on earth. Estimates range from 1,500 to 3,000. The possible combinations are beyond calculation.

As in the classification of plants and animals, the different kinds of minerals are known as species. The most common are the silicates – combinations of oxygen and silicon, which is a glass-like solid. Silicates alone make up about 90% of all material in the crust of the earth, and more than a quarter of all known species of minerals. Oxygen is also present in carbonates (chalk, lime), and in most precious stones, though not in diamonds, which are almost pure carbon.

Learning to recognise minerals is like playing a parlour game out of doors. The best way to start is by eliminating everything that is *not* a mineral. According to the definition, minerals have never been alive. Although they are necessary to all forms of life, once they are incorporated into living tissue, they are no longer considered minerals. This presents some interesting paradoxes. For example, oyster shells and pearls are composed of the same substance as a mineral called aragonite, but oyster shells are produced by animals.

All man-made substances can also be discounted, because minerals must occur naturally. A diamond found in the earth is a mineral, but a man-made diamond – although it may be identical in composition – is not. This part of the definition has caused arguments among the experts. One controversy concerns a substance called larium, found in the sea off Greece. Larium was formed when sea water reacted with slag (residue from lead mines) dumped in the sea more than 2,000 years ago. So is larium a natural substance?

The structure of a mineral is one of its most distinctive characteristics. Minerals are made up of symmetrical shapes called crystals; for example, there are crystals of salt and, on the inside of a geode, crystals of quartz (see below). Though most crystals are microscopic, the crystalline structure of minerals can often be seen in large formations.

A certain purity of chemical composition is one way to identify a mineral, but there are other tests. Hardness, lustre, colour and melting temperature all aid in mineral identification. Some minerals produce an electrical current when heated or put under pressure. Then, too, there are various specific tests – such as reactions to acids and to burning. Other minerals glow (fluoresce) when placed under "black" (ultra-violet) light, giving them a dramatic look when shown this way.

Geodes – the surprise within

Geodes, sometimes called thunder eggs, begin as bubbles in rock-forming material. In sedimentary rock (which is usually laid down as mud on the sea floor), the bubble may be a pocket of water. After the mud hardens into rock, the centre fills with water-borne minerals (usually silicates). The minerals crystallise on the interior walls. Later, when the surrounding rock is worn away, the geode is left behind. If you pick up a plain round stone that weighs much less than you expected, it may be worth splitting open – perhaps it is actually a geode.

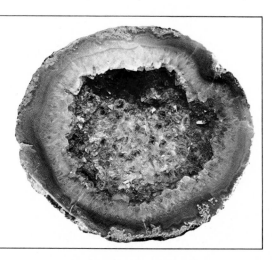

Start with silicates – they are easy to identify and often beautiful

Because there are so many kinds of minerals (some difficult even for mineralogists to identify except with laboratory equipment), it is a good idea to start with something abundant and relatively obvious. Silicates are ideal because two of their components – oxygen and silicon – are the most abundant elements in the earth's crust. Nearly all of the rock-forming minerals are combinations of silicon, oxygen and one or more metals. Silicates may differ widely, ranging from crystal-clear quartz to coal-black obsidian (which is volcanic glass, thrown out during an eruption). But most silicate specimens of any size are relatively hard and have a definite glass-like sheen. Sand is primarily quartz, but this is not obvious because the grains are tiny. Manufacturing processes use silicates for products as diverse as ordinary glass (which is made from sand), porcelain, filaments for sensitive electronic instruments, and roofing materials. Many silicates are considered to be gems – agate, onyx, jasper, opal, jade and others.

White veins of glassy quartz, above, are found in many rocks, particularly granite. (The red spots are lichens.) Such veins may indicate to prospectors that valuable ores are present.

Wavy bands of jasper coat a streamside rock in the Australian Outback. Jasper is an opaque, fine-grained variety of quartz; an iron-rich mineral called hematite gives jasper its red colour.

Vivid rings of agate, below, were formed when water deposited silicates inside a rock cavity (a similar process creates geodes).

The hunt for valuable ores

In the 1960s, an oceanographic ship cruising in the Red Sea made an amazing discovery – parts of the sea bed were "paved" with valuable metals. Deep-sea drilling brought up one sample that indicated some of the sea bed was about 30% iron, with lesser amounts of zinc, copper, lead, silver and gold. Even more surprising than the original discovery of the metals was the discovery of how they got there. The metals along zones in the Red Sea and many similar areas are the result of refining – not refineries operated by humans, but by vast natural processes that operate on the crust of the earth.

The explanation for the existence of such deposits of metals goes back to the theory of continental drift. The hard outer crust of the earth is fractured into gigantic plates that shift like chunks of ice in a river. Where hot rock rises from the earth's interior into the sea (as it does in the Red Sea and certain other places), the material cools and then cracks. Sea water invades the fissures and dissolves the many kinds of metals that occur naturally in the basalt (volcanic rock). As the water becomes heated, it rises and is replaced by more cold water, and the process continues. The metals, which are present in only small amounts in basalt, become concentrated in the mud on the sea floor. Near some rifts, this refining process has even created veins of pure metal.

The many forms of copper

Copper is termed one of the seven metals of antiquity because it was one of the relatively few metals known and used in primitive times. The others, which were also either available in a free state or in easily melted ores, were tin, gold, silver, mercury, iron and lead. When copper was mixed with tin (about 90% copper to 10% tin), the result was bronze. Bronze Age implements were stronger than other tools, and brought about drastic changes in warfare, farming and early civilisation in general.

The growing plates on the globe are, in effect, like slow-moving conveyor belts. As new material is welded to the plates along a rift, the plates are enlarged. The metals that are concentrated at the rift are carried outwards, to the opposite margin of the plate. When the outer edges of two plates collide, the heavier plate may slip beneath the lighter one. It is believed that the lower plate is pushed downwards into the earth's molten interior, where it melts. As the plate descends, metals concentrated on its upper surface may be scraped off by the edge of the upper plate, thus creating an even greater concentration of metals. (Sometimes the intense pressures that occur where plates collide transform common minerals into precious stones, including emeralds and jade.) In other areas, the metals may be carried downwards with the plate.

As these ideas developed, geologists began to see that continental drift might be a clue to finding valuable ores (ores are metal-bearing deposits). Traditionally, looking for ores was a hit-or-miss proposition that depended mainly on a lucky prospector discovering an obvious outcrop. As maps were checked, the theory was strengthened; it became apparent that most existing mines are located along the borders of plates. For example, it was discovered that the Mediterranean island of Cyprus, which has been a major copper-producing area for thousands of years, was once under water. In fact, Cyprus is near a former rift that has been raised above sea level. The great metallic wealth of western South America occurs where a plate has been sliding under the continent for millions of years. Gold deposits, such as those in Alaska and California, are associated with plate boundaries.

The new knowledge is already beginning to bear fruit. In 1972 a copper mine began production on Bougainville, an island in the South Pacific that stands beside an active ocean rift; the mine is estimated to hold some 900 million tons of ore. The exploration of similar areas in other parts of the world is under way.

The Red Sea lies over an active fissure, which is gradually pushing Africa away from Asia. But the search is also being made along ancient plate boundaries such as the trough running across the bulge of Africa between Algeria and Nigeria. This has the advantage of traversing dry land. As can be seen from the map, many of the richest areas must lie at the bottom of the ocean. Progress in undersea research may bring them within man's grasp.

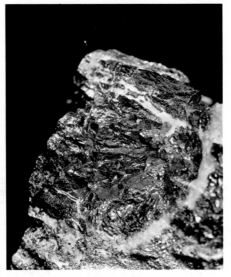

The iridescent tarnish on rock called bornite reminded miners of peacock feathers – hence bornite's common name of peacock ore. To a chemist, peacock ore is copper iron sulphide.

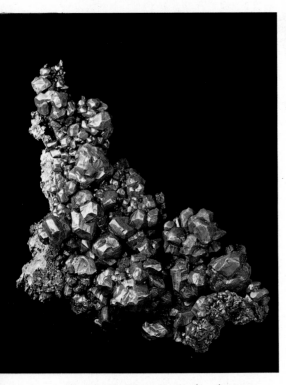

The burnished hue of native (pure) copper makes it easy to identify. The ore came from a lava flow in Michigan, which was worked by Indians long before Europeans arrived.

The brilliant colour and striking bands of this African malachite make it seem quite different from other types of copper. But malachite is indeed a form of copper – copper carbonate.

Ores are more abundant at the boundaries of the plates

The edges of the earth's crustal plates are vast treasurehouses of metal ores, especially near chains of volcanic islands. This map shows the margins of the major plates. As water on the ocean floor is heated, it dissolves and then deposits ores along ridges in the middle of the ocean. The slow expansion of the plates carries metals upwards and outwards from the ridges. Thus concentrations of metals increase. Two plates that grow outwards from a common ridge are often alike in mineral content. Ores found in one plate can lead prospectors to ores in a nearby plate. Metals such as zinc, copper and gold are deposited separately – often in a predictable sequence. In the case where one plate goes underneath another (subduction), some metals are concentrated above the surface; others are carried down.

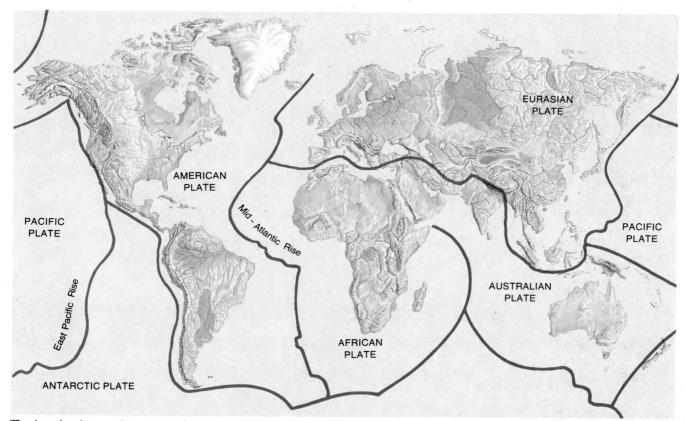

The six major plates, and two mid-ocean rises, are still being charted. In addition to the plates shown, there are many active smaller plates.

Hot, molten basaltic rock wells up from deep within the earth, at the ridges where the earth's crustal plates are formed. When the basalt reaches the sea floor, it cools and cracks. Sea water infiltrates the cracks and dissolves metals contained in the basalt. The water itself is heated and rises back up to the sea floor, where it cools again. Cold water is not as good a solvent as hot water, so most of the dissolved metals are deposited as silt on the sea floor. Much the same process takes place at the opposite edges of the plates, where they collide. One plate is usually deflected deep into the earth, carrying the metal-bearing silt and some sea water with it. When this water is heated in the earth's interior, it rises and deposits the metals once again, in a more concentrated form. Huge deposits await discovery.

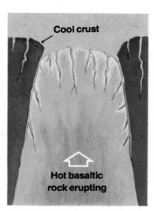

A column of hot basalt rises between two crustal plates where the sea floor spreads.

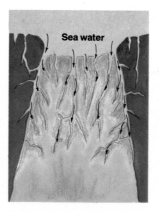

As basalt reaches the top, it cools and cracks. Invading sea water dissolves many metals.

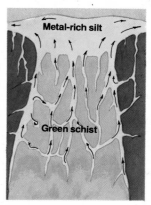

Metals are deposited in silt on the ocean floor. Here, the rock has cooled into schist.

273

Why some minerals are called gems

What most gems have in common is their beauty. A cut diamond will refract light into dazzling, fiery flashes; polished rubies and sapphires may show a star pattern when light strikes them; opals are famous for their rainbows of shimmering flecks and dots. Gems generally share two other characteristics – they are rare and durable.

The definition of a gem is influenced by history. Long before chemists classified minerals by features such as crystalline structure, many small bits of hard materials – often shiny or colourful – were prized in the making of jewellery. Thus some gems are not stones at all. Amber is fossilised sap, pearls are produced by oysters, and coral is the skeletal remains of marine animals.

In common usage, a gem is any mineral (except a metal, such as gold) that is used as jewellery. Fewer than 100 kinds of minerals are classified as gems. A particular mineral, such as beryl, may provide a variety of gemstones. Some specimens of beryl are green, because of the presence of minute quantities of chromic oxide. In a way, chromic oxide might be considered an imperfection, although a valuable one – emeralds are stones of green beryl. Aquamarine is beryl with small amounts of iron; morganite (another gemstone) is beryl coloured pink by lithium.

Similarly, rubies and sapphires are both coloured forms of the mineral corundum, which is to be found in the tool-shed or garage of most homes as emery paper. The hue of these gemstones varies with the amount of the colouring substance they contain, or, in the case of diamonds, with the crystalline structure.

Though important in the past, the distinction between precious and semi-precious stones is not particularly significant today. The value of a gem may change with time, depending on fashion and the relative rarity of the stone. (At present, rubies are the most highly prized.) Technological advances also influence the value of a gem. Perhaps the greatest breakthrough came in 1955, when genuine crystals of diamonds were made in the laboratory for the first time. Diamonds are a form of pure carbon. To make them, scientists heated carbon-containing substances to nearly 2,000°C (3,632°F) and applied a pressure of 1 million lb. per square inch. To date, the diamonds synthesised in the laboratory have been made for industrial purposes, such as the cutting points of drills, and not as gemstones. (The artificial diamonds sold in jewellery shops do not have the same chemical and physical properties as genuine diamonds.)

In nature, as in the laboratory, diamonds are produced by intense heat and pressure. What apparently happens in the earth's interior is that magma, or molten rock, pushes its way up through weak areas to the surface. For diamond formation, carbon and large amounts of gas have to be present. Because of the heat and pressure, some of the carbon may be crystallised into rough diamonds, more or less

The cutting of a diamond is the key to its brilliance

In their natural condition, diamonds look like dull pieces of glass (see below). The ultimate value of a diamond depends on several factors – its colour and weight (measured in carats after the stone has been cut), and whether it is without serious flaws. There is considerable risk involved in the cutting of any potentially valuable stone. If it is struck correctly, its maximum size can be retained, and further cutting can enhance its brilliance. However, if struck at the wrong angle, the stone may shatter. The diamond (right) is a splendid, well-cut specimen of approximately 5 carats.

Ideally, a diamond will reflect light whether it is seen from above or from the side. Many of the famous stones of royalty are surprisingly dull, by modern standards. This is because the art of diamond-cutting (or the cutting of other jewels) was not perfected until relatively recent times. But though some crown jewels may have less lustre than their fame might suggest, no one would risk changing them.

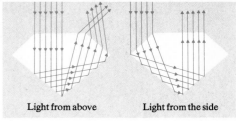

Light from above   Light from the side

the way sand can be melted to form glass. As the gas erupts at the surface, the diamond crystals are propelled upwards. When the core of magma cools, it forms a diamond-rich plug, or pipe, in the earth. Such pipes are made of a rock called kimberlite, first found in Africa.

Diamonds do not always stay in the kimberlite pipes awaiting discovery by man. Those near the surface may be carried great distances by streams and glaciers, and can often be traced back to their source. Near the middle of the 19th century, some farm children found a pretty pebble along the banks of a South African river. The pebble, which turned out to be a valuable diamond, led to the discovery of the now-famous diamond mines of South Africa. A number of diamonds have been found near the Great Lakes, in North America. It seems reasonable to suppose that these diamonds were carried to the spot by glaciers (from kimberlite pipes further north). But so far no one has found their source.

The rounded cut of this ruby brings out the brilliance of the star. This effect, which is called asterism, is caused by gas bubbles trapped inside the stone during formation.

The Burmese Star of Asia, a sapphire, differs from a star ruby not in crystal form, but in the presence of trace elements that give colour.

PHOTO TIPS
Capturing the essence of mineral structure

To create a striking photograph of a mineral, emphasise the special qualities of your subject, such as its crystalline structure, cleavage planes and colour. For example, white mica (below) has minute "terraces" that project at the edges of the crystals. Each terrace is a fracture plane that can be split open with a sharp blade. Mica is often found in "books" with large transparent "pages".

• The best place to photograph a mineral is at home or in a studio – not out in the field. You can adjust the position of the mineral to show the maximum detail of its surface. Use a steady light source, such as photofloods. The light from a flash is generally too brief to let you see all the reflections and shadows.
• Make sure the camera is steady during the exposure; a tripod is ideal.

White mica reflects light like glass, and requires careful placement of the light source. The natural, tilted structure of this mineral creates "caves" that add mystery to the photo.

Selenite crystals often form in caves. The branching form results when crystals of gypsum are free to grow in any direction.

Fibrous green crystals of pyromorphite seem to grow like moss, but the mineral is actually a type of lead ore, shaped and coloured like a plant.

How caves are formed

Typical cave scenery surrounds this cave entrance in West Virginia in America – well-watered vegetation, gently rolling hillsides, and outcroppings of the underlying limestone rock.

Caves invade the earth as the water level drops

Like most formations of stratified rock, the large beds of limestone that underlie many parts of the world are riddled with tiny cracks and seams. The fracture zones run in two directions, vertically and horizontally. (In many illustrations, limestone is shown like brickwork, which is close to reality.) Acidic groundwater, which dissolves limestone, infiltrates these slim channels and slowly undermines the entire limestone formation.

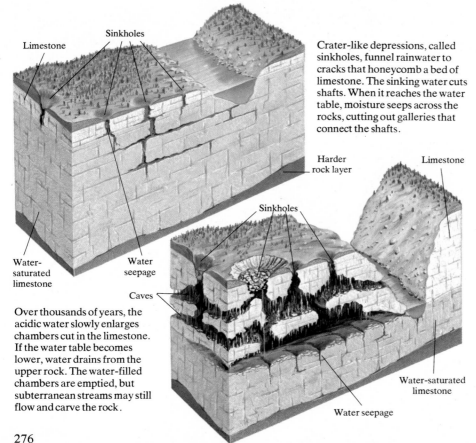

Crater-like depressions, called sinkholes, funnel rainwater to cracks that honeycomb a bed of limestone. The sinking water cuts shafts. When it reaches the water table, moisture seeps across the rocks, cutting out galleries that connect the shafts.

Over thousands of years, the acidic water slowly enlarges chambers cut in the limestone. If the water table becomes lower, water drains from the upper rock. The water-filled chambers are emptied, but subterranean streams may still flow and carve the rock.

Caves are usually formed by water, and most of them are cut in limestone. This kind of rock differs from others because it is formed from the remains of tiny marine plants and animals, and also coral and shellfish. These organisms, which were more common millions of years ago than they are today, absorbed calcium compounds from the sea and concentrated them within skeletal tissues. When the organisms died, the chalk-like materials accumulated and hardened into thick beds of limestone. (Some limestone is formed by other processes, such as evaporation.) As the crust of the earth shifted, many of these former sea beds became part of the continents. Today limestone is especially abundant in parts of Britain, Ireland, France, Yugoslavia and China, and in the south-eastern corner of the United States.

A limestone deposit on dry land is still affected by water. As rain falls through the air and seeps into the soil it picks up carbon dioxide and forms a mild acid. The acidic rainwater dissolves limestone, slowly enlarging its numerous cracks.

Most of this activity occurs in underground layers of rock within the water table – the zone that is saturated with groundwater. Water percolates slowly through limestone formations, carrying substances dissolved from the rock into rivers, and ultimately to the sea. Water-filled cavities are created in the limestone. Some are like huge pits or chimneys; they were formed along vertical cracks in the rock. Others are horizontal chambers, which developed as water oozed along planes of weakness between thick layers of limestone.

As the cavities increase in size, they may connect and form extensive labyrinths filled with slowly moving water. Sometimes the water table drops, because of drought or shifts in the earth's crust. This drains the chambers, leaving the caves dry. Water may still flow through parts of the cave as an underground stream, although other sections may remain completely dry.

At this stage, the flow of a stream may be swift, and a different force may begin to shape the cave. Often, water seeping into the cave is heavily laden with silt and debris, which acts as an abrasive on the underground stream bed. Thus the rate of erosion is increased.

Not all caves are cut in limestone. Some are formed from lava flows. As lava streams downhill, the surface usually cools and hardens before the lava underneath it. When the flow of lava stops, a shell may be left behind that resembles a long tunnel.

Such chambers have an appropriate name – lava-tube caves. Many are small, but at least two, Ape Cave in America and Kazumura Cave in Hawaii, are more than 2 miles long.

The sea also scoops out caves on rugged coasts. Famous examples are Fingal's Cave on the island of Staffa, in the Hebrides, and the Blue Grotto on the island of Capri.

Some of the most spectacular caves are carved in the ice of large glaciers. One room in an ice cave in the North American Rockies was about 250 ft high. Scientists believe ice caves are cut primarily by meltwater, or perhaps by warm air flowing through cracks and crevices. Such caves grow and collapse quickly – sometimes within a few years. Ice caves are hazardous to explore because so-called flakes of ice, weighing up to several tons, may fall from the ceiling.

The Dead Sea Scrolls were found in a cave in Jordan similar to those shown right. Relatively cool and dry conditions in the caves preserved the religious texts for some 2,000 years.

SAFETY AND SURVIVAL
Do's and don'ts of cave exploration

Cave explorers, who are called speleologists, say that the greatest danger underground comes not from natural hazards, but from faulty equipment and negligence on the part of the explorers themselves. The first rule of caving is: "Never enter a cave alone." Join a caving club so that you will always have experienced companions.

• Someone on the outside should be given all the details of your planned cave expedition – the number of people in your party, where you are planning to go and, most especially, when and where you expect to come out. This ensures that help will be sent if you do not turn up at the appointed time and place.

• Be sure that you are in good physical condition, and recognise your limitations. Do not explore an unknown cave if you suspect it will be beyond your capabilities.

• Cave exploration bears a resemblance to mountain climbing, and calls for some of the same equipment. For example, you will need a nylon rope that will support at least 1 ton, wire ladders, pitons, mooring pins and a well-stocked first-aid kit. Proper caving equipment includes more than one light source – a carbide lamp, a torch, candles and waterproof matches.

• Protecting your head with a helmet of the kind used by miners is a good idea. Wear fairly tight-fitting, snag-proof clothing, so as not to be encumbered when you wriggle through narrow passages. Speleologists sometimes haul equipment behind them in a special container – a bullet-shaped metal cylinder 10 in. across and 3 - 4 ft long. Extended cave exploration will require a lightweight sleeping bag, plenty of water in canteens, dehydrated meals and a stove.

• Take along a map of the cave, if one is available. If not, sketch your route as you explore. Note landmarks by looking backwards, this is the way they will appear if you return the way you went in. As an extra safety measure, you might take along a packet of small aluminium squares with a piece of double-sided adhesive tape on the back. Use these squares to mark your trail. Remember to remove such tapes as you leave the cave.

• Do not make a descent if you are not sure you will be able to climb out again.

• Never explore a cave with sinkholes (or in low-lying ground) if there is a chance of rain. There may be no escape from a cave flood. Leave a weather-watcher at the cave entrance to warn the exploring party if heavy rain does threaten.

A waterfall pours into a cave in Colorado, America, with the force of a fire hose. Such a gallery is unusual, and changes shape rapidly.

Strange, silent worlds

Some of the world's most spectacular scenery lies hidden in the dark recesses of caves. In windless chambers, rivers and pools as smooth as glass reflect formations that look like waterfalls, icicles, flowers and lily pads. Although many of the shapes suggest life and movement, they are all made of stone. Sometimes the only sound to be heard is a ceaseless dripping – the tapping note of water.

Water not only removes material from a cave, but also makes a contribution. As water drips from the ceiling, it evaporates and many minerals (dissolved from the limestone rock) are left behind. As each drop adds its load, an "icicle" may form. Like a straw, it has a hollow centre – a slender channel through which the drops flow. When the "straw" reaches several inches in length, the hollow centre usually becomes plugged; water begins to trickle down the outside. The straw becomes a solid, carrot-shaped stalactite, one of the most familiar of cave formations.

Frequently, some water falls to the cave floor before it evaporates. On the floor, another type of formation – a stalagmite – builds up. Stalagmites are usually thick and rounded, because the drops of water splash over a fairly wide area. Many people confuse stalactites and stalagmites. To remember which is which, think of a stalac*tite* as *holding tight* to the ceiling; and of how a stalag*mite might* one day reach it. A stalactite and a stalagmite may grow together, forming a column. Some columns grow to immense proportions and resemble the fluted pillars of a Greek temple. One column in the Cueva de Nerja, near Málaga, in Spain, is nearly 200 ft high.

A free-hanging stalactite in the Poll an Ionain Cave in County Clare, Ireland, is 38 ft long; the tallest known stalagmite is in the Aven Armand Cave at Lozère, in France, and measures 98 ft.

Some cave formations represent growth that occurred over thousands, perhaps millions, of years. But the growth may be quite rapid, if the rate of evaporation is fast and the concentration of minerals in the water is high. Newly abandoned mining machinery in a British cave has stalactites that are already about 6 ft long.

Dream Lake in Luray Caverns in America is a good example of the world of silent beauty to be found in caves, many of which are open to the public. On a guided tour, hidden rivers, exquisite cave formations, gaping chasms and vaulted domes can be inspected in safety – nearly all caves are naturally "air-conditioned" by their structure.

Occasionally, water seeping through the ceiling trickles downwards along the contour of the cave roof. In such cases, the deposits may form draperies with flowing folds and wrinkles. Slow seepage may produce small corkscrew-like shapes called helictites. If a crack is filled with deposits from evaporating water, a slight pressure apparently develops and squeezes the material from the crack. Curving, petal-like formations called cave flowers are the result.

Most of these curious forms are made up of calcium salts dissolved from the surrounding limestone. They are usually white, with sheens of other colours, almost like a coat of gloss paint. Occasionally, other dissolved substances, such as iron or copper, will show up. These impurities may colour the cave formations beautiful tints of red or blue. (In caves where there are guided tours, any green tints you may see are probably algae – encouraged to grow by the presence of lights.)

A cave pool may contain lovely subterranean sculpture. A rocky projection

above the pool sometimes develops a wafer-thin collar of mineral deposits that looks like a lily pad. In especially quiet pools, small mineral rafts actually float on the surface of the water. Minerals are sometimes deposited around grains of sand at the bottom of the pool, forming exquisite shapes called cave pearls. Where the pools spill over, minerals are deposited and may form ornate sculptures that resemble waterfalls. Like the other cave formations, these waterfalls are permanently frozen into their dream-like shapes.

The fanciful sculptures of water and minerals

Stalactites never grow to great lengths – the longest one known measured less than 40 ft. Calcite, the chalky mineral of which most cave formations are made, lacks tensile strength; this means that it cannot sustain much weight. Therefore, when a stalactite reaches a certain size, it usually breaks and falls from the ceiling. If you visit a cave, you will probably notice stalactite fragments on the floor. On the other hand, stalagmites and columns often grow to truly gigantic proportions.

The mineral-bearing water that formed the dripstone above created a series of tiny dykes on the stone's surface. As water flowed around the obstructions, it produced the many ornate, drapery-like ridges.

Unusually delicate, needle-like "flowers", often called helictites, grow in clumps along walls in many cave systems.

Three variations on a single theme

How fast the water drips and evaporates affects the shape of cave formations. Here, most of it evaporated on the stalactite.

This stalagmite (on the ground) has grown faster than the stalactite above it. The two forms may eventually merge.

Columns that look like wedding cakes may develop if there is a great amount of dripping water. Note the frozen appearance of drips.

279

Cave-dwelling creatures

Caves are nature's time capsules. Their vast underground chambers harbour many kinds of animals that have not been seen on the surface of the earth for thousands or even millions of years. Caves have become refuges because, unlike the earth's surface, caves change very little. Ice Ages come and go, forests dry up and become deserts – but underground life goes on just as usual.

If you have ever visited a cave, you probably noticed that various parts of it differed greatly. For example, the opening of a cave is very much like the exterior – sunlight, rainfall and temperature are virtually the same as on the outside. But as you go deeper into a cave, the light intensity lessens and the air becomes damp and cool. This is called the twilight zone – a halfway world between the outside environment and the interior. As the last rays of light fade away, you enter the unchanging world of the deep cave, where the temperature remains nearly the same throughout the year, usually around 10°C (50°F).

The inhabitants of the cave change with the zones. Most of those that live at the mouth of the cave are also found in the outside world. Mosses, ferns, lichens and vines cling to the walls. Swallows nest in the crevices near the cave's mouth. Frogs, mice and other small animals scurry through the accumulation of dead leaves and twigs. Many of these creatures regularly venture into the shelter of the twilight zone, as do snakes, salamanders and hosts of crickets. Perhaps the best-known of all cave residents are bats. Although bats may show a preference for using the twilight zone as shelter, these animals return regularly to the outside world to hunt for food.

The most specialised cave animals are those that never leave the inner cave. These animals, which include certain species of fish, crayfish and flatworms, resemble their counterparts outside the cave. But many of the cave-dwelling species have a ghost-like pallor and cannot see. Some of them do not have eyes at all. The animals are born, reproduce and die without ever leaving the cave, unless they are accidentally carried out. They are called troglodytes – cave-dwellers.

The study of cave life is one of the newest sciences. Apparently, many cave animals are "living fossils". In fact, most troglodytes that live on and in cave soil (such as cave crickets) are believed to be descendants of similar species that inhabited the forest floor during the last Ice Age. As the earth's climate warmed, these creatures took refuge in caves, where conditions continued to resemble their original habitat. During countless generations, they "lost" their colour and their eyes, which served no function in a lightless environment. Numerous cave-dwellers developed enlarged, sensitive feelers (such as the unusually large antennae of cave crickets) which enabled them to perceive their surroundings. Many cave animals respond instantly to the slightest vibration.

In old caves where the fauna have been isolated for many generations, endemic species – that is species that exist only there – have developed. Notable examples occur in Dalmatia, Yugoslavia, where there are many caves, each with its own species of beetle.

All life depends on water, and this is true of cave life as elsewhere. Dry caves not only are devoid of life, they are often like museums, where mummified animals and plants are preserved in dried form. A wet cave is sometimes called "live" – meaning that it can support an animal community. Ultimately, all caves depend on replenishment from the outside world, whether through underground streams, or food brought in by other animals.

Life-styles vary in the three different zones

Living conditions, especially the amount of light, change dramatically from a cave's entrance to the dark interior. Though the zones are not sharply defined, and animals move about from zone to zone, different species usually prefer different zones. Near the entrance, certain creatures may use the cave only temporarily. A cave swallow seeks a site for its cup-shaped nest. A snail will find a dark, moist refuge here. Reddish salamanders favour the slippery rocks of the twilight zone, their climbing activities aided by long tails. Cave crickets and harvestmen feed on decaying material in this region. Contrast the brown crayfish with its close relative from deeper in the cave; the cave crayfish is colourless and has much longer antennae. Similarly, the blind salamander lacks pigment and functional eyes, which would be of little use in the dark interior.

1. Cave swallow
2. Cellar glass snail
3. Cave salamander
4. Cave cricket
5. Harvestman
6. Brown crayfish
7. Cave crayfish
8. Blind salamander

Cave entrance

Twilight zone

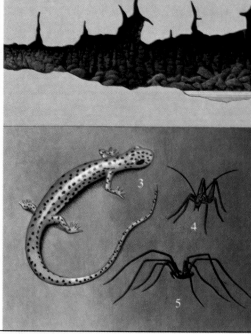

Eerie blue threads hang from the roof of the Waitomo Caves in New Zealand. The sticky, luminescent threads are lures spun by glow-worms – the larvae of certain gnats. Insects which stick to the lures are reeled in.

Swooping through the dark, a European bat locates insect prey by sending out sound waves. Many kinds of bats roost in caves during the day and emerge in great numbers at night. In winter, certain species of bats hibernate in huge colonies inside caves.

Inner cave

Oilbirds nest on ledges inside caves. Like other winged residents of caves, oilbirds bring in food (fruit) from outside. Palm nuts transported from a nearby forest have sprouted inside this Trinidad cave. The bird sees well in the dark; its clicks also act as a kind of sonar.

Following ancient clues

Clues to the mystery of the earth's past are all around us. Steep-walled valleys, glacier-scarred mountain slopes, outcroppings of rocks – all these are full of information. As in every good mystery, the challenge is in recognising what the clues reveal.

The first great geological sleuth was an 18th-century British surveyor named William Smith, who became intrigued by the layers of rocks he saw while building canals in the south of England. He was the first person to notice that the layers (strata) occurred in the same sequence in various locations – as he put it, "like slices of bread and butter". Smith, nicknamed "Strata" by his friends, also noticed that each layer had "fossils peculiar to itself", and that these fossils could be used to identify the layers.

Such an idea seems obvious today, but before Smith's time, few people had realised that the earth had passed through many stages of development, and that each stage had its own characteristic forms of life, which were often preserved in layers of sedimentary rock.

Smith did not realise the full significance of his discoveries, but later scientists did. Earlier conceptions about the history of our planet – including estimates that the earth was only 6,000 years old – were effectively overthrown.

For about a century, fossils were used to establish the age of a particular rock stratum. But it was soon discovered that fossils alone did not explain the records in stone. Climate was part of the story. For example, a period of tropical climate resulted in the formation of great swamps which produced not only characteristic fossils, but also, ultimately, deposits of coal as well. Periods of colder climate produced different fossils, and also other clues, such as the ice-cut valleys and low hills left by glaciers.

By using the evidence from both geological and biological sources, scientists divided earth's history into the Precambrian, the earliest; the Paleozoic (old life); the Mesozoic (middle life), when dinosaurs existed; and the Cenozoic (modern life), which includes the present stage in the world's development.

The earth's fossil time-clock is a relative one. It lets us know which rocks and fossils are older than others, but does not tell us absolute time – the total age of the earth. This could not be detected until the 20th century. The discovery that radioactivity in rocks (such as uranium) changes at a particular rate opened the way to more accurate dating methods.

By studying these radioactive changes, scientists have calculated that the earth is about 4,600 million years old. The earliest fossil record, of one-celled bacteria, is believed to be about 3,400 million years old. Thus life has been present for most of earth's history; human beings, however, have been in existence for only a relatively short part of that time.

NATURE OBSERVER
Ice-Age evidence

The periods of time in historical geology are so great, they seem unreal to many people. One of the few "landmarks" that can be checked is evidence left over from the Ice Ages. About a million years ago, late in the Cenozoic Era, ice began to pile up and travel. There were four major advances and withdrawals of massive glaciers (and any number of minor ones). They left a great deal of evidence as they moved over the land. There are grooves and gouges in rock, and huge amounts of gravel, which is called glacial till. The effect of the Ice Ages is less apparent in the Southern Hemisphere.

Glacial deposits are used all over the world to make boundary walls (left). Grazing is possible, but ploughing is clearly not.

Melting glacial snows left Geiranger Fjord in Norway (above) with the characteristic steep walls of such "drowned" valleys.

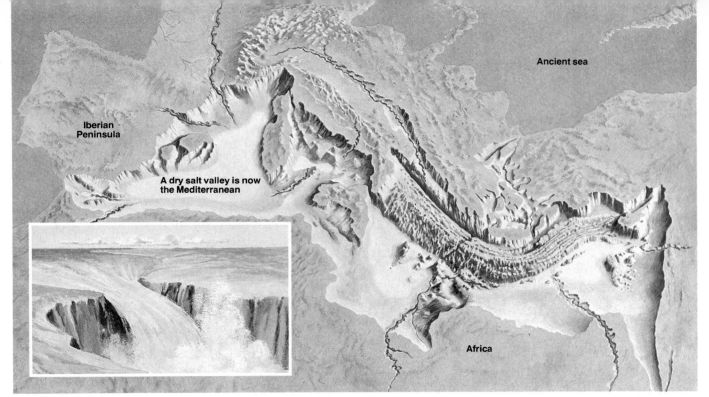

Ancient sea

Iberian
Peninsula

A dry salt valley is now
the Mediterranean

Africa

About 6 million years ago the Mediterranean probably looked as it does in the painting above – like a huge, dry valley lying some 10,000 ft below sea level. Its waters had evaporated because the sea's connection with the Atlantic (at what is now the Strait of Gibraltar) had been blocked by a shifting in the earth's crust. A later shift re-opened the Gibraltar tap. Water thundered in over a waterfall (inset), in a flow estimated at several hundred times greater than that of Niagara. But it took about a century for water to fill the basin.

Tilted layers of rock, millions of years old, are on view at Capitol Reef

It is obvious from the colourful formations at Capitol Reef, in Utah, why the Navajo Indians called this area "the land of the sleeping rainbow". Striations of different colours in the photograph on the right show some of the major strata depicted in the diagram below. (At the top of the photo is the Kayenta formation, then the Wingate, the Chinle and the Moenkopi.) The diagram – of a region not far from where the photograph was taken – is a transect. That is, the diagram takes a straight course across the land and records all the formations along the way. Because the crust shifted, the formations are like so many tipped-up dominoes. They range in age from the Permian Period, which began about 270 million years ago, to the Cretaceous, which ended 65 million years ago. More than once, ocean waves washed inland, covering the area. These seas laid down the major layers of silt. Each in turn hardened into sedimentary rock – mostly shale, sandstone and limestone. The seas receded and eventually the land turned to desert.

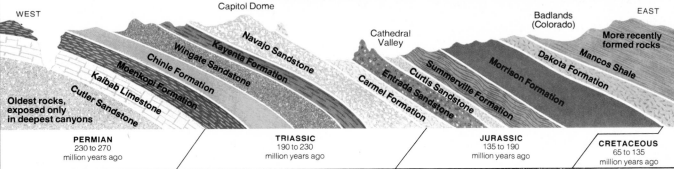

WEST

Capitol Dome

Cathedral
Valley

Badlands
(Colorado)

EAST

More recently
formed rocks

Navajo Sandstone

Kayenta Formation

Wingate Sandstone

Chinle Formation

Moenkopi Formation

Kaibab Limestone

Cutler Sandstone

Oldest rocks,
exposed only
in deepest canyons

Carmel Formation

Entrada Sandstone

Curtis Sandstone

Summerville Formation

Morrison Formation

Dakota Formation

Mancos Shale

PERMIAN	TRIASSIC	JURASSIC	CRETACEOUS
230 to 270 million years ago	190 to 230 million years ago	135 to 190 million years ago	65 to 135 million years ago

Where and how fossils were formed

Everyone knows what a dinosaur looks like, but have you ever wondered how we know? After all, dinosaurs have been extinct for 60 million years. We derive our knowledge of dinosaurs – and countless other animals and plants, some extinct for 3,000 million years – from fossil records.

A fossil is a relic, a trace of ancient life. Usually, a relic must be at least 12,000 years old to be called a fossil. Some fossils are circumstantial evidence: that is, nothing remains of the animal itself except footprints. For example, about 180 million years ago large numbers of dinosaurs walked on huge, claw-like feet over the region now known as the Connecticut Valley in the United States. Their tracks in mud are now fossil imprints in stone.

To become a fossil, a plant or animal usually has to have been buried; this prevents it from decaying quickly or being eaten by scavengers. A few fossils exist because of freezing: the woolly mammoths and other animals frozen during the last Ice Age are the most perfectly preserved animals ever found. Unfortunately, these frozen fossils are rare and perish quickly once they have thawed. Other well-preserved fossils have been mummified by drying.

Moulds and casts make up the majority of fossils. The original plant or animal was covered by sediment, which later hardened. The organism decayed and its materials shrank, leaving a cavity. This empty space became a natural mould. The mould then filled with clay, sand or other fine material, which hardened into a cast.

The most remarkable moulds are found in northern Europe, near the Baltic Sea. There, insects were entombed in the sap of now-extinct coniferous trees. The resinous sap turned into amber, a very hard substance. Though the insects themselves may have decomposed, a look at an amber mould under a microscope reveals incredibly fine details.

The process of petrifaction makes fossils that are actually stone. The soft portions of the organisms, buried in moist soil, soon decay, and water permeates the hard parts that remain. The water deposits minerals in the fine structure of bone or shell, thus reinforcing the strength of the structures. Some fossilised shells of marine animals and bones of land animals were preserved in this way.

Petrified forests are groups of fossil trees whose cellular structure was invaded and preserved by the mineral silica. This type of petrifaction is called replacement. One unusual thing about certain specimens is that some of the original wood has remained intact. The preservation has been so perfect that the cellular structure and annual growth rings of these trees are clearly visible.

Fossils reveal change, presenting a tantalising chain of evidence of the evolution from simple to advanced forms of life. Some, called index fossils, also give the age of rock formations. The extinct trilobites – three-lobed marine animals sometimes called fossil butterflies – are index fossils. Trilobites gradually evolved longer tails and more ornate structures. Because scientists know when the different types of trilobites were common, they can tell the age of rocks containing these fossils.

The earliest-known fossils of vertebrates date back to 500–430 million years ago and are of aquatic animals. Later fossils show the development of amphibians, that lived both in water and on land, then reptiles and mammals.

Fossils lend support to the drifting-continent theory of geology, which includes the idea that all the continents were once joined in a single supercontinent. Fossils of related animals have been found oceans apart. Because these animals could not have travelled such distances, scientists assume the continents must have done the travelling.

Trilobites, which flourished in the Paleozoic Era (600 to 200 million years ago) ranged in size from ¼ in. to 27 in.

Amber is fossilised sap, which often contains preserved insects. The largest amber deposits are along the coasts of the Baltic Sea.

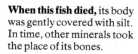

When this fish died, its body was gently covered with silt. In time, other minerals took the place of its bones.

The petrified stumps (below) are of ancient trees. Some of the specimens are in amazing condition; when the silica was dissolved, the wood was still well preserved.

Many amateur fossil-hunters have made important discoveries in the field. By following a few simple rules, anyone can join in the exciting journey back through geological time to the very dawn of life on earth.

● First check to see if you need a permit to dig. Some sites are strictly forbidden, as for example, the region in Africa where traces of early man are still being found.

● Fossils of animals with backbones are discovered comparatively rarely. If you find one, ask for help from a paleontologist (you can get in touch with one through any local college or university).

● But beyond this, the field is wide open and very inviting. All you need is a geologist's pick, large and small chisels for freeing the specimens, old newspapers for wrapping fossils, and a knapsack to carry your finds back to your home.

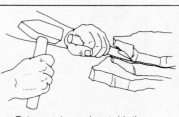

To be certain you do not chip the fossil, insert your chisel along the grain of the rock formation, rather than across it. There are often two fossils in one find – the cast and the mould that formed around it.

Piecing together the evidence

In the long period of human history before evolution was understood, man was beset with puzzles. Huge, inexplicable bones kept coming to the surface, and there was no theory to account for their existence. Gradually, as prehistory came into focus (which explained, among other things, how sea-shell remains found their way to the tops of mountains), the pieces began to fall into place. A backbone, such as the one above, being extracted from its stone bed, is part of just such a detective story. No doubt bones and other remains exist that have not yet been found. More can be expected to turn up in the future. The pursuit never ends.

How can you read footprints? Animals, ancient and modern, leave distinctive markings. Spacing reveals stride, which gives a clue to height and weight.

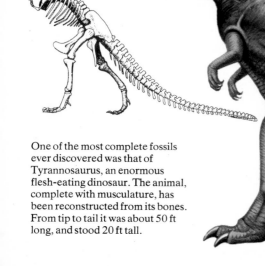

One of the most complete fossils ever discovered was that of Tyrannosaurus, an enormous flesh-eating dinosaur. The animal, complete with musculature, has been reconstructed from its bones. From tip to tail it was about 50 ft long, and stood 20 ft tall.

● Nearly all fossils are found in one general type of rock – the sedimentary layers of sandstone, shale and limestone. These rocks were originally deposited in fine films of sediment – gently, layer on layer. Eventually, the pressure of the accumulated layers turned this relatively soft material to stone. But the layers remain, almost like pages in a book.

● A good place for fossil-hunting is where roads are being built. Any site where layered rock is exposed, new or old, is a likely place. This includes stream beds, building sites and quarries. (Be careful, of course, not to get in the way of bulldozers, or set off an avalanche of loose sand.)

● Keep a record of when and where a specimen was found. The identity of the fossil is usually easy to determine from reference books on the subject.

● This is a hobby that can be enjoyed alone, but often there is a club you can join, where you can get tips on good sites, help in identifying finds, and perhaps swap specimens.

Coal and petroleum: a precious legacy

The energy stored in coal and petroleum originally came to the earth from the sun. The bulk of the present-day supplies was laid down some 600 to 200 million years ago, when tropical conditions were widespread. Lush, swampy forests produced huge trees; warm coastal seas swarmed with microscopic forms of life. When these organisms died, much of their tissue was recycled as it is today – through scavenging and decay. But a significant amount of dead plant and animal material was covered with mud, which prevented complete decomposition.

With the passage of time, as layer upon layer of fine sediment was deposited over the once-living material, the sheer weight turned the sediments to rock. Sandwiched between the layers, both coal and petroleum were produced and preserved under pressure. Coal was formed mostly of giant fern-like plants that have only small counterparts today. (Coal may still be forming here and there on earth, but conditions are not right for the production of significant quantities.)

The weight of the sedimentary rock gradually caused some changes in the coal lying beneath it – pressure produces heat, and heat accelerates chemical reactions. The coal subjected to less pressure is softer and more porous; this type is called bituminous coal. Anthracite is harder, burns more cleanly, and is generally found deeper in the earth; it may occasionally be found near the surface. But anthracite is always the product of great pressure.

Under the microscope, coal's origins are astoundingly clear. It is not uncommon to find the imprint of a perfect fern frond in a piece of coal that has split open along the seam, where the frond settled gently in the mud.

Petroleum is mainly of animal, rather than plant, origin. It has been known and used since ancient times, but more as a medicine and a curiosity than anything else. Not until the development of the internal combustion engine did petroleum assume any great importance in the lives of human beings. Today, petroleum fuels provide most of our energy needs; coal is second. There is now worldwide concern that known reserves of both liquid and solid fuels are in danger of being exhausted.

Petroleum was formed mostly of single-celled marine animals, similar to the planktonic (or floating) animals found today. These microscopic animals ate plants, such as algae, which had originally captured the energy of the sun by photosynthesis.

Unlike coal, petroleum may not be found where it was formed. Being a liquid, it readily flows through the porous rocks around it, sometimes collecting in so-called traps. These traps usually occur where layers of impervious rock cap a segment of porous rock, holding the petroleum the way you hold something in your cupped hands.

Although geologists speak of "pools" of petroleum, it is usually stored in countless, minute pores of rock such as sandstone. When these rocks are drilled, the petroleum, which is often under huge pressure, flows out as if from a sponge. Sometimes, a gusher results, literally raining buried sunshine.

Coal was formed in swamps millions of years ago

Coal varies so greatly in its composition that geologists classify it simply as a sedimentary rock – one of the few rocks that will burn. The purest coal, containing up to 95% carbon, may have been formed from a swampy forest such as the one in the illustration on the right. Ideal conditions for the formation of coal were forests that grew continuously for many centuries, free of muddy inundations. If the plant remains were later buried at a great depth, under tremendous pressures, the result would be the finest coal (anthracite). In international trade, coal is divided into about a dozen different kinds on the basis of hardness and other physical and chemical properties. Impurities in coal, such as clay, produce most of the ash and cinder left behind when coal is burned. When coal has sulphur in it, smog may be the result. That is why there are laws controlling the use of coal.

Key to ancient coal forest

1. Tree fern	4. Giant horsetail
2. Giant dragonfly	5. Giant cockroach
3. Scale tree (Lepidodendron)	6. Scale tree (Sigillaria)

What all fossil fuels have in common . . .

Refining can transform crude petroleum into a wide array of products – from asphalt for roads to lubricating oils or gases for fuel.

Wherever life is present (or has left its remains), you will find hydrogen and carbon – in chemical compounds called hydrocarbons. Materials as diverse as paraffin, benzine, naphtha and asphalt are all hydrocarbons. So are the petrol that powers cars and the coal that heats the furnaces of home and industry. With a skill that would make the ancient alchemists green with envy, modern chemists are able to transform hydrocarbons to the kinds of substances needed for many particular functions. The simplest hydrocarbon has one carbon atom and four hydrogen atoms. It is so light, it is a gas – methane. The heaviest hydrocarbons – such as pitch and asphalt – have immense molecules with as many as 100 carbon atoms. Some, called aromatics, give off a distinct odour.

CHAPTER TEN

Participation is the key to enjoyment

The time to enjoy the out of doors is today, rain or shine. The place is up to you. Wherever you venture, here are thoughts to take along.

Human beings belong out of doors as much as stars and flowers. But there is no denying that the rush of living and working has had the effect of making many of us unfamiliar with the natural world. And, in one important way, many of us *are* aliens. We need to relearn what our forefathers knew, and native peoples still seem to understand intuitively – and that is the practice of frugality. That is what conservation means – never taking more from nature than we really need, never leaving behind unnecessary traces of our presence, and not inflicting wounds on the earth.

There are many, many things to do out of doors that are both pleasant and sound from the standpoint of preserving nature. But because the growth of human populations throughout the world is putting stress on the resources of our planet, we need to be more careful. The undiscovered wilderness is more a wish than a reality; most of the land is already in use.

Where to go, then, to enjoy nature? If you are careful, there is no reason *not* to go to wilderness areas, but nature is also close by – as near as your window or your back garden. City parks and farm roads are rich in natural dramas. Nature is always ready to reclaim land and occupy nooks and crannies. Little natural communities will spring up wherever there is the slightest chance to do so. But we do have to be friends to the land, to plants and to animals. We have to look at them as earlier people did, with sympathy and respect. Being out of doors is good for the human spirit – and nature can use all the friends it can find in its struggle to survive.

It is fun to go out on a walk with others, because people seldom see the same thing in exactly the same way. For one person, the sighting of a particular bird may be a first; for another, it may be a renewed acquaintance; for a third, there may be amusement in hearing the notions of others, accurate or not.

Ways to help preserve nature

So simple a thing as a closed gate is important to keeping the world in order. Animals that live within the gates – dogs and livestock – are thereby spared dangerous forays on to roads, where they may be killed or do damage. Respecting fences is not mere conformity, but a sensible recognition that few people would put up a fence without having a good reason.

The key to protecting nature is just that – respect. All creatures, great and small, have a fair claim to existence. Animals should be allowed to live their lives unmolested. The same goes for plants, which deserve protection from damage by unthinking passers-by. It is, of course, acceptable to pick up fallen leaves and take them home. But all too often, people will casually pull off a leaf or a branch for no apparent reason. One branch may not seem to count, but there are multitudes of people out of doors these days, and such injuries add up. For much the same reason, it is a form of conservation to stay on pathways, wherever they are clearly marked. In this way, the compacting of the soil from human footsteps is confined to a single track, and the rest of the area can remain in its natural condition.

Nature is made up of marvellous surprises. Half the fun is in finding rare species of caterpillars and plants, for instance, or discovering your own caves and rock sculptures. One possible explanation of why people paint graffiti on rocky outcrops is the human need to establish a connection with nature. The need is real and strong, but there are any number of better ways to touch the pulse of nature than to mark the land or take home plants or animals. Photography is the easiest way to capture nature, but sketching, taking notes, and recording sounds on tape are also satisfying, lasting – and cause no damage. Part of keeping nature at its best is being considerate about playing portable radios. Listen to them with earphones or, better still, leave them at home.

What you do influences everyone who sees you. If children or inexperienced holidaymakers see you carefully picking up rubbish and cleaning up a camp site, they will be more likely to do the same thing. Everyone has heard about preventing forest fires, but it is a point that can hardly be over-emphasised – a careless match, cigarette or untended campfire can cause truly horrifying damage. Your own behaviour can make conservation seem more important than all the lectures in the world.

This applies to parks and the other pockets of natural life, such as grassy, tree-lined squares, in towns and cities. Teaching youngsters to enjoy what is there, without spoiling or littering it for those who come later, is good training for treks into the countryside.

At home, there are many simple but effective conservation measures you can put into practice. For example, pile fallen leaves into a compost heap instead of burning them. By doing this, you will recycle the nutrients in the leaves, and gain fertile soil for your garden at the same time. When you use pesticides, follow directions carefully; use chemicals sparingly. Instead of spraying with pesticides, many people plant marigolds or geraniums to discourage harmful insects.

If you can spare space in your garden, why not let nature have its way? Letting an area run wild is an important means of preserving the native plants and animals of a region. A thicket is especially inviting to birds. You might build a pile of branches, starting with the greenery left over from Christmas (including the tree itself). Choose a clear space for such a pile – not too near buildings or trees, where it might be a fire hazard. Another way to encourage wildlife is in the plants you choose. Some kinds are attractive to birds and butterflies because of their flowers, seeds or berries.

Your local garden club or the information office of a botanical garden can tell you which species of plants are appropriate for your region.

This newly hatched tropical gecko will soon go about its business of eating moths, flies and mosquitoes. All animals merit consideration, but this little creature offers an additional attraction – it utters loud, startling sounds that have earned for it the name of Guam canary.

A healthy, vigorous common mullein (left) has caused many a passer-by in America to engage in a tug-of-war with it – and win. But there is an unfortunate side-effect to such casual weed-pulling. For when the mullein dries out in winter, its seed stalk provides food for wild animals, including such birds as the chickadee (above) that has found an unmolested specimen of this unappreciated plant.

PHOTO TIPS
If you can't get rid of them, catch them on film

Since fox raids are unavoidable in many suburban areas, you might as well take advantage of the situation and try to get a good photograph of the culprit. If you exercise a little patience, nature will come to you.
• Put your dustbin close to an area where you can hide, such as near the garage.
• Use a telephoto lens so that you can focus on the animals without being so close that you frighten them. Use an electronic flash or flashbulbs for illumination.
• If there is not enough light from street lamps or neighbouring houses, you may need an extra light to see when your subjects arrive. A red floodlight, such as those sold for outdoor holiday displays, may serve the purpose. Direct the light at the bins and put it just close enough so that you are able to see. Many animals' eyes perceive red light poorly, and the animals will behave as if it were dark. This set-up will also allow you to observe them from a nearby window.
• At camping grounds, too, keep your camera ready. Badgers and squirrels may nose around looking for food.

Tracks, trails and traces

The chances of your seeing the nocturnal hunting of a fox, or the narrow escape of its prey, are slight. But in the clear light of day, you may be able to reconstruct the movements of each animal by reading the tracks it left in snow or moist earth. By knowing where to look and what to look for, you can come to know all sorts of animals you may never actually see. A field guide to animal tracks is a must for precise identification. The size and shape of animal droppings are also a help in identification.

The techniques of tracking animals in this way were evolved by hunters. They can also be used, however, by nature-lovers who wish only to observe.

By following animal tracks, scientists have gained information about animals that was not known by direct observation. For example, when biologists followed many miles of fox trails, they were surprised to find out – from evidence left on the trail – that the foxes ate mostly small rodents and carrion, rather than chickens and pheasants (as had been thought earlier).

You can find animal tracks almost everywhere – including cities. Squirrels have even left tracks on the wet cement of new pavements. In open areas, you can usually find tracks wherever there is cover (around trees, bushes and fallen logs) and along barriers such as cliffs, fences and stone walls. The edges of ponds and streams are good places to look, too, because the animals seek water. Once you find tracks, look for more in the same place on later outings. Some animals habitually follow the same "highways"; in Britain, many badger paths are known to be centuries old.

Mud and snow usually carry the clearest tracks, but you may also find them in dust, sand and clay. Rocks and logs may be stamped with the muddy footprints of animals that came from a nearby stream. A particularly good time to look for tracks is just after rain or a snowfall. Of course, you must get close to tracks in order to examine them, but you should do so carefully, to avoid destroying them. Almost every animal makes some sort of tracks – from a snail (which leaves a glistening trail) to an otter (which can be identified by its large footprints).

In learning to recognise tracks of different species, start with some of the basic types you are likely to encounter. Mice, squirrels and rabbits commonly travel by bounding, with the back feet usually landing ahead of the front feet. Many mammals, such as squirrels and badgers, press their whole foot – heel and toes – in the ground when walking. Predators such as cats and foxes, which depend on speed, run mainly on their toes; the forward part of their footprint makes the deepest impression.

Deer and other cloven-hoofed animals walk on their toes, which are modified into hoofs; they leave easily recognisable tracks.

Some trails tell tales. If the two toes of a hoofprint are far apart, the animal was probably running. On a sandy beach you may see the innumerable tracks of sandpipers, and the little holes where they pecked in the sand for food. Birds are hard to identify from their tracks alone, but you can often tell if the tracks were made by birds with webbed feet (such as ducks), with lobed feet (coots), or with long toes (herons). If the prints of the two feet are side by side, the bird was hopping; if the footprints are staggered, the bird was walking.

 COLLECTOR'S TIPS
Preserving animal tracks in plaster

Casts of animal tracks can be made with a mixture of two parts of plaster of Paris and one part of water. The plaster will harden quickly and must be mixed just before use. The original cast is called a negative. To make an exact duplicate of the track – a positive – you must make a cast of the negative. With deep, muddy tracks, there may be a lip or overhang that would lock the cast together after you have made the positive. In this case, you should use paraffin wax for the original cast. A plaster positive is then made, and the paraffin can be melted out in a warm oven.

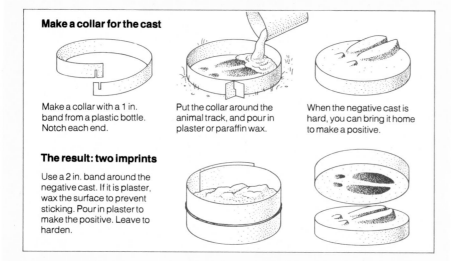

Make a collar for the cast

Make a collar with a 1 in. band from a plastic bottle. Notch each end.

Put the collar around the animal track, and pour in plaster or paraffin wax.

When the negative cast is hard, you can bring it home to make a positive.

The result: two imprints

Use a 2 in. band around the negative cast. If it is plaster, wax the surface to prevent sticking. Pour in plaster to make the positive. Leave to harden.

Identifying mammal prints

From foxes to finches to frogs, most animals make tracks. Mammal prints are the easiest to identify – which is fortunate indeed, as the wild creatures themselves may seldom be visible. As the prints shown here indicate, species with similar feet and methods of locomotion make similar tracks. First learn the similarities, and then the differences.

Compare the shapes and sizes

The size and shape of a track reveal a lot about an animal. Hand-like prints, such as those made by squirrels and badgers, indicate an inquisitive, dextrous creature. Note the hare's footprints. When hopping, the heel of the hind foot shows; when running, only the toes touch.

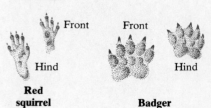

Front
Front
Hind
Hind
Red squirrel
Badger

The common adder moves over sand much as an eel swims through water. Its tracks are a record of the lithe movements of its body.

Heavier animals, like these red deer, make deep tracks, especially when the ground is soft after rain. As they run, the two toes in each hoof spread; the wider the toe marks, the faster the deer are travelling. Look also for signs that they have lain down.

Bird tracks are hard to identify. Look at their overall size and shape, the length and number of toes, and whether or not feet are webbed.

Some hoofprints are split in two

Hoofed animals, called ungulates, have toes enclosed in horny sheaths. Most ungulates – deer, antelope, goats and cattle – have two toes on each foot. When these animals run or jump, their tracks show the pair of toes spread apart. Single-toed ungulates include horses and zebras.

Domestic sheep

Roe deer

Red deer

Reindeer

Tracks in dry soil differ from those in mud

Tracks made by the same animal vary dramatically, depending on the material in which they are left. Some surfaces hold a detailed imprint, but others register only a vague blob that is harder to identify.

Wood mouse in sand **Wood mouse in mud**

Front

Hind

Front

Hind

Hedgehog

Front

Hind

Hind

Front

Hind

Hare **Common rat** **Otter**

How to tell cats from dogs

Cat and dog tracks have large heel pads and four toes. House cats make miniature versions of tiger prints. As cats usually keep their claws retracted, claws do not show in their tracks. Most prints from members of the dog family have toenails.

Cocker spaniel

Red fox

House cat

Wild cat

Birds – where and when

The wings of birds make them the most mobile of all animals, even more widely distributed over the globe than insects. Birds have populated every habitat on earth. Penguins flourish in Antarctica; sandgrouse and larks survive in deserts; seabirds live on the open ocean for months at a time. Wherever there is food to sustain life, some birds will take advantage of it for themselves and their families.

The key to finding birds is knowing what they eat. Each major habitat – such as grassland or forest – provides different foods and attracts a distinctive community of birds. Where two or more habitats meet, plant food is especially plentiful. This attracts not only plant-eating birds but also insects – and therefore insect-eaters. Swamps, forest edges and meadows are smaller neighbourhoods that are especially good for birdwatching.

A birdwatcher soon learns to recognise sites that are attractive to birds, and to predict which species might be found there. Sparrows favour weedy fields; thrushes, blackbirds and robins haunt bushy areas. In spring, warblers and greenfinches seek blossoming trees; in winter, finches flock around seed-bearing birches. When in fruit, wild cherries attract robins and bullfinches. Old apple orchards draw warblers and pine groves shelter owls. Certain times and places, of course, are easier than others for actually seeing the birds; visibility is better over water than in a forest.

Almost invariably, birds nest close to their food supply. Resident (nesting) birds in any locality seldom vary from one year to the next; if the environment remains unchanged, the same kind of bird will return again and again, say, to a bird-box or nesting territory. Once you are familiar with an area, you will be able to predict which birds will be there at the same time next year.

Patterns of bird behaviour change, however, and it is often the devoted local birdwatcher who is the first to record a trend of great scientific interest.

Spring and autumn are the migration seasons. At these times, you are most likely to see species you have not seen before. After a storm, migrating birds may appear in unexpected places, far from their usual range. Normally shy and elusive birds often seem fearless during migration. For example, in autumn, St James's Park, in the heart of London, teems with hungry birds chasing insects directly over people's heads.

Most of Britain's summer visitors, and all the winter ones, are migrants. In summer, warblers, nightingales, cuckoos and swallows travel north from Africa. Winter visitors, such as ducks, geese and waders, go north to the Arctic. There is also an east-west migration to Britain in autumn, of winter thrushes, starlings and occasionally waxwings from northern Europe.

Migration seasons are actually longer than you might expect, because different birds start out at different times. Arctic shorebirds start south in July, at a time when the tundra-nesting ducks and geese are still busy raising their broods. The northward movement is faster and more direct than the southern migration because in spring birds feel a sense of urgency to mate and nest.

Most migrants fly by night. (With a telescope, you can sometimes see them silhouetted against the full moon.) Fortunately for birdwatchers, nocturnal migrants usually stop to rest and feed during the day. Certain coastal resting areas are well known to birdwatchers. For huge flocks of snow geese and sea ducks, visit the bays and estuaries of East Anglia, or along the flat coastlines of Belgium and Holland. In America, the lakes and marshes of Oregon and California offer similar concentrations of waterfowl. Further south, on the Caribbean coast of Texas shorebirds from the Arctic mingle with species from western marshes; long-legged tree ducks, which are residents of the area, share their living space with ducks that come from all parts of North America.

In a sun-flecked cypress swamp, a little blue heron, still in white, first-year plumage, takes a rest from its feeding activities (right). Later, its snowy feathers will be replaced by the slate-blue plumage of the adult bird.

Three birds, all called robins

The common names of birds are a source of much confusion. The same bird may have different names, depending on the locality – and entirely different birds may have the same name. When the English colonists went to America and saw a thrush with a red breast, they called it a robin, after their own familiar bird. In Australia, European settlers applied the name to a group of birds related to flycatchers

Erithacus rubecula

The original robin, a native of Europe, is a small cousin of the thrush

Turdus migratorius

The American robin is a typical thrush, with close relatives in Europe and tropical America

Petroica phoenicea

The flame robin is an Australian flycatcher. Females lack red breasts

A bird-table invites birds to visit you

 BIRDWATCHING TIPS
Keeping a life list

"What is a life list, and why should I keep one?" new birdwatchers ask. A life list is a written record of every bird species you have seen and identified. With such a list, you will not have to depend on your memory.

• To be included in a life list, a bird must be alive and in the wild. (Visitors to a bird-table also count.) Get an experienced watcher to confirm the identifications if you are not sure.

• When you go on a trip, take a notebook and record birds as you see them. Or use the field cards published by a local bird club. These notes will be the source material for your life list.

• You can keep your life list in a scrapbook alongside the descriptions of the species, or in the index pages.

• For permanent records, use file cards and boxes. One large card for each species is preferable to several small ones that fill up quickly. Or you may want to use a looseleaf notebook. Type the bird's common and scientific names in the upper left corner – for example, THRUSH, SONG (*Turdus philomelos*). Note the date and place of your first sighting; add later ones.

• File the cards alphabetically by the bird's common name. Later, you will probably want to organise the cards according to bird families.

• Other kinds of lists may appeal: a garden list; trip lists; yearly lists; county, regional, or continental lists. Your life list will provide the data.

The songthrush, a handsome winter visitor, consumes large quantities of seeds

A male chaffinch will fight for its place at a bird-table. It stays all year round

If a quarrelsome jay arrives, other birds leave

Blue tits boldly snatch a bite from an occupied table and sometimes attack milk bottles for the cream

The nuthatch is an insect-eater, but it also relishes nuts and seeds

Food draws birds – if you want lively company in your garden put up a bird-table. Plans for tables, advice on bird food, and lists of food-bearing plants are available in many books. In addition to food, be sure to supply water. Plant shrubs near the table so that the birds will have hiding places from predators

House sparrows scratch on the ground for fallen food

The hedge sparrow, or dunnock, forages on the ground for food

How to recognise birds

The easiest way to learn about birds is to start with your local species. This automatically gives you both a clearly identified habitat (coast, forest, park, meadow), and also many opportunities to see a fairly stable population of birds. The problem of large numbers of bird species is immediately scaled down by the place. (This is true whether you are near home or on holiday in an unfamiliar area.)

It is also best to turn to local experts or a bird club, where a local bird list may be available. Birdwatchers welcome beginners. They will help you by pointing out field marks, and confirming your tentative identifications. A few walks with these experts and you will learn which birds can be recognised from a distance (a soaring hawk, for example), and which need a closer look through binoculars (a warbler in a tree-top or a member of the sparrow family, seen briefly in a bush).

Size and shape, field marks and behaviour are the major means of recognition. In a short time, you will find you can pinpoint a species by going straight to its major identification points.

Size and shape

Overall proportions: estimating size is the first step in recognition. Choose three common birds and learn their relative sizes and shapes. Then you can compare other birds with them

Bills: the shape and length of a bird's bill are clues to its habits and identity. Waders have long, probing bills; seed-eaters, thick, stubby bills; insect-eaters, thin, sharply pointed bills

Necks: how do you recognise two dark birds swimming at a distance? Look at the neck. If it is long and thin, the bird is a cormorant; if short and thick, it is a great northern diver

Legs: length of legs helps in sorting out the shorebirds. Sandpipers' legs vary from the lanky limbs of the greenshank to the stockier build of the snipe. Plovers have short legs

Wings and tails: many birds can be told in flight by their silhouettes overhead. A deeply forked tail separates the swallow from the martin. Contrast the falcon's pointed wings and long tail with the hawk's broader wings and tail

Behaviour and flight patterns

What a bird does may tell more about it than looks. Both the lesser spotted woodpecker and the nuthatch cling to trees, but one feeds head up, the other often hangs head down. The spotted flycatcher sits erect and wags its tail; a wren usually cocks its tail. The hedge sparrow hops and scratches with both feet while a songthrush walks and runs

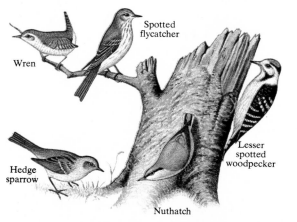

Take off: dabbling ducks and coots often feed together. To tell them apart, watch them rise from the water. Ducks climb vertically; coots patter along before becoming airborne

Field marks

Crested tit

Waxwing

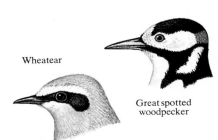

Wheatear

Great spotted woodpecker

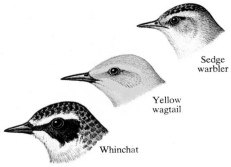

Sedge warbler

Yellow wagtail

Whinchat

Crests: birds with pointed crests, like the species above, are easily recognised. In other birds, modified feathers form plumes (quail), horns (horned lark), and "ears" (owls)

Face patterns: bright cheek patches combined with black eye markings aid in sorting out the many warblers, as well as other birds. Check your bird guide to become familiar with them

Eye lines, eye rings, spectacles: you will need binoculars to pick up the field marks of these birds. All three have close relatives that lack the eye markings

Mistle thrush

Song-thrush

Goldcrest

Tree sparrow

House martin

Bullfinch

Breast spots: to identify sparrows and thrushes, look at the number of spots. The mistle thrush is heavily spotted, other thrushes less so. Sparrows have a central spot, or "bib"

Caps and crowns: rusty caps are worn by tree sparrows. This goldcrest's vivid crown is always visible; but less brilliant head markings may be quite hard to spot

Rump patches: as a bird flies from you, a light rump is a conspicuous recognition signal – you can hardly mistake a martin. And in any plumage a bullfinch's back stands out

Hawfinch

Common redstart

Avocet

Common teal

Collared flycatcher

Tail marks: conspicuous white outside tail feathers occur in some birds such as the finches. In courtship, the redstart splays its tail to show a blaze of flame-red

Wing patterns: many waterbirds show conspicuous wing patches – it helps to learn the markings of some of the common species. The shelduck, like the goosander and avocet, flashes a striking all-over design

Wing bars: these light markings identify some of the numerous species of flycatchers. Some warblers have wing bars too

Canada goose

Long-tailed duck

Kestrel

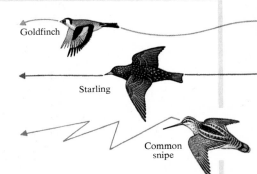

Goldfinch

Starling

Common snipe

Formation flying: Canada geese, well known for their precise V-flights, are champions of this art. Cormorants and white pelicans often form V's. Brown pelicans fly in long lines

Hovering and diving: one of the few birds able to hang with beating wings above one spot is the kestrel; a plunging dive follows. This is a feat of aeronautics shared with the much smaller kingfisher

Flight lines: a bird's flight line is a useful behaviour trait. Finches – and woodpeckers too – have a bounding, undulant flight. A starling's flight is direct. A snipe zigzags away

Watching bird behaviour

Did you know that a car makes an excellent observation hide? Open-country birds, especially those that feed or nest near a road, accept a car as a natural object. A hawk perched on a telephone pole will allow you to examine it closely through your binoculars – as long as you stay inside the car. But just step outside, and off it flies! The small wire-perchers (such as swallows, yellowhammers and sparrows) and the fence-post sitters, such as meadowlarks, can best be seen from a

Royal terns are evenly spaced along a seaside railing – an arrangement that could easily be reshuffled by a persistent newcomer. Spacing behaviour can be seen among many species.

car moving slowly along a country road. Birdwatching by car is an ideal rainy-day occupation for the entire family.

Watching holes is another activity that allows you to observe bird behaviour without disturbing a nest or alarming parent birds. Almost every woodland or wild-life sanctuary has a few dead trees with one or more holes. During the breeding season, most of these holes will be occupied – perhaps by a great spotted woodpecker, a nuthatch or a tawny owl. Station yourself where you have an unobstructed view, and wait until a head pops out or a parent flies in with food.

A variety of songbirds undoubtedly nest in your locality – even in your garden. It is usually easy to locate their nests, whether they are high in an elm, like the oriole's swinging hammock, or inside your garage, like those of the swallow and robin. You can discover the nests by keeping an eye out for birds carrying nesting materials early in the season. Later in the year, you will see them carrying food for the young. Most birds that nest close to human beings develop considerable tolerance and do not seem to mind being watched from a reasonable distance. But use your binoculars, and never disturb a nest.

Remember, that if you stay near a nest and keep the birds away too long, their eggs or young may become too chilled for life to survive.

Identifying a bird, or even locating its nest, is not all there is to observing bird behaviour. Nesting activities, incubation,

feeding of young, and general social behaviour differ for each of the major groups, such as shorebirds or birds of prey. Most bird books arrange species in such groups.

For the most rewarding experiences, be prepared to devote some time to watching a bird in action. Note its method of feeding. A flycatcher will sit motionless on a bare twig until an insect passes by; after a quick foray, the successful hunter will return to the same twig. A gull will drop a mussel or a crab on to a paved surface, cracking the shell to get at the meat.

Courtship behaviour is easier to observe in a colony of birds than among individual pairs of small woodland birds. For example, from a suitable distance you can watch how a female tern receives the ritual gift of a small fish, and how the males protect their nesting sites with stabbing beaks. Noisy squabbling and fights characterise the early settlement of a sea-bird colony. Later, the birds coexist in relative peace.

Hawks and eagles have distinctive courtship displays – thrilling sky shows where the partners may circle higher and higher, crossing and recrossing each other's path until they are almost out of sight, then closing their wings in a power dive. It is not difficult to locate the bulky nest of a pair of hawks; once you have, these proud birds, which often nest in partially wooded areas, are always worth watching. Britain's few eagles are found only in the Scottish Highlands.

BIRDWATCHING TIPS
What to do when a baby bird falls from its nest

A baby bird that has fallen from its nest arouses everyone's sympathy. Parents and teachers are often faced with a tearful child carefully holding a tiny robin. If this happens to you, reassure the child and ask where he or she found it.
● Happily for the bird, the best thing to do is the simplest. If the nest can be found, put the bird back. If you cannot reach the nest, place the bird on the lower limb of a tree or on top of a tall shrub where a prowling cat is unlikely to find it. A hungry young bird cheeps continuously, and its parents will soon find and feed it. If the nestling is able to fly, the adults will encourage it to flutter to safety. Parent birds do not desert a nestling simply because it has been handled by a human being.
● If the baby bird cannot be returned to the

vicinity of its nest, call the nearest nature centre, or ask the advice of an experienced ornithologist; for feeding a young bird is a full-time occupation. A nestling must be fed every 15 to 20 minutes from early morning to dusk. That is not the only problem – you also have to give it the appropriate diet, duplicating as nearly as possible its natural food. A young robin, for instance, needs a continuous supply of earthworms (finely chopped beef can be substituted). Drop the food in its beak as its mother would.
● It is hopeless even to consider caring for a tiny, blind nestling that has not yet developed feathers. Added to the feeding problem is the need to keep it warm. The chances that you will rear it successfully are very slight, so do not be disappointed if you cannot save it.

Dislodged from its nest, perhaps blown down by a spring storm, a fluffy nestling finds comfort in a human hand.

The ballet of sandhill cranes takes place in early spring, as the birds migrate northwards. Both sexes take part in courtship rituals that help the birds to determine which are males and which are females. Cranes are champion dancers. Loud trumpeting accompanies the bowing, leaping and strutting. Other species in which the sexes are similar, such as herons and storks, pair off for quieter displays in private.

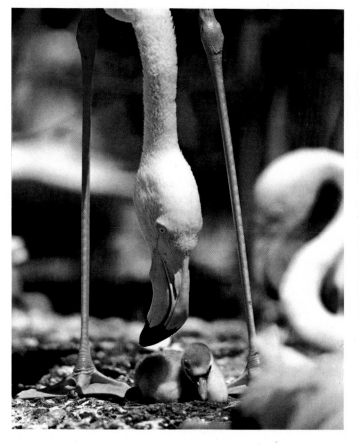

What appears to be a squabble among different gulls is actually a family discussion. The dark juvenile on the ground is clamouring for food. As the youngster matures, parents are less willing to feed it.

Tender loving care for the small downy chick is evident in the attitude of this adult African flamingo. Note that the chick's bill is straight, quite unlike the angular and bent bill of its long-legged parent.

Special tips for nature subjects

When you focus your camera, you also focus your mind. A camera opens your eyes to nature, allowing you to observe with greater clarity the details of a scene you may pass every day. Trees and meadows, mountains and valleys, lakes and streams, the expansive dome of the sky are all seen in a new way.

A photographer is an artist who paints with light; it is light that produces chemical changes in the film. When using a camera you must constantly judge the quality of light – the softness of morning and evening, the brilliance of midday, and the astounding differences between the light of one region and that of another. You must also consider how clouds, fog and haze influence the mood of the scene.

Time is on your side when you are photographing landscapes or scenic details. With animals in motion, however, you may have only an instant in which to compose and shoot. Unless the light is changing rapidly, at dawn or dusk, you have time to plan your shot carefully. If conditions are not right, you will often have the opportunity of photographing at another time.

Take pictures of scenes and subjects *you* like; work for results that please *you*. By sticking to your own standards, and not trying to imitate someone else's photographic style, the results will express your personality.

Try to tell a story. If, for example, the subject is very small, such as a "forest" of moss, include a leaf or other natural object that will reveal scale. If you want to capture the mood of autumn – perhaps the last leaf on a tree – be sure to include a section of bare branch to emphasise the isolation of the leaf. A timberline tree, with all its branches straining in one direction, is the very portrait of a prevailing wind.

Put colour to work in your photographs. Frame brilliant subjects against a dull-coloured background. If you are taking a close-up of an iridescent beetle, the insect will show up best against a pale leaf or petal, or the bark of a tree. Or, if your subject is a meadow of golden flowers, look for a note of contrast – one blossom of a different colour, a butterfly – to set off the vivid display.

Lines and curves add interest to a composition. Look for the graceful C or S-curve of a flowering branch or a stream meandering through a valley. Strong, sharp angles, like those of the letters L and Y, give the subject a more architectural look. Stone fences and forked tree trunks are examples of this. Make sure that the strongest line in a scene (the horizon, for example) does not cut your photograph in half. A mountain peak or other focal point may look better if a little off-centre.

When photographing groups of objects, remember that odd numbers tend to be more interesting than even numbers. No one is quite sure why, but pictures of one, three or five objects (especially when they are about the same size) are more pleasing than twos, fours or sixes. You can test this for yourself: try photographing two flowers, then three. Any odd-even contrast will do. Do you agree that "odd man" is *in*, not *out*, in this situation?

While capturing nature at its best and most interesting with your camera, there is nothing to stop you incorporating your family or friends in the compositions. They can help to indicate the size and scale of your subjects, as well as making your shots pleasant souvenirs.

If you are a novice photographer, the best practice is simply to become familiar and comfortable with your camera equipment. Work with one or two types of film; you will soon come to prefer one kind, whether you choose colour prints, colour slides or black-and-white.

Remember, your eye is the most important element in photography. What you see and how you see it are what make good pictures.

Following the seasons with your camera

A photo story is sometimes more convincing if told in a series of pictures – for example, the changing of seasons as shown on the right. This is how you can follow a tree through its yearly changes.

Select a conspicuous reference point, such as the distinctive form of a tree, large rock or fence post. Notice the distinctive branching of the tree (right). You will see that such a repeated element is important in putting the emphasis on the changing colours of the foliage. Take the shot from the same place each time, or ensure a good match by bringing a copy of the first photo in the series.

Take all of the photographs at about the same time of day, so that lighting and shadows remain similar. To accentuate seasonal differences, try to take pictures when the season is at its peak – for example, when autumn colours are brightest, or after a snowfall.

PHOTO TIPS
Know your camera

Experimenting with your camera will enable you to become a more creative photographer. After you have adjusted to the mechanics of your camera, you can concentrate on composition.
● Read the manual that comes with your camera so that you will know what the camera can and cannot do.
● Proper lighting is an essential part of photography. Location and time of day can make a great difference in how your pictures look. Learn when and where to take certain shots for different effects. For example, the bright light of high noon creates strong contrasts.
● Use a light meter to help you set proper lens aperture and shutter speed. If there are both dark and light area in the scene (such as a white lighthouse on a rocky shore), you can emphasise the contrasting areas by using slightly different settings from those indicated by the meter.

● Bracket the exposure. To do this, first make an exposure as the meter indicates. Then take another at an f/stop wider, and a third at an f/stop smaller. This can produce three entirely different effects.
● Check your focus just before shooting.
● Make notes of the subjects and settings for each shot, and use them as references for studying your pictures when they are developed. You can learn from your errors as well as your successful shots.
● Practise all year round, and do not be afraid to use lots of film.

Use the shutter and lens opening to create different effects. On the left, a small lens opening and slow shutter speed were used. Note that the background is comparatively sharp. On the right, a large aperture and fast speed brought the daisies into focus, and the background is blurred.

Photographing animals – wild and tame

What distinguishes animal photographs from scenes is the challenge of capturing a moving subject. A photo of a soaring gull is more dynamic than a shot of a shoreline. (A telephoto lens is a great asset – some people consider it essential for animal photography.) A subject with story potential is a photographer's delight. It may be a flotilla of geese on a pond or a procession of ducks crossing a road to reach the water.

A bird's nest in an unusual location – perhaps on the arm of a statue – is another possibility. If you have a bird family nesting in your garden you can follow the drama of their lives in a series of pictures. But always be careful not to get so close to the nest that you frighten the parent birds or their nestlings.

You can frequently get quite near an animal when it is engaged in some activity – eating, courting, singing or calling. Sometimes during the spring breeding season, a frog may be so preoccupied that you can walk right up to it and touch its head – or take its picture. When stalking an animal, do not attract attention to yourself. Always try to move quietly, slowly and steadily.

If you have camera equipment around your neck, make sure it does not rattle. It is generally better to wear natural-tone clothing that blends with the background, rather than bright colours.

One of the best techniques for getting close to wildlife is "bait and wait". Take along small amounts of sunflower seeds, nuts or bird-seed. Put the bait in a place where you think animals will come, or where you have seen them on previous occasions. Then find a comfortable spot near by – partially concealed, if possible. Focus your camera on the food and wait. You will probably be surprised at the different animals that may arrive – birds, mice, badgers, deer and others. Take advantage of natural bait. An oak tree with acorns will attract squirrels; a field of flowers attracts insects (and also the birds that feed on them).

You can get closer to your subject by using a hide. If you are going to make a lengthy study you can build an elaborate hide but, otherwise, you can improvise one by throwing a length of dark-coloured fabric over a bush or a makeshift frame of poles. Sometimes merely a blanket over your head and body will do.

For general use on a 35 mm. camera, the most versatile telephoto lens is one with a focal length of from 135 to 250 mm. Unless the camera is on a tripod, a telephoto lens usually requires shooting at a shutter speed of 1/250th of a second or faster, in order to prevent blurring from camera motion. This will probably require a faster film.

There are three strategies for photographing elusive species – a hide, a telephoto lens, and a remote shutter release (such shutter releases are made in lengths of up to 200 ft). Of course, you can use more than one of these techniques at the same time.

Review your photographs with special attention to outstanding successes or recurring failures. If the animals in your photos seem to be walking into walls, it is because you have forgotten that the edges of the view-finder are, in fact, visual walls. Do not stop with reviewing your own pictures. Analyse everything you see in magazine illustrations and advertisements. Look for compositions that create interesting effects. Take notes, then experiment to see how you can apply what you have learned to your own compositions.

Photographs help to save species. In fact, photography can be considered the conservationist's best friend. Numerous species of plants and animals have been endangered by the very people who love them most. Every rare butterfly triumphantly collected by an enthusiast is a serious loss to its small population. So when the capture is only on film, the species gets a reprieve.

Camouflaged hides are frequently used by professional photographers to allow a close approach to wildlife. You do not need an elaborate hide to use this technique. Because some animals may wait until you have left the hide, you may have to resort to trickery. Have a friend go in with you and then leave.

Adjusting your camera to a moving target

A graceful, soaring bird caught in full flight makes an exciting photograph. Find an area where birds roost or feed. "Freezing" the bird with a fast shutter speed (see below) may produce a fascinating study of flight positions. Sometimes you may want to turn the camera to follow the bird as it flies. The bird in the photograph may be in sharp focus and the background blurred – as if the background and not the bird were speeding by. To avoid this blurred effect, use a film with a high ASA rating. If you are using a telephoto lens, set the shutter at 1/250 or faster if possible.

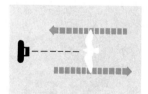

When a bird flies directly at the camera, shoot at a speed of at least 1/125.

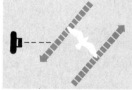

A diagonal approach requires a shutter speed of 1/250 to stop the action.

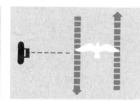

For crosswise flight, use a speed of 1/500 or faster to register a sharp image.

PHOTO TIPS
Opportunities at zoos, aquariums and game parks

Some of the most interesting portraits of animals in action can be obtained close to home – at your local zoo or aquarium. Even an ordinary camera can get good pictures there, although most action shots require specialised equipment such as adjustable lenses and fast film.

• Plan your trip for a time when the zoo will not be too crowded. Many animals are active in early morning or late afternoon; also lighting is usually more favourable at this time of day. Feeding time is also good.

• Observe the animal's behaviour before you start photographing. Many large zoo animals have regular walking patterns; some pace up and down constantly. Just get your camera ready and wait until the subject comes towards you again.

• Bars on cages and mesh fences can sometimes be avoided by standing very close and centring the lens through one of the openings. Or use a large aperture that will throw the mesh out of focus. A telephoto lens can be ideal for this situation, especially if the animal is at a great distance from the photographer.

• Indoor aquariums usually have glass enclosures, which give off reflections from flashes. (Some aquariums prohibit the use of flashes.) You can avoid these reflections by directing the flash through the front glass; never shoot from an angle. Wear dark-toned clothing to reduce reflections.

1. A camera angle from above is especially effective if you are photographing marine animals such as this bewhiskered walrus.

2. A telephoto lens was used to get a close-up effect of these frogmouths, although the birds were actually about 15 ft away.

3. For the special effect of a downpour, the photographer's helper sprayed water from a hose while the duck obligingly posed.

4. This passing school of fish was photographed with a camera placed very close to the glass enclosure of an observation tank.

Planning a camping holiday

The most important part of any camping trip takes place before you leave home. Success depends on careful planning. When you are miles into the woods, it is too late to do anything about necessities you have left at home – such as matches or a knife. This is why old hands at camping use checklists to help organise their trips.

What equipment you need depends on the kind of camping you intend to do, and also on your mode of transportation. For example, if you are travelling in a car, you can take along almost anything that will fit into it – a roomy tent, a cooler, and plenty of food, even canned goods. If you plan to camp at a site accessible only to hikers, you should take only what you can comfortably carry on your back.

Each type of camping requires certain tools or equipment. If you are a novice, it is a good idea to ease into camping gradually. In the beginning, rent your equipment, and go camping with experienced people, perhaps with a club. In this way, you will have a chance to see what style of camping suits you before buying equipment.

If you have children, it can be a good idea to hold your first camp in your own garden. The whole family can then find out how to use the equipment and what they would really need on an isolated site.

Camping simplifies life. Your daily requirements are reduced to the basic necessities: shelter, food, and clothing. Your shelter can be anything from a caravan to a sleeping bag.

If your campsite can be reached by car, you can choose a tent that is built for roominess and comfort rather than compactness and minimal weight. The best types of tents are those with a sewn-in floor, large windows with mosquito netting, and roll-down flaps for protection against bad weather. Tents with umbrella frames are favoured by many because they require few stakes and ropes, and can be set up on almost any kind of ground. Most are also sturdy enough to withstand fairly strong winds. On a long trip, there is much to be said for a tent with enough headroom for an adult to stand upright.

Fabrics with plastic coatings are usually more weatherproof than those made of treated cotton. Make sure the tent has a label clearly specifying that it is flame-resistant. No matter what kind of tent you have, never allow any kind of fire inside it – not even a lighted match.

A picnic cooler keeps perishables fresh as long as the ice is replenished. If foods such as vegetables or meats are packed while still frozen, they will act as coolants, and will also stay cold a day or two longer. Drinking water, milk, and juices can also be frozen in plastic containers before the start of the trip. If you are sure there will be plenty of water at your campsite, take along the makings of casseroles or stews. They are especially advantageous when rains or high winds make more elaborate meals impractical.

Plan for the unexpected – a downpour, a swarm of insects, or a midsummer cold snap. This is particularly important when you choose your clothing. Guidebooks and brochures for most recreational areas give the average high and low temperatures for each month, and the amount of rainfall to be expected. It is always better to take along a little more clothing, rather than get caught with too little. Clothes that can be worn in layers, such as shirts, sweaters, and jackets, are more convenient than one large, heavy coat. Remember that mountains can be chilly even on sweltering summer days.

Keep your camp site clean. Take along several plastic bags for storage. Food odours attract animals, so put all food in tightly closed containers. Follow local regulations in disposing of refuse. Never store food inside your tent. Many undesirable encounters with animals and with insects can be avoided by taking these precautions.

HIKING AND CAMPING
▲ A checklist for your camping trip

There are more items here than you are likely to want. Each camper should tailor a checklist to match individual preferences, means of transportation, length of time you will be out on your trip, and the season of the year. Obviously, a separate checklist is needed for a trip centred on fishing or some other specific activity. Once you have your own list (perhaps typed), make a few copies of it for future holidays. Then update it as you decide what was really necessary and what can be omitted.

Camping equipment
- ☐ Tent
- ☐ Fly sheet
- ☐ Ground sheet
- ☐ Blankets
- ☐ Sleeping bag
- ☐ Air mattress
- ☐ Camp chair
- ☐ Whisk broom
- ☐ Torch
- ☐ Extra batteries
- ☐ Lamp and extra mantles
- ☐ Canteens
- ☐ Bucket
- ☐ Maps
- ☐ Compass
- ☐ Rope
- ☐ First-aid kit (see page 312)
- ☐ Water-purification tablets
- ☐ Tool kit (including pliers and hammer)
- ☐ Axe (or small saw)
- ☐ Spade
- ☐ Portable lavatory
- ☐ Toilet tissue
- ☐ Plastic rubbish bags

Cooking equipment
- ☐ Camp stove
- ☐ Fuel
- ☐ Grill
- ☐ Funnel for fuel
- ☐ Charcoal
- ☐ Fire extinguisher
- ☐ Potholder
- ☐ Matches
- ☐ Cooking utensils
- ☐ Coffee or tea pot
- ☐ Cups and dishes
- ☐ Knives, forks, spoons
- ☐ Tin and bottle opener
- ☐ Cooler
- ☐ Cooler pack
- ☐ Aluminium foil
- ☐ Paper towels
- ☐ Wash bowl
- ☐ Plastic water container
- ☐ Detergent (in plastic container)
- ☐ Pot scrubber

Food supplies
- ☐ Bread
- ☐ Butter
- ☐ Bacon
- ☐ Eggs
- ☐ Porridge
- ☐ Coffee
- ☐ Tea
- ☐ Milk (powdered)
- ☐ Fruit juices
- ☐ Cooking oil
- ☐ Salt
- ☐ Pepper
- ☐ Seasonings
- ☐ Mustard
- ☐ Sauces
- ☐ Sugar
- ☐ Fruits
- ☐ Cheese
- ☐ Soups (dehydrated)
- ☐ Potatoes (dehydrated)
- ☐ Onions (dehydrated)
- ☐ Tinned stews
- ☐ Quick desserts
- ☐ Frozen meats
- ☐ Cereals (hot and cold)
- ☐ Raisins
- ☐ Fresh fruit
- ☐ Chocolate

Personal items
- ☐ Clothes
- ☐ Warm jacket
- ☐ Rain clothes
- ☐ Toilet articles
- ☐ Towels
- ☐ Insect repellent
- ☐ Suntan lotion
- ☐ Sewing kit
- ☐ Sunglasses
- ☐ Camera
- ☐ Film
- ☐ Guidebooks
- ☐ Leisure items (games, books, etc.)
- ☐ Sports equipment
- ☐ Binoculars
- ☐ Notebook and pencils

Choosing a campsite is of great importance to the enjoyment of your holiday. Unless you already know exactly where you want to camp, consult guidebooks for camping grounds – public and private. If bookings are accepted, make yours as soon as you know when your trip will be.

A safe campfire – where, when and how

If carefully made and properly tended, a campfire can be the centre of warmth and cheer. Some campsites may already have fire facilities. Otherwise, choose a spot out in the open, away from tents, trees and bushes. (Do not build fires during windy weather, especially during a dry spell.) Dig a hole about 18 in. across and 6 in. deep. Circle the hole with fairly large stones. Build the fire in the centre of the hole, using twigs and leaves as kindling and larger branches to keep the fire going.

Keep a bucket of water and a spade handy in case it becomes windy after your fire is started; put the fire out if there is any danger of it spreading. Never leave the fire untended. When putting a fire out, use lots of water; separate the burning pieces and soak each one thoroughly. Throw water into the fire hole, stirring the ashes until they are thoroughly wet. Before leaving the campsite, replace the soil and turf over the ashes. A good camper leaves no traces of his presence when he moves on.

Hiking and walking

⚠️ HIKING AND CAMPING
Using a compass

An orienteering type of compass is best for beginners. There are a number of different models with a transparent base, a direction-finder, and a liquid-filled housing for fast and accurate readings. The key to learning how to use any compass is differentiating between *magnetic* north (to which a compass needle is attracted) and *geographical* north (to which maps are drawn). The difference – in degrees – between the two is called declination.

• **To follow a compass reading,** first locate the degree direction (say, 20 degrees NE) on the compass rim. Hold the compass about waist level; move around slowly until the red end of the magnetic needle lies directly over the orienteering arrow (within the circular housing). Once you have the desired degree, look straight ahead, pinpoint a landmark such as a tree, and go to it.

• **To take a bearing,** face the desired direction and turn the housing until the needle points to "N".

• **To set a direction** from compass to map, align the compass edge with your present position and your destination on the map. Turn the compass housing until the orienteering arrow is parallel to the meridian on the map.

• **To relate a map to a compass** of the orienteering kind, set the compass at 360 degrees. Place the compass on the map so that the housing arrow points north (to match the map); turn the map (with the compass on it) until the needle of the compass points to "N".

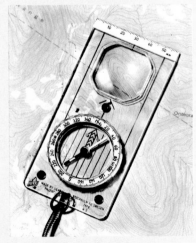

A map and a compass can work together. Practise using both in a familiar location before going out into the wilds. Familiarise yourself with the features of your map before setting out on a trip.

To see nature at close quarters, go on your two feet. From car, bus or train you will form a reasonable general impression of the landscape; everything whizzes by. Of course, car, bus and train are ideal means of reaching places. But once arrived, you will see wildlife in all its beauty and complexity only by hiking.

You may choose to take a simple stroll away from your car for an hour or so, or you may decide to go on a week or more's trek, carrying all you need to make yourself self-sufficient away from the comforts of urban life.

Footwear is of the utmost importance. Walking boots should be strong, comfortable, and broken in *before* you go on a long hike. Weight is not synonymous with strength; every 3 oz. on your feet requires that you exert as much energy as if you were carrying 1 lb. on your back. Boots should be roomy enough to be worn over two pairs of socks (which help keep feet warmer and drier). Try out the boots on a few long walks, perhaps with a rucksack; this will help you – and your boots – to get broken in.

A steady pace is the key to comfortable, long-distance walking, so you should consciously develop a rhythm to your stride. At the start of your trek, set a moderate pace that will allow the slowest (youngest, oldest or least experienced) member of your group to keep up without undue exertion. About 2 mph is a good pace for the average walker. A moderate pace also means you will have to make fewer rest stops. When you rest, it is better to lean against a tree or rock than to sit down. Sitting has a way of ruining your walking rhythm. (Some people believe sitting interferes with circulation and stiffens muscles.) It is generally best to wait until a full rest stop to eat or drink, rather than having a snack along the way. Eat and drink sparingly – a full stomach can be positively uncomfortable when you are hiking. A pack should feel good on your back, and not swing loosely. Packs with waist belts help distribute the weight evenly.

How warm or cold you are greatly influences your endurance. Most experienced walkers agree that the best way to stay warm is not to get hot. In other words, keep making adjustments – wear your clothing in layers, which you can peel off or add as needed. Wear a hat to protect against a hot sun. In cool weather, one way to keep your hands and feet warm is to button your jacket, and perhaps tighten your belt. If your torso is warm, heat goes to your extremities.

Soft, roomy clothing is sensible because any constriction (say, snug-fitting trousers) restricts your movements and tires your muscles. Long sleeves and long trousers offer protection from brambles and scraping against rocks. A good insect repellent will also add immeasurably to your comfort.

Hiking is for seasoned walkers. Most of the techniques and equipment are the same, except for a sleeping bag, tent and stove. Down-filled sleeping bags offer the most warmth for the least weight. Fibre-filled bags are less expensive and will often suffice. Sleeping bags are rated for temperature and come in different sizes; do not buy a larger bag than you need. (It will not be warmer, but *will* add weight.)

A lightweight tent offers protection against rain, cold and insects. Make sure the tent is not too complicated to put up. The material should be flame-resistant and waterproof, but also porous enough to "breathe".

Dehydrated and freeze-dried foods offer the most nutrition per ounce. (The weight of tinned foods makes them unsuitable for hiking.) In an ordinary grocery shop you can find many dried foods that are inexpensive and just as tasty as special camping foods.

Whether you are on a day's walk or a week-long hike, you will discover the truth of the old saying: "Problems are solved by walking." Nature will soon help you to see them in perspective.

This hiker is wearing a knapsack, designed for short jaunts. When you pause for lunch or a rest, take a moment to look at your map.

A comfortable rucksack is important to the enjoyment of a hike. Proper loading is the key. The zone method of loading a pack helps you align the additional weight of a pack with your own centre of gravity (along the spine). Keep the load high and forward. The illustration above is a guide to the three vertical zones that help you do this. Zone A is closest to you; place the heaviest items here – tent on top, then stove, pegs, poles and utensils. Zone B, in the middle, should have the medium-weight objects – clothes, food, sleeping bag. Pockets are in this zone; distribute the weight of small items among them. Carry the lightest objects – maps, permits, medicines and snacks – in Zone C, the furthest from you. You can tell your pack is correctly loaded if you can walk upright in relative comfort, without it pulling you backwards.

When breaking camp, a hiker should store small items first (to make sure nothing gets left) and larger items, such as tents, last. Leave no trace of your presence, so that others can enjoy the campsite.

Orienteering tests your skill in reading maps

Orienteering, a sport which has become popular all over the world, originated in Scandinavia in 1920. Combining skill with an element of adventure, it gives young and old a chance to compete on equal terms. Contestants need only to be reasonably fit and able to use a compass and read a map.

The aim is to find the quickest route over unfamiliar terrain. Contestants can choose the way they go, but must pass through control points in the correct sequence, leaving a mark or picking up a token at each point. The score depends on the time taken to complete the course.

At the start of the race, each contestant is given a map on which all the control points are shown by number. Each person's starting time is noted and set intervals are kept between each departure so that contestants do not overlap. Usually, several races are held.

For all but very inexperienced people, orienteering is a sport best done alone. It is up to the individual to decide whether to cross a swamp or go the 3 miles round it. A steady pace is advisable: the skilled orienteer never runs when he can walk. If he misses a control point or gets lost, he looks for a recognisable land feature and re-orients himself.

The section of map on the right is a typical example of the maps now drawn specially for orienteering. Unlike conventional maps they employ symbols and shades of green and yellow to denote different sorts of terrain and vegetation and the difficulty that contestants will experience in crossing them.

For information on orienteering clubs in Britain, write to:
British Orienteering Federation,
Lea Green, near Matlock,
Derbyshire DE4 5GJ.

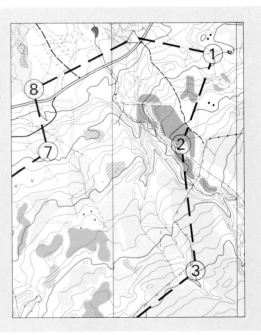

Water, water everywhere

It is pleasant to splash your face in the cool water of a sparkling stream, especially after a long hike. But even if it looks clean, such water is not necessarily safe enough to drink.

Water is so much a part of nature that it is often taken for granted. But there are different rules for its different uses, depending on whether you are going to drink it, swim in it, or go boating on it.

The water in springs and streams often seems so fresh that you may be tempted to scoop it up and drink. No matter how clear the water looks, however, you have no way of knowing whether it is pure. Unless you are going to be near an approved source of drinking water, take your water with you. Water of unknown quality can be boiled for a few minutes, or use purification tablets. Rainwater is an exception. If caught in a clean container, it is safe for drinking.

Whenever you go swimming, whether in a lake or in the ocean, observe the rules. You should never swim alone, no matter how good a swimmer you are or how safe the water seems to be. A stream or river may have currents that vary from place to place, unexpected deep holes and underwater snags. It is especially unsafe to dive in an unfamiliar place. If you have been exerting yourself – hiking, for example – give your body a chance to cool off before swimming in cold water. It is also wise to wait a while after a meal before swimming.

A good general rule is: "The more you ate, the longer you should wait."

In areas where there are lifeguards, heed their instructions and swim only in designated areas. Flotation devices such as air mattresses are suitable only for shallow, quiet waters. Poor swimmers are the ones most inclined to take them into deep water; if a child or non-swimming adult falls off a floating raft, or if the raft collapses, there is real danger of drowning.

At the seashore, judge the surf by watching at least a dozen breakers; if the waves seem too high, postpone your swim. Even wading can be dangerous in a strong surf. A powerful backwash can sweep waders – especially children – off their feet and carry them out into deeper water.

"Undertow" is created when waves cut through an underwater sandbar and form a channel. As water runs out through this breach, the current becomes localised and extremely powerful. If you are caught in an undertow, do not try to swim against it, even if it carries you far beyond your normal swimming distance. You will only be wasting your strength. Once the current eases, swim parallel to the beach to avoid getting caught again.

Another safety measure is an aware-

SAFETY AND SURVIVAL
Learning to float now can save your life later

Protect yourself and your family whenever you are out on the water – whether you are swimming or boating. Most drowning victims knew how to swim, but found themselves in a situation beyond their skill or endurance. If you follow this procedure for staying afloat – even if you are a non-swimmer – you can survive for several hours until rescued. Practise this drill in a local swimming pool before going on holiday. Begin in shoulder-deep water, spending three to five seconds underwater. As you gain confidence, move into deeper water. Below are the basic steps.

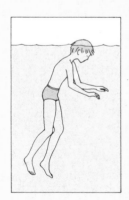   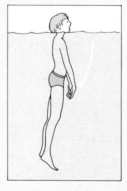 

1. Take a deep breath and hold it. Put your face in the water. Relax and float vertically with your arms and legs dangling.

2. To take another breath, raise your arms straight out in front of you; at the same time bring a foot forward in a scissors kick.

3. Raise your head until your mouth is out of water. Press down with your hands in a circular motion. Bring your legs together.

4. With your chin level with the surface, exhale through your nose. Then inhale deeply through your mouth.

5. Return to resting position. If you sink too deep, push down with your hands. A kick will also raise you.

ness of the direction in which you are drifting. (In the ocean, the water travels parallel to the beach, in addition to its motion in and out.) Pick a landmark and keep an eye on it, so as not to drift too far from where you entered the water. In unfamiliar waters, try to touch bottom every so often, to make sure you are not in too deep.

Whenever you venture on to the water in any kind of boat, wear a life jacket. Even if you are a good swimmer (and you should never go boating if you cannot swim), a life jacket is essential. If a mishap occurs, you may need this support. Expert boaters and canoeists never go down an unfamiliar river without first surveying it on foot – there could be a steep drop or dangerous rapids just around the bend.

Each kind of boating has its special equipment, skills and rules. Learn techniques from qualified instructors. Rowing looks easy, but it is taxing – you may have to row back against the wind. Canoeing waters are classified as brown water and white water; that is, relatively slow-moving rivers versus foaming rapids. Kayaks are the most unstable of all the small freshwater boats, and no one who has not mastered white-water canoeing should try them.

Even in the calm of a "narrow boat" trip on a canal, an increasingly popular way of spending a holiday in Britain and elsewhere in Europe there can be perilous moments. Locks can be tricky to man-oeuvre and it is easy to have a "man overboard". It is only sensible to prepare for emergencies. Do not think it is the sort of thing that can never happen to you.

A canoe ride across calm waters is always a relaxing interlude during a day of hiking and setting up camp. Here, at Upper Kachess Lake in America, the shores are inaccessible by road, which makes this an ideal spot for canoe camping. Note that both paddlers are wearing life jackets – a vital precaution, especially if children are included in the group.

Handling a canoe

Every year more people discover the joy of canoeing. Canoes are easily transported and do not cause pollution. To ensure stability, balance a canoe when loading; equipment and people should be placed so that weight is evenly distributed. It is important to learn how to get into and out of a canoe (see right). When paddling, sit or kneel; if you are alone, kneel in the middle of the canoe. When two are paddling, the one at the rear steers. You will find that each stroke of the paddle turns the canoe slightly off course. An experienced canoeist can demonstrate various strokes to correct this tendency, to move the canoe backwards or sideways, or to stop its forward motion. Non-swimmers should never enter a canoe, and no one should stand up or shift seats while the canoe is in motion.

When getting into (or out of) a canoe, face forwards. Grip the nearest rim with one hand; place one foot in the centre of the canoe. Reach for the distant rim while shifting your weight on to the foot already in the canoe.

To tow a canoe upstream, tie a 50 ft rope to forward and stern thwarts. Navigate around obstructions by pulling on the stern line. Pull on the forward line to bring it closer.

What is safe? What is dangerous?

Nobody can learn anything about nature without being curious, but curiosity needs to be tempered with common sense. Approach animals with caution or you run the risk of being hurt. For instance, a young calf in a field looks very appealing, especially to children who will want to cuddle it. Besides, natural inquisitiveness will often tempt it to come and stare at passers-by. But this curiosity may suddenly turn to fear if it is handled. Near by, the mother cow will usually be keeping an eye on her offspring, and if the calf gives cries of distress, she may well attack – just as a human mother would attack a strange creature threatening her baby. Unprovoked, father bull is not often dangerous. But some bulls are testy, so treat all of them with caution.

Dragonflies are beautiful to see and harmless to human beings. They probably got their bad reputation because they dart so swiftly, and may remind people of insects that do sting, such as wasps and bees. Spiders, like dragonflies, have an undeserved reputation for being dangerous. Europe's only dangerous species is Italy's tarantula. Victims of its bite used to sweat out the poison in a frantic dance – the origin of the tarantella. Other spiders are natural allies of man because they eat insects.

The common saying that wild animals are more afraid of you than you are of them is generally true. Animals are usually aware of your presence long before you see them. Most will avoid you, if possible. If you come across a snake, for example, the chances are that the reptile will slip away even before you have been able to react. Few snakes are poisonous. However, if you are not sure that a snake is harmless, move away slowly and quietly.

If a snake does bite you or one of your party, kill it and take it to hospital with you for identification.

Encounters with some wild animals may be involuntary – you just stumble across them. Usually, this is the situation in which animals inflict injuries. Always inform yourself about the wildlife of a region where you will be camping or hiking. When climbing, try to avoid putting your hands or feet where you cannot see. You should never reach into holes or crevices in trees, cliffs or rocks. Such places may conceal snakes or scorpions. Before stepping over a log, look on the other side.

Pushing your way through tall grass or thick brush can also be hazardous. In some brushy and grassy areas, small insects called ticks can be a problem. When they bite, they become embedded in the skin and are difficult to remove. Clothing can help protect you – wear long sleeves and trousers, and tie a scarf around your neck.

When you get home, look yourself over carefully and apply rubbing alcohol to any ticks you find; this will loosen their grip. Another method is to light a safety match, blow it out, and then apply the still-hot tip to the insect's body.

Stinging nettles and other rash-causing plants probably cause more discomfort than anything else in the wild. The techniques for avoiding a rash are simple. Learn to identify the poisonous plants in your region (see illustrations, far right). Avoid touching any part of the plants, including the leafless twigs. Some of these plants should not even be burned in autumn, as the irritant may be carried on the wind.

Certain types of terrain may seem safer than they actually are. The edge of a cliff or a ravine may be disguised by vegetation. The smooth, green surface of a bog may conceal danger. Quicksand may form alongside water courses, and even in relatively dry places. Part of the hazard is that it is frequently temporary, and so not charted on maps. It can look flat and rather inviting. One clue to the presence of quicksand may be a glint of moisture. Quicksand forms where water has been trapped in a depression, with particles of sand or clay suspended in it like a thick soup. If your foot ever goes into the ground suddenly, go back immediately and look for another route.

Dragonfly, devil's darning-needle, snake-doctor, mule-killer – every name applied to this insect denotes danger. Actually it is harmless except to prey, such as mosquitoes.

The garden spider in its delicate web (right) deserves respect. Spiders' bites can be painful, but only a few species are dangerous. It is a clear case of "look, but do not touch".

This venturesome bear cub looks lovable enough to hug. But it may have been chased up the tree by its mother, which is almost always near by. Female bears are ferocious in defence of their young. The only sensible approach is with a telephoto lens from inside a car.

The few poisonous spiders include these three

Black widow spiders and their relatives are found almost world-wide, but those of Australia and North America are the most poisonous. Fortunately, these spiders are secretive and do not bite unless they are molested. Only the bite of the female is dangerous. Brown recluses, which occur in the central and south-western United States and in South America, are somewhat less poisonous. As with snakes, young children and people in poor health are in greater danger from the spiders' poison.

The European tarantula is the region's only poisonous spider. It is found in Italy. The frantic dance called the tarantella is named after it.

The black widow is famous for the red hourglass on its underside. Its name comes from the female's habit of eating the male after mating.

The red-back spider from Australia is closely related to the black widow, but its red marking is located on its back instead of its belly.

NATURE OBSERVER
Poisonous plants

Deaths from poisonous plants are extremely rare in Britain and Europe, although many of the region's plants and fungi are poisonous, and some can be lethal. The bitter taste of some plants stops people eating them; so while poisoning may cause pain and sickness, it is rarely fatal. Children are particularly vulnerable, but adults may eat a poisonous plant by accident. Deadly nightshade berries, for example, resemble cherries, and death has been caused by mistaking monkshood roots for horseradish. Other plants, such as stinging nettles, produce rashes.

The pain-relieving drug atropine is made from poisonous deadly nightshade (above).

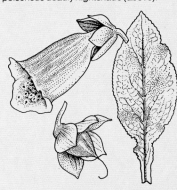

Digitalis, a heart stimulant drug, comes from the poisonous foxglove flower.

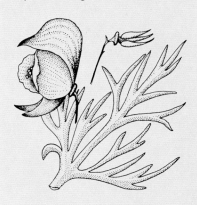

Monkshood, also called wolfsbane, was used to tip arrows for hunting animals.

Precautions and practice

SAFETY AND SURVIVAL
First-aid kit

A first-aid kit is like a mobile medicine cabinet, and should be equipped for all minor emergencies. Make sure that it includes a first-aid manual, with detailed instructions on how to take care of such emergencies as shock, food poisoning and insect bites.

• Assemble the items well before your trip to allow time to buy whatever items are missing.

• Label all items clearly, and put them together in a container. A tool chest with a hinged cover is ideal, but do not lock it with a key (the key might be missing just when you need it most).

• Be certain to include medicines for any particular ailments of individual family members. If any are vital, carry a reserve supply in a separate place.

• Check the kit before each trip, and re-stock used items.

• Keep medicines out of the reach of children.

• Below is a list of suggested items. You may want to supplement it for your own special needs.

☐ Roll of gauze, 2 in. wide
☐ Gauze dressings, 3 in. square
☐ Box of small adhesive dressings
☐ Roll of cotton wool
☐ Elastic bandages
☐ Bottle of antiseptic
☐ Lotion (calamine) for insect bites, rashes and sunburn
☐ Petroleum jelly
☐ Aspirin
☐ Bicarbonate of soda or baking soda
☐ Remedies for digestive upsets
☐ Rubbing alcohol
☐ Ampoules of ammonia (for fainting)
☐ Scissors
☐ Tweezers
☐ Package of needles (for removing splinters)
☐ Safety pins
☐ Small, sharp knife (or single-edged razor blades)
☐ Medicine dropper
☐ Wooden safety matches
☐ Torch
☐ Thermometer

• Do not assume that because you have not had recent occasion to use a particular medicine or salve that it will continue to be in good condition from one camping trip to the next. If a medicine has changed colour, replace it.

• Be especially careful about the condition of sterile materials, such as bandages. They should be kept dry (put them in plastic bags), or they may pick up moisture from the air and lose their value as sterile dressings.

The carefree exuberance of camping and hiking often causes people to take needless risks. It is important to develop an "outdoor sense" that anticipates (and thereby avoids) potential mishaps. A careful approach to nature does not get in the way of enjoyment – it enhances your feeling of confidence.

Experienced hikers and campers always make a point of knowing exactly where they are. If you consult a topographical map of the region where you will be hiking or camping, you will gain a familiarity that will make your trip more rewarding. At the same time, you can note places where help is available in case you need it – the nearest town, a Red Cross post, or a house where there may be a telephone. The map may indicate areas to avoid, such as a treacherous ravine or cliff, or a swamp.

Though maps will help you avoid getting lost, there are other precautions you can take to be sure no member of your party strays too far. If you are staying at a campsite, show children a few landmarks so they will know where they are when they wander around. No one should leave the campsite for a solitary swim or a long walk. Always tell someone if you are leaving the group. It is a good idea for everyone to carry a whistle, to be used in case of emergency. (Three whistle blasts mean distress.) Children may be tempted to blow their whistles when there is no emergency, but a brief period of "whistle testing" once or twice a day may help prevent this. Parents can use the whistle for an "assemble here immediately" signal.

Successful camping in a group depends on a fair and cheerful division of the many tasks necessary on a site. Children tend to enjoy being made responsible for particular jobs. It is good training for when they go away later to school, scout or guide

A secure bandage for an injured hand

Gently wipe the area around the wound (and the wound itself) with soap, water and a clean cloth. The strokes should be away from the cut. Cover the wound with sterile gauze, held in place with plaster. An injury on the hand can be bandaged with the figure-of-eight method (see below). Form the knot by splitting the bandage.

How to bandage a hand with rolled gauze

Leave it to the experts:

It can be dangerous to allow a broken leg to be treated by the first person to arrive on the scene. The best advice is to leave the injured limb alone, and wait for the arrival of a doctor or ambulance man. On no account should an unqualified person attempt to set a broken bone, or even to clean the wound. This kind of well-meaning action can be harmful – a layman may not even be able to tell whether a bone is broken or merely dislocated or sprained. A broken arm can safely be treated by placing it in a sling, improvised from a scarf, shirt or any other large piece of clean cloth, as in the illustration on the right. But a broken leg should be left to the experts. The lower illustration shows what they will do to give the limb temporary support with an inflatable splint, until the victim can be got into a hospital.

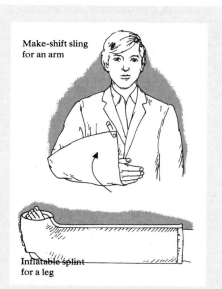

Make-shift sling for an arm

Inflatable splint for a leg

camps without their parents to help them.

Fires deserve respect. Build them away from tents – flames and sparks travel surprisingly far on a windy day. Clear the area to stop the fire spreading. Watch out, too, for overhanging branches. If you are cold and damp, approach a campfire gradually; shoes and clothing may quickly become too hot for comfort. When you extinguish your campfire, be thorough, and use lots of water. To make sure it is out, douse the fire an hour or so before you leave.

Make sure the supports for kettles or grills are sturdy enough to carry the weight. Never put liquid lighter fuel on a burning fire or even one that is warm and glowing. If you carry a paraffin supply for camp stoves or lanterns, make sure it is kept in an approved container, well away from fire or excessive heat. Never remove the fuel cap of an appliance such as a paraffin stove while it is still warm. Heaters, even flameless ones, use up oxygen and also produce poisonous gases, and so should not be used in a closed tent or unventilated shelter.

Be prepared for any changes in the weather. Take such changes into consideration in setting up a campsite. If possible, avoid low ground where you may be flooded, or ground that is too high, where you will be exposed to blasts of wind. During an electrical storm, stay away from trees. One of the biggest rainy-day problems is boredom, particularly for children. Take along some simple games or a few books to help pass the time in a rainy spell.

Much of the safety and enjoyment of nature outings depends on what you do before you leave home. Test the condition of items such as torches and stoves before your trip; if they do not work, you will have a chance to fix them. If you have new appliances, be sure to read the instructions and warnings for their use.

If someone in your party is injured, or if you come across someone who needs help, here are five first-aid measures recommended by the Red Cross. **First,** give urgently needed aid – such as restoring breathing or heartbeat, and stopping bleeding – before attending to other injuries (see illustrations, right). **Second,** keep the victim lying down. It is often a temptation to get the victim up and walking around if the injury is not obvious – the victim may even insist on it – but this could do serious harm. **Third,** check for the location and seriousness of the injury. (There may be more than one.) **Fourth,** decide what needs to be done. **Fifth,** carry out your plan of action promptly.

Restore breathing – mouth-to-mouth

The mouth-to-mouth technique is now considered the most practical method to restore breathing. First check to see if the air passage is clear. Look into the mouth and remove any obstruction. If the individual is a victim of electric shock, make sure contact with the current is disconnected before you even touch the person. Place the victim face up. Put one of your hands under the victim's neck, and tilt the head backwards, chin upwards (see steps 1 and 2 below). Pinch the nostrils shut, to make sure that the air you force in does not escape. Place your mouth over the victim's; if it is a child, cover both nose and mouth with your mouth. Blow hard enough to make the chest rise (3). Turn your head to the side and listen for exhalations (4). For adults, give a strong breath every five seconds; for children, a shallow breath every three seconds. Continue this procedure even if you see no result.

1. Lift up neck and tilt head partially back

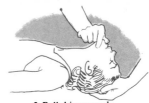
2. Pull chin upwards

3. Pinch nostrils and blow into open mouth

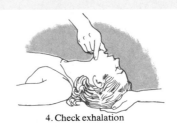
4. Check exhalation

Applying pressure to stop bleeding

Severe bleeding should be stopped by the fastest means possible. Keep the victim lying down. Press the wound firmly with sterile gauze or a clean piece of cloth (see below). Constant pressure is important, so hold the cloth while someone else acts as your assistant. If the gauze becomes saturated, put another piece directly over it and continue the pressure. If bleeding persists, apply pressure *above* the wound. When bleeding stops, bandage the dressed wound firmly, but not tightly.

Direct pressure over wound

If pressure over a wound does not stop the bleeding from an arm or leg, block the circulation from the supplying artery. There are four locations on the body to which arterial pressure can be applied (see diagram, right). Press firmly on the spot closest to the wound. Do not apply arterial pressure to wounds of the neck, head or torso. In case of severe bleeding, watch for signs of shock.

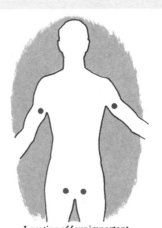
Location of four important pressure points to stop arterial bleeding

Bringing nature into your home

It is a good general rule to think about your own convenience before you bring any part of nature indoors. This may sound obvious (perhaps even a bit hard-hearted), but if you are not ready to give a plant or animal the care it needs in order to keep it healthy, you will more than likely regret the whole thing. For example, if you are one of the multitudes of people who hate to get up in the morning, even a pet dog may be a strain. (Dogs are keen for food, attention, and early-morning walks.) A more suitable animal compan-ion might be one that is naturally nocturnal, such as a hamster, which will whir around on its exercise wheel throughout the evening.

Watching a butterfly develop

The metamorphosis of a butterfly – the change it undergoes from egg, through caterpillar and pupal stages, to its final emergence – can be observed and photographed in your home. If you look at the undersides of nettle leaves, you may find butterfly eggs. The photographs below show you what to look for.

Tiny aquamarine-blue eggs were attached to this leaf by a female painted-lady butterfly.

An aquarium is ideal for people who enjoy observing the habits of small living things rather than the noisy and vigorous activities of larger pets. Salamanders, chameleons and certain species of frogs are some of the few wild creatures that do reasonably well under household conditions.

Exotic pets are always a bad idea. Such animals, including ocelots and monkeys, cannot be house-trained. Wild animals are seldom healthy or contented in captivity (except in zoos where the keepers have been trained to deal with their needs – on a full-time basis). It is better not to encourage the trade in exotic animals – their capture may deplete an already endangered population. The monkey you see in a pet shop should be left there; if you buy it, the shopkeeper will replace it. You are not "saving" one animal – you are encouraging the capture of more of these creatures.

Then, too, if an exotic animal becomes ill, your local veterinary surgeon will not necessarily be able to help. Even zoo specialists are stumped occasionally when their charges develop fevers, or simply stop eating. Many people who buy exotic animals during trips abroad discover on arrival at their home airport that importation of the particular species is prohibited; regulations forbid entry of many species. Even if they are admitted, your neighbours may take you to court for housing objectionable wild animals – or even domesticated farm animals.

The attractive Easter chick or duckling that someone gave your children is destined to become a full-grown adult. (Or the animal may die before reaching maturity – in which case your children will be miserable.) A pink piglet is even more of a disaster – when mature, it is generally large and never fragrant.

What *can* you bring home and enjoy? Besides the domesticated pets that are familiar to us all – dogs, cats, canaries and fish – insects are good candidates for house pets. They are surprisingly amenable to living with human beings. However, picking up insect eggs in the wild might result in your bringing a pest into your house. Unless you are sure of your species identification, it is probably safest to obtain insect eggs from a supplier of biological or educational materials. If you buy from a catalogue, you will not only have a chance to become familiar with different types of insect eggs, but will also receive specific instructions for their care – temperature, amount of light, and kinds of food that may be needed when the insects hatch.

Many people enjoy rearing butterflies from egg to adult. If, at the end of the "experiment", the season is right, all you have to do is open the window, and your guests will be free to live in the wild – if the habitat is suitable.

What about plants? There are so many species, it would seem that no room need be without a house plant. As with animals, it is generally better to grow "domesticated" (cultivated) species rather than taking plants from the wild. If you would like advice on what to plant, all you have to do is ask a plant lover. People with "green fingers" are generally delighted to enlist others into their ranks – and they might even give you cuttings from their own treasures.

After hatching, the caterpillar gorges on leaves, and eventually grows to an inch or longer.

The caterpillar attaches itself to a twig, head downwards.

The caterpillar's furry skin gives way to a smooth pupa.

During the pupal stage, the insect changes drastically.

HOW TO
Set up and maintain a terrarium

Why have a terrarium? To many people, a garden growing under glass seems more representative of the natural world than bits of isolated greenery. As a bonus, such a clustered arrangement is actually better for many plants than growing them in separate pots. After watering a newly planted terrarium, it becomes relatively self-supporting – you may not have to water it for weeks.

● Almost any clear, uncoloured glass or plastic container can be turned into a terrarium – sweet jars, fish bowls and aquariums. Containers with wide mouths are easiest to plant. A terrarium in a narrow-necked bottle is more difficult not only to set up, but also to rearrange if you want to add or remove plants. Woodland terrariums should have a cover (transparent), which will give the plants the necessary humidity.

● Though just about any species will thrive in a terrarium, it is best to stay with species that remain small. For a woodland terrarium, choose plants such as small ferns, mosses, ivies and creepers. Or choose among the many miniature varieties sold in garden shops. You may even have suitable candidates already at hand.

● Line the bottom of the terrarium with crushed gravel, for drainage. On top of this, distribute charcoal (of a type sold specifically for plants). This will "sweeten" the soil.

Key to Plants

1. Pilea depressa
2. Dracaena sanderiana
3. Nephrolepsis exaltata
4. Tortula muralis
5. Fittonia verschaffeltii
6. Peperomia argyeia

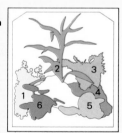

Metamorphosis varies with temperature. In a week or so, the pupa begins to wriggle.

The adult breaks free, crawls out and hangs upside-down, filling its crumpled wings.

Its wings firm and dry, the painted lady is now ready to fly. The life-cycle is completed.

Nature pursuits for a lifetime

An interest in nature is one of the few human activities that can endure for a lifetime. School ends, friends move to other places (or you do), and even your ambitions change. But an interest in nature is inborn – as you can easily see when you watch small children playing outdoors. Paradoxically, we tell children to stop gazing out of schoolroom windows and to look only at the blackboard, in order that they may learn to live in the real world. With some reluctance, they do this.

Ultimately, it becomes necessary for human beings to return to the wonder of nature. It is not so much the amount of time you have as how you use it. If a train is delayed at a country station, instead of fuming, use the time to look at any thick-

Grasses taller than a child may seem like private forests. In time, the child outgrows the grasses, but the remembrance of outdoor expeditions remains. The magic light of late afternoon, the tickling fronds of grass, the tangy cold air – such things confer a love of nature, and a lifetime sense of belonging.

ets near by. You are sure to find sparrows, and in spring or autumn, migrating birds often take shelter in such places.

Once you are on your way, look at the landscape as though you were a visiting geologist or botanist. (It is all too easy to be distracted by human habitations.) You can start with simple observation, but you can also go on to discover more about the area through which you are passing. Guidebooks are generally small enough to fit into a briefcase or duffel bag. Perhaps you will spot a place where you might like to go for a hike, thus becoming more familiar with your own region. The first step in studying natural history is to learn as much as you can about your immediate surroundings. You can add to that knowledge later.

Whenever you travel, at home or abroad, be sure to allow time to visit the countryside and look at wildlife and geological formations. Visit zoos, parks and wildlife refuges; compare them with ones you already know. Zoos are ideal places to see elusive or rare animals. If you live near a zoo, you may even be able to watch a young animal grow up over a period of months.

Sharing – learning from others, encouraging children, and teaching them to teach their own – is part of the enjoyment of nature. Would you not be delighted to find a journal written by one of your great-grandparents, telling about a journey or giving details of life long ago? The suggestion that such a record might exist would send most of us on an intensive search for it. Your own children and grandchildren would surely value such a journal from your hand. Why not consider keeping a log of a holiday, or an animal's life cycle (enacted within sight of your window), or notes on whatever aspects of nature interest you? If you see something fascinating, it is no time for false modesty about your skills as a writer. You might even illustrate your writings as you go, using simple line drawings.

You might contribute to the sum of human knowledge – there are a great number of plants and animals that have not yet had the full attention of scientists. Many small habitats await a biographer. Keen interest in a subject can make up for a lack of formal training. You may even become an expert in your field – whatever it may be. Do not be afraid to embark on something long-term; choose an activity that can be picked up and put down as your time allows – whether studying a particular plant or animal or learning to sketch.

Many stamps are true works of art – miniatures that are commissioned to be as accurate in detail as they are beautiful in effect. When you become a nature-stamp collector, you are taken on a treasure hunt. Say you have a stamp with a green turtle on it. This leads you to learn more about these endangered animals and their lives; you are likely to become one of their defenders. A collection of butterflies on stamps is far better than real ones. You can enjoy them and learn about them without depleting the natural populations.

HOW TO
Sharpen your powers of observation by sketching

The basic difference between a photograph and a sketch is not just in the end product. A skilled artist may produce a drawing remarkably like the image on film. The difference is in the kind of work that goes into the image and what you get out of it . An artist – experienced or not – must notice details more closely.

• Do not worry about accuracy at first, or about showing friends what you have done. Be prepared for a certain amount of clumsiness in your drawings. Sketching is like any other art. The less self-conscious you are – and the more you concentrate on what you are doing – the better your results. You can look on your sketching as a kind of private diary.

• Take a small, inexpensive sketch-pad along whenever you think you will have time to do a sketch or two. Many people are inhibited from drawing by the belief that you must have a certain amount of something known as talent to be successful. In fact, what you need is practice and persistence.

• If you find one kind of sketching too cumbersome (such as carrying a box of watercolours), switch to something else. Felt-tipped pens are convenient as artists' tools, though the products are less durable than charcoal or oils. A quick pencil sketch is pleasing and satisfying for many artists. Or use pen and ink.

• It helps to specialise in a particular subject – scenery, plants, birds – in order to develop proficiency in your sketching.

• Then give yourself time to enjoy this very personal kind of self-expression. Many people have found peace of mind in sketching out of doors.

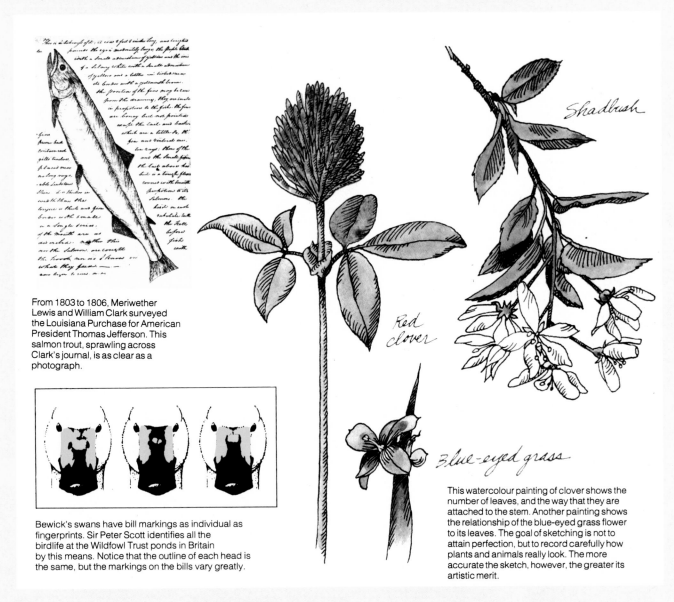

From 1803 to 1806, Meriwether Lewis and William Clark surveyed the Louisiana Purchase for American President Thomas Jefferson. This salmon trout, sprawling across Clark's journal, is as clear as a photograph.

Bewick's swans have bill markings as individual as fingerprints. Sir Peter Scott identifies all the birdlife at the Wildfowl Trust ponds in Britain by this means. Notice that the outline of each head is the same, but the markings on the bills vary greatly.

This watercolour painting of clover shows the number of leaves, and the way that they are attached to the stem. Another painting shows the relationship of the blue-eyed grass flower to its leaves. The goal of sketching is not to attain perfection, but to record carefully how plants and animals really look. The more accurate the sketch, however, the greater its artistic merit.

Glossary-Index

*This section provides definitions of nature terms
and an index to the contents of the book. Special box features
are here for future reference – and for your entertainment.*

What distinguishes this Glossary-Index from the index and glossary of most other books is that, here, the two have been combined. In addition, there are many special box features. (For further information on the subjects covered, consult the contents list on pp. 5, 6 and 7. And also look at the features on pp. 8 and 9, which subdivides these features into eight categories: photo tips, birdwatching tips, nature observer, hiking and camping, safety and survival, how to, collector's tips, and living with nature.)

General index entries

Many topics are so familiar – bark, roots, whales – that they do not require definition. Where appropriate, the scientific name of a species is given (there are many local variations in common names, but scientific names are fairly standardised). The index states what *aspect* of a subject is discussed in this book, which should save your time (or, conversely, arouse your interest). **Boldface** page numbers indicate illustrations.

Definitions that supplement the text

In many instances, a topic is discussed in the text, but the formal definition is reserved for the Glossary-Index. For example, symmetry is discussed on p. 14, illustrated on p. **15,** but not defined in either place (the objective of these pages is to call attention to the beauty of patterns in nature). Nevertheless, some readers may want to

Impressions on the human mind are like the channel of a stream, deepened by constant flow. The flow, for us, is experience – listening to the wind, feeling the warmth of the sun, watching the play of light on cascading water. All that we have learned makes each new experience richer.

know how symmetry is defined, if not at first, then perhaps when the subject comes up later; they can find it in the Glossary-Index.

Box features of general interest

Topics that are referred to in many parts of the book, such as energy, have been brought together as box features. Enjoyable oddities, such as correct collective nouns for different species, have been added. Then there are general references, such as the box that gives you the two sets of formulae for converting the old system of measure to the metric, and the metric to inches, pounds, and so on. On the next page, you will find a box on one of the most misunderstood of all subjects – scientific classification. Many people believe that the classification of plants, animals and minerals is all settled. In fact, the reverse is true; it is full of spirited debate. The purpose of classification is to make a subject easier to understand and to put new information in perspective with what we already know.

Science is ever-changing, open to all

Science influences our lives too profoundly for us to leave it to the experts. For instance, there is a real need to know about the land – our lives depend upon it. But practicality alone is not why we are interested in nature. For many people, birdwatching, hiking, or just sitting outdoors taking in the sounds and scents of nature is a recreation of the pleasantest kind. Once you get started, the more experience you have as a nature explorer, the easier it is to learn more. Probably the most exciting discovery you can make – whether in childhood or as an adult – is that there are aspects of nature that still need investigating, and that *you* can join in the expedition.

The key to classification: King Philip came over for ginger snaps

The nonsense sentence in the title is a memory device for the basic sequence in classification – **K**ingdom, **P**hylum, **C**lass, **O**rder, **F**amily, **G**enus, **S**pecies. This system, designed by Carolus Linnaeus, an 18th-century Swedish botanist, is a means of categorising the diverse components of the natural world – plants, animals and minerals.

Linnaeus made it possible for people of many nationalities to speak the language of science. The system is based on Latin, but there are many words and parts of words borrowed from Greek and other languages. Therefore, it is more accurate to speak of *scientific* names, rather than *Latin* names.

The broadest categories

The system starts with gross differences. In Linnaeus's time, there was a sharp dividing line between plants and animals. Animals were generally capable of independent movement, and dependent on other living matter, either plant or animal, for their food. Thus there were two living *kingdoms*, and one separate, non-living kingdom of minerals.

With the later development of high-powered microscopes, the betwixt-and-between organisms came to light. For example, there is a one-celled organism called Euglena, which moves like an animal (using one or more whip-like tails), and also has chlorophyll within its body (which is a plant characteristic).

Nowadays, many scientists recognise four living kingdoms – the Monera (which includes bacteria and blue-green algae), Protista (other algae, fungi and protozoa), Metaphyta (complex plants), and Metazoa (complex animals). If minerals are included, the total number of kingdoms is five.

Ever finer distinctions

The first division under kingdom is *phylum*. Though this word may seem unfamiliar, we use the idea daily – molluscs, such as mussels, make up one phylum, sponges another, and animals with backbones yet another.

The next subdivision is *class*. For example, among complex plants, all flowering plants form a single class. Because all distinctions in classification are based on similarities and differences, the number of members in a particular class varies greatly. For example, the class Insecta contains about 3 million species, but the millipedes, which are in a class by themselves, number only 6,000 or so. This disparity in numbers runs through the whole system of classification.

Within each class, there are one or more *orders*. For example, the class Mammalia contains the order Rodentia, which includes mice, chinchillas and other rodents. Another order is Primates, which includes monkeys.

A family resemblance

It is at the *family* level that most people begin to feel comfortable about classification (not even the most dedicated scientist knows all the subdivisions, which include super-groups and sub-groups at each level). Anyone can see that cats belong to one family, Felidae, and dogs to another, Canidae.

However, there are always oddities to keep things interesting. For example, the giant panda is a problem in classification. It has some claim to membership in the bear family (Ursidae). Its brain, blood proteins, and the tiny size of its cubs at birth are fairly close to bear types. But it is also a candidate for the raccoon family (Procyonidae) because its calls are like some members of the raccoon family. The giant panda does not sleep in winter as bears do, but remains active like the raccoon family.

After the name of many a pretty flower, you are likely to find a long, unfamiliar, double name. This includes the *genus* and *species*, which form the scientific name of the species. These words are frequently given in *italic* type after the common name; the genus is capitalised, the species not. (You will find the genus and species throughout this Glossary-Index. In some instances, species will be abbreviated to *sp.* This means the reference applies to more than one species within the genus.)

Genus and species are rather like names for individual people – they are quite specific forms of identification. They are especially practical when referring to plants and animals on different continents. On p. 294, there are three birds called robins; even though they were all named by English-speaking people, the birds are different. Thus the word robin is insufficient.

When it comes to different languages, the problem of common names becomes even greater. What is called butterfly in English is called mariposa in Spanish, papillon in French, farfalla in Italian, and Schmetterling in German. But every nationality is able to follow – and make use of – scientific names in study and correspondence. Here is the biological classification of a monarch butterfly:

Category	Name
Kingdom	Metazoa
Phylum	Arthropoda
Class	Insecta
Order	Lepidoptera
Family	Danaidae
Genus	*Danaus*
Species	*plexippus*

The monarch butterfly appears on p. 17, together with the viceroy butterfly. Like all butterflies, the viceroy belongs to the same kingdom, phylum, class and order. But it is in a different family (Nymphalidae) and its specific name – genus and species – is *Limenitis archippus*.

Traditionally, a species has been defined as a group of related organisms that can interbreed and produce fertile offspring. But this is not a flawless definition because some organisms, especially plants, hybridise and produce fertile offspring – for example, some ferns.

Recent revisions

Biologists are constantly reclassifying the species. The great blue heron and the great white heron, once thought to be two different species, are now considered to be colour variations of the same species.

Recently, ornithologists compared characteristics of a large number of Traill's flycatchers. They discovered that there were really two bird species involved – the willow flycatcher and alder flycatcher, differing in habitat and song.

To birdwatchers, this reclassification had more than theoretical importance; it gave them one more species to be counted on their "life lists" (see p. 295). Numerically minded birdwatchers greatly appreciate classification changes that split species, and bemoan changes that lump species and cause them to lose a bird entry from their life lists, built up so painstakingly.

For most plant and animal entries in this index, the scientific name follows the common name. When the name appears in *italics*, it is the genus and species. The genus is in capital letters and the species is sometimes abbreviated to *sp.* (when it refers to more than one species). If the scientific name is *not* italicised, the reference is to a larger grouping, such as family, order, or class. Definitions are included to supplement the information given elsewhere. Illustrations are noted in **bold** type.

A

B

basalt – volcanic rock that comes from the molten layer below the crust of the earth (in its molten state, the material is called magma, and is located in the earth's upper mantle).

Basalt rises in liquid form. As lava, it varies in consistency from place to place, depending on what other substances are

ABCs of scientific names

Translating a scientific name – made up of the genus and species – can be both informative and entertaining. For example, the second part of the scientific name – the species – of the 7-spot ladybird is *7-punctata;* a more heavily spotted relative is *22-punctata.* The species name of the ruffed grouse is *umbellus,* meaning parasol – a description of the ruff of feathers raised during courtship.

Prefixes, suffixes, and roots in scientific names are worth learning because they recur throughout the plant and animal kingdoms. For example, many names include the suffix *-phaga,* from the Greek word meaning eater. The prefix *pitheco-* means monkey, and *Pithecophaga* is the genus of the monkey-eating eagle. (The bird is actually more of a pig-eater than a monkey-eater.) *Lagos* means hare. Surprisingly, ptarmigan belong to the genus *Lagopus,* or hare-footed. What the construction of this name points out is that the birds have "fuzzy" feet like hares (especially in winter).

Scientific names are usually combinations of Latin or Greek syllables. Here are approximate translations for some syllables that make up scientific names in this index. The actual spellings vary from name to name. For example, *Vulgaris* means common. The red squirrel is *Sciurus vulgaris;* the common limpet is *Patella vulgata;* and a widespread species of barley is *Hordeum vulgare.* Though two unrelated creatures may have the same species name (the starling is *Sturnus vulgaris*), their first (genus) names are never the same.

Some of the names refer to nations – *Branta canadensis* is the Canada goose. Others refer to people – *Gazella granti,* for instance, is the Grant's gazelle.

PARTS

capill	hair	*Eolophus rosei**capill**us* (galah)
caud	tail	*Stercorarius longi**caud**us* (long-tailed jaeger)
folium	leaf	*Campanula rotundi**folia*** (harebell)
gnath	jaw	*Pero**gnath**us pencillatus* (desert pocket mouse)
pod	foot	*Poly**pod**ium vulgare* (common polypody)
pter	wing	*Mega**pter**a novaeangliae* (humpback whale)
rhiz	root	*Spirodela poly**rhiz**a* (great duckweed)
rhynch	snout	*Anas platy**rhynch**os* (mallard)
rostrum	beak	*Phloea longi**rostris*** (Brazilian stink bug)
		*Rallus longi**rostris*** (clapper rail)

COLOUR AND LIGHT

alb	white	*Casmerodius **alb**us* (great egret)
		*Crocethia **alb**a* (sanderling)
argent	silver	*Larus **argent**atus* (herring gull)
aur	gold	*Mesocricetus **aur**atus* (golden hamster)
		*Seirus **aur**ocapillus* (ovenbird)
cerulean	sky blue	*Florida **caerulea*** (little blue heron)
chrys	gold	*Aquila **chrys**aetos* (golden eagle)
		***Chrys**opsis falcata* (sickle-leaved golden aster)
ciner	ashes	*Gibbula **ciner**aria* (grey topshell)
cyan	dark blue	*Circus **cyan**eus* (marsh hawk)
fulg	bright	*Haliotis **fulg**ens* (green abalone)
fulva	yellow-brown	*Hemerocallis **fulva*** (day lily)
		*Petrochelidon **fulva*** (cave swallow)
fusca	dark, tawny	*Dendroica **fusca*** (blackburnian warbler)
		*Ranatra **fusca*** (water scorpion)
gris	grey	*Limnodromus **gris**eus* (short-billed dowitcher)
leuc	white	*Lagopus **leuc**urus* (white-tailed ptarmigan)
		*Loxia **leuc**optera* (white-winged crossbill)
mel	black	*Ameirus **mel**os* (black bullhead)
rubr	red	*Phoenicopterus **rubr**er* (greater flamingo)
		*Pseudotriton **rubr**er* (red salamander)
virescens	green	*Alnus **virid**is* (green alder)
		*Picus **virid**is* (green woodpecker)

SIZE SHAPE AND NUMBER

arista	spiny	*Pinus **arista**ta* (bristlecone pine)
brachy	short	*Corvus **brachy**rhynchos* (common crow)
brevi	short	*Yucca **brevi**folia* (Joshua tree)
campana	bell	***Campan**ula rotundifolia* (harebell)
elongato	elongated	*Mammillaria **elongata*** (lady-finger cactus)
falcate	sickle-shaped	*Chrysopsis **falcata*** (sickle-leaved golden aster)
gibbous	humpbacked	***Gibbula** cineraria* (grey topshell)
lati	broad	*Cynanthus **lati**rostris* (broad-billed hummingbird)
nan	dwarf	*Eritrichium **nan**um* (alpine forget-me-not)
onco	tumour	***Onco**rhynchus nerka* (sockeye salmon)
oxy	pointed	*Acipenser **oxy**rhynchus* (Atlantic sturgeon)
pero	pouch	***Pero**gnathus pencillatus* (desert pocket mouse)
platy	flat	*Anas **platy**rhynchos* (mallard)
poly	many	***Poly**podium vulgare* (common polypody)
vesic	bladder	*Fucus **vesic**ulosis* (bladder wrack)

BEHAVIOUR AND HABITS

ceutho	hide	***Ceutho**philus stygius* (cave cricket)
decidua	deciduous	*Larix **decidua*** (European larch)
garrulous	talkative	***Garrulus** glandarius* (European jay)
pugnax	aggressive	*Uca **pugnax*** (marsh fiddler crab)
tremulous	quivering	*Populus **tremul**oides* (quaking aspen)

HABITAT

dendr	trees	***Dendr**oica fusca* (blackburnian warbler)
hal	sea	***Hal**iotis fulgens* (green abalone)
limn	lake	***Limn**odromus griseus* (short-billed dowitcher)
nival	snow	*Microtus **nival**is* (snow vole)
palustris	swamp	*Telmatodytes **palustris*** (long-billed marsh wren)
pelagic	open ocean	*Physalia **pelagica*** (Portuguese man-of-war)
petr	rock	***Petr**ochelidon fulva* (cave swallow)
stygian	subterranean	*Ceuthophilus **stygius*** (cave cricket)
sylva	woods	*Myosotis **sylva**tica* (cultivated forget-me-not)

Yearly census of British birds

Since 1962 there has been a census of birds in Britain. Volunteers at more than 250 sites all over the country make a careful count of numbers of each species in spring and summer and compare them with figures for the previous year. When the information is assembled at Tring, Hertfordshire, it produces a national picture of bird life. For instance, the census showed that the bitter winter of early 1963 killed about 79% of British wrens, 59% of moorhens and 59% of song thrushes. The census also gives a clear pattern of the damage wreaked on our bird population by pollution and some farm chemicals. Armed with undisputable figures, provided in this way, ornithologists can campaign effectively for the protection of birds and suggest ways in which human progress can be made without annihilating wildlife.

Blackbirds head the list

To the surprise of many town-dwellers, the census shows that the house sparrow is not our most common bird, despite the numbers in which it congregates around our town houses. The leader is the blackbird, once a woodland dweller, that has adapted itself happily to life close to human beings in town and country alike. Included in the census are summer visitors from the Continent – and some who stayed on. Forty years ago the nearest collared doves lived in the Balkans. The first "tourists" flew over to Lincolnshire in 1952 and since then there is hardly a district in the country where they have not settled. A close eye is also kept on birds that are in danger of extinction in Britain, such as the Dartford warbler, which requires gorsy heathland – now being swallowed up by spreading farms and housing developments – and the eagles and falcons threatened by pesticides.

climate – the description of precipitation and temperature over a relatively large area, covering a substantial period of time. Hours of sunlight (which vary greatly according to the latitude) and the force, frequency, and direction of winds are all part of the general description of climate. *Weather* may fluctuate a great deal from one year to another, but *climate*, considered as an average of decades, may remain fairly constant for centuries.

composite – a large family of flowering plants, technically known as the Compositae. A typical composite flower is made up of a number of florets, hence the name. Some florets are clustered in a central disc, and others form rays that extend outwards from the centre of the disc. Daisies, sunflowers, asters, and thistles are all composites.

The full array of constellations

Though the word constellation comes from the Latin meaning "stars together", the constellations are really human inventions. (See pages 252-253, and notice the illustration on page **253** that shows the great distances among the stars in the Plough. Such distances are characteristic of all constellations.)

Nevertheless, constellations are useful reference points in the sky, whether for navigation or the identification of a particular star. Here are the 88 official constellations, with their technical (Latin) and common English names. There is no point anywhere on the globe from which all of the constellations can be seen.

Latin name	English name
Andromeda	Andromeda
Antlia	Pump
Apus	Bird of Paradise
Aquarius	Water Carrier
Aquila	Eagle
Ara	Altar
Aries	Ram
Auriga	Charioteer
Boötes	Herdsman
Caelum	Chisel
Camelopardalis	Giraffe
Cancer	Crab
Canes Venatici	Hunting Dogs
Canis Major	Bigger Dog
Canis Minor	Smaller Dog
Capricornus	Horned Goat
Carina	Keel
Cassiopeia	Cassiopeia
Centaurus	Centaur
Cepheus	Cepheus
Cetus	Whale
Chamaeleon	Chameleon
Circinus	Pair of Compasses
Columba	Dove
Coma Berenices	Berenice's Hair
Corona Australis	Southern Crown
Corona Borealis	Northern Crown
Corvus	Crow
Crater	Cup
Crux	(Southern) Cross
Cygnus	Swan
Delphinus	Dolphin
Dorado	Dorado
Draco	Dragon
Equuleus	Colt
Eridanus	Eridanus
Fornax	Furnace
Gemini	Twins
Grus	Crane
Hercules	Hercules
Horologium	Clock
Hydra	Water Monster
Hydrus	Male Water Monster
Indus	Indian

Latin name	English name
Lacerta	Lizard
Leo	Lion
Leo Minor	Smaller Lion
Lepus	Hare
Libra	Balance
Lupus	Wolf
Lynx	Lynx
Lyra	Lyre
Mensa	Table
Microscopium	Microscope
Monoceros	Unicorn
Musca	Fly
Norma	Square
Octans	Octant
Ophiuchus	Serpent Holder
Orion	Orion
Pavo	Peacock
Pegasus	Pegasus
Perseus	Perseus
Phoenix	Phoenix
Pictor	Easel
Pisces	Fishes
Piscis Austrinus	Southern Fish
Puppis	Stern
Pyxis	Mariner's Compass
Reticulum	Net
Sagitta	Arrow
Sagittarius	Archer
Scorpius	Scorpion
Sculptor	Sculptor
Scutum	Shield
Serpens	Serpent
Sextans	Sextant
Taurus	Bull
Telescopium	Telescope
Triangulum	Triangle
Triangulum Australe	Southern Triangle
Tucana	Toucan
Ursa Major	Great Bear
Ursa Minor	Little Bear
Vela	Sails
Virgo	Virgin
Volans	Flying Fish
Vulpecula	Little Fox

Endangered species

Everyone has heard of the plight of certain animals, endangered because their
habitats are being destroyed and their
populations over-hunted. In the crowded
world of South-east Asia, there is no
longer room for tigers to roam (see page
150). In different places, but for similar
reasons, orang-utans, snow leopards,
whooping cranes, and California condors
are becoming extinct. Other large mammals have been eliminated from certain
regions – for example, wolves, lynxes,
and brown bears no longer live in the
Swiss Alps (see the chart on page **89**).

Status report

This book is mainly concerned with plants
and animals you are likely to see. Therefore, we have shown only a few of the
endangered species. For illustrations of
some that are listed as threatened by the
International Union of Conservation of
Nature and Natural Resources (I.U.C.N.),
see the following entries in this index:
hunting dog (African), peregrine falcon
(American), bighorn sheep, whale (the
blue, humpback, and right are
threatened), cheetah, chinchilla, and
Malayan tapir.

ecology – the study of the interaction of living things with their environment (the prefix eco- means house). Therefore, a book about nature, such as this one, is really a book about ecology. In addition to a close-up view of nature, you can also take a global approach. There are six regions, or realms, set off by notable differences in animal life. For example, the *Australian Realm* (including New Zealand and New Guinea) has unique marsupials – kangaroos, koalas, and many more. Their presence is evidence that Australia broke away from the other continents before the rise of the more advanced mammals, which have replaced most marsupial populations elsewhere. The *Palaearctic Realm* extends from western Europe to the Pacific, as far south as the Sahara and the Himalayas. The *Nearctic*, which takes in Greenland and North America (down into Mexico), has species that are more closely related to animals in the Palaearctic than to species in the *Neotropic Realm* – which includes Central and South America. This is because the Nearctic and Palaearctic have been connected to one another by land bridges on several occasions. The *Ethiopian Realm* takes in most of the African continent. The *Oriental Realm* includes India, Indochina, and Malaysia. Within each of these realms are many biomes. The factors which have to be considered in an ecological study are air, water, soil, climate and every kind of living thing, plant or animal, all of which are closely intertwined. The word "ecology" is often used incorrectly to mean concern for the environment and its preservation, rather than the study of natural history.

ecotone – the border region between two neighbouring ecological communities.

environment – the total surroundings of an organism. We are accustomed to taking into account the non-living aspects of the environment – soil, water, air, climate, and the like. But the environment also includes plants and animals – all the forms of life that may influence an organism, whether through predation, competition, or some other interaction.

epiphyte – a plant that grows on top of another plant, such as on the limb of a tree. This helps the epiphyte (also called an air plant) to absorb the sunlight necessary for photosynthesis. Epiphytes, which are common in tropical rain forests, include Spanish moss (a type of lichen), staghorn fern, and many species of orchid.

The recovery of the trumpeter swan (a bird that is pictured on page **187**) can be considered an ecological success story. Though still rare, this bird has undergone a tremendous population increase during the last decades – thanks to a ban on hunting, the establishment of a refuge in Wyoming, and also the transplanting of colonies to new locations.

Small species are also waning
Not all endangered animals are large and spectacular ones. Certain butterflies, molluscs, fish, salamanders, and representatives of nearly every major group are disappearing, some without even being noticed. About 10% of the world's flowering plants are threatened with extinction (see common flowers versus rarities, page 156).

What is needed is an understanding of the relationship between the environment and the life-style of a particular species, and also an awareness that each species is a unique product of countless evolutionary changes. In the words of William Beebe, the American explorer and naturalist, "When the last individual of a race of living things breathes no more, another heaven and another earth must pass before such a one can be again."

Energy in many forms
The earth is daily supplied with a great influx of energy from the sun. The problem for those who would make use of it is in its storage. Solar panels, of the kind that power space satellites, are still expensive to manufacture, but solar technology is making progress as the supply of fossil fuels decreases. France, in particular, has made great advances in this field.

Efficient power plants
Plants capture energy from the sun in their green pigment – chlorophyll (see page 46). The plants, in turn, supply energy to animals (see food chains and webs, pages 148, **148,** 149). Fossil fuels – coal and petroleum – are the remains of once-living things. What makes these fuels so valuable is their capacity to store energy for millions of years. The energy of coal and petroleum is available whenever it is needed, and it can be kept in reserve indefinitely. (See the discussion of coal and petroleum formation on pages 286, **286, 287**.)

Water power
Hydroelectric power is created by water rushing through generators at the sites of waterfalls and dams. This energy is used rapidly, travelling with great speed through power lines. Like the chemical energy in batteries and fuel cells, the problem with this kind of energy is how to store it.

Tapping internal pressures
Geothermal energy uses the heat given off by the molten interior of the earth. This technology is well developed in certain geothermal regions where the crust of the earth makes such steam heat readily available (see pages 268, **268, 269**). In some places, all the buildings – dwellings, offices, schools, and factories alike – are linked to a central-heating system, based on this natural heat.

The newest and the oldest
Atomic energy is tremendously powerful. However, many people consider this source to be too hazardous, and the disposal of nuclear waste material does pose serious problems. Harnessing the winds is frequently proposed. Windmills are an ancient means of doing just that, but they fell into disuse with the arrival of inexpensive electricity. Windmills are now enjoying a renaissance. Tides, too, are under consideration as sources of power, but they are often strong and erratic. At the moment, they do not seem as promising as other energy sources, but research into the possibilities continues, and may bear fruit in the future.

How birds are adapted to flight

Few animals change their environment as drastically as a bird does every time it becomes airborne. With few exceptions – the ostrich, rhea, emu, kiwi and penguin, which walk, waddle, or swim rather than fly – birds fly with amazing grace. Their flying capability is a result of their light weight, streamlined bodies, and remarkable plumage. Large bones – in wings, legs, and skull – are thin and hollow. For example, the bones of one frigatebird, a tropical flier with a 7 ft wingspan, weighed only 4 oz. In soaring birds, such as vultures, air-filled wing bones have interior crosspieces, or struts, like those that support the wings of a plane.

The air within
Another extraordinary adaptation to flight is a system of air sacs, which fill much of a bird's abdominal cavity and are linked with the air spaces in the bones, as well as with the lungs. A mallard, for example, has five air sacs. A bird actually breathes throughout its body. In a continuous, one-way flow, air passes directly from the bronchial tubes into the sacs and then into the lungs. (In mammals, air flows into and out of the lungs, rather than through them.) This means that the blood of birds is richly supplied with oxygen. Flight also depends on the structure of a bird's wings, and the way it uses them. Joints where wings meet shoulders enable the wings to be moved up and down. These vertical movements supply the power that propels the bird along. The large primary feathers on a bird's wings are what supports its weight in the air.

Varied patterns of flight
Small birds tend to have large wings in proportion to their size, and so are able to take to the air without much effort. Because of its shoulder joints, a hummingbird can hover before a flower and even fly backwards – something no other bird can do (see the photo of a broad-billed hummingbird on page 21). Heavy birds, such as vultures and storks, must supplement the lifting power of their wings. They do this by springing into the air (preferably from a height), by running to gain momentum, or by taking advantage of thermal updraughts in a combination of flapping and gliding. There is a broad spectrum of flying patterns, ranging from the rapid beating of a hummingbird's wings to the gliding flight of an albatross. An albatross, such as the one shown on page 108, seems not to flap its wings at all. Two closely related groups, the gulls and the terns, have different flight patterns. (See pages **122-123**.)

For most birds, landing is just as complex as taking off. Birds usually land against the wind. They create resistance to the air stream while in flight by changing their posture so that the body is erect. They also spread their wings and tail feathers to slow down their flying speed.

Perhaps the most astonishing aspect of these techniques of flight is that birds evolved originally from reptiles. At some unknown point many millions of years ago the scales of a reptile developed into feathers. It was more millions of years, however, before what we recognise as birds appeared on earth.

The sparrowhawk – an accipiter, or typical hawk – is a bird of rapid flight. It can dash through a wooded area in pursuit of its prey, or soar with intermittent wing flaps over open country. This bird, in its habitat, appears in colour on page 52.

The marsh harrier (or marsh hawk, as it is called in America) often sails a few feet above the vegetation, holding its wings in a V and tilting from side to side. It may hover briefly over land or water before swooping down to strike its prey (see page 131).

G

Comfort on a day's outing

Most people these days go into the countryside by car and spend only a few hours at a time on their feet. Here are some tips for this sort of expedition:

• Always carry a packet of elastic stick-on dressings to end the misery of walking with a blistered heel. Keep the packet permanently in a glove pocket. It can also be useful for small cuts.

• Take a big plastic bottle of fresh water. The one bottle will serve for giving the dog a drink, washing, washing up and topping up the radiator.

• One or two large towels seldom come home unused. They may be wanted for swimming, or washing and drying someone who puts his foot in a stream.

• Tea carried for hours in a vacuum flask tastes awful. Carry hot water in the flask and make your tea fresh with tea bags. Big flasks have a compartment for a milk bottle. Coffee also tastes better freshly made.

• Keep a paper bag for your rubbish. Throw it into a waste basket if you find one. If not, take it home and put it in your own dustbin.

• The big, plastic sheet sold as a car luggage-cover makes an excellent groundsheet if held down with stones.

Geological time – its divisions and characteristic life-forms

This chart shows the *sequence* of geological events, starting with the earliest at the bottom and ending with the most recent at the top. The number of years within each span of time is still a matter of speculation. New techniques of measurement have brought greater precision to the establishing of actual dates.

But because geological time is so long the precise dates are not of vital importance to appreciation. What do these divisions of time really mean? Rock is recycled constantly as the surface of the earth is steadily worn away and the rock particles are redeposited.

The name of a rock stratum refers to the most recent time the rock was deposited. For example, Cambrian rock was deposited in the Cambrian Period, and may contain trilobites (see page 285 for a picture of a fossil trilobite and more about the use of fossils in establishing the age of rocks). Few rock layers seem to have remained stationary since their original deposition. On page **283,** you will see how some layers have been tilted. (Notice that several rock formations have been laid down within a single period. Also note irregularities in the thickness of layers and the rate of erosion.)

ERA A major division of time	PERIOD Mainly associated with rock deposits	EPOCH Only two periods are subdivided into epochs
CENOZOIC (65 million years to the present) We are living in the Cenozoic Era, which is shorter than the other eras. (The prefix ceno- means new or recent; -zoic refers to life.) For the most part, the climate has been colder in the Cenozoic than in earlier eras. The four major Ice Ages have profoundly influenced life-forms, and at the same time reshaped the land over which the icy masses travelled. During the Cenozoic, mammals have dominated the land. When the last of the great glaciers retreated, man emerged as the most important animal on earth. He has become the main agent of ecological change, transforming the world's vegetation and often destroying the habitats of other creatures.	**QUATERNARY PERIOD** The onset of glaciation marked the beginning of this period.	**HOLOCENE** The rise of civilisation.
		PLEISTOCENE Ice Ages. Mastodons died out.
	TERTIARY PERIOD Tertiary means third, and is a legacy from the 18th-century convention of dividing geological time into four parts. Two great mountain chains developed during the Tertiary. According to the continental-drift theory, the Alps resulted from a collision between Europe and Africa; the Himalayas developed when India collided with Asia.	**PLIOCENE** Large carnivores were prevalent.
		MIOCENE Mammals diversified.
		OLIGOCENE Primitive apes appeared.
		EOCENE Rise of grasses (which yield grain).
		PALEOCENE Appearance of earliest horses.
MESOZOIC (225 to 65 million years ago) "Mesos" is the Greek word for middle. This era is known as the Age of Reptiles, for they conquered the land, air, and water.	**CRETACEOUS PERIOD** Dinosaurs died out. Flowering plants developed.	
	JURASSIC PERIOD Dinosaurs were abundant. The first birds appeared.	
	TRIASSIC PERIOD Earliest dinosaurs and mammals developed.	
PALEOZOIC (600 to 225 million years ago) Marine invertebrates were the dominant life-forms during the early part of the Paleozoic Era; later in this era, some animals gradually colonised the land. The Paleozoic was once considered the earliest division of geological time (paleo- means ancient). The fossil record before the start of this era is so incomplete that the chronology of events (when certain plants and animals evolved, and in what sequence) has not yet been established precisely by scientists.	**PERMIAN PERIOD** Insects appeared, amphibians increased, and trilobites died out.	
	CARBONIFEROUS PERIOD Enormous coal-forming forests flourished.	
	DEVONIAN PERIOD Sharks and other large fish were widespread.	
	SILURIAN PERIOD First land plants; some air-breathing animals.	
	ORDOVICIAN PERIOD Fish appeared, as well as coral and animals with shells.	
	CAMBRIAN PERIOD Trilobites prevalent; North America mostly covered by seas.	

PRECAMBRIAN – once a blanket term for the earliest time in earth's history – has been subdivided. The Proterozoic Era began about 1,200 million years ago; sponges and jellyfish lived in the water. The Archeozoic Era began 2,000 million years ago, when bacteria and algae drifted in warm seas. The Azoic Era (meaning without life) started when the earth formed, some 5,000 million years ago. Precambrian rocks are found in Britain in the "Lewisian Complex" along the north-western coast of Scotland. The Outer Hebrides, together with the islands of Coll and Tiree, are also composed of Precambrian rock. The oldest examples have been put at 2,600 million to 2,400 million years old.

gypsum – a common, commercially important mineral used in the manufacture of plaster of Paris. (Early gypsum quarries were in Paris – hence the name plaster of Paris.) Chemically, gypsum is known as hydrous calcium sulphate. Alabaster and selenite are two forms of the mineral gypsum.
  —**213**
  —See also selenite

H

Horns versus antlers

Deer and antelope are confused in many people's minds because of their obvious similarities. They are graceful, hoofed animals with striking head adornments. Actually, their headgear is the easiest way to tell them apart. Every child knows that Santa's reindeer have *antlers*. These are impressive and complex structures of solid bone. Usually antlers have many branches, called points or tines. Antelope, on the other hand, have *horns*, which may be long or short, spiral, straight, or curved.

Antlers are shed annually

New antlers appear as small velvety knobs filled with blood vessels. The bony structure forms inside this velvet covering; after several months, the antler hardens and the velvet peels off. Males of the deer family – Cervidae – are antlered; females may have smaller bony growths. In two species, the Chinese water deer and the musk deer, the males have no antlers.

Horns are permanent

Hollow and bony, horns grow throughout the animal's life and are not replaced if lost or injured. Members of the large family Bovidae, which includes antelope, bison, goats, sheep, and cattle, have true horns, Giraffes and their relative, the okapi, have short, skin-covered horns. Old males of some giraffe species may have a extra horn or even an extra pair. The different kinds of rhinoceros have one or two solid horns of a fibrous material.

In a family by itself

The North American pronghorn looks and behaves like an antelope (see page **147**). Because of its peculiarities, the pronghorn is placed in a family of its own, the Antilocapridae (meaning antelope-goat). It has short, erect horns that develop over a permanent bony core. The outer, horny covering is replaced each year by a new horn that pushes up underneath it.

Continents apart

Geography separates the many species of deer from the antelopes. Deer are spread over Europe, North and South America, and Asia; they are missing from Africa except for the north-western corner. South of the Sahara, the large and small antelopes fill the niche occupied by deer on the other continents.

The subcontinent of India is one place where the ranges of deer and antelope overlap, but they do not compete in the same habitat.

Introduced species – plants and animals transported by man

Living things do not stay put. Plants move about as seeds, carried by wind and water; animals make their own way to new homes. And ever since man began travelling around the globe, human beings have moved plants and animals from one place to another. Some transplants, such as zoo animals, are not released into the wild, and so they cannot be considered colonists of a new land. But others, called introduced species, become an established part of the flora or fauna. House sparrows are a clas-sic example. These birds, which were set free in New York to add a touch of Britain to the New World, now breed over most of North America. The Indian mongoose was transplanted to the West Indies (and other places) for a different reason – its habit of eating rodents. A variety of garden flowers have "escaped" and proliferated in the wild. The forget-me-not (page **91**), Queen Anne's lace (page **154**), and ox-eye daisy (page **137**) are all introduced species in North America. In reality, the expression "introduced species" can be misleading. It implies deliberate human action, which is not always the case. For example, no one *wanted* the Japanese beetle in North America. Apparently it went over in a shipment of plants to a New Jersey nursery, found conditions to its liking, and spread across the land. A number of introduced species – some welcome, some not – are listed below. The list is by no means comprehensive, but serves to show that many introduced species have flourished.

North America
Tiger lily
(from Asia)

Water hyacinth
(from South America)

Japanese beetle
(from Asia)

Gypsy moth
(from Europe)

Cabbage butterfly
(from Europe)

Fire ant
(from South America)

Giant snail
(from Africa)

Ring-necked pheasant
(from Asia)

Starling
(from Europe)

Nutria
(from South America)

South America

Mosquito fish
(from North America)

Rabbit
(from Europe)

Europe
Himalayan balsam
(from Asia)

Chinese crab
(from Asia)

Colorado beetle
(from North America)

Slipper limpet
(from North America)

Mosquito fish
(from North America)

Reeves's pheasant
(from Asia)

Grey squirrel
(from North America)

Muskrat
(from North America)

Africa
Water hyacinth
(from South America)

Mosquito fish
(from North America)

Starling
(from Europe)

Grey squirrel
(from North America)

Asia
Water hyacinth
(from South America)

Cabbage butterfly
(from Europe)

Giant snail
(from Africa)

Mosquito fish
(from North America)

**Australia
and New Zealand**

Water hyacinth
(from South America)

Cabbage butterfly
(from Europe)

Fire ant
(from South America)

Mosquito fish
(from North America)

Chinook salmon
(from North America)

Rabbit
(from Europe)

hot spring, 268, **268, 269**
hummingbird, broad-billed *(Cynanthus latirostris),* **21**
hurricane, 230, 244-245, **244-245**
hydra *(Hydra oligactis)*
  Special feature: assembling and caring for a pond aquarium, **179**
hydrocarbon, **286**
hyena, spotted *(Crocuta crocuta),* **148**
hyrax, rock *(Heterohyrax sp.),* **95**

I J K

ibex *(Capra ibex),* **89**
ice, 240, **241**
  See also glaciers
ice cave, 277
ice lens, **99**
igneous rock (volcanic), 78-79, **78, 79,** 260
  Special feature: specialising in volcanic rocks, **79**
  See also basalt
Iguaçu Falls, Brazil-Argentina, **172**
impala *(Aepyceros melampus),* **27**
Indian grass *(Sorghastrum nutans),* **142**
insectivorous plants, 184-185, **185**

invertebrate – an animal without a spinal column, such as an insect, jellyfish, or worm. About 95% of all animal species are invertebrates, although they may seem less important than the vertebrates because they are not as large.
  — See individual groups or species

iridescence, 20, **21**
isobar, 234, **234-235**

jack-knife clam, Atlantic *(Ensis directus),* **119**
jackrabbit, antelope *(Lepus alleni),* **214**
jaeger, long-tailed *(Stercorarius longicaudus),* **8**
jasper, **271**
jay,
  European *(Garrulus gladarius),* **89, 295**
  Steller's *(Cyanocitta stelleri),* **88**
jellyfish
  moon jelly *(Aurelia aurita)*
  Special feature: beware of sea creatures that sting and pinch, **110**
jerboa,
  desert *(Jaculus jaculus),* **206**
  long-eared *(Euchoreutes naso),* **207**
Joshua tree *(Yucca brevifolia),* 212, **213**

jungle – a commonly used synonym for tropical rain forest (the term that ecolo-

gists prefer). Jungle is a misleading word because it conveys the image of impenetrable thickets, which actually occur only at the border of a rain forest. The phrase "law of the jungle" – meaning eat or be eaten – is also inappropriate because this expression is equally valid for any other biome.
  —See rain forest, tropical

juniper *(juniperus sp.),* **40**
  Special feature: different ways of identifying conifers, **41**
Jupiter
  Special feature: the word planet means "wanderer", **253**

kangaroo, red *(macropus rufus),* 146, **146**
kelp
  See tangles
kingfisher *(Alcedo atthis),* **180-181, 297**
kites
  Special feature: the ancient sport of flying a kite, **231**
krummholz, 97, **97**

L

lake – a relatively large, inland body of standing water. Characteristically, a lake has a deep, dark zone, where light does not penetrate. Therefore, plants do not grow on the entire bottom of a lake. A pond, which may be as wide as many a lake, is shallower and has plants rooted all along the bottom.
  —170-177, **170-177**
  Special feature: clues from maps, **174**
  —salt lakes, 204, **204, 205**
lapwing *(Vanellus vanellus),* **152-153**
larch,
  American *(Larix laricina),* **40**
  European *(Larix decidua),* **89**
  sky *(Alauda arvensis),* **55, 152-153**
  Special feature: different ways of identifying conifers, **41**
  western *(Larix occidentalis),* **88**

larva – an immature stage of an animal that is drastically different (not just in size) from the adult form. The larvae of some marine invertebrates, such as barnacles, drift in the sea, then attach to a surface and develop into the sedentary adults. Insect larvae, though always wingless, come in a variety of forms and are called caterpillars, grubs, maggots, or

nymphs, depending on the species. The larvae of amphibians are usually aquatic; a tadpole is the larval stage of a frog.
  —butterfly larva (caterpillar), **314-315**
  —caddisfly larva, **180-181**
  —dragonfly nymph, *Special feature:* assembling and caring for a pond aquarium, **179**
  —firefly larva, *Special feature:* watching the flashing patterns of fireflies, **20**
  —glowworm (gnat larva), **281**
  —japanese beetle larva, **162**
  —long-horned leaf beetle larva, 178
  —mayfly larva, *Special feature:* specialised lives in streams and torrents, **191**
  —mosquito larva, **23**
  —net-winged midge larva, *Special feature:* specialised lives in streams and torrents, **191**
  —red salamander larva, **180-181**
  —tadpole, **180-181,** *Special feature:* assembling and caring for a pond aquarium, **179**

lava, 78-79, **78**
  See also igneous rock
lava-tube cave, 277
lawn
  Special feature: grow a better lawn, 143

legume – a plant belonging to the family Leguminoseae (Fabaceae), such as sweet pea, alfalfa, honey locust, and acacia. A legume can be recognised by its flower (a butterfly-shaped blossom with five petals), and by its fruit (a dry or leathery bean-like pod that splits into two separate halves). Most legumes also have compound leaves; in other words, several leaflets grew from a common leaf-stalk. Legumes are extremely important to agriculture and to the world's food supply. On their roots grow large clusters of special types of bacteria, called nitrogen-fixing bacteria. These micro-organisms absorb nitrogen from the air and convert the gas to a form that plants can use. Since both bacteria and legume benefit from this relationship, their close association is an example of commensalism (see entry under symbiosis).
  —general discussion of legume family, 42-43
  —*See also* clover, lupine, mulga

lemming, Norway *(Lemmus lemmus),* **101**
lichen, 57, 88-89, **88**
  British soldier *(Cladonia cristatella),* **57**
  pixie cup *(Cladonia pyxidata),* 57

M

malachite – a green mineral made of copper carbonate. Malachite is a product of the weathering of other copper formations; the green tarnish that forms on copper and bronze is actually malachite. Large quantities have been found in Africa, the south-western United States, in the Ural Mountains of Russia, and in other places throughout the world.
—272

metamorphosis – a dramatic change (or series of changes) in the form of an animal after hatching. Meta- means beyond, and morph refers to form. (Morphology is the study of forms.) Amphibians and insects undergo such transformations. Among in-

Murmuration, exaltation or pod?

Collective nouns (or nouns of congregation) are often used to describe groupings of animals, whether they live in societies or come together only at certain times, such as the breeding season or during migration. Often, the very use of these words enhances the pleasure of watching the animals – you see how the names may have been derived from their behaviour.

Birds

cranes, herons	sedge, siege
crows	hover, murder
ducks	brace (a pair), flush, brood
eagles	convocation
falcons	cast
finches	charm
geese	gaggle, flock, skein (flying)
grouse	covey, pack
hawks	cast
lapwings	deceit
larks	exaltation, bevy
magpies	tiding
murres	bazaar
nightingales	watch
peacocks	muster
pheasants	nye, nest, nide, brood, flock
plovers	congregation, wing
quail	bevy, covey
ravens	unkindness
snipe	wisp, walk
sparrows	host
starlings	murmuration
swans	herd, game, bevy, drift, sounder
teal	spring
turkeys	rafter
wigeon	company
woodcock	fall, covey, flight

Mammals

beavers	colony
cats	clutter
cattle	herd, drove
deer	herd, leash (set of three)
elk	gang
ferrets	business
foxes	skulk
goats	tribe
hares	drove, kindle
horses	string
hounds	pack
kittens	litter
lions	pride
moles	company, labour
mules	pack
rabbits	colony, kindle
seals	herd
whales	pod, school
wolves	pack

Amphibians and reptiles

frogs	colony
toads	knot
snakes	den
vipers	nest

sects, there are two major types of metamorphosis – complete and simple (also called incomplete). Species with complete metamorphosis, such as butterflies and moths, have a pupal stage; insects with simple metamorphosis, such as dragonflies and grasshoppers, do not pass through this prolonged quiescent stage. One of the most interesting examples of metamorphosis, and one of the easiest to observe, is the development of the tadpole. You can watch it in your own aquarium (see page 179). Gradually it grows legs and, from an aquatic creature, develops into a land-living frog.

mica, white – a common, rock-forming mineral, also called muscovite. White mica, which is a compound of aluminium silicate, is an important component of granitic rock.

mirage – the reflection of light through layers of air of different densities, which creates the illusion of an object in a different place; or the illusion that something is wet when, in fact, all you are seeing is a shimmer of light.

Mammals – a highly diversified group

From platypus to peccary, from bat to bison, what makes a mammal different from other animals is that mammals nourish their young with milk. This characteristic plays more than a nutritional role in a mammal's world, for it often creates a strong relationship between mother and offspring.

In certain species, this relationship is short-lived; some mice are weaned 2 weeks after birth and breed at 5 weeks. At the other extreme is the walrus, which is believed to nurse for 2 years.

Mammals, like birds, are "warm-blooded". What this term means is that their body temperatures are relatively independent of the surroundings. Because of this, mammals are able to live in the coldest of climates and move about in practically any temperature. (Cold-blooded species require a certain amount of heat to become active.) Of course, this does not mean that all mammals are active at all times. Hibernators conserve energy by resting throughout the winter (see page 65); certain species, such as desert jerboas, become torpid in summer (see illustration on page 206). Estivation is the name for this summer torpor.

Most mammals have two sets of limbs. (Whales, manatees, and dugongs are the exceptions.) But the method of locomotion varies tremendously from species to species. Cheetahs run, rabbits jump, monkeys climb, beavers swim, gibbons swing, bats fly, and "flying" lemurs glide. Other mammals simply walk on all fours.

The successful rodents
Present-day mammals are classified into about 20 orders, depending on the system of classification used. A similar number of orders contains only extinct species. For example, the order Pantodonta is composed of the pantodonts – large hoofed creatures that died out about 35 million years ago.

As you can see from the list here, the different orders vary greatly in importance. Among mammals, rodents dominate the earth, in both number of species and total population. (There are some 2,000 kinds of rodents – about half of all mammalian species. And there may be more rodents on earth than all the other mammals put together.) In contrast, the aardvark, or earth-pig – an African termite-eater – has an order all to itself. The name of its order, Tubulidentata, refers to the microscopic tubules in aardvark teeth.

Teeth are highly significant in the classification of mammals. For one thing, they indicate an animal's eating habits. For example, aardvarks, like other mammals that eat termites or ants, have only a few teeth. The tropical animals known as anteaters have no teeth. (They are in the order Edentata, which means lacking teeth.)

Fortunately for taxonomists, teeth are durable structures that are frequently preserved as fossils. And fossils are perhaps *the* most important clue to relationships between groups of animals. Fossil evidence was a major reason for the reclassification of rabbits and their relatives. Once part of the order Rodentia, rabbits, hares and the tiny pikas of the Russian steppes are now in a separate order called Lagomorpha.

Mammalian orders

Monotremata: platypus, spiny anteater
Marsupialia: opossums, pouched "mice" and "rats", koala, wombats, kangaroos, wallabies, Tasmanian devil
Insectivora: hedgehogs, shrews, desmans, moles
Dermoptera: cobegos (flying lemurs)
Chiroptera: bats
Primates: lemurs, lorises, galagos, monkeys, gibbons, gorillas, chimpanzees
Edentata: sloths, anteaters, armadillos
Pholidota: pangolins
Lagomorpha: pikas, rabbits, hares
Rodentia: squirrels, chipmunks, cavies, chinchillas, mice, rats, beavers, muskrat, voles, kangaroo rats, hamsters, gerbils, porcupines, pacas, hutias
Cetacea: whales, dolphins, porpoises, narwhals
Carnivora: dogs, foxes, wolves, bears, raccoons, kinkajous, pandas, weasels, ferrets, minks, martens, fisher, wolverine, badgers, skunks, otters, genets, civets, mongooses, fossa, aardwolves, hyenas, lynxes, cats, caracal
Pinnipedia: sea lions, seals, walruses
Tubulidentata: aardvark
Proboscidea: elephants
Hyracoidea: rock hyraxes, dassies
Sirenia: manatees, dugong
Perissodactyla: horse, tapirs, rhinoceroses, zebras, burros, mules
Artiodactyla: pigs, peccaries, hippopotamuses, camels, chevrotains, antelopes, deer, giraffes, sheep, goats, cattle, musk ox, takin

Measurement: how to convert from one system to another

Measurement is the language of numbers. At present, the metric system is the official system of most of the world. Britain and America still operate halfway on the old system of feet, miles, pounds, etc., but the metric system is gaining ground. To use the equations here, take, say 5 inches, multiply by 25.4 to get the metric equivalent – 127 millimetres. Now do the reverse (pocket calculators are a great help). Multiply the 127 millimetres by the conversion figure for Imperial measure – 0.039. The result is 4.953 inches, which can be rounded off to 5 inches. In other words, there is a discrepancy in conversion. The relatively long conversion numbers try to compensate for this. The results are sufficiently accurate for most practical purposes.

IMPERIAL MEASURE	MULTIPLY BY	TO GET METRIC
Length and Distance		
inches	× 25.4	= millimetres
inches	× 2.54	= centimetres
feet	× 0.305	= metres
yards	× 0.9144	= metres
miles	× 1.609	= kilometres
Surface Area		
square inches	× 6.452	= square centimetres
square feet	× 0.093	= square metres
square yards	× 0.836	= square metres
acres	× 0.405	= hectares
square miles	× 2.58999	= square kilometres
Volume		
cubic inches	× 16.387	= cubic centimetres
cubic feet	× 0.028	= cubic metres
cubic yards	× 0.765	= cubic metres
Capacity		
fluid ounces	× 28.41	= millilitres
pints	× 0.568	= litres
quarts	× 1.136	= litres
gallons	× 4.546	= litres
bushels	× 36.4	= litres
Weight		
grains	× 0.0648	= grammes
ounces avdp.	× 28.35	= grammes
pounds avdp.	× 0.45359	= kilogrammes
tons	× 0.907	= metric tons
Temperature		
(degrees Fahrenheit −32) × $\frac{5}{9}$ =degrees Celsius		

METRIC MEASURE	MULTIPLY BY	TO GET IMPERIAL
Length and Distance		
millimetres	× 0.039	= inches
centimetres	× 0.3937	= inches
metres	× 3.281	= feet
metres	× 1.094	= yards
kilometres	× 0.621	= miles
Surface Area		
square centimetres	× 0.155	= square inches
square metres	× 10.764	= square feet
square metres	× 1.196	= square yards
hectares	× 2.471	= acres
square kilometres	× 0.3861	= square miles
Volume		
cubic centimetres	× 0.061	= cubic inches
cubic metres	× 35.315	= cubic feet
cubic metres	× 1.308	= cubic yards
Capacity		
millilitres	× 0.0351	= fluid ounces
litres	× 1.76	= pints
litres	× 0.88	= quarts
litres	× 0.22	= gallons
litres	× 0.0275	= bushels
Weight		
grammes	× 15.43	= grains
grammes	× 0.035	= ounces avdp.
kilogrammes	× 2.205	= pounds avdp.
metric tons	× 1.102	= tons
Temperature		
(degrees Celsius ×1.8) + 32 = degrees Fahrenheit		

N

O

Navigation and orientation among animals

How animals find their way is remarkable for at least two reasons – the variety of methods used, and the skill with which the different species navigate. For example, whales and seals produce pulsing sounds underwater. When such sounds are reflected back from some object – perhaps a reef or other obstruction – the animal can determine the location and navigate accordingly. Similarly, bats find their way in the dark by emitting high-pitched sounds (which cannot be heard by human beings without the aid of special equipment). The sounds bounce off any object – wall or potential prey – and the bat adjusts course. The speed with which its cries are sent and received, as well as the swiftness of response, are extraordinary.

Steering by smell and sound

Many marine animals are renowned for their ability to return to specific breeding grounds after a spell in the open ocean. For example, the migrations of salmon have been well documented by tagging the fish and then recapturing them. Ichthyologists (fish scientists) believe that once salmon reach the coast, they may recognise their native freshwater stream by the smell of the water. But this ability does not explain how salmon find their way the entire distance from the middle of the ocean to the coast. Perhaps, as some experiments indicate, the fish may use the sun as a compass.

Sea turtles are also long-distance migrators. Green turtles tagged on Ascension Island (their breeding site in the South Atlantic) have been recovered at a number of sites on the Brazilian coast, which is about 1,400 miles away. Turtles released in Brazil have returned to their tagging sites on Ascension Island. Archie Carr, a scientist who has studied green turtles extensively, believes that these reptiles use a variety of directional aids. Ocean currents and stars may be involved. Perhaps green turtles may even be guided by a sense of smell.

The homing ability of tame pigeons – their extraordinary capacity to return to home base after being released at a distant point – was known to the ancient Greeks and Egyptians. These birds were surely the first species to raise the question of how an animal could accomplish such a navigational feat. Thousands of years – and numerous experiments – later, ornithologists are still not in agreement on any one particular theory.

In the study of homing ability, banding techniques have been particularly useful, for they make it possible to recognise individual birds upon recapture. (In banding, a bird is captured in a net. A numbered band – or bands – is placed around its leg, and the bird is then released.) One Manx shearwater was banded on an island off the coast of Wales and released at Boston in America. In 12½ days, it was back at its burrow in Wales. These seabirds, and a variety of land species, have demonstrated that at least some birds possess an innate sense of direction.

This genetic tendency may be reinforced by experience. For example, a group of starlings were captured in Holland and released in Switzerland at the start of their autumn migration. The adults veered west, reaching their customary wintering grounds by taking a different direction. But the juveniles flew southeast, which is the direction in which the species normally migrates. They ended up in a new wintering area.

Such experiments document a bird's success in returning to familiar places. But they do little to explain just how first-year migrants, unguided by adults, reach distant goals, or how champion long-distance migrants find their way over half a world.

Arctic terns commute between the far north and the shores of Antarctica; some golden plovers home in on small mid-Pacific islands after a nonstop flight from Alaska. These navigational exploits are still largely unexplained.

Theory on theory

In addition to their directional instinct, birds are believed to be guided by prevailing wind directions. They seem to maintain a course by referring to the changing positions of the sun and constellations.

Many biologists think that keen-sighted birds store up topographical details of landscapes, and even ocean wave patterns, on their outward journeys. On the homeward trip, the birds may recall such details in reverse order.

But many birds travel on overcast nights, when celestial clues are not clearly visible. (See page 294 for a discussion of bird migration.) Recent experiments have suggested that birds respond in some way – not yet understood – to the influence of the earth's magnetic field and gravitational forces.

organic – material of plant or animal origin. Organic compounds contain hydrogen and carbon, and may have other elements such as oxygen and nitrogen. Through photosynthesis, plants make organic molecules (sugar) from inorganic substances (carbon dioxide and water).
—*See* coal, petroleum

P Q

Pangaea – the theoretical supercontinent from which all the continents of today are believed to have been formed. This land mass began to split apart, and, according to the theory (supported by a great deal of evidence), the continents are still drifting.
—*See* plate tectonics

permeability – how readily a fluid such as water can pass through pores or small channels in rock or layers of soil. The porosity of rock relates to how large the pores may be, and how much water can be retained.
—*See* water table

Comparing the other planets with the Earth

Geologically speaking, the earth is not a particularly distinguished planet. But it is the only planet we inhabit at the present time, so scientists frequently use it as a standard of comparison for the other eight planets in our solar system. Thus the chart below gives all periods of time in *earth units* – earth days, earth hours, earth minutes. (An earth day is 24 hours – the time the earth takes to make one complete rotation on its axis. As you can see from the chart, the period of rotation of Mars – a *Martian day* – is slightly longer; a day on Jupiter is shorter.) In a similar way, the chart gives a planet's

mass relative to the earth, instead of the actual mass in grammes. Mercury has much less mass than the earth; Jupiter has much more. In another column, the surface gravity ("pull") of each planet is given, also relative to the earth. A number greater than 1.00 means that any object on that particular planet would weigh more than its weight on earth. For addi-tional information about our solar system and this illustration, see pages **246-247**. The planets are discussed on page **253**. On page **248** there is a *special feature:* How to get your bearings in the night sky, and on page **249** there is a star map.

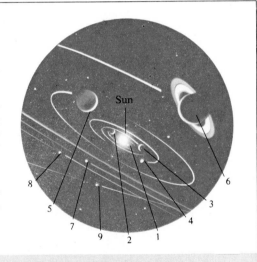

Planets and Moon	Mean Distance from Sun in Millions of Miles	Period of Orbit Earth Units	Period of Rotation in Earth Units	Diameter in Miles	Mass Relative to Earth	Density in Pounds per Cubic Foot	Surface Gravity Relative to Earth	Surface Temperature Range
1. Mercury	36	88 days	46 or 59 days	3,100	0.05	355	0.38	+750°F
2. Venus	67	225 days	247 days	7,700	0.81	322	0.89	+800°F
3. Earth	93	1 year	24 hours	7,927	1.00	344	1.00	−127°F to +136°F
4. Mars	141.5	687 days	24 hr., 37 min.	4,200	0.10	243	0.38	− 50°F to + 90°F
5. Jupiter	483	11.9 years	9 hr., 50 min.	88,800	317	81	2.54	−280°F to −200°F
6. Saturn	886	29.5 years	10 hr., 14 min.	75,100	95	45	1.2	−330°F to −240°F
7. Uranus	1,783	84 years	10 hr., 45 min.	31,000	14	100	1.07	−380°F to −270°F
8. Neptune	2,797	165 years	15 hr., 48 min.	28,000	17	138	1.4	−400°F to −330°F
9. Pluto	3,660	248.4 years	6 days, 10 hr.	3,600	0.8	200	0.7	−370°F
Earth's Moon	239,000 miles from earth	28 days	27 days, 7 hr., 43 min.	2,160	0.012	208	0.165	−200°F to +200°F

Plants: variations in root and stem

Many plants depend for survival on their roots, which supply them with water and essential nutrients from the surroundings (usually, but not always, the soil). Some roots are fibrous and branching (see diagram of a grass plant on page **142**). Others, called taproots, are thickened structures that store food. They anchor tall, spreading trees such as oaks (see pages **46** and **47**). Carrots and beets are also examples of taproots.

Bulbs and corms

Another type of food-storage system is represented by bulbs and corms. These underground structures are actually modified stems. Their function is to carry the plant through the non-growing season, and to produce rapid growth when conditions are favourable. A *bulb* consists of layers of closely folded, fleshy leaves or scales; a flower bud is enclosed at the centre, and roots develop from the base. Tulips, lilies, and onions are bulbous plants. A *corm*, also a modified stem, is solid and either round or flattish; the bud is at the top. Unlike a bulb, a corm shrivels as the food it contains is used up. Crocuses and gladioli propagate by corms.

Tubers, rhizomes, stolons

A *tuber* is a thickened underground shoot; eyes or buds produce new growth. Dahlias and white potatoes are tuberous plants.

A *rhizome* is a horizontal underground stem; new shoots develop from buds at the joints. Bamboo and grasses propagate by rhizomes (see pages **44** and **142**); so do ferns, irises, and some orchids. A *stolon* (page **142**) is an aboveground runner. Strawberry plants send out stolons; where these horizontal stems touch the ground, they develop roots.

Oddities abound

Fungi are unlike most other plants because what looks like a root system – a network of fine hairs called a mycelium – is all there is to the plant. (See page **59**.) The mushrooms we see above ground are transient; they produce the spores, which are similar to seeds. (Some of the other spore-producers, such as mosses and algae, lack true roots.)

Epiphytes, often known as air plants, appear to live on nothing at all. Many orchids and bromeliads have fleshy, knotted roots that take in water from the humid air. (See pages **66** and **67**.)

These plants are not parasites – they take no nourishment from the trees on which they grow.

pollution – the contamination of land, air, or water, which may eventually render a place uninhabitable for its usual residents – plant and animal. What distinguishes present-day problems of waste disposal from those of the past is that – owing to the rapid expansion of human populations – we are producing *more* waste products. And the debris of today differs in kind from that of times past. Many materials produced by advanced technology are extremely durable, and are beyond the capabilities of natural agents of decomposition to break down and recycle. For example, aluminium, which is a relatively abundant element in the crust of the earth, is difficult to extract from its ores. However, once extracted and made into a product, aluminium is more permanent than a metal such as iron (which rusts and is thereby recycled). In addition to solid wastes, pollution problems extend to such situations as the overheating of rivers. The warming of waters near cities and industrial installations makes many rivers unsuitable for the species that usually live there. This is called thermal pollution, and it may also affect estuaries and seashores. Chemical contaminants and oil spills damage the environment, too. Excessive noise can also be considered pollution.
—*See* ways to help preserve nature, 290, **290, 291**

pupa – in the development of certain insects, the stage between larva and adult. An insect in the pupal stage does not eat or move about, but undergoes extensive structural and physiological changes. The pupae of many moth species are protected by a silken cocoon. Butterfly pupae, which tend to be more colourful and intricately sculptured than moth pupae, are often called chrysalids (the singular is chrysalis).
   —pupa of butterfly, **314-315**
   —pupa of Japanese beetle, **163**

R

S

saprophyte – a plant that obtains nourishment from decaying matter. Sapro- means decay, and -phyte refers to plant.

A rain forest in a surprising place

The words "rain forest" conjure up a steaming world where slender trees soar to heights of a hundred feet and a canopy of leaves creates a dark, vine-covered gymnasium for monkeys. But not all rain forests are in the tropics. North America has one – in the Pacific Northwest there is a rain forest that is distinctively different from its tropical "cousins".

The Olympic rain forest

This temperate-zone rain forest is the product of warm ocean currents that flow across the Pacific from Japan, bringing mild breezes with them. As the waves lap the shores of the Olympic Peninsula, the accompanying winds move inland and strike the mighty peaks of the Cascade Mountains. The moisture in the sultry air condenses over the Olympic region; about 150 inches of rain and snow drench the area each year.

Types of vegetation

Few woody vines grow in the Olympic forest, and most of the trees are conifers. Nurtured by years of gentle weather, they are gigantic. The world's largest western hemlock, Douglas fir and red cedar (along with the red alder) are found here. And everywhere there are ferns and mosses – on the forest floor, on fallen logs, even high up on the trunks of living trees.

rock – a general term that refers to solid, non-living material in the crust of the earth. There are three basic types – igneous (volcanic), sedimentary (from fine deposits that have been compressed), and metamorphic (rock that has been transformed by extreme heat and pressure, affecting the crystalline structure to a great extent).

Science: methods and subdivisions

Science means knowledge. Every branch of science is dynamic, ever-changing; as questions are answered, new ones are asked. Problems are solved by a five-part scientific method, which begins with careful, repeated *observations*. Then a *problem* is defined, in the form of a question that can be tested. Formulating a *hypothesis* – a tentative answer to the question – is the next step. If *experimentation* proves that this hypothesis is wrong, another hypothesis must be set up.

Experimentation always involves a control, which provides a reference against which to judge the results. For example, in testing the effectiveness of a medicine, certain individuals are given a substance that is known to have no effect; these are called controls. Other individuals are given the medicine being tested. All other aspects of the experiment are the same for the two groups. Thus, it is reasonable to assume that differences in the results can be attributed to the medication. Based on the results of an experiment (or a series of experiments), the scientist formulates a *theory*. This is the last step in the scientific method. So the "final" product is a broad statement that leads to further research.

A sampling of -ologies

The names of many sciences are "-ologies". Here are some that are concerned with natural history:

Science	Subject
anthropology	human beings
apiology	honeybees
biology	life
bryology	mosses
cetology	whales
dendrology	trees
ecology	environment
entomology	insects
ethology	animal behaviour
herpetology	amphibians, reptiles
ichthyology	fishes
limnology	fresh water
malacology	molluscs
meteorology	weather, atmosphere
mycology	fungi
myrmecology	ants
ornithology	birds
paleontology	life of the past
pedology	soil
phycology	algae
phytology	botany
pteridology	ferns
speleology	caves
zoology	animals

stratum – in geology, a distinct layer of rock that usually differs in composition from the adjacent layers. (The plural is strata.) Strata are most easily seen in sedimentary rock, but can sometimes be seen in igneous (volcanic) rock.
—*Special feature:* roads are prime places to see geological formations, 81

Territories – claims and advertisements among animals

Of all the claims to space made by animals, territorial behaviour is probably the most widely discussed and best understood. A territory has been defined as an area defended by its occupant against competing members of the same species. Territorial behaviour has been studied in many animals. Male sticklebacks and other nest-building fish are famous examples. They dig a nesting site and clear it of debris, then entice a female of the species to come and lay her eggs. Thereafter, the eggs, and later the hatchlings, are vigorously defended by the parent fish.

Territories and birds

The singing of a male bird from a prominent perch in spring is territorial behaviour. He is singing to attract a mate and also to warn off other males. In most cases, the division of an area into territories helps to ensure adequate food for adults and offspring (although the adults may also feed outside the territorial boundaries). This space also provides nesting materials, and sometimes shelter and escape routes from predators. Territories have the effect of spreading out the populations of birds, which prevents overcrowding. Of course, for colonial-nesting birds such as gannets (see pages 120-121), the food supply is concentrated in the ocean, and the territory is really only a nesting site.

Variation by species and season

Bald eagles have been known to drive off other eagles from a square-mile area, but territorial defence is most intense near the nest during the breeding season. Most other birds, such as blue tits, have much smaller territorial demands, and a hummingbird may claim only part of a garden. Songbirds may favour only one layer of a tree. The same tree can contain a warbler's nest at the top, and a finch's nest in the middle or lower branches. Year after year, birds tend to return to the same breeding grounds, and often to the same nest. This phenomenon is known as site attachment. Each year, a territory is likely to have a slightly different shape, depending on the number and vigour of the competing neighbours. But when the breeding season is over, the birds – even year-round residents – tend to become less militant in defence of space. Territorial behaviour gives way to a more relaxed claim to roosts and feeding areas.

Territorial behaviour is triggered by glandular responses to the amount of sunlight. The hypothalamus, at the base of the brain, registers changes in the amount of sunlight as the seasons progress. Increased sunlight in spring stimulates birds to many activities, and to physical changes, such as the development of breeding plumage. It sets off migration in many species, and makes male birds more aggressive. In general, diverse species live amicably near one another – mainly because they are usually not competing either for the same food or for the same kind of nesting sites. In instances where two different species of birds compete for the same nesting site or food, the result is usually an immediate settlement – the more powerful bird drives off the other, but without the ceremonial behaviour usually employed in competing with a bird of the same species. Once in possession, the bird will defend its territory against all comers.

Mammals have different patterns

There is always a temptation to take what is learned from one behavioural study and apply it to another. But mammals (which are less mobile for the simple reason that most do not fly) cannot be compared directly with birds. Their claims to space are often difficult to see (because of the foliage), and there is a real question about the purpose served by their "territorial" markings. Mammals frequently use droppings, urine, or secretions from scent glands to establish their presence. But we do not know if this marking is more important as warning or advertisement. The rabbit leaves small piles of pellets around its central den. Does this frighten off other rabbits, or does it attract them? The behaviour of domestic dogs, as they are taken for a walk on their leashes, is not simply elimination, it is communication.

Home range or familiar route?

How a mammal sets up the area needed for its use still requires study. For example, a shrew will establish a path to which it adheres without variation, and along which it can travel swiftly. But this fixed pattern differs greatly from the behaviour of otters, which seem at home everywhere. (See pages 26, 27.) The fighting among large mammals – as, for example, deer – has led to the idea that the behaviour is territorial. But in fact, the fight is often over possession of females, not for ownership of a certain site. As with other factors in the complicated pattern of nature, the two can also be interlinked.

U V

ungulates – a broad category within the mammalian class, where the animals are grouped according to the number of toes on their hoofs. The odd-toed ungulates (Perissodactyla) include tapirs, rhinos, horses, and zebras. Then there are the Artiodactyla (which have an even number of toes), including pigs, camels, deer, antelope, giraffe, and cattle. Elephants are related, but are in a different, smaller group of ungulates.
—*See specific animals*

vertebrate – an animal with an internal backbone (spinal column) made of bone or cartilage. The five major groups of vertebrates are fish, amphibians, reptiles, birds, and mammals. All vertebrates have additional characteristics in common – a two-part nervous system consisting of a brain and spinal cord, a head with a mouth and sense organs, and no more than two pairs of limbs.
—*See individual groups or species*

Volcanoes on the ring of fire

The areas of greatest geological unrest have been identified and are shown here. These regions are dotted with many volcanoes, where the hot magma under the crust has broken through and reached the surface.

The area surrounding the Pacific Ocean is called the ring of fire because it accounts for about 90% of all major earthquakes. Both earthquakes and volcanoes are products of the same forces – crustal movements, heat, and the build-up of pressures deep within the earth (see pages 78-79, and 266-267). Scientists monitor earthquakes by recording shifts in the earth's crust, exchanging information internationally. The natural magnetism of rock and its electrical conductivity reflect crustal movements.

A local change in the earth's magnetism is almost always followed by slight tremors, which can be detected by sensitive instruments. Most major earthquakes are preceded by several small tremors. Scientists are tracing such tremors as extensively as possible to discover pre-quake patterns that will aid in predicting serious earthquakes.

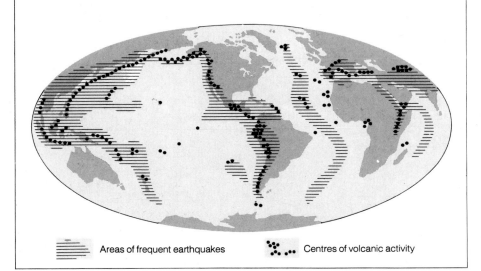

——— Areas of frequent earthquakes   :·: ··· Centres of volcanic activity

W

water table – refers to the upper boundary of the underground water supply of a particular region. In digging a well, for example, the shaft may have to be sunk to a depth of 50 or 100 ft to reach the water table. If too much water is extracted from a particular area, the water table may drop, and all the wells of a region may run dry. Groundwater, which occupies chinks and cracks in rock and gravel, is replenished by rain and by underground flow. Much is still to be learned about the extent of this naturally occurring source of fresh water. In some regions it is abundant; in others, the water table is so deep as to be impractical to reach. One thing is certain – groundwater is being extracted faster than it is being replaced. Britain, for instance, is only beginning to realise the effects of the dry summers of 1975 and 1976.

Wind-chill factor: a combination of temperature and wind speed

The weather outside may be a tolerable 35°F., but if the wind is blowing at 20 mph, the temperature will feel much lower – more like 12°F. This chart gives thermometer readings at the top, and how the wind speed causes these figures to seem much lower. In effect, the wind carries heat off at different speeds, and your body must work harder to replace the lost warmth. Windproof outer clothes are the answer.

Wind speed	Actual temperature in degrees Fahrenheit									
	35°	30°	25°	20°	15°	10°	5°	0°	−5°	−10°
	Wind-chill temperatures – how cold it seems to be									
5 mph	33°	27°	21°	16°	12°	7°	1°	−6°	−11°	−15°
10 mph	21°	16°	9°	2°	−2°	−9°	−15°	−22°	−27°	−31°
15 mph	16°	11°	1°	−6°	−11°	−18°	−25°	−33°	−40°	−45°
20 mph	12°	3°	−4°	−9°	−17°	−24°	−32°	−40°	−46°	−52°
25 mph	7°	0°	−7°	−15°	−22°	−29°	−37°	−45°	−52°	−58°
30 mph	5°	−2°	−11°	−18°	−26°	−33°	−41°	−49°	−56°	−63°
35 mph	3°	−4°	−13°	−20°	−27°	−35°	−43°	−52°	−60°	−67°
40 mph	1°	−4°	−15°	−22°	−29°	−36°	−45°	−54°	−62°	−69°
45 mph	1°	−6°	−17°	−24°	−31°	−38°	−46°	−54°	−63°	−70°
50 mph	0°	−7°	−17°	−24°	−31°	−38°	−47°	−56°	−63°	−70°

Recommended reading for reference and pleasure

These books are suggested for your further enjoyment of nature, especially if you wish to enlarge your knowledge by taking a specialist interest in any particular field. Ranging from the learned to the popular, they make fascinating reading. You should be able to obtain them from your library or bookshop.

ECOLOGY AND GENERAL INTEREST

AA Book of the British Countryside, London, Drive Publications for the Automobile Association, 1973.

ARDREY, ROBERT, The Territorial Imperative, London, Collins, 1967.

BOURLIÈRE, FRANÇOIS, The Land and Wildlife of Eurasia, New York, Time Inc., 1964.

BROOKS, MAURICE, The Life of the Mountains, McGraw Hill, 1968.

BURTON, MAURICE (ed.), The Shell Natural History of Britain, London, Rainbird, 1970.

CARSON, RACHEL, The Sea Around Us, Oxford University Press, 1961.

CARTHY, J. D., Animal Behaviour, London, Aldus, 1965.

CLOUDSLEY-THOMSON, J., Life in Deserts, London, G. T. Foulis, 1964.

CONDRY, WILLIAM, Woodlands, London, Collins, 1974.

DE HAAS, W., and KNORR, F., Marine Life, London, Burke, 1966.

ENGELHARDT, WOLFGANG, Pond-Life, London, Burke, 1964.

EVANS, I. O., The Observer's Book of Sea and Seashore, London, Frederick Warne, 1976.

FARB, PETER, Living Earth, London, Constable, 1960.

FITTER, R. and LEIGH-PEMBERTON, J., Britain's Wildlife – Rarities and Introductions, London, Nicholas Kaye, 1966.

GARMS, HARRY, The Natural History of Europe, London, Hamlyn, 1967.

GRAHAM, MICHAEL, A Natural Ecology, Manchester University Press, 1975.

HICKIN, NORMAN, The Natural History of an English Forest, London, Hutchinson, 1971.

HOKE, JOHN, Man's Effects on his Environment, London, Franklin Watts, 1971.

INGLE, RAY, A Guide to the Seashore, London, Hamlyn, 1969.

KIRMIZ, J. P., Adaptation of Desert Environment, London, Butterworths, 1962.

LEUTSCHER, ALFRED, Field Natural History – A Guide to Ecology, London, Bell, 1969.

LYNEBORG, LEIF, Field and Meadow Life, London, Blandford, 1968.

MACAN, T. T. and WORTHINGTON, E. B., Life in Lakes and Rivers, London, Collins, 1951.

MILES, P. M. and H. B., Freshwater Ecology, London, Hulton Educational Publications, 1967.

NEAL, ERNEST, Woodland Ecology, London, Heinemann, 1958.

ODUM, E. P., Fundamentals of Ecology, Eastbourne, W. B. Saunders, 1971.

Our Magnificent Wildlife, London, The Reader's Digest Association, 1975.

PEARSALL, W. H., Mountains and Moorlands, London, Fontana, 1971.

REID, LESLIE, Earth's Company, London, John Murray, 1958.

SANKEY, JOHN, Guide to Field Biology, London, Longman, 1964.

The Fascinating Secrets of Oceans & Islands, London, The Reader's Digest Association, 1972

VEVERS, GWYNNE, Seashore Life in Colour, London, Blandford, 1969.

WHITE, GILBERT, Natural History of Selborne, London, Everyman Dent, 1960.

Wildlife in Britain, a guide to natural habitats, safari parks and zoos, Basingstoke, The Automobile Association, 1976.

YONGE, C. M., The Seashore, London, Collins, 1967.

BIRDS AND MAMMALS

AUSTIN, O. and SINGER, A., Birds of the World, London, Hamlyn, 1967.

Book of British Birds, London, Drive Publications for The Reader's Digest Association and the Automobile Association, 1972.

BOORER, MICHAEL, Mammals of the World, London, Hamlyn paperback 1970.

BRINK, F. H. VAN DEN, Field Guide to the Birds of Britain and Europe, London, Collins, 1966.

BRUUN, BERTEL, Guide to the Birds of Britain and Europe, London, Hamlyn, 1975.

BRUUN, BERTEL and SINGER, PAUL, Concise Encyclopedia of Birds, London, Octopus Books, 1976.

BURTON, JANE, Animals of the African Year, London, Peter Lowe, 1972.

BURTON, MAURICE, Systematic Dictionary of Mammals of the World, London, Museum Press, 1965.

BURTON, MAURICE and ROBERT, Encyclopedia of Mammals, London, Octopus Books, 1975.

CAMPBELL, BRUCE, Dictionary of Birds in Colour, London, Michael Joseph, 1974.

Larousse Encyclopedia of Animal Life, London, Hamlyn, 1974.

LAWRENCE, M. J. and BROWN, R. W., Mammals of Britain – their Tracks, Trails and Signs, London, Blandford, 1970.

LORENZ, KONRAD, King Solomon's Ring, London, Methuen, 1955.

LORENZ, KONRAD, On Aggression, London, Methuen, 1966.

Marvels and Mysteries of our Animal World, New York, Reader's Digest Inc., 1964.

MITCHELL, ALAN, Birds of Garden and Woodland, London, Collins, 1976.

PETERSON, R., MOUNTFORT, G. and HOLLOM, P. A. D., Field Guide to the Birds of Britain and Europe, London, Collins, 1954.

SOPER, TONY, New Bird Table Book, Newton Abbott, David and Charles, 1974.

SOUTHERN, H. N. (ed.), Handbook of British Mammals, Oxford, Blackwell Scientific Publications, 1964.

STOKES, TED and SHACKLETON, KEITH, Birds of the Atlantic Ocean, London, Country Life, 1968.

STOKOE, W. J. (revised BURTON, MAURICE), The Observer's Book of Wild Animals of the British Isles, London, Frederick Warne, 1968.

STONEHOUSE, BERNARD, Animals of the Antarctic, London, Methuen, 1972.

STONEHOUSE, BERNARD, Animals of the Arctic, London, Methuen, 1955.

WELTY, C. J., Life of Birds, London, Constable, 1964.

YOUNG, JOHN Z., Life of Mammals: Their Anatomy and Physiology, Oxford University Press, 1975

YOUNG, JOHN Z., Life of Vertebrates, Oxford University Press, 1962.

Recommended reading (continued)

REPTILES, FISHES, INSECTS AND OTHER ANIMALS

BAGENAL, T. B., *The Observer's Book of Freshwater Fishes*, London, Frederick Warne, 1970.

BELLAIRS, ANGUS and CARRINGTON, RICHARD, *The World of Reptiles*, London, Chatto & Windus, 1966.

BUCHSBAUM, RALPH, *Animals Without Backbones* (2 vols), London, Pelican, 1972.

BURTON, JOHN, *The Oxford Book of Insects*, Oxford University Press, 1968.

BURTON, MAURICE, *Life under the Sea*, London, Spring Books, 1961.

CAMPBELL, A. C., *Guide to the Seashore and Shallow Seas of Britain and Europe*, London, Hamlyn, 1977.

CLARK, AILSA, *Starfishes and Their Relations*, London, British Museum, 1962.

CLEGG, JOHN, *Freshwater Life of the British Isles*, London, Frederick Warne, 1965.

COLYER, CHARLES and HAMMOND, CYRIL, *Flies of the British Isles*, London, Frederick Warne, 1968.

ENGELHARDT, WOLFGANG and MAXMULLER, HERMANN (transl. Heather Fisher), *Woodland Insects*, London, Burke, 1964.

FORD, E. B., *Butterflies*, London, Collins, 1946.

FRANK, S., *The Pictorial Encyclopedia of Fishes*, London, Hamlyn, 1969.

JANUS, HORST, *Molluscs*, London, Burke, 1965.

LEUTSCHER, ALFRED, *A Study of Reptiles and Amphibians*, London, Blandford, 1963.

LINSSEN, E. F. and NEWMAN, HUGH, *The Observer's Book of Common Insects and Spiders*, London, Frederick Warne, 1973.

MANDAHL-BARTH, G. (ed. Arnold Darlington), *Woodland Life*, Poole, Blandford Press, 1972.

NEWMAN, HUGH, *Man and Insects*, London, Aldus, 1965.

NEWMAN, HUGH and MANSELL, E., *Complete British Butterflies in Colour*, London, Ebury and Michael Joseph, 1968.

OLDROYD, HAROLD, *Insects and Their World*, London, British Museum, 1966.

RILEY, N. D. (ed.), *Insects in Colour*, London, Blandford, 1977.

SMITH, MALCOLM, *British Amphibians and Reptiles*, London, Collins, 1960.

TWEEDIE, MICHAEL, *Atlas of Insects*, London, Heinemann, 1974.

WHEELER, ALWYNE, *Fishes of the World – an illustrated dictionary*, New York, Macmillan Inc., 1975.

BOTANY AND PLANT IDENTIFICATION

ALVIN, K. L. and KERSHAW, K. A., *The Observer's Book of Lichens*, London, Frederick Warne, 1963.

BLAMEY, M., FITTER, M. and FITTER, A., *Wildflowers of Britain*, London, Collins, 1977.

BRIGHTMAN, FRANK, *The Oxford Book of Flowerless Plants*, Oxford University Press, 1966.

CLAPHAM, A. R., TUTIN, T. G. and WARBURG, E. F., *Flora of the British Isles*, Cambridge University Press, 1962.

FITTER, R. S. R., *Finding Wild Flowers*, London, Collins, 1971.

HADFIELD, MILES, *Your Book of Trees*, London, Faber and Faber, 1964.

HUBBARD, C. E., *Grasses*, London, Pelican, 1954.

HUTCHINSON, JOHN, *British Wild Flowers* (2 vols), London, Pelican, 1955.

HUXLEY, ANTHONY, *Mountain Flowers*, London, Blandford, 1967.

KEBLE-MARTIN, W., *A Concise British Flora in Colour*, London, Ebury Press, 1965.

LANGE, MORTEN and HORA, F. B., *Guide to Mushrooms and Toadstools*, London, Collins, 1967.

McCLINTOCK, DAVID and FITTER, R. S. R., *Pocket Guide to Wild Flowers*, London, Collins, 1956.

Mushrooms and Toadstools – how to identify them, London, Orbis Books, 1972.

ROSE, FRANCIS, *The Observer's Book of Grasses, Sedges and Rushes*, London, Frederick Warne, 1966.

WILLIS, J. C., *Dictionary of Flowering Plants and Ferns*, Cambridge University Press, 1966.

GEOLOGY AND MINERALOGY

CALDER, NIGEL, *Restless Earth*, London, B.B.C., 1972.

DEESON, A. F. L. (ed.), *The Collector's Encyclopedia of Rocks and Minerals*, Newton Abbott, David and Charles.

EVANS, I. O., *The Observer's Book of Geology*, London, Frederick Warne, 1971.

KIRKALDY, J. F., *Minerals and Rocks*, London, Blandford, 1970.

New Larousse Encyclopedia of the Earth, London, Hamlyn, 1974.

ROGERS, CEDRIC, *Rocks and Minerals*, London, Ward Lock, 1973.

SCHUMANN, W., *Stones and Minerals*, London, Lutterworth Press.

STEERS, J. A., *Coasts and Beaches*, Edinburgh, Oliver & Boyd, 1969.

TARLING, DON and MAUREEN, *Continental Drift*, London, Bell 1971, Pelican 1971.

WEATHER AND ASTRONOMY

ASIMOV, ISAAC, *The Universe*, London, Pelican, 1971.

BIGGS, JOHN S., *Discovering Weather*, University of London Press, 1965.

Elementary Meteorology, London, H. M. Stationery Office, 1962.

HOLFORD, INGRID, *Interpreting the Weather*, Newton Abbott, David and Charles, 1973.

HOYLE, FRED, *Galaxies, Nuclei and Quasars*, London, Heinemann, 1966.

Larousse Encyclopedia of Astronomy, London, Hamlyn, 1959.

LESTER, REGINALD M., *The Observer's Book of Weather*, London, Frederick Warne, 1967.

MANLEY, GORDON, *Climate and the British Scene*, London, Fontana, 1952.

SCORER, R. S., *Weather*, London, Phoenix House, 1959.

OUTDOOR ACTIVITIES

DENNIS, EVE (ed.), *Everyman's Nature Reserve – ideas for action*, Newton Abbott, David and Charles, 1972.

FITTER, R. S. R., *Guide to Birdwatching*, London, Collins, 1963.

HARRIS, REG, *Natural History Collecting*, London, Hamlyn paperback, 1969.

KNIGHT, MAXWELL, *Bird Gardening – how to attract birds*, London, Routledge & Kegan Paul, 1954.

KNOX, JOHNSON, *Sailing*, London, Collins, 1975.

LEUTSCHER, ALFRED, *Tracks and Signs of British Animals*, London, Macmillan, 1960.

RAND, JIM and WALKER, TONY, *This is Orienteering*, London, Pelham Books, 1976.

Credits and acknowledgments

We wish to express our gratitude to the artists and photographers who have contributed to this book. In the course of their work, many have become naturalists in the old tradition – interested in every aspect of the subjects they have painted or captured on film. Most of the persons named here have generously contributed background information about the animals, plants, places, and situations that they have portrayed. We would like to give particular thanks to Alan Linn, who, in addition to providing us with photographs, has made a substantial contribution to the text.

Front cover S. Chirol. **1** David Muench. **2-3** (mountain avens) S. J. Krasemann. **4** Bill McRae. **8** Mary Sue Ubben. **9** *top* The Coleman Company; *bottom* George H. Harrison/Grant Heilman.

CHAPTER ONE

10-11 Robert Perron. **12** *top left* David Hiser; *upper right* Kathy & Alan Linn; *bottom* Larry West. **13** *top* Arthur Christiansen; *bottom* John Mason/Ardea. **14** Ed Cooper. **15** *top left* Davis W. Finch; *top right* Robert B. Evans/Tom Stack & Associates; *middle* Douglas Faulkner; *bottom left* Jeff Foott; *bottom right* Nick Drahos. **16** *top* Phoebe Dunn; *bottom left* E. S. Ross; *bottom right* David G. Allen. **17** *top* Robert S. Simmons; *bottom* Enid Kotschnig. **18** *left* Karl H. Himmer. **19** Walter Linsenmaier. **20** Kathy & Alan Linn. **21** *top left* Wardene Weisser; *top right* Kjell B. Sandved; *bottom left* Nick Drahos; *bottom right* B. M. Shaub. **22** Douglas Faulkner. **23** *top* E. S. Ross; *lower right* Enid Kotschnig; *left* David Doubilet/Animals Animals. **24** C. Allan Morgan. **25** *upper left* Enid Kotschnig; *top right* Thase Daniel; *bottom* E. S. Ross. **26** *left* Nicholas de Vore III/Bruce Coleman Inc.; *right* C. Haagner/Bruce Coleman Inc. **27** *top left* Hans Reinhard/Bruce Coleman Inc.; *top right* Karl Maslowski/National Audubon Society/Photo Researchers; *bottom right* J. Markham/Bruce Coleman Inc.; *bottom left* Enid Kotschnig. **28** J. P. Varin/Jacana. **29** *top left* Rafael Macia/Photo Researchers; *top right* Illustration from WILD GREEN THINGS IN THE CITY by Anne Ophelia Dowden, 1972, reprinted by permission of the author & Thomas Y. Crowell Company, Inc., publisher; *bottom* Kathy & Alan Linn. **30** *left* Ed Cooper; *right* Olive Glasgow. **31** *top* Brian Payne; *bottom left* Documerica; *bottom right* Ed Cooper.

CHAPTER TWO

32-33 Ray Atkeson. **34** Ed Cooper. **35** *top left* Stan & Kay Breeden; *top right* André Martin; *bottom left* Ed Cooper; *bottom right* Jussi Pohjakallio, Studio Pohjakallio Co Oy. **36-37** Antonio Petruccelli. **38** Michael Ramus. **39** *top* Rebecca Merrilees; *bottom left* Michael Ramus; *bottom centre* Joy Spurr/Bruce Coleman Inc.; *bottom right* Grant Heilman. **40** *left* Olive Glasgow; *upper right* David Muench; *lower right* Thase Daniel. **41** Rebecca Merrilees/Richard Robson. **42** Marcel Sire. **43** *top* E. R. Degginger; *bottom* Enid Kotschnig. **44** *left* Mulvey Associates; *right* Simon Trevor/Bruce Coleman Inc. **45** *left* Thomas Blagden, Jr.; *right* J.-P. Hervy/Jacana. **46-47** John Murphy. **48** *left* Olive Glasgow; *others* E. S. Barnard. **49** *top* Firestone Tyre and Rubber Co.; *middle left* Thase Daniel; *bottom left* R. F. Thomas/Bruce Coleman Inc.; *right* Richard Bonson. **50-51** John Murphy. **52-53** Darrell K. Sweet. **53** *upper right inset* Gerald Bishop; *lower right* Reprinted from BIOLOGY by Karl von Frisch by permission of Harper & Row. **54** Grant Heilman. **55** Anne Savage. **56** *top left* Heather Angel; *bottom left* Hans Reinhard/Bruce Coleman; *others* G. A. Mathews/Natural Science Photos. **57** *centre* Larry West; *others* Enid Kotschnig. **58** *top* E. R. Degginger. **59** *top* Hans Reinhard/Bruce Coleman; *top and upper right* Olive Glasgow; *bottom right* R. K. Murton/Bruce Coleman. **58-59** *bottom* From "The Most Poisonous Mushrooms" by Walter Litten. © March 1975 by Scientific American, Inc. All rights reserved; *others* E. R. Degginger. **60-61** *top* Richard Bonson; *bottom* Stan and Kay Breeden. **62-63** *bottom* John Murphy. **63** *top* Kathy & Alan Linn; *middle left* Phoebe Dunn; *middle right* John Murphy. **64** *left* Olive Glasgow; *right* J. J. Craighead. **65** *upper left* Larry West; *lower left* William J. Jahoda/National Audubon Society; *right* From "Annual Biological Clocks" by Eric T. Rengelley and Sally Asmundson. © April 1971 by Scientific American, Inc. All rights reserved. **66** Renoux/Holmes Lebel. **67** *top left & centre* E. S. Ross; *lower left* Jacques Jangoux; *right* Enid Kotschnig. **68** *left* Reprinted from TROPICAL QUEENSLAND by Stanley and Kay Breeden by permission of Collins Publishers. **68-69** *bottom* Jacques Jangoux. **69** *top left* Jacques Jangoux; *right* Eva Cellini.

CHAPTER THREE

70-71 G. Rebuffat/Rapho/Photo Researchers. **72** Loren McIntyre. **73** *top* John R. Brownlie/Bruce Coleman Inc., *middle* Grant Heilman; *bottom* David Muench. **74** David Muench. **75** *top left* Ed Cooper; *top right* Paul Chesley; *lower left* Eva Cellini; *lower right* Jerome Wyckoff. **76-77** Antonio Petruccelli. **78** *left* Loren McIntyre; *right* Howard S. Friedman. **79** *bottom left* David Muench; *bottom right* G. F. Allen/Bruce Coleman Inc.; *others* Jerome Wyckoff. **80** *left* David Muench; *right* Howard S. Friedman. **81** *middle* Howard S. Friedman; *others* Jerome Wyckoff. **82** H. Flygare/Bruce Coleman Inc. **83** *left & upper right* Howard S. Friedman; *others* Jerome Wyckoff. **84-85** *bottom* Howard S. Friedman. **85** *top left* M. Terrasse; *upper right* David Muench. **86** Ray Atkeson. **87** *left* Russell D. Lamb; *right* Howard S. Friedman. **88-89** Eva Cellini. **90** *left* H. Reinhard/Bruce Coleman Inc.; *right* E. R. Degginger. **91** *left* Russell D. Lamb; *top right* G. D. Plage/Bruce Coleman Inc.; *bottom right* Enid Kotschnig. **92** *bottom* Barry Driscoll. **93** *top* Noel Habgood; *bottom left* G. Nystrand/Bruce Coleman Inc.; *bottom centre* Keith Gunnar/Bruce Coleman Inc.; *bottom right* Harry Engels/Bruce Coleman Inc. **94** Darrell K. Sweet. **95** *top* W. Bayer/Bruce Coleman Inc.; *bottom* Darrell K. Sweet. **96** *left* Bill Ratcliffe; *right* From "The Fungi of Lichens" by Vernon Ahmadjian. Copyright © February 1963 by Scientific American, Inc. All rights reserved. **97** *top* Ed Cooper; *bottom* John Murphy. **98-99** *bottom* Howard S. Friedman. **99** *top* Pete Martin. **100** (map) Howard S. Friedman; *bottom* Eva Cellini. **101** *top left* Eric Hosking/Bruce Coleman Inc.; *top right* Edgar T. Jones; *bottom* Charlie Ott/National Audubon Society.

CHAPTER FOUR

102-103 & 104 Ray Atkeson. **105** *top* Bonnie Muench; *middle* Robert Walch; *bottom* Richard Frear/National Park Service. **106-107** Howard Koslow. **108** *upper* M. F. Soper/Bruce Coleman Inc.; *bottom* Karen Lukas/Group IV/National Audubon Society. **109** Courtesy of the Atmospheric Environment Service, Canada. **110** *left* Carl Roessler/Sea Library; *right* George Lower/National Audubon Society. **111** *top* Douglas Faulkner; *middle* Enid Kotschnig; *bottom* Howard S. Friedman. **112** *left* Howard S. Friedman; *right* Paul Chesley. **113** Ed Cooper. **114** Dennis Brokaw. **115** *top* William H. Amos; *bottom*

Howard S. Friedman. **116** *upper* William H. Amos; *bottom* Jeff Foott. **117** Denis Brokaw. **118-119** *bottom* Howard S. Friedman. **119** *top* George H. Harrison/Grant Heilman. **120 & 121** E. R. Degginger. **122** William D. Griffin. **123** *left* Darrell K. Sweet; *right* Dennis Brokaw. **124** *upper* Heather Angel; *bottom* Runk/Schoenberger/Grant Heilman. **125** *top* Dennis Brokaw; *bottom* John Murphy. **126** Howard S. Friedman. **127** *top* Grant Heilman; *middle left* G. R. Roberts; *lower right* Howard S. Friedman; *bottom* Ed Cooper. **128** *upper* Grant Heilman; *bottom* Dennis Brokaw. **129** ©1969 by Ian McHarg, permission of Doubleday & Company, Inc. **130-131** Richard Robson. **132** *upper* Caulion Singletary. **132-133** *bottom* John Murphy. **133** *top* Caulion Singletary; *middle* Valerie Taylor/Sea Library.

CHAPTER FIVE

134-135 Paul Chesley. **136** Len Rue, Jr. **137** *top* S. Zand; *bottom left* M. P. Kahl; *right* Grant Heilman. **138-139** *top* Antonio Petruccelli; *bottom* Enid Kotschnig. **140** *upper* Leonard Lee Rue III; *bottom* Andre Durenceau. **141** John Murphy. **142** *left* Enid Kotschnig *right* Patricia D. Duncan. **143** Illustration from WILD GREEN THINGS IN THE CITY by Anne Ophelia Dowden, 1972, reprinted by permission of the author & Thomas Y. Crowell Company, Inc., publisher. **144** George H. Harrison/Bruce Coleman Inc. **145** *left* Norman Myers/Bruce Coleman Inc.; *upper right* Grant Heilman; *bottom right* Howard S. Friedman. **146** *upper left* C. Haagner/Bruce Coleman Inc.; *upper right* Australian Information Service; *bottom* Jane Burton/Bruce Coleman Inc. **147** *top* Norman Myers/Bruce Coleman Inc.; *bottom* C. Allan Morgan. **148** Enid Kotschnig. **149** *top* Guy Coheleach; *centre* H. Reinhard/Bruce Coleman Inc. **150** John Schoenherr. **151** *top* Nicholas de Vore III/Bruce Coleman Inc.; *right* Rod Allin; *bottom* C. Haagner/Bruce Coleman Inc. **152-153** Eric Robson. **154** Grant Heilman. **155** *top* Lowell Hess; *bottom left* Howard S. Friedman; *bottom right* Grant Heilman. **156** Enid Kotschnig. **157** Edward S. Barnard. **158** *top* C. Allan Morgan; *others* E. S. Ross. **159** *top* John Dawson from BIOLOGY TODAY © 1972 by Communications Research Machines, Inc., used with permission of CRM Books, Del Mar, Calif.; *bottom* Runk/Schoenberger/Grant Heilman. **160** *top* Edward S. Barnard; *bottom* Kjell B. Sandved. **161** Kjell B. Sandved. **162** *top* Kathy & Alan Linn; *bottom left* John Murphy; *bottom right* E. S. Ross. **163** *left* Kathy & Alan Linn; *right* J. Markham/Bruce Coleman Inc. **164** *left* Howard S. Friedman; *right* G. R. Roberts. **165** *top* S. Rayfield/Bruce Coleman Inc.; *bottom left* Grant Heilman; *lower right* Howard S. Friedman. **166** Kathy & Alan Linn. **167** *top left* Thomas Blagden, Jr.; *top right* Ed Cooper; *bottom* Paul Chesley.

CHAPTER SIX

168-169 Steve C. Wilson/DPI. **170** Ed Cooper. **171** *top* Peter F. R. Jackson/Bruce Coleman Inc.; *bottom left* Ed Cooper; *bottom right* David Muench. **172-173** Antonio Petruccelli. **174** *left* Howard S. Friedman; *bottom right* Ed Cooper. **175** *top right* Len Rue, Jr.; *middle left* Enid Kotschnig; *others* Leonard Lee Rue III. **176** Biological Sciences Curriculum Study. **177** *top* Bill Ratcliffe; *bottom* M. P. Kahl. **178** *top* Ray Shaw; *bottom* N. Smythe. **179** Enid Kotschnig. **180-181** Eric Robson. **182** *left* Enid Kotschnig; *right* Dennis Brokaw. **183** *upper left* E. S. Ross; *bottom left* Kathy & Alan Linn; *right* E. R. Degginger. **184** *top* Olive Glasgow; *bottom* John Murphy. **185** *top* William M. Harlow; *bottom left* David Overcash/Bruce Coleman Inc.; *bottom right* Robert L. Dunne/Bruce Coleman Inc. **186** *bottom left* Michael Wotton; *bottom right* J. H. Carmichael, Jr./Bruce Coleman Inc. **187** *top* Michael G. Anderson; *bottom* Darrell K. Sweet. **188** *left* Jeff Foott. **189** *left* Enid Kotschnig, *right* Howard S. Friedman. **190** Richard Montague. **191** *top* David Muench; *bottom left* From THE ECOLOGY OF RUNNING WATER by H. B. N. Hynes, published by the Liverpool University Press; *centre & bottom right* Jeff Foott/Bruce Coleman Inc. **192** *bottom* Ed Cooper. **193** *top left & right* David Muench; *bottom left* Howard S. Friedman. **194-195** Howard S. Friedman. **195** *top* E. R. Degginger. **196** *left* David Muench; *right* © Philip Hyde. **197** *top* Howard S. Friedman; *bottom left* David Muench; *bottom right* Ed Cooper. **198** *top* Peter G. Sanchez; *bottom* G. R. Roberts. **199** *left* Howard S. Friedman; *right* Consulate-General of the Netherlands.

CHAPTER SEVEN

200-201 David Muench. **202** *left* Ed Cooper; *right* J. S. Zand. **203** *top* Giorgio Gualco/Bruce Coleman Inc.; *bottom* R. R. Pawlowski/Bruce Coleman Inc. **204** Loren McIntyre. **205** *top* David Muench; *bottom left* Howard S. Friedman; *bottom right* Ed Cooper. **206-207** *top* Antonio Petruccelli; *bottom* Darrell K. Sweet. **208** George Gerster/Rapho/Photo Researchers. **209** *top right* Clem Haagner/Bruce Coleman Inc.; *left* Howard S. Friedman; *middle right* Joseph Van Wormer/Bruce Coleman Inc.; *bottom right* Clem Haagner/Bruce Coleman Inc. **210** *left* V. Serventy/Bruce Coleman Inc.; *right* John Brownlie/Bruce Coleman Inc. **211** *top* John Brownlie/Bruce Coleman Inc.; *middle & bottom left* R. R. Pawlowski/Bruce Coleman Inc.; *bottom right* V. Serventy/Bruce Coleman Inc. **212** *left* Howard S. Friedman; *right* Jen & Des Bartlett/Bruce Coleman Inc. **213** *top & bottom left* M. P. L. Fogden/Bruce Coleman Inc.; *bottom right* Ed Cooper. **214-215** Darrell K. Sweet. **216** *top* C. Haagner/Bruce Coleman Inc.; *bottom* Jen & Des Bartlett/Bruce Coleman Inc. **217** *top* Howard S. Friedman; *bottom* Toni Schneiders/Bruce Coleman Inc. **218** Clem Haagner/Bruce Coleman Inc. **219** *top* Jack Dermid; *middle* Jane Burton/Bruce Coleman Inc.; *bottom* Howard S. Friedman. **220** Darrell K. Sweet. **221** *bottom right* G. R. Roberts; *others* Ed Cooper. **222** Ed Cooper. **223** *top* John Brownlie/Bruce Coleman Inc.; *middle* E. R. Degginger; *bottom* Enid Kotschnig. **224** *left* Rod Allin; *right* Jack Dermid. **225** *top* Biological Sciences Curriculum Study; *bottom left* Jane Burton/Bruce Coleman Inc.; *bottom right* Robert L. Dunne.

CHAPTER EIGHT

226-227 NASA. **228** *bottom* John Deeks. **228-229** *top* John Gronert. **229** *bottom left* John Deeks; *bottom right* Peter G. Sanchez. **230** E. R. Degginger. **231 & 232** *left* Enid Kotschnig. **232-233** *centre* Al Giosa. **233** *top left* Environmental Picture Services; *top right* John Deeks; *upper middle left* John Deeks; *upper middle right* Environmental Picture Services; *lower middle left* John Deeks; *lower middle right* Donna Harris; *bottom left* John Deeks; *bottom right* E. R. Degginger. **234** *left & 234-235 centre* National Oceanic & Atmospheric Administration. **235** *upper right* Howard Sochurek/Woodfin Camp & Assoc.; *bottom right* Enid Kotschnig. **236** *bottom* Howard S. Friedman. **236-237** *top* Thomas Blagden, Jr. **237** *bottom* Ed Cooper. **238** *top* Dennis Brokaw; *bottom* Kathy & Alan Linn. **239** *top* Paul Chesley; *lower* Kathy & Alan Linn. **240** *left* Paul Chesley; *right* Edward S. Barnard. **241** *top left* National Oceanic & Atmospheric Administration; *bottom left* Sonja Bullaty; *middle* From CLIMATE AND WEATHER by John A. Day & Gilbert L. Sternes. 1970, reprinted by permission of the publisher, Addison-Wesley, Reading, Mass.; *right* Helmut K. Wimmer. **242-243** John Deeks. **243** *right* Enid Kotschnig. **244-245** Helmut K. Wimmer. **246** *left* NASA. **247** Helmut K. Wimmer. **248** *left* Howard S. Friedman; *others* Darrell K. Sweet. **249** Astronomy Magazine artwork by Adolph Schaller © 1975 by AstroMedia Corp. **250** *top* Howard S. Friedman. **250-251** *bottom* Patricia Ryan. **251** *top* Peter Gill. **252** *left* The Granger Collection; *right* Helmut K. Wimmer. **253** *left* Patricia Ryan; *upper right* Lick Observatory; *bottom right* NASA. **254** *top* Photograph by Don Dean ©1974 by AstroMedia Corp.; *bottom left* American Museum of Natural History, Hayden Planetarium; *right* Willard MacCalla/Sky Publishing Corp. **255** *centre* Patricia Ryan; *others* Lick Observatory. **256** *top* C. Kussner/Tom Stack & Associates; *bottom* Helmut K. Wimmer. **257** *top* Hale Observatories; *middle* American Museum of Natural History; *bottom* G. R. Roberts.

CHAPTER NINE

258-259 David Muench. **260** *left* Ed Cooper. **260-261** *centre & bottom right* Photographic Library of Australia. **261** *upper right* J. Spurr/Bruce Coleman Inc. **262-263 & 264** Richard Edes Harrison © Smithsonian Magazine. **265** *top* Luis Villota; *bottom* Richard Edes Harrison © Smithsonian Magazine. **266** Michael W. Quearry. **267** *upper left* Howard S. Friedman; *bottom left* National Oceanic & Atmospheric Administration; *right* Jon Brenneis. **268** Paul Chesley. **269** *left* Paul Chesley; *top right* Howard S. Friedman; *bottom right* Ed Cooper. **270** *left* Jack Dermid/Bruce Coleman Inc.; *right* Lee Boltin. **271** *top* Jack Dermid/Bruce Coleman Inc.; *bottom left* J. R. Brownlie/Bruce Coleman Inc.; *bottom right* Joy Spurr Bruce Coleman Inc. **272** *left* Henry Janson; *upper right* Jane Burton/Bruce Coleman Inc.; *bottom right* E. R. Degginger/Bruce Coleman Inc. **273** *top* Antonio Petruccelli; *bottom* Richard Edes Harrison © Smithsonian Magazine. **274** *left* Lee Boltin; *upper right* Gemological Institute of America; *bottom right* Patricia Ryan. **275** *left* Lee Boltin; *upper right* Neville Fox-Davis/Bruce Coleman Inc.; *bottom middle* Roger & Joy Spurr/Bruce Coleman Inc.; *bottom right* Jane Burton/Bruce Coleman Inc. **276** *top* D. Lyons/Bruce Coleman Inc.; *bottom* Howard S. Friedman. **277** *top* S. C. Bisserot/Bruce Coleman Inc.; *bottom* Paul Chesley. **278-279** *bottom* Gene Ahrens/Bruce Coleman Inc. **279** *upper & middle right* D. Lyons/Bruce Coleman Inc.; *bottom* Howard S. Friedman. **280-281** *bottom* John Murphy. **281** *top left* Photographic Library of Australia; *top right* S. C. Bisserot/Bruce Coleman Inc.; *bottom right* Walter Dawn. **282** *left* G. R. Roberts; *right* Norwegian Information Service in the United States. **283** *top* Davis Meltzer; *lower right* R. N. Mariscal/Bruce Coleman Inc.; *bottom* Howard S. Friedman (after CAPITOL REEF – THE STORY BEHIND THE SCENERY, KC Publications). **284** *upper left* Grant Heilman, Specimen from North Museum, Franklin & Marshall College; *upper right & middle* Runk-Schoenberger/Grant Heilman, Specimen from North Museum, Franklin & Marshall College; *bottom* M. P. L. Fogden/Bruce Coleman Inc. **285** *top* Runk-Schoenberger/Grant Heilman, Specimen from North Museum, Franklin & Marshall College; *centre* Norman Myers/Bruce Coleman Inc.; *right* Enid Kotschnig; *bottom* John Murphy. **286** *top* Irving Kaufman; *bottom left* Kathy & Alan Linn. **287** Painting by Alex Ebel ©1974 Field Enterprises Educational Corporation.

CHAPTER TEN

288-289 Jack Zehrt. **290** Nick Drahos. **291** *top left* Grant Heilman; *top right* C. Allan Morgan; *bottom* Ian Beams/Ardea. **292-293** *bottom left* Enid Kotschnig; *bottom right* Richard Bonson. **293** *top left* C. Mylne; *top right* Richard Bonson. **294** Anne Savage. **295** *top* Thase Daniel. **298** *left* Mary Sue Ubben; *right* Phoebe Dunn. **299** *top* George Silk. *bottom left* M. P. Kahl; *bottom right* E. R. Degginger. **300-301** *bottom* John H. Gerard. **301** *upper* Kathy & Alan Linn. **302** *left* Gilbert Nielsen; *right* C. Allan Morgan. **303** *upper right* Steve C. Wilson/DPI; *others* Gilbert Nielsen. **305** *top* The Coleman Company; *bottom* Kathy & Alan Linn. **306** *left* Silva, Stockholm, Sweden; *right* John S. Flannery/Bruce Coleman Inc. **307** *left* K. Gunnar/Bruce Coleman Inc.; *upper right* Camp Trails Co. **308** *top* David Muench; *bottom* Enid Kotschnig. **309** *top* K. Gunnar/Bruce Coleman Inc.; *bottom* Enid Kotschnig. **310** *left* Kathy & Alan Linn; *right* David Cavagnaro. **311** *top left* Warren Garst/Tom Stack & Assoc.; *right* Anne Savage. **312-313** Edward Vebell. **314** Kathy & Alan Linn. **315** *top* Enid Kotschnig; *bottom* Kathy & Alan Linn. **316** *top* Kathy & Alan Linn; (stamps) Private Collection. **317** *upper left* Missouri Historical Society; *bottom left* The Wildfowl Trust, Slimbridge; *right* Earl Thollander. **318** David Muench.

TYPESETTING: Vantage Photosetting Ltd., Southampton
PRINTING and BINDING: Poligrafici Editoriale, Bologna